D[...] [...]E BUND GAIDEN:
[...]PIRE BUND

NOZOMU TAMAKI

Per me si va ne la città dolente,

per me si va ne l'etterno dolore,

per me si va tra la perduta gente.

Giustizia mosse il mio alto fattore:

fecemi la divina podestate,

la somma sapienza e 'l primo amore.

Dinanzi a me non fuor cose create

se non etterne, e io etterno duro.

Lasciate ogne speranza, voi ch'entrate.

Through me, you pass into the city of woe:
Through me, you pass into eternal pain:
Through me, among the people lost for aye.

Justice the founder of my fabric mov'd:
To rear me was the task of power divine,
Supremest wisdom, and primeval love.

Before me, things create were none, save things
Eternal, and eternal I shall endure.
All hope abandon, ye who enter here.

—Dante's Inferno, Canto III

Dive In The Vampire Bund 1

Contents

Tamaki Nozomu Presents Dive In The Vampire Bund 1

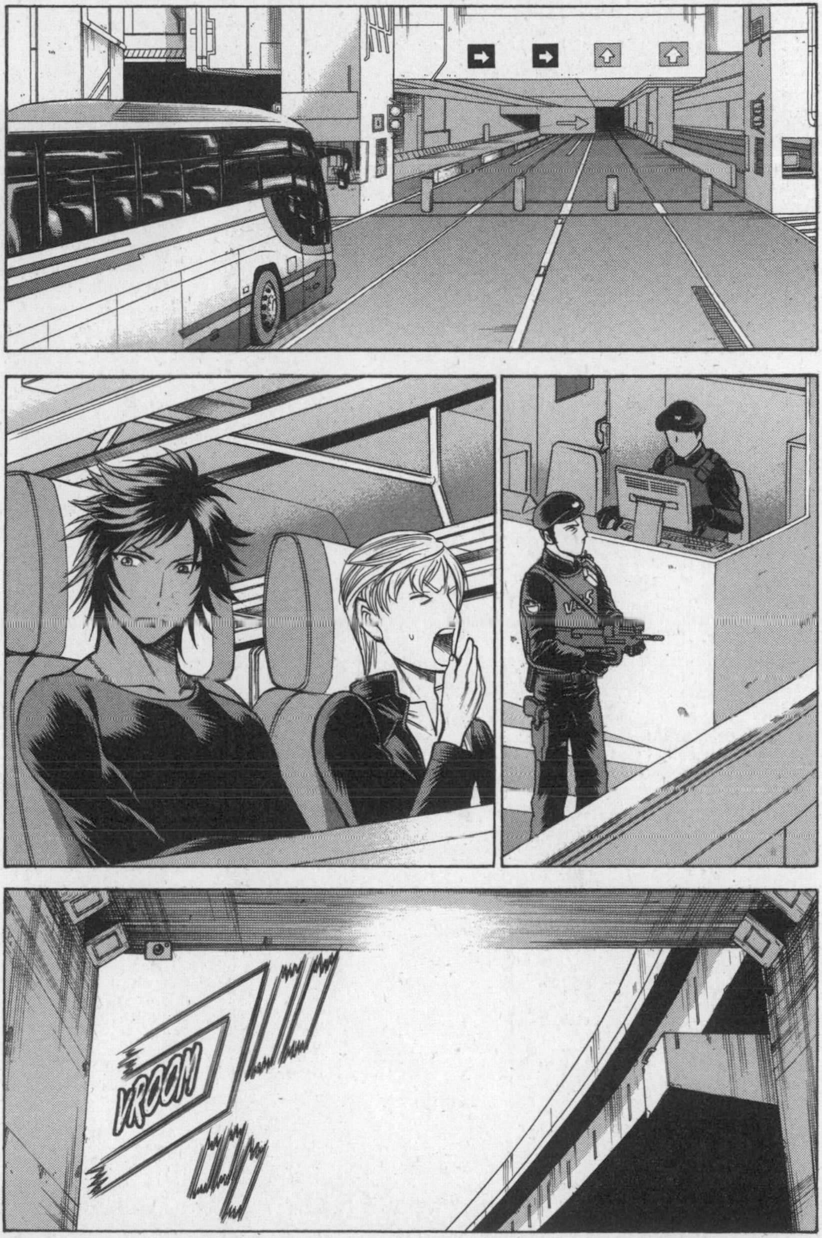
VROOM

Chapter 1: Magical Mystery Tour

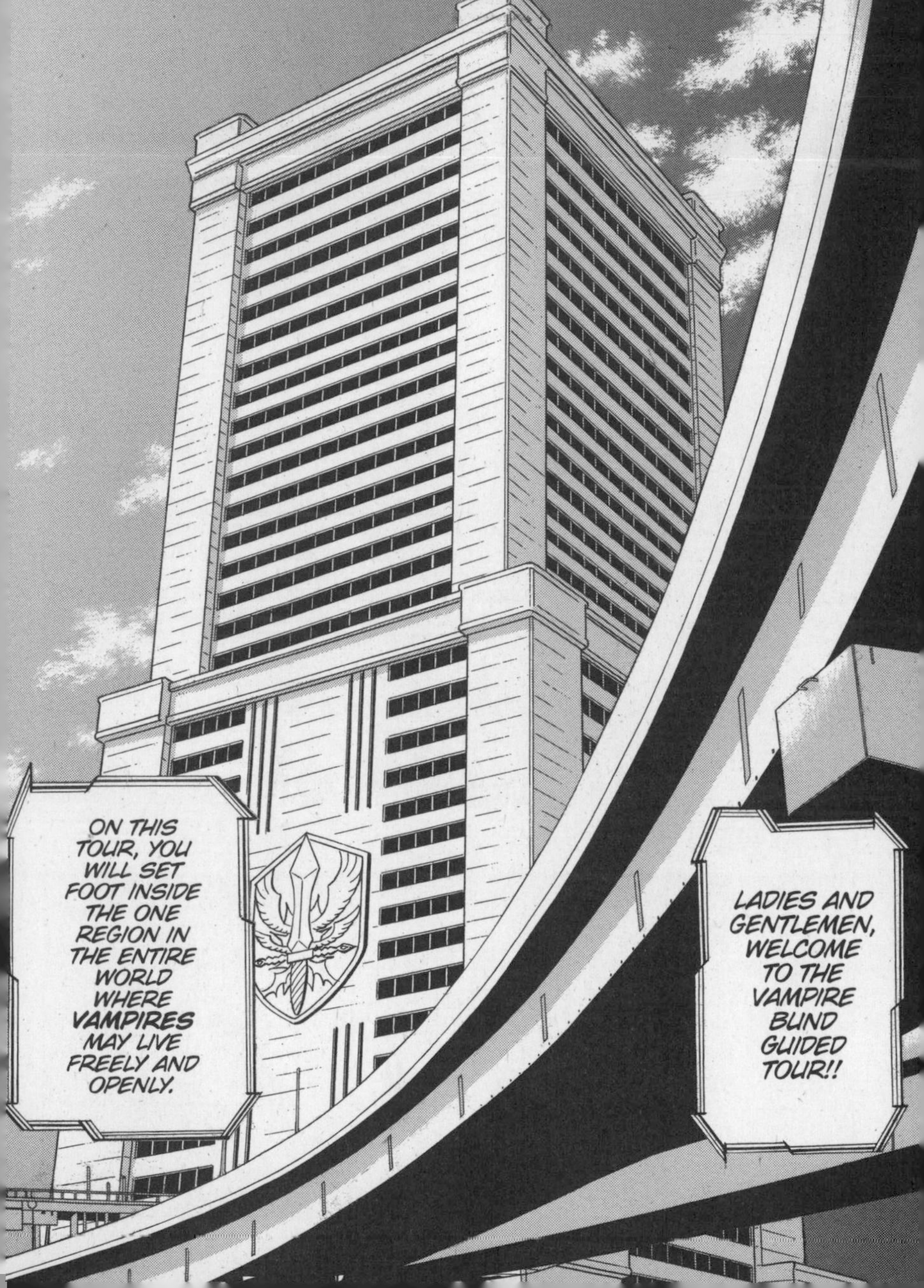
LADIES AND GENTLEMEN, WELCOME TO THE VAMPIRE BUND GUIDED TOUR!!
ON THIS TOUR, YOU WILL SET FOOT INSIDE THE ONE REGION IN THE ENTIRE WORLD WHERE **VAMPIRES** MAY LIVE FREELY AND OPENLY.

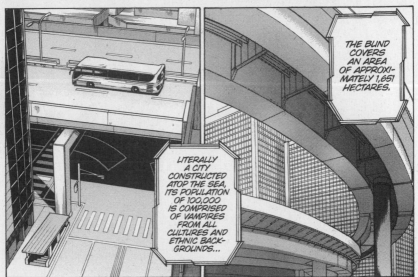

THE BUND COVERS AN AREA OF APPROXIMATELY 1,651 HECTARES.

LITERALLY A CITY CONSTRUCTED ATOP THE SEA, ITS POPULATION OF 100,000 IS COMPRISED OF VAMPIRES FROM ALL CULTURES AND ETHNIC BACKGROUNDS...

MAN, WHAT THE HELL?

I DON'T SEE A SINGLE BLOOD-SUCKER ANYWHERE. BOR~RIING!

WELL, *DUH*. IT'S STILL DAYLIGHT.

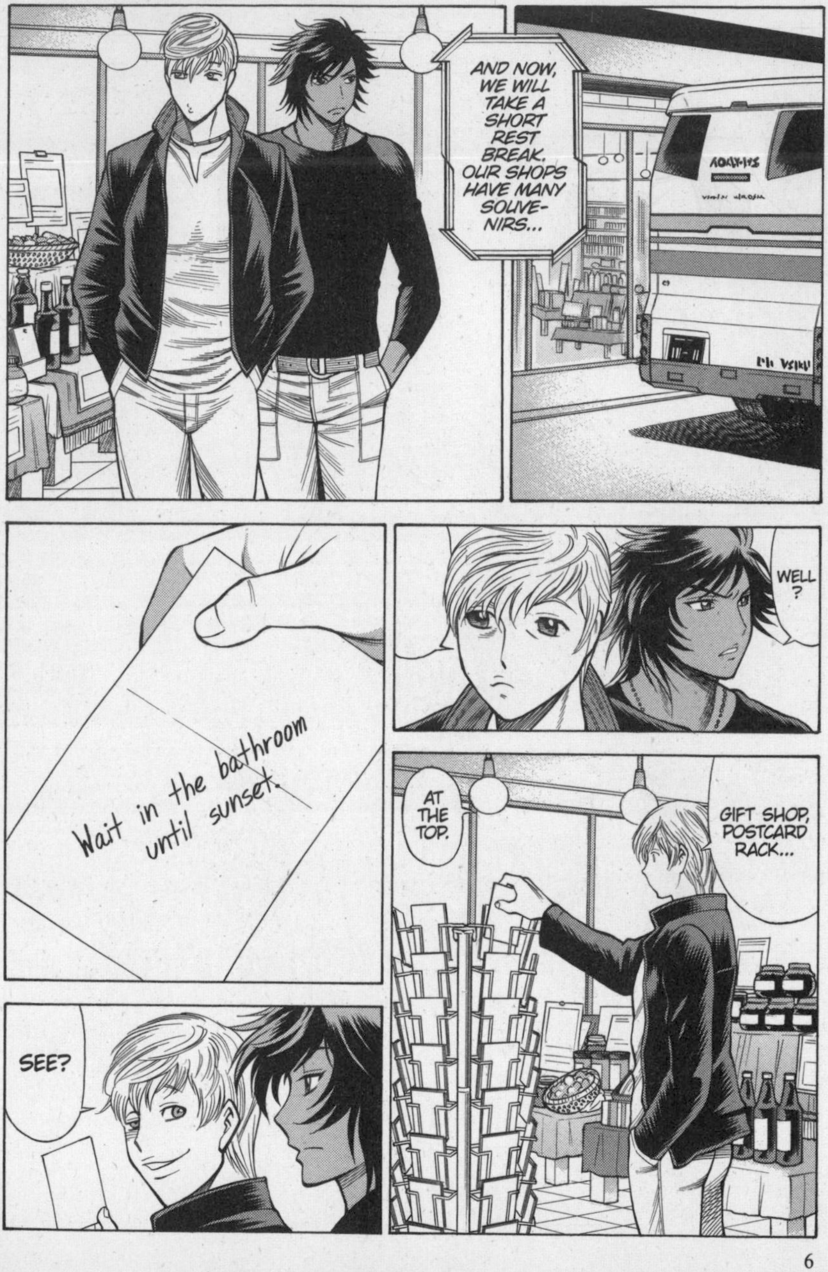
AND NOW, WE WILL TAKE A SHORT REST BREAK. OUR SHOPS HAVE MANY SOUVE-NIRS...
WELL?
GIFT SHOP, POSTCARD RACK...
AT THE TOP.
Wait in the bathroom until sunset.
SEE?

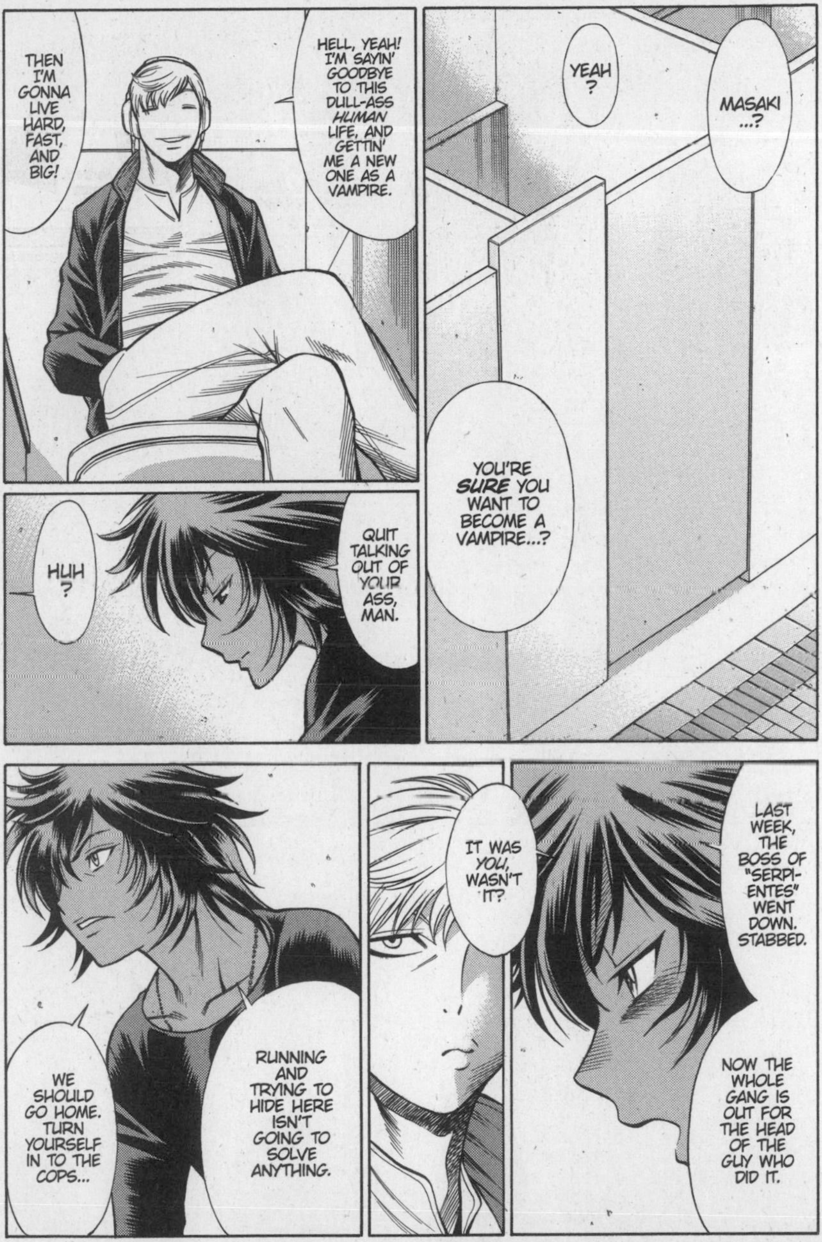
MASAKI ...?
YEAH ?
YOU'RE SURE YOU WANT TO BECOME A VAMPIRE...?
HELL, YEAH! I'M SAYIN' GOODBYE TO THIS DULL-ASS HUMAN LIFE, AND GETTIN' ME A NEW ONE AS A VAMPIRE.
THEN I'M GONNA LIVE HARD, FAST, AND BIG!
QUIT TALKING OUT OF YOUR ASS, MAN.
HUH ?
LAST WEEK, THE BOSS OF "SERPI-ENTES" WENT DOWN. STABBED.
NOW THE WHOLE GANG IS OUT FOR THE HEAD OF THE GUY WHO DID IT.
IT WAS YOU, WASN'T IT?
RUNNING AND TRYING TO HIDE HERE ISN'T GOING TO SOLVE ANYTHING.
WE SHOULD GO HOME. TURN YOURSELF IN TO THE COPS...

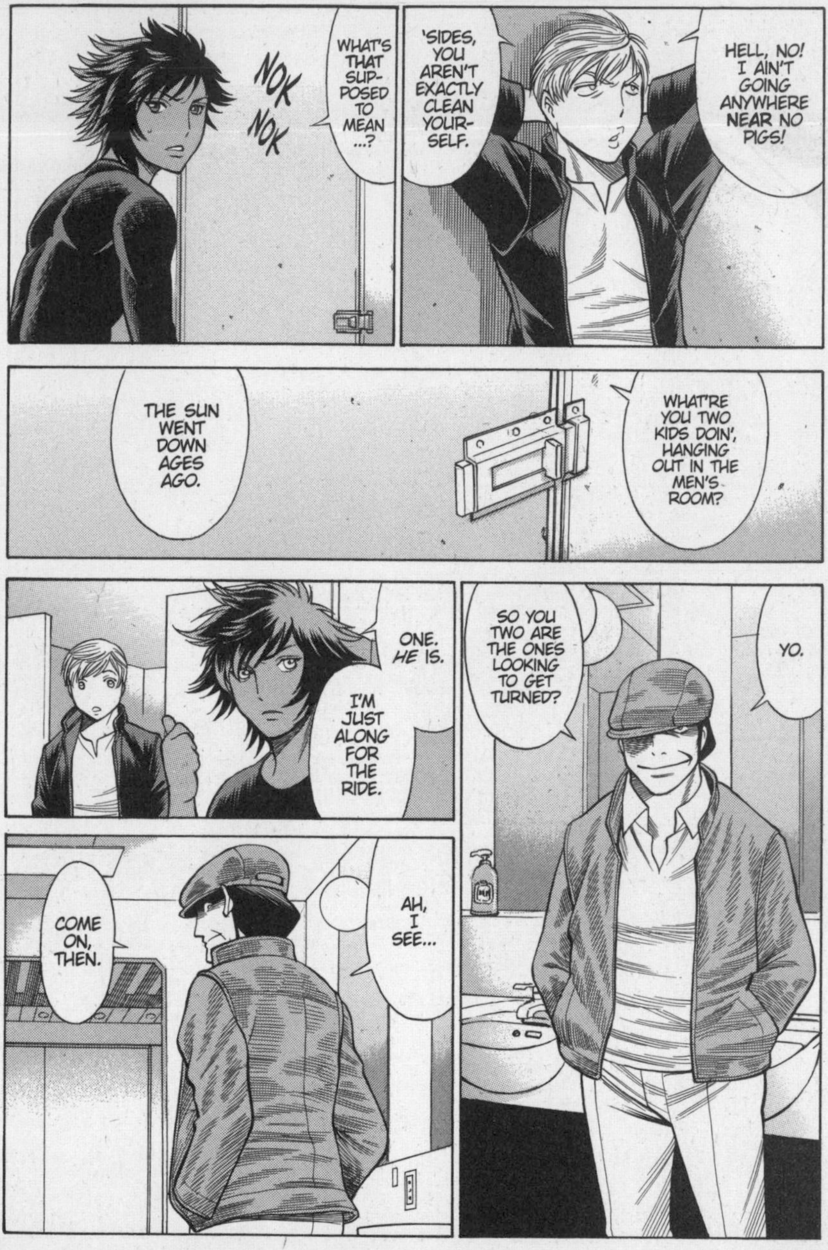
HELL, NO! I AIN'T GOING ANYWHERE NEAR NO PIGS!
'SIDES, YOU AREN'T EXACTLY CLEAN YOURSELF.
NOK NOK
WHAT'S THAT SUPPOSED TO MEAN ...?
WHAT'RE YOU TWO KIDS DOIN', HANGING OUT IN THE MEN'S ROOM?
THE SUN WENT DOWN AGES AGO.
YO.
SO YOU TWO ARE THE ONES LOOKING TO GET TURNED?
ONE. *HE* IS.
I'M JUST ALONG FOR THE RIDE.
AH, I SEE...
COME ON, THEN.

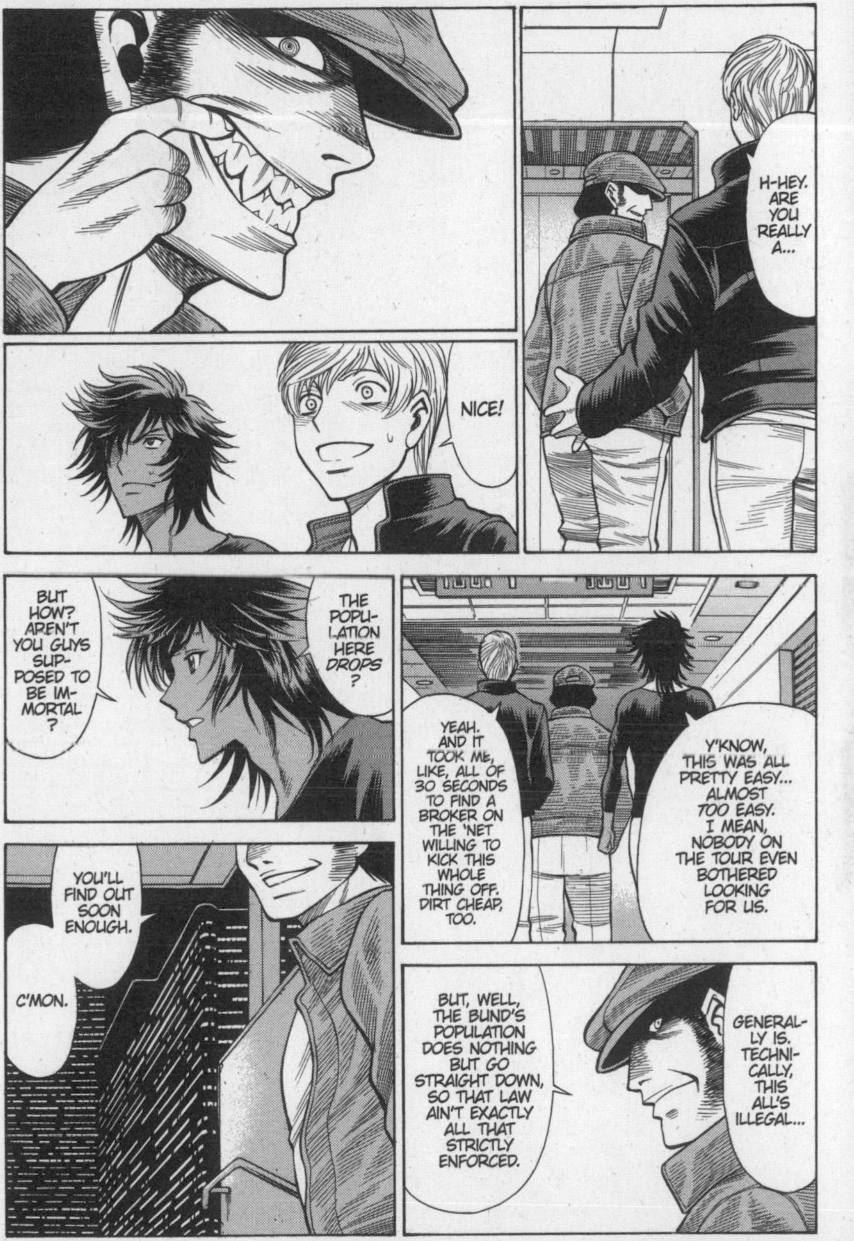

H-HEY. ARE YOU REALLY A...
NICE!
Y'KNOW, THIS WAS ALL PRETTY EASY... ALMOST *TOO* EASY. I MEAN, NOBODY ON THE TOUR EVEN BOTHERED LOOKING FOR US.
YEAH. AND IT TOOK ME, LIKE, ALL OF 30 SECONDS TO FIND A BROKER ON THE 'NET WILLING TO KICK THIS WHOLE THING OFF. DIRT CHEAP, TOO.
GENERAL-LY IS. TECHNI-CALLY, THIS ALL'S ILLEGAL...
BUT, WELL, THE BUND'S POPULATION DOES NOTHING BUT GO STRAIGHT DOWN, SO THAT LAW AIN'T EXACTLY ALL THAT STRICTLY ENFORCED.
THE POPU-LATION HERE *DROPS*?
BUT HOW? AREN'T YOU GUYS SUP-POSED TO BE IM-MORTAL?
YOU'LL FIND OUT SOON ENOUGH.
C'MON.

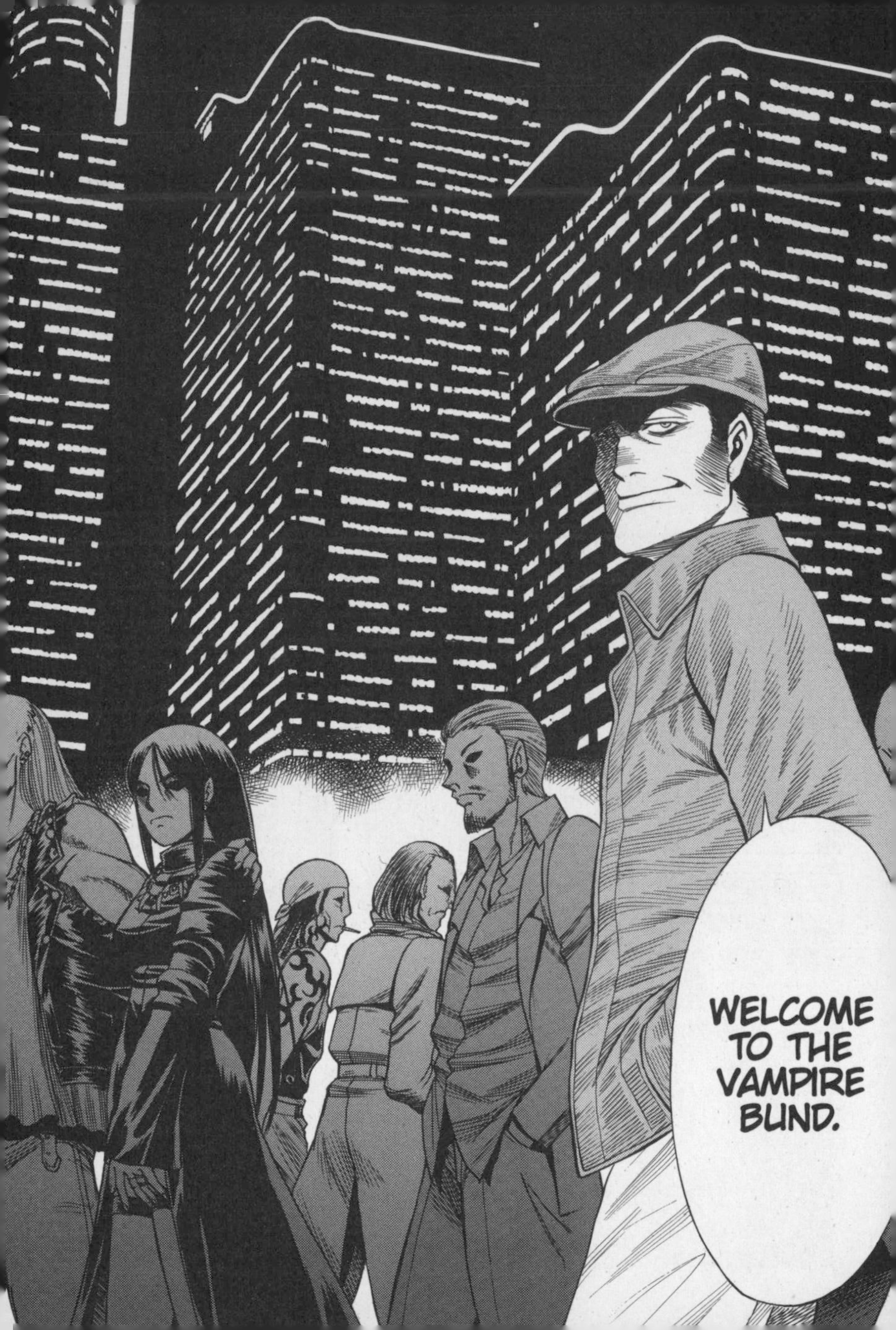
WELCOME TO THE VAMPIRE BUND.

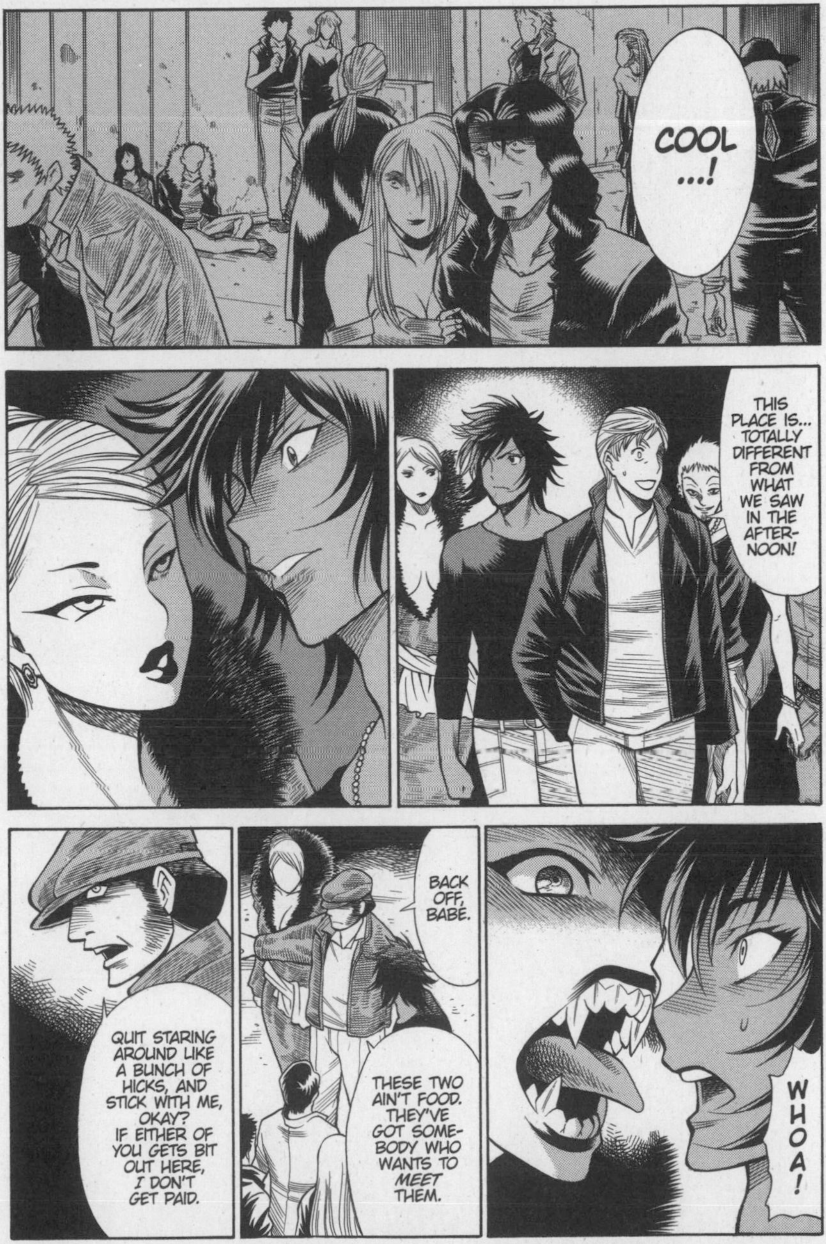
COOL ...!
THIS PLACE IS... TOTALLY DIFFERENT FROM WHAT WE SAW IN THE AFTER-NOON!
WHOA!
BACK OFF, BABE.
THESE TWO AIN'T FOOD. THEY'VE GOT SOME-BODY WHO WANTS TO *MEET* THEM.
QUIT STARING AROUND LIKE A BUNCH OF HICKS, AND STICK WITH ME, OKAY? IF EITHER OF YOU GETS BIT OUT HERE, *I* DON'T GET PAID.

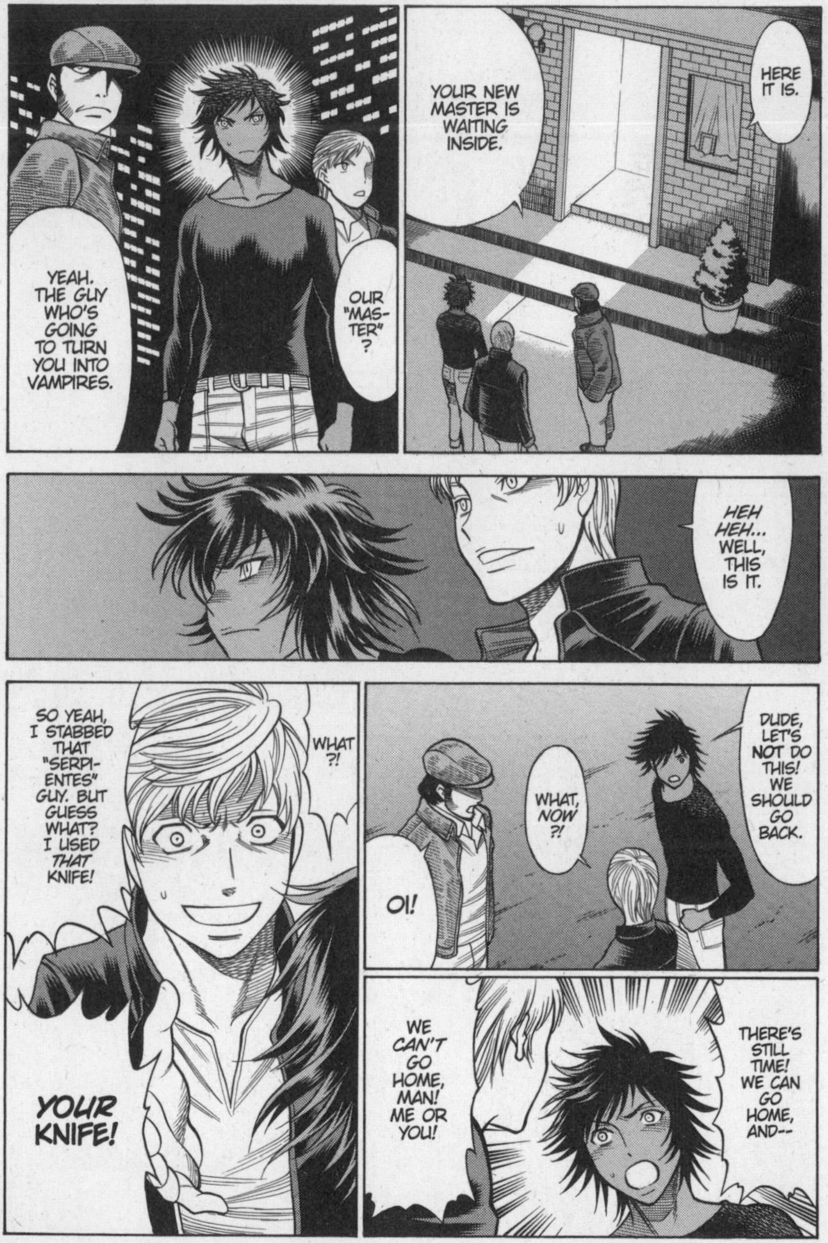
HERE IT IS.
YOUR NEW MASTER IS WAITING INSIDE.
OUR "MASTER"?
YEAH. THE GUY WHO'S GOING TO TURN YOU INTO VAMPIRES.
HEH HEH... WELL, THIS IS IT.
DUDE, LET'S NOT DO THIS! WE SHOULD GO BACK.
WHAT, NOW?!
OI!
THERE'S STILL TIME! WE CAN GO HOME, AND--
WE CAN'T GO HOME, MAN! ME OR YOU!
WHAT?!
SO YEAH, I STABBED THAT "SERPIENTES" GUY. BUT GUESS WHAT? I USED THAT KNIFE!
YOUR KNIFE!

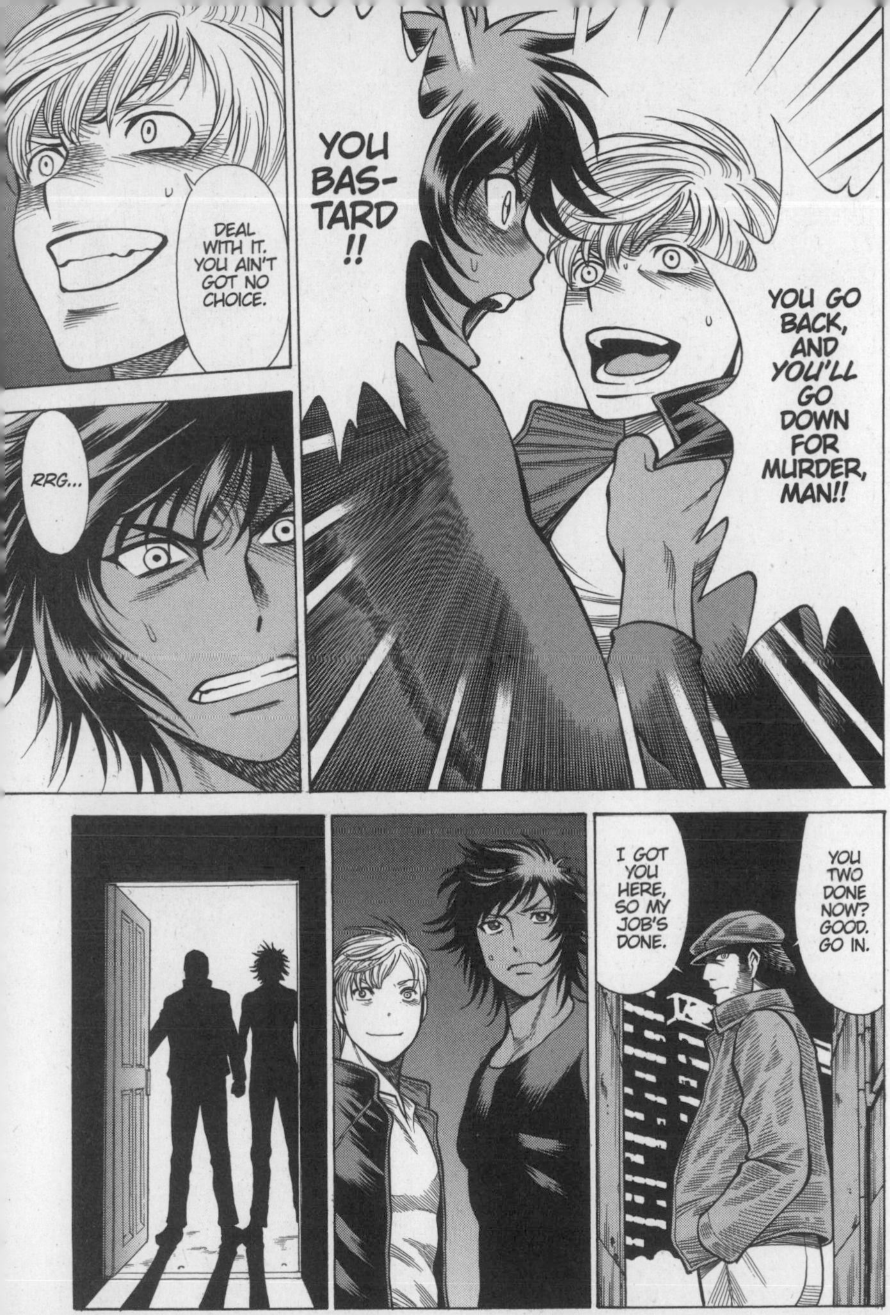
YOU GO BACK, AND YOU'LL GO DOWN FOR MURDER, MAN!!
YOU BASTARD!!
DEAL WITH IT. YOU AIN'T GOT NO CHOICE.
RRG...
YOU TWO DONE NOW? GOOD. GO IN.
I GOT YOU HERE, SO MY JOB'S DONE.

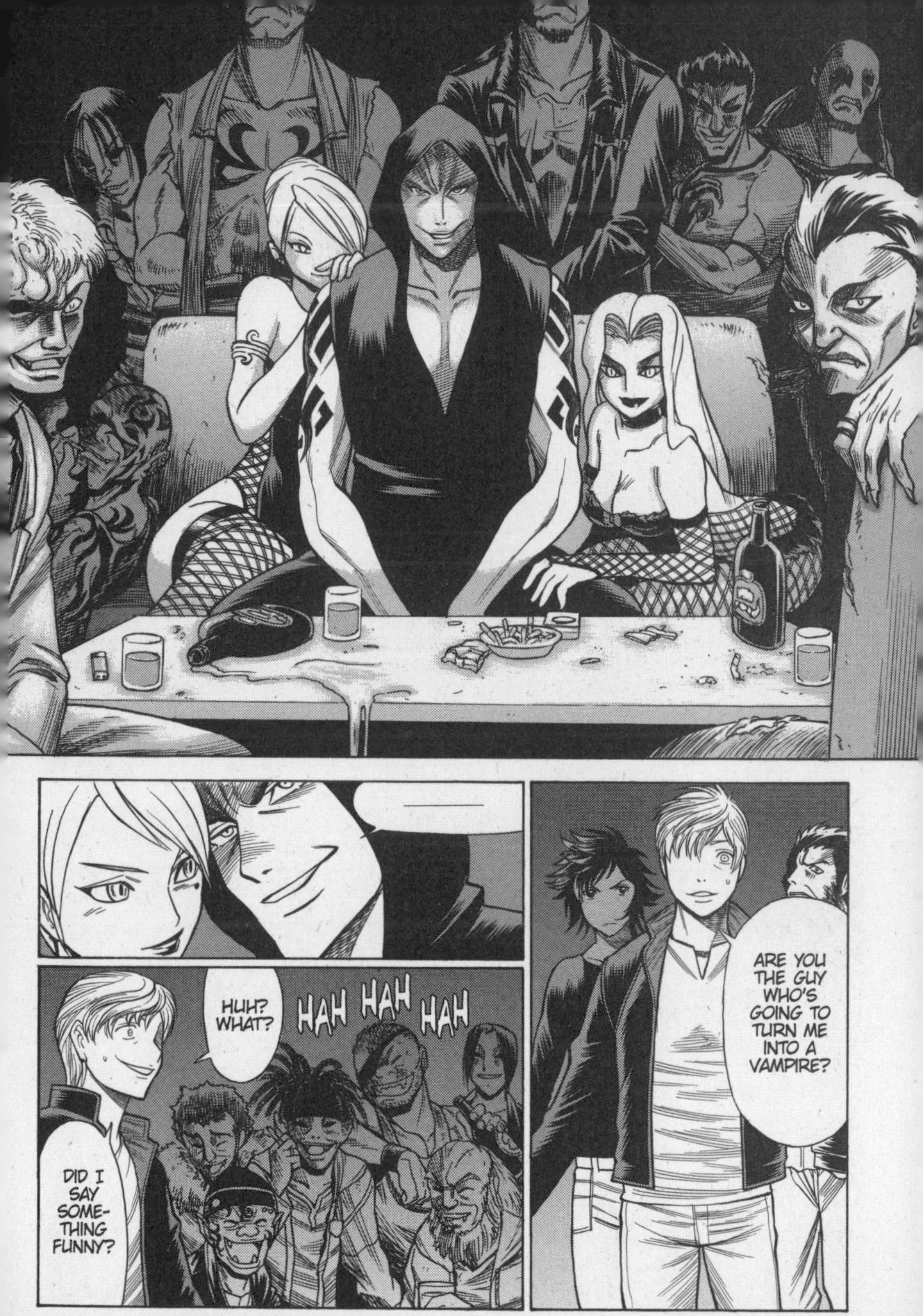
ARE YOU THE GUY WHO'S GOING TO TURN ME INTO A VAMPIRE?
——
HAH HAH HAH
HUH? WHAT?
DID I SAY SOME-THING FUNNY?

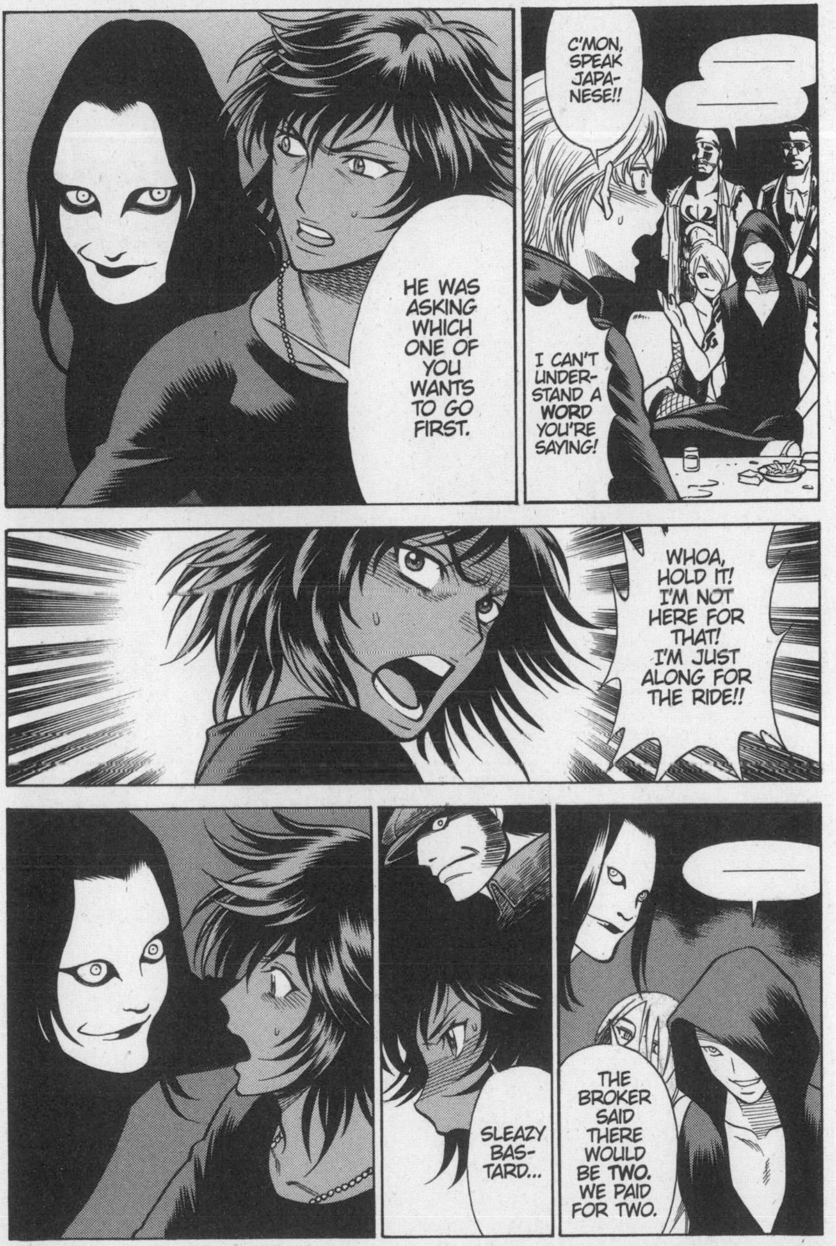
C'MON, SPEAK JAPA-NESE!!
I CAN'T UNDER-STAND A WORD YOU'RE SAYING!
HE WAS ASKING WHICH ONE OF YOU WANTS TO GO FIRST.
WHOA, HOLD IT! I'M NOT HERE FOR THAT! I'M JUST ALONG FOR THE RIDE!!
THE BROKER SAID THERE WOULD BE TWO. WE PAID FOR TWO.
SLEAZY BAS-TARD...

JOIN US AND LET US DRINK YOUR BLOOD. OR REFUSE, AND DIE.
MAKE YOUR CHOICE.

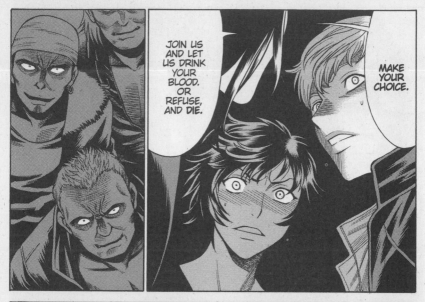

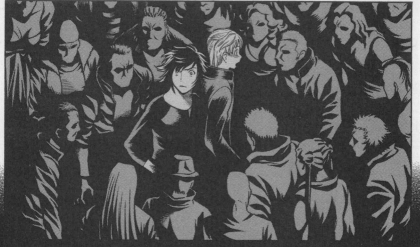

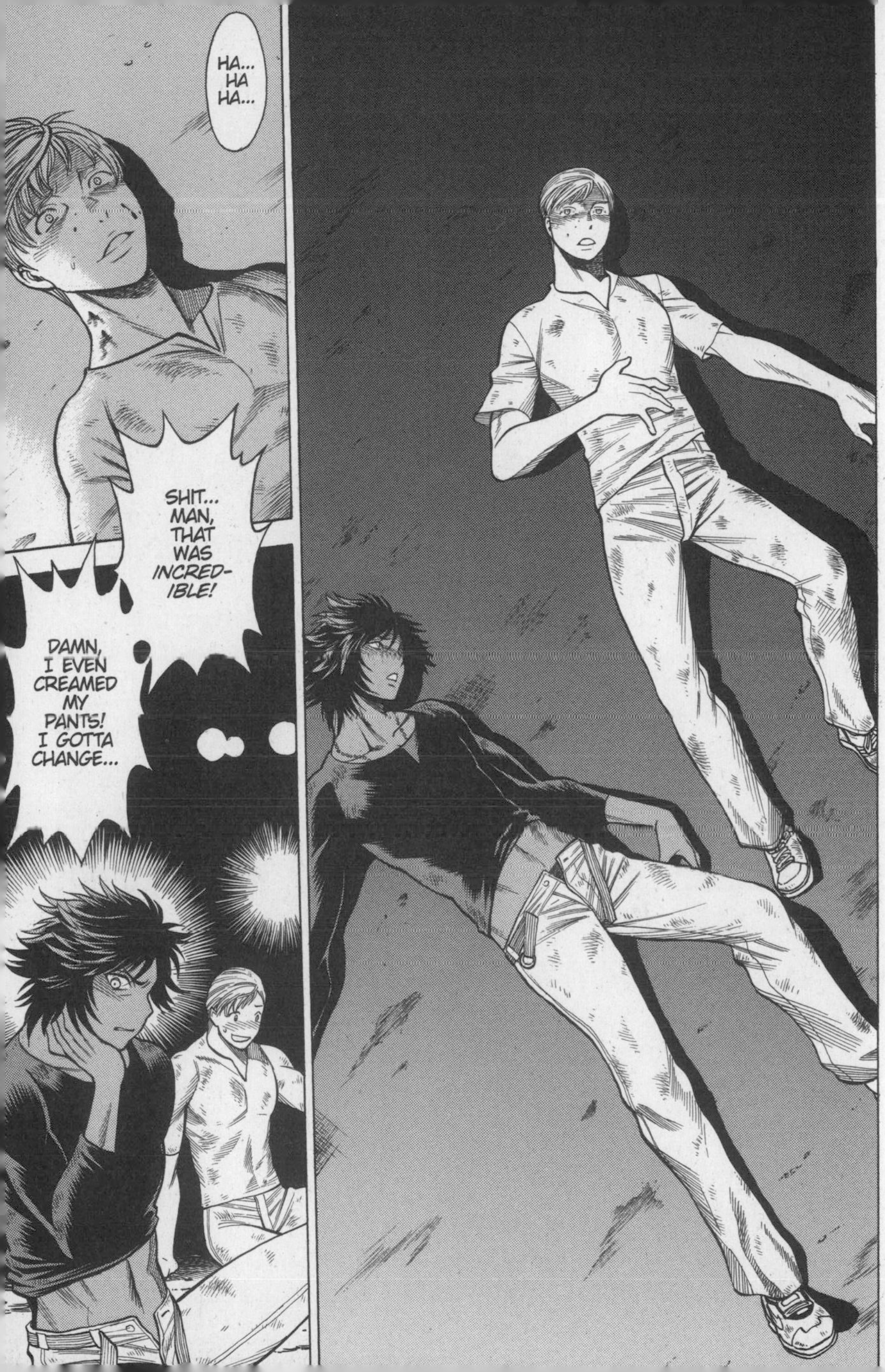
HA... HA HA...
SHIT... MAN, THAT WAS INCRED-IBLE!
DAMN, I EVEN CREAMED MY PANTS! I GOTTA CHANGE...

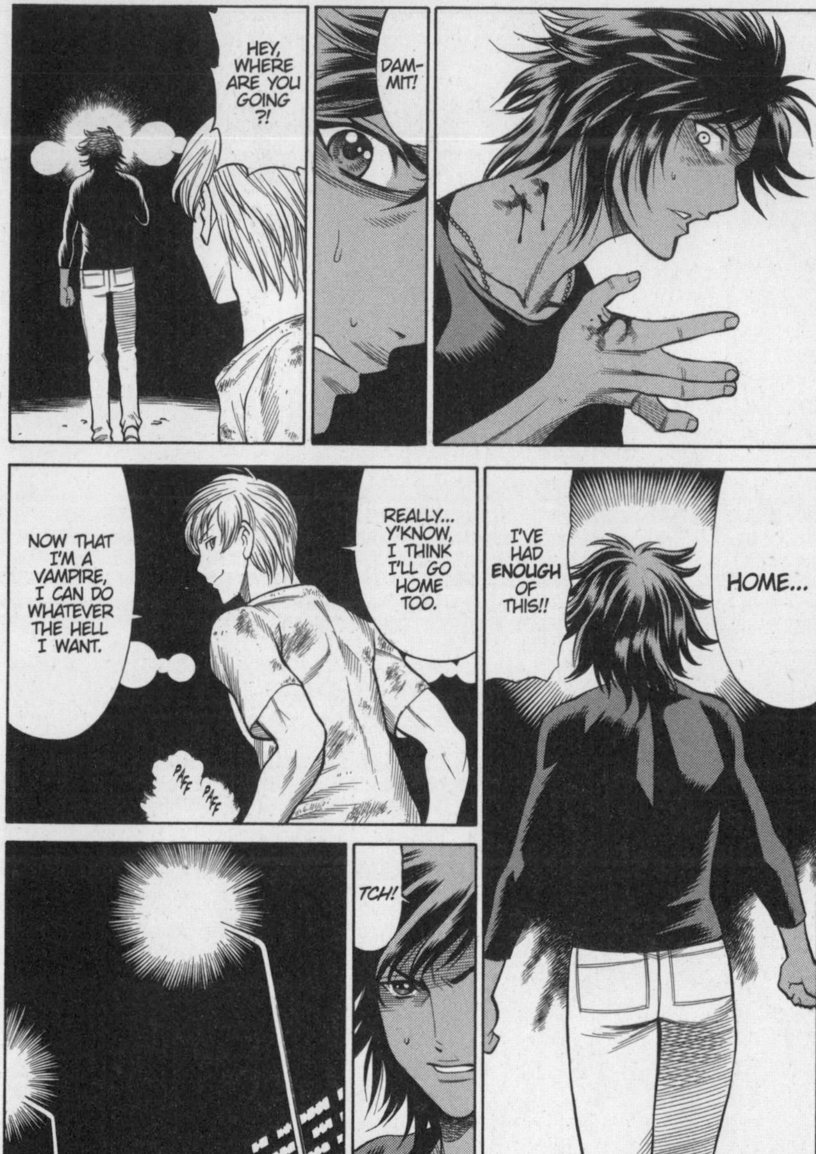
DAM-MIT!
HEY, WHERE ARE YOU GOING ?!
HOME...
I'VE HAD ENOUGH OF THIS!!
REALLY... Y'KNOW, I THINK I'LL GO HOME TOO.
NOW THAT I'M A VAMPIRE, I CAN DO WHATEVER THE HELL I WANT.
PAFF PAFF
TCH!

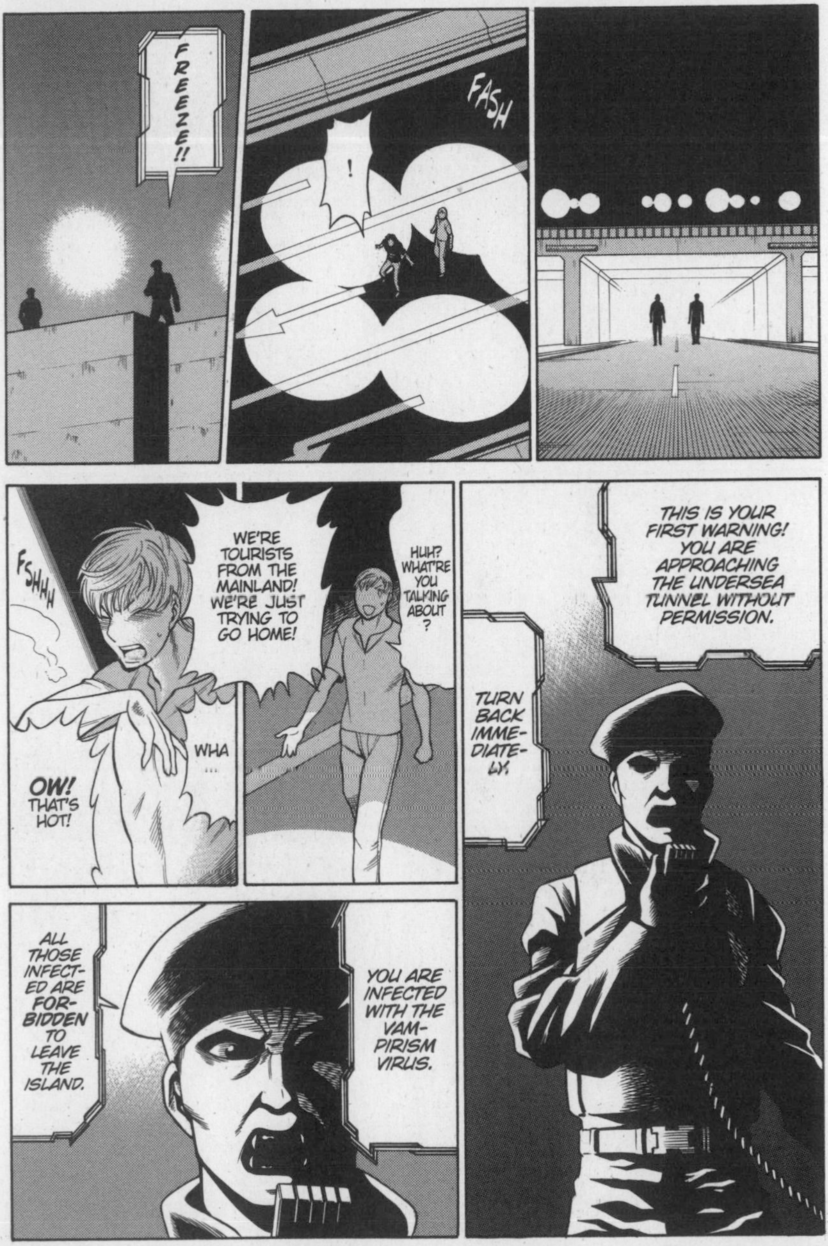
FASH
!
FREEZE!!
THIS IS YOUR FIRST WARNING! YOU ARE APPROACHING THE UNDERSEA TUNNEL WITHOUT PERMISSION.
TURN BACK IMMEDIATELY.
HUH? WHAT'RE YOU TALKING ABOUT?
WE'RE TOURISTS FROM THE MAINLAND! WE'RE JUST TRYING TO GO HOME!
FSHHH
WHA...
OW! THAT'S HOT!
YOU ARE INFECTED WITH THE VAMPIRISM VIRUS.
ALL THOSE INFECTED ARE FORBIDDEN TO LEAVE THE ISLAND.

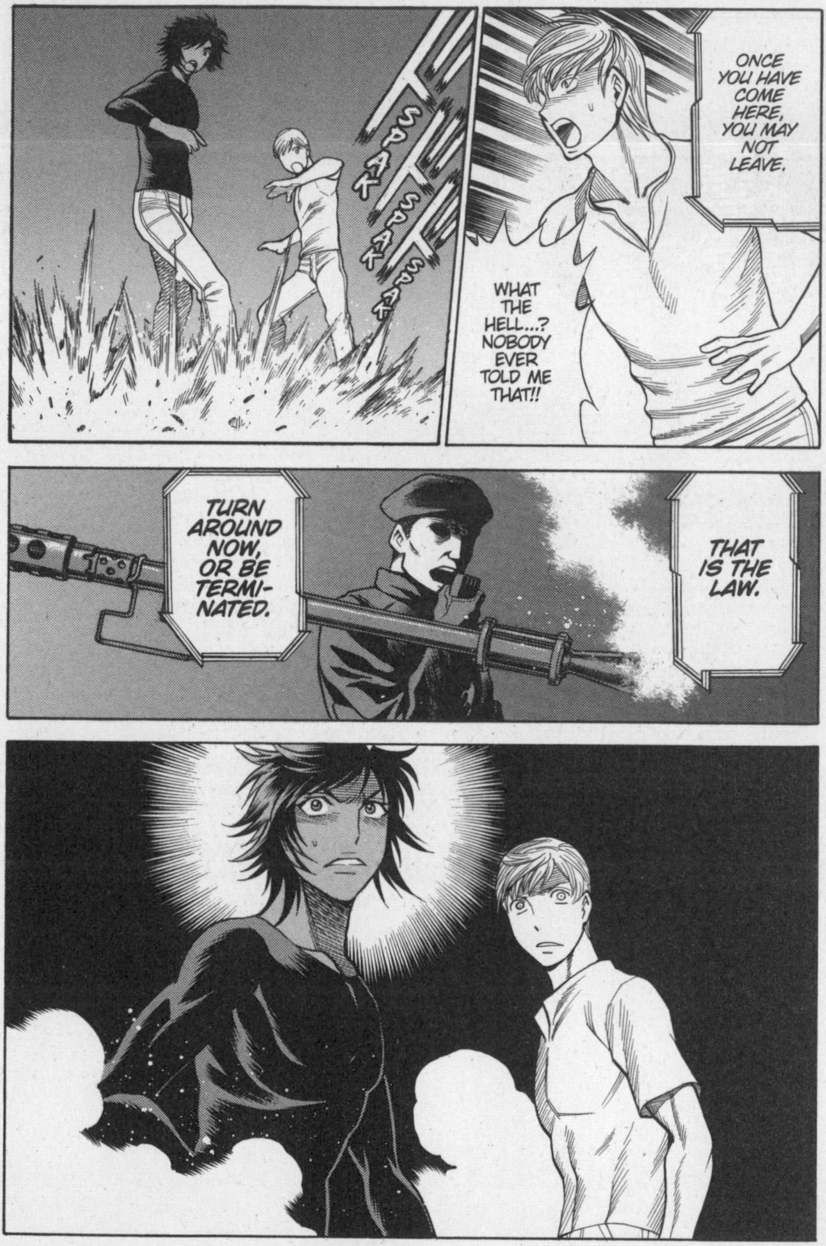
ONCE YOU HAVE COME HERE, YOU MAY NOT LEAVE.
WHAT THE HELL...? NOBODY EVER TOLD ME THAT!!
SPAK SPAK SPAK
THAT IS THE LAW.
TURN AROUND NOW, OR BE TERMI-NATED.

Chapter 2: Baptism

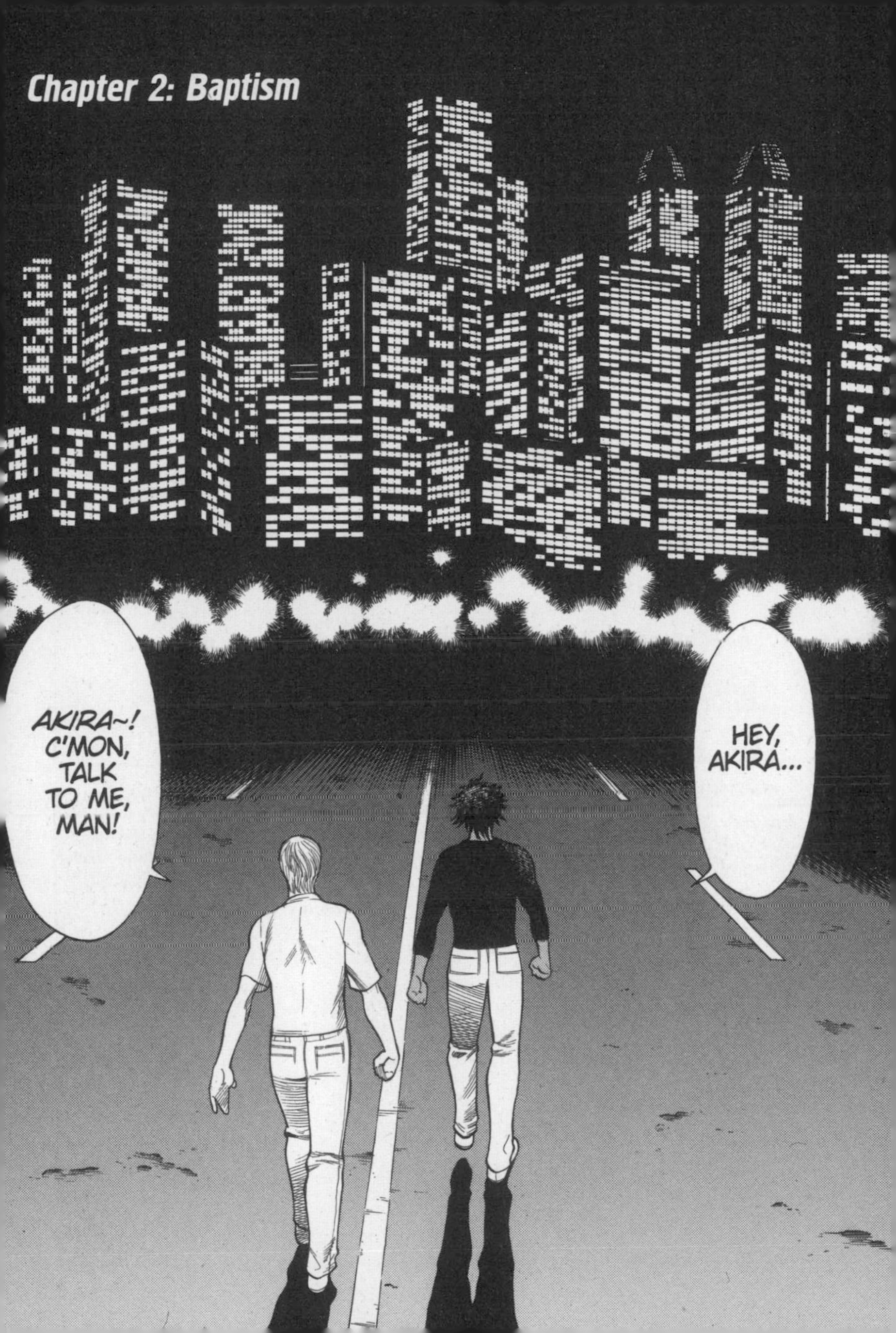
HEY, AKIRA...
AKIRA~! C'MON, TALK TO ME, MAN!

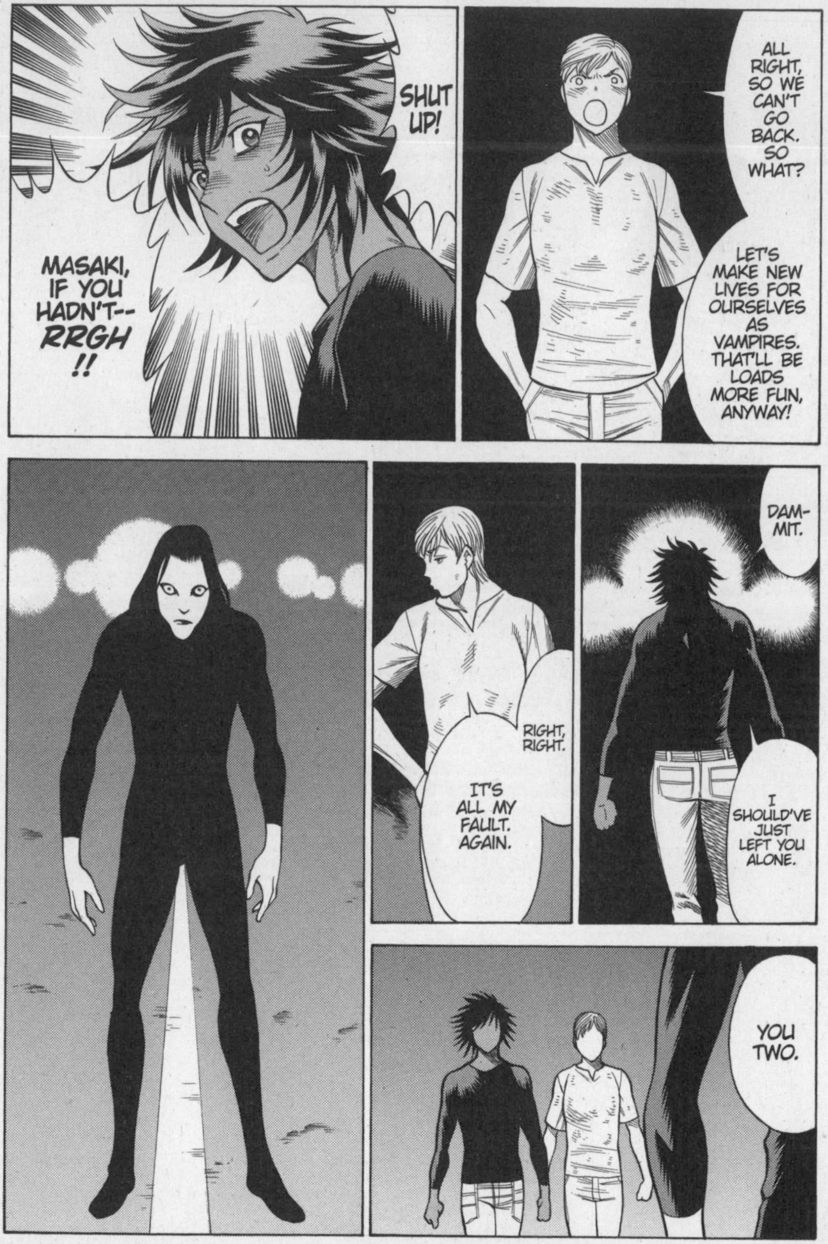
ALL RIGHT, SO WE CAN'T GO BACK. SO WHAT?
LET'S MAKE NEW LIVES FOR OURSELVES AS VAMPIRES. THAT'LL BE LOADS MORE FUN, ANYWAY!
SHUT UP!
MASAKI, IF YOU HADN'T-- RRGH!!
DAM-MIT.
I SHOULD'VE JUST LEFT YOU ALONE.
RIGHT, RIGHT.
IT'S ALL MY FAULT. AGAIN.
YOU TWO.

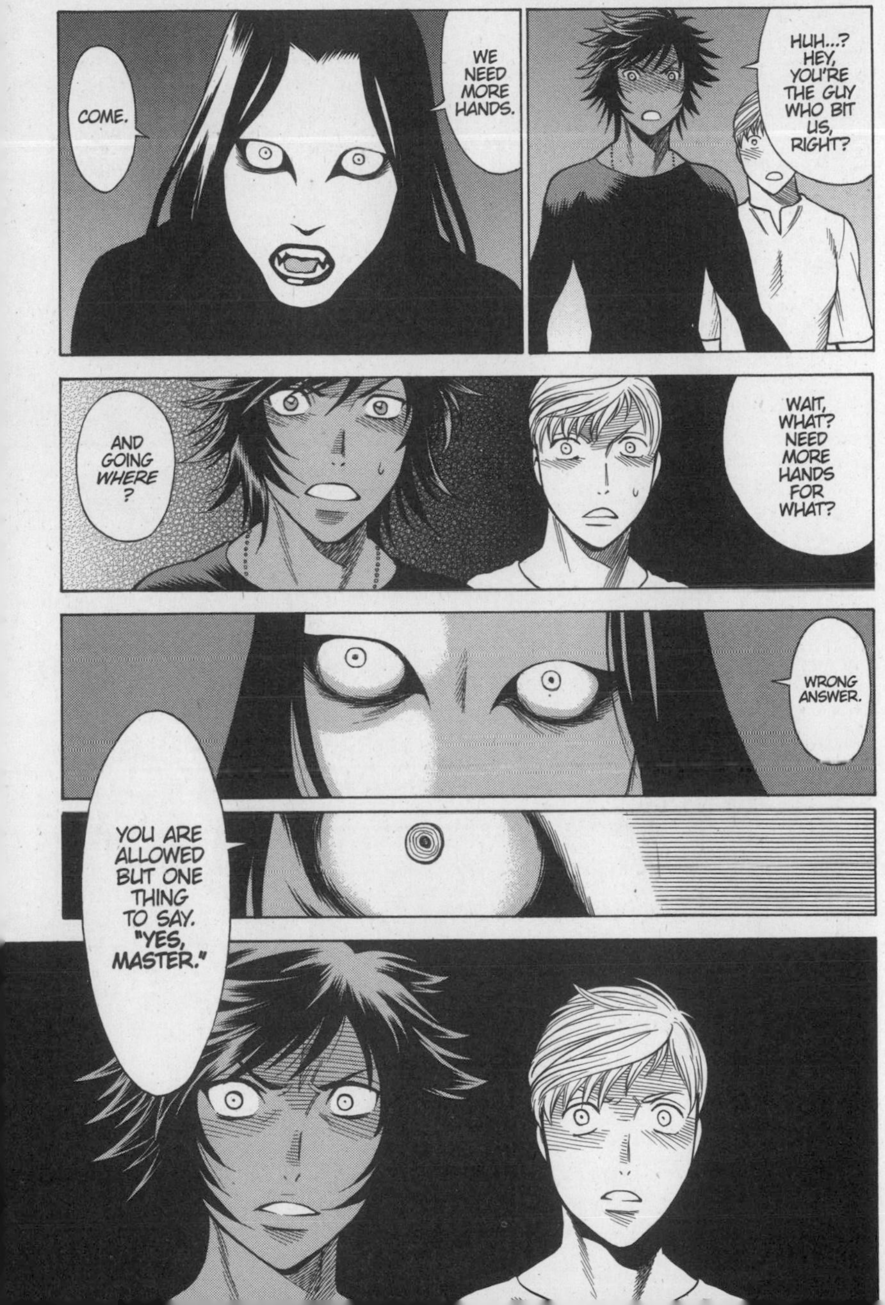
HUH...? HEY, YOU'RE THE GUY WHO BIT US, RIGHT?
WE NEED MORE HANDS.
COME.
WAIT, WHAT? NEED MORE HANDS FOR WHAT?
AND GOING *WHERE*?
WRONG ANSWER.
YOU ARE ALLOWED BUT ONE THING TO SAY. "YES, MASTER."

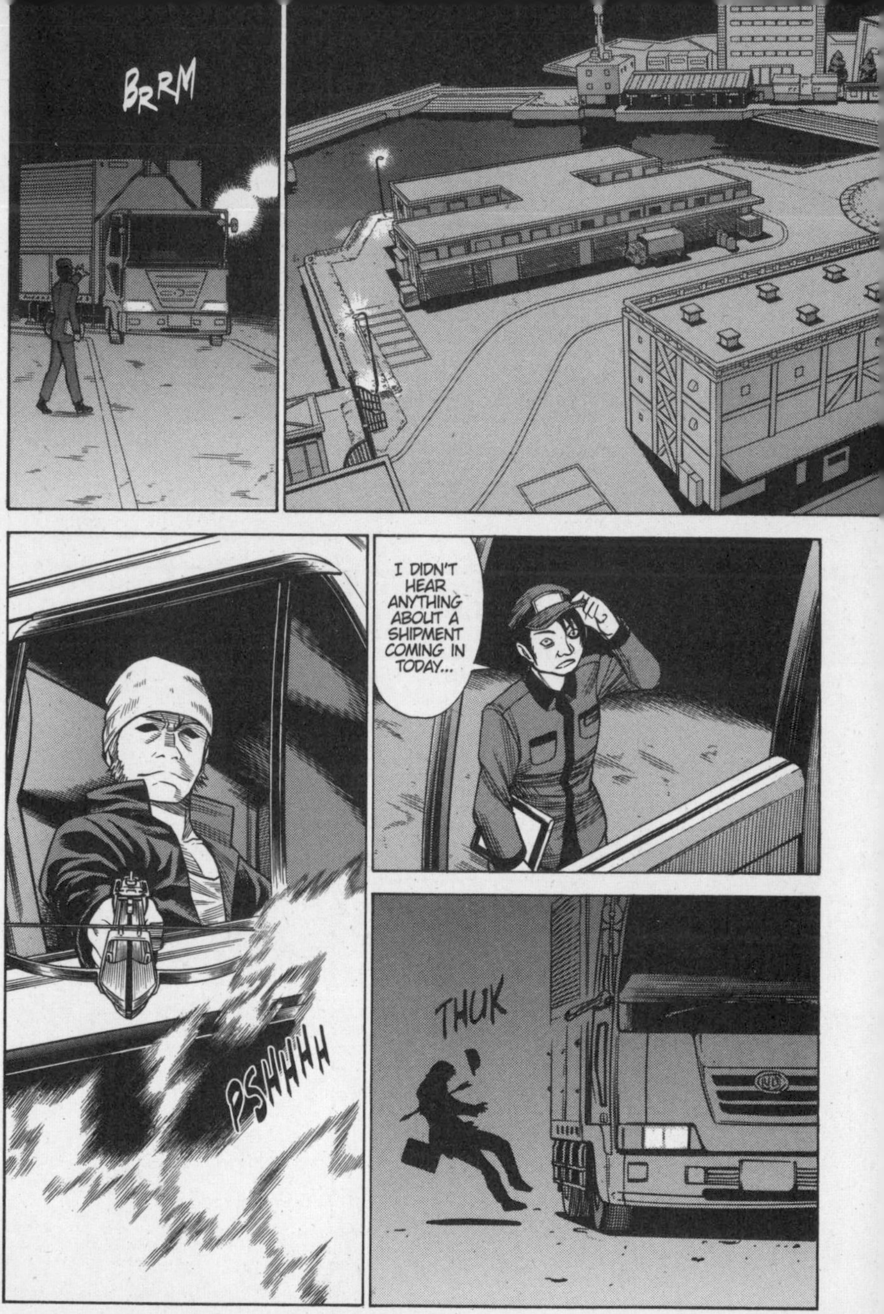
BRRM
I DIDN'T HEAR ANYTHING ABOUT A SHIPMENT COMING IN TODAY...
THUK
PSHHHH

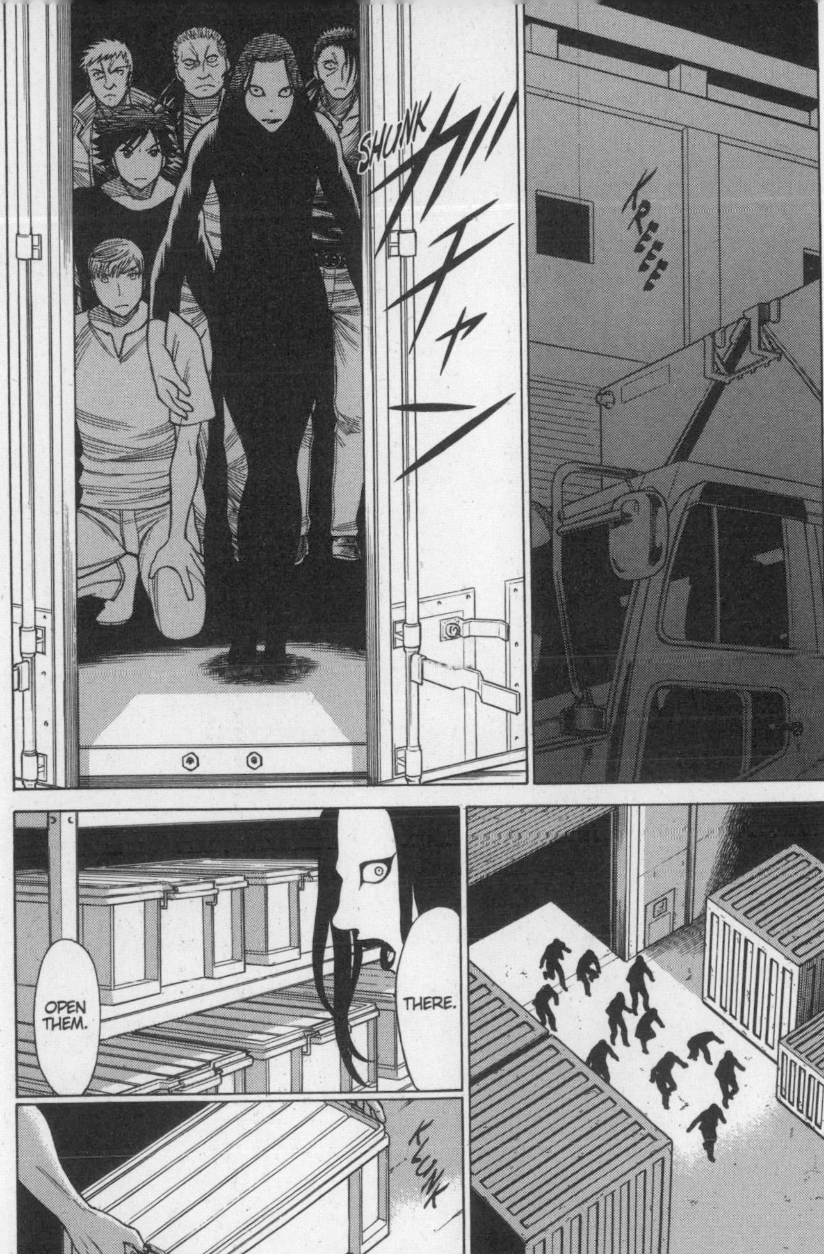
KREEEE
SHUNK
ガチャーン
THERE.
OPEN THEM.
KLUNK

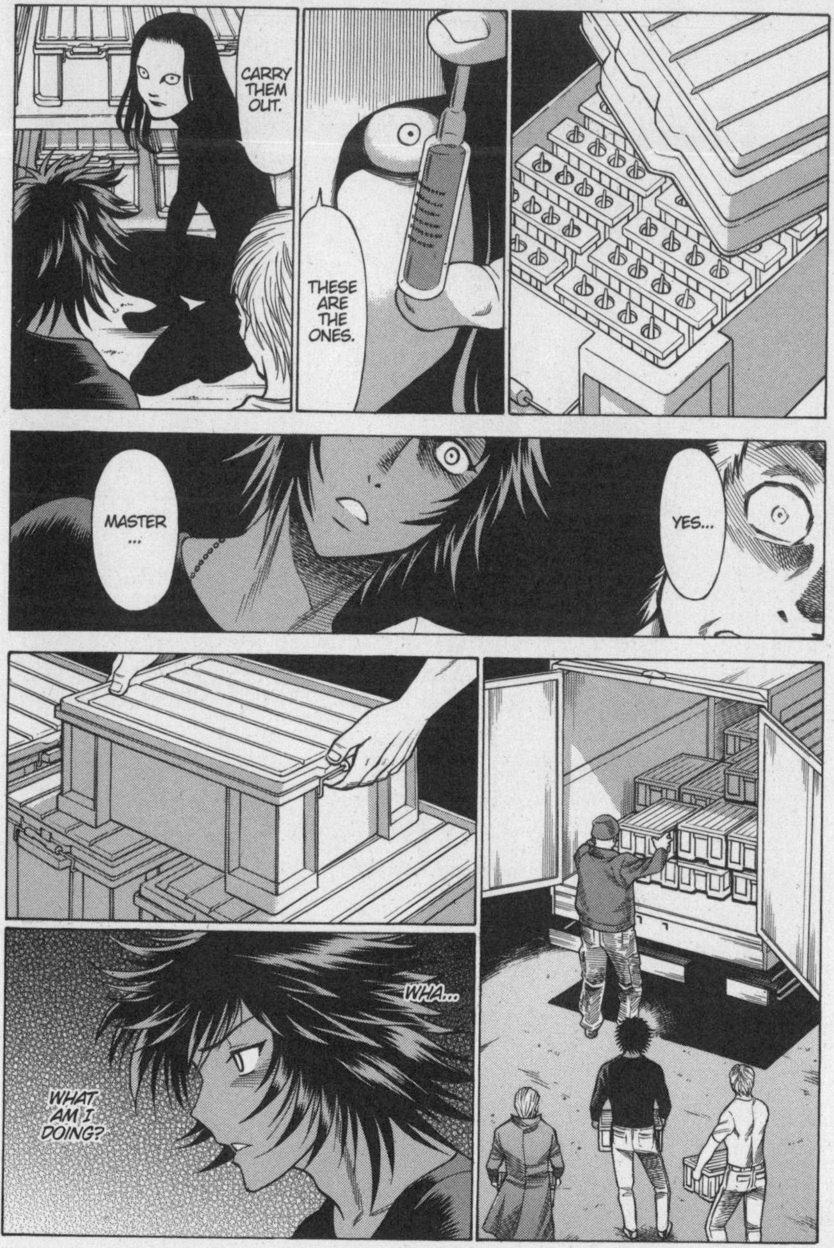

THESE ARE THE ONES.
CARRY THEM OUT.
YES...
MASTER ...
WHA...
WHAT AM I DOING?

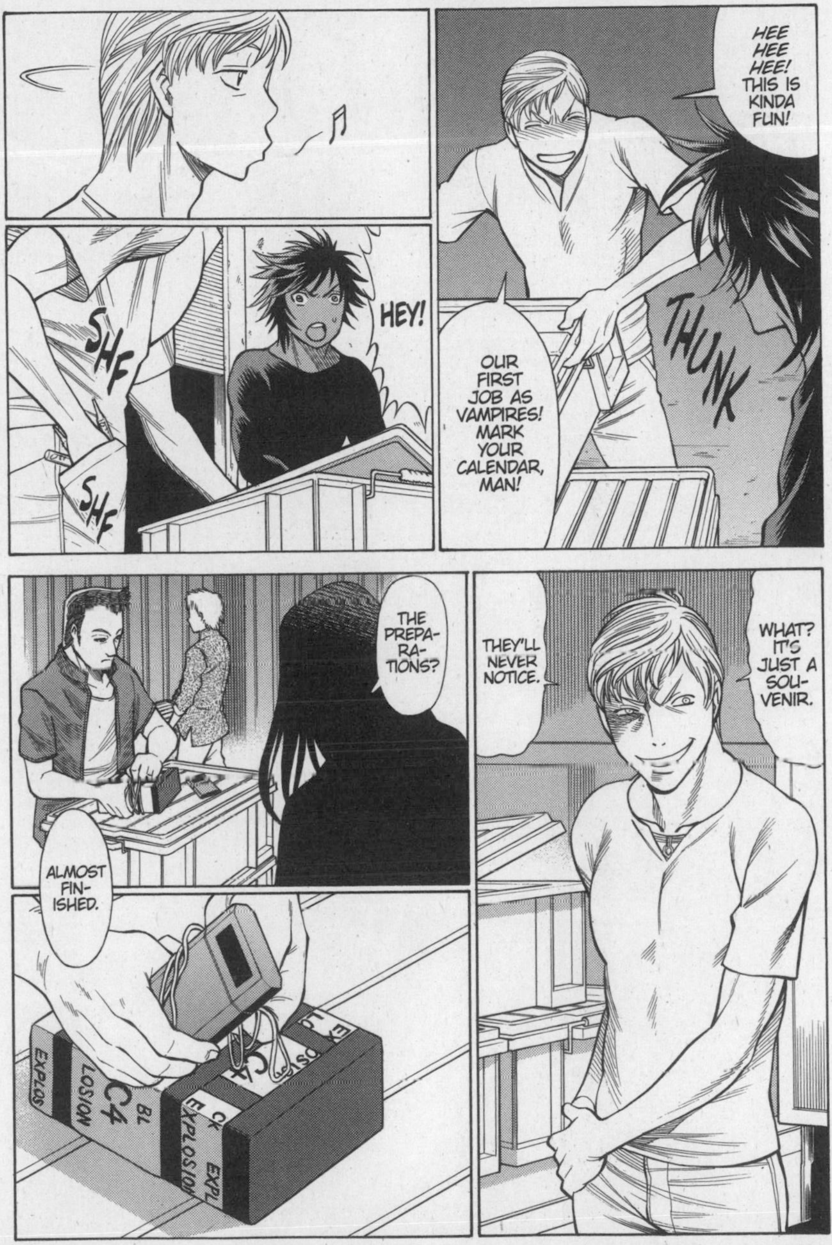
HEE HEE HEE! THIS IS KINDA FUN!
OUR FIRST JOB AS VAMPIRES! MARK YOUR CALENDAR, MAN!
THUNK
SHF
SHF
HEY!
WHAT? IT'S JUST A SOUVENIR.
THEY'LL NEVER NOTICE.
THE PREPARATIONS?
ALMOST FINISHED.
C4
EXPLOSION

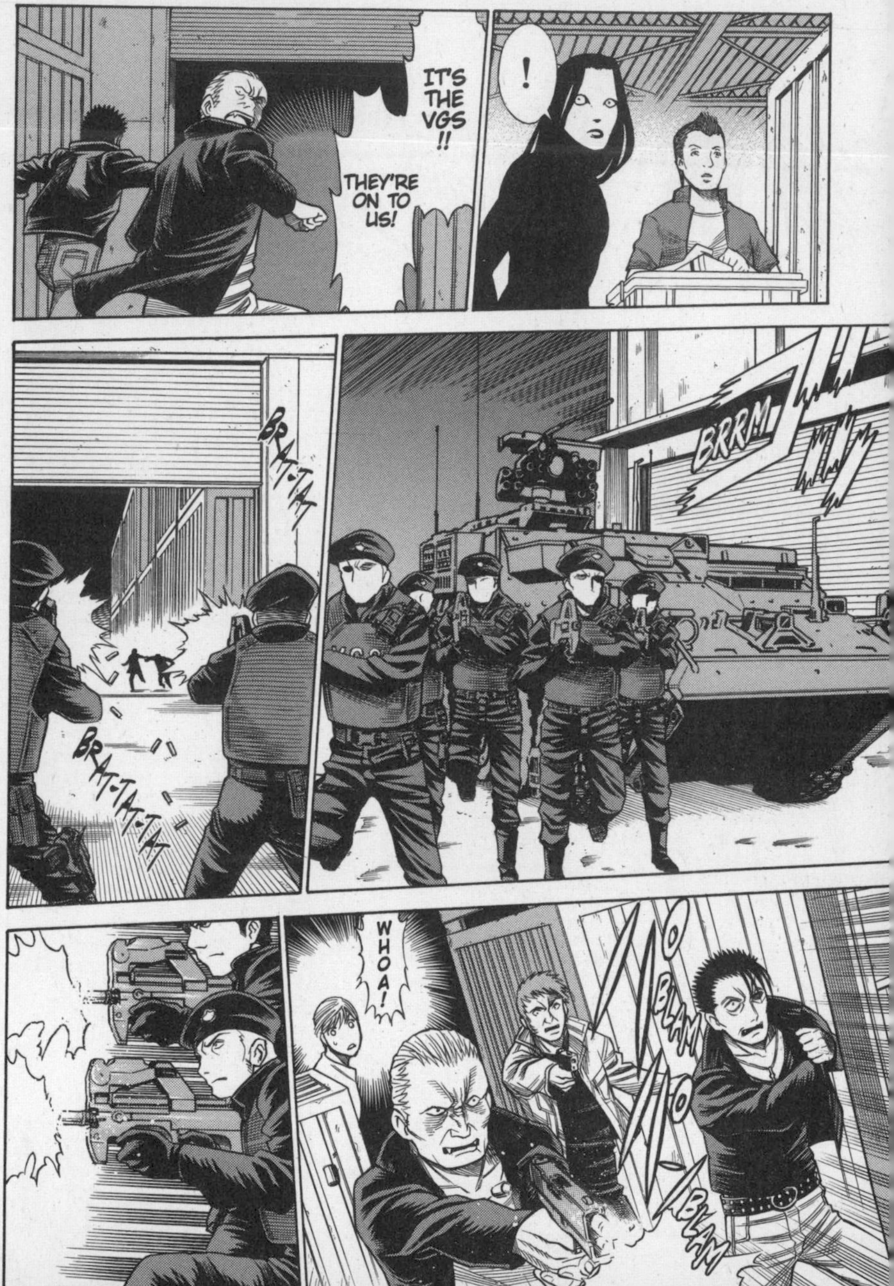
!
IT'S THE VGS!!
THEY'RE ON TO US!
BRRM
BRAT-TAT
BRAT-TAT-TAT
WHOA!
BLAM
BLAM

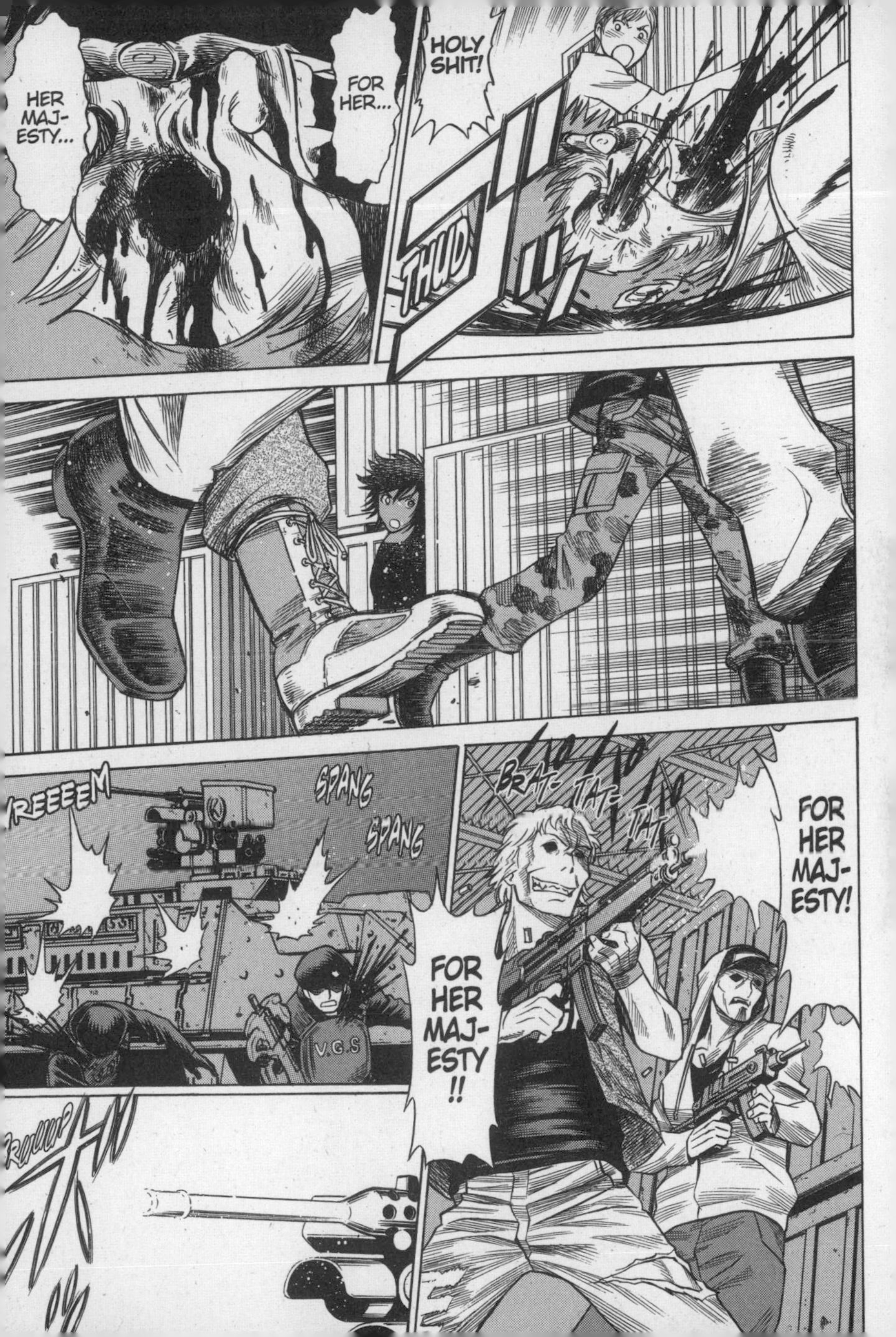
HOLY SHIT!
THUD
FOR HER...
HER MAJ-ESTY...
BRAT-TAT-TAT
FOR HER MAJ-ESTY!
FOR HER MAJ-ESTY !!
SPANG
SPANG
VREEEEM
V.G.S

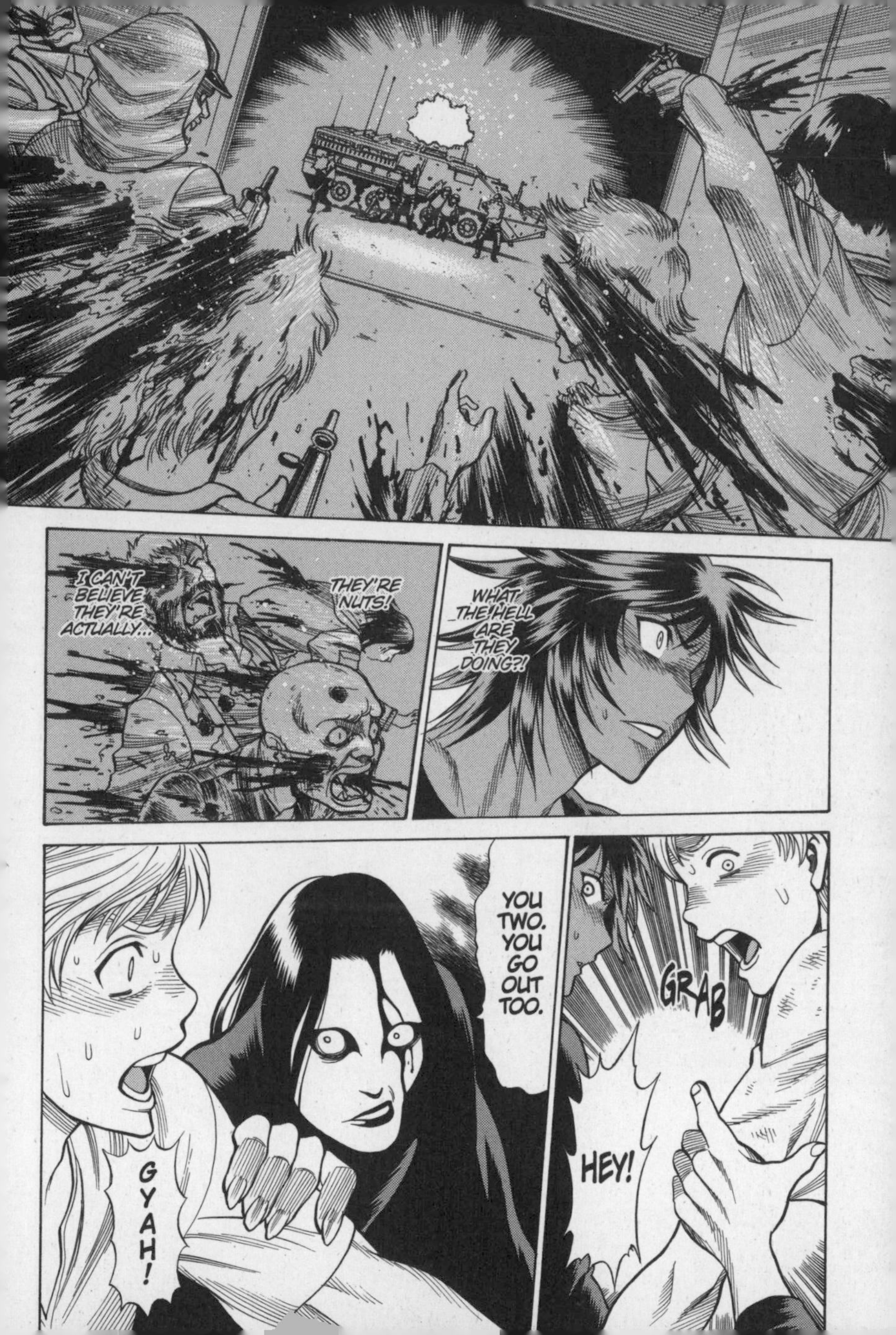
WHAT THE HELL ARE THEY DOING?!
THEY'RE NUTS!
I CAN'T BELIEVE THEY'RE ACTUALLY...
GRAB
HEY!
YOU TWO. YOU GO OUT TOO.
GYAH!

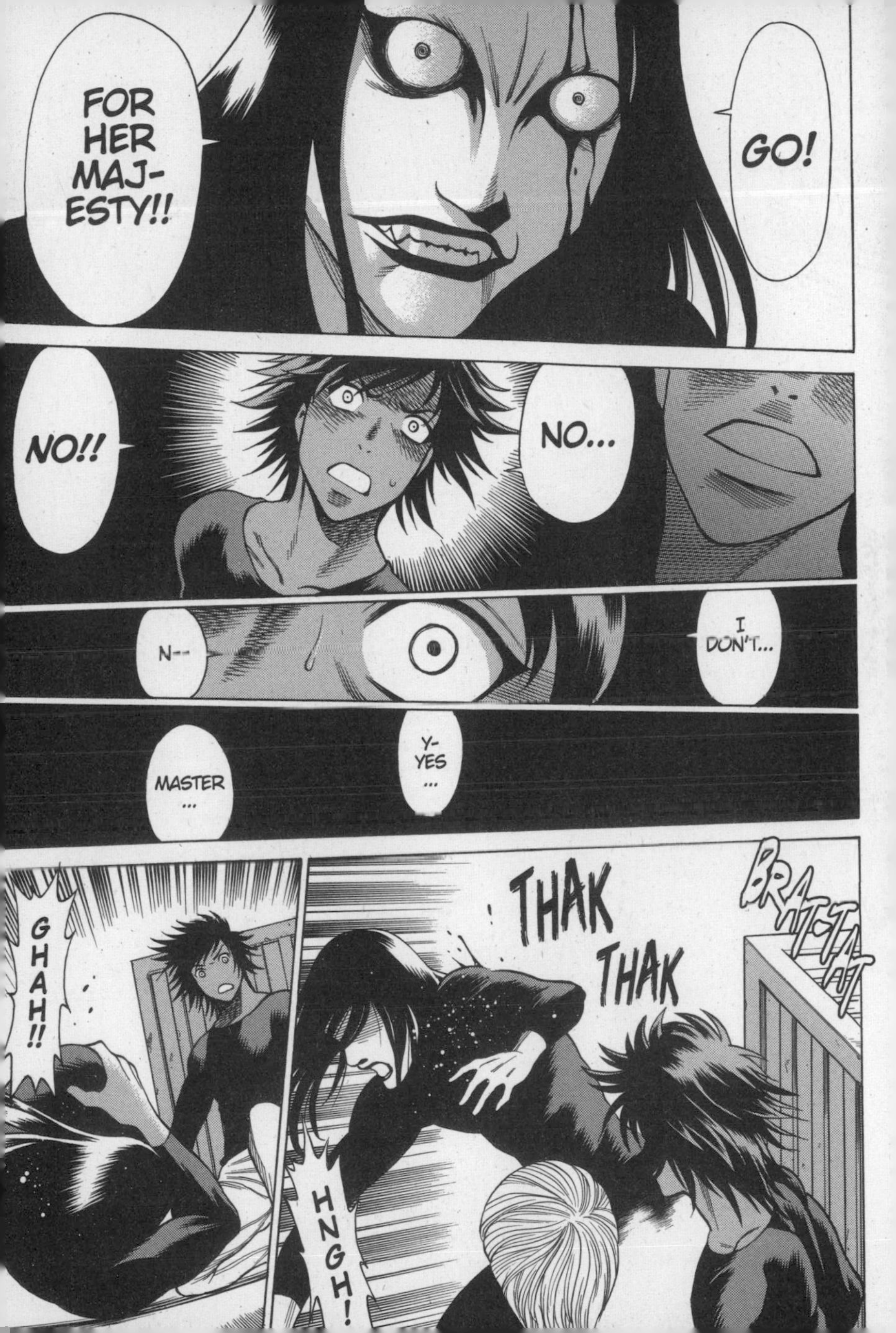
GO!
FOR HER MAJ- ESTY!!
NO...
NO!!
I DON'T...
N--
Y- YES ...
MASTER ...
BRATATAT
THAK
THAK
HNGH!
GHAH!!

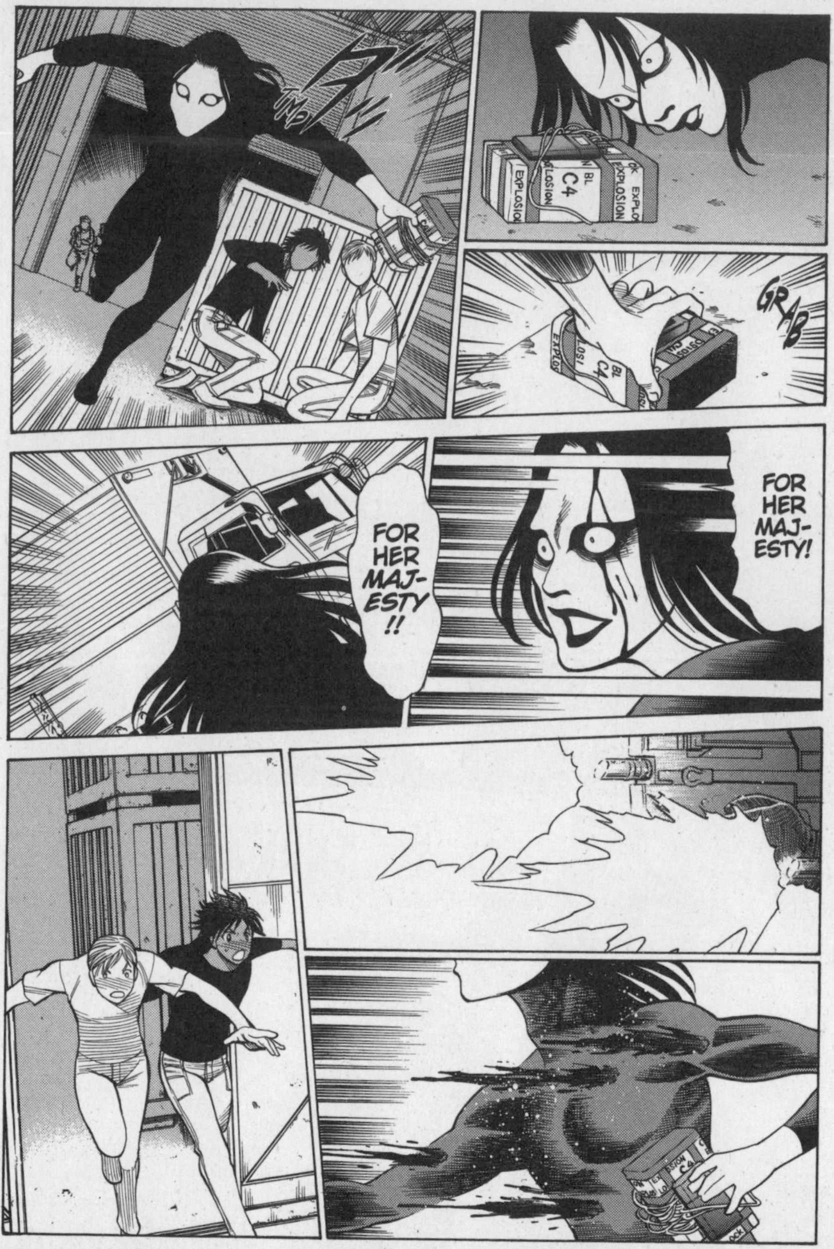
C4
EXPLOSION
GRAB
FOR HER MAJ- ESTY!
FOR HER MAJ- ESTY !!

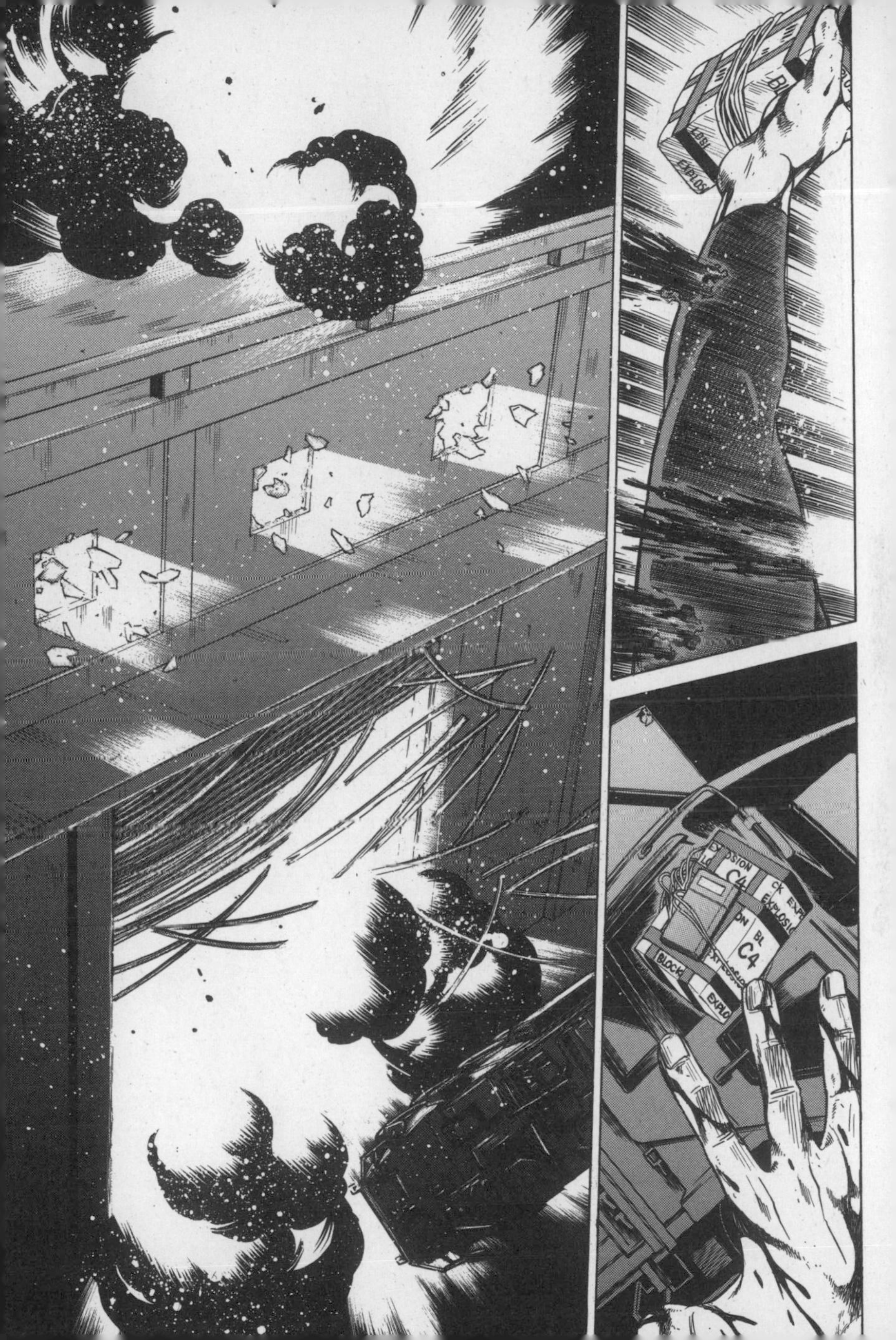
EXPLOSION
C4
C4
BLOCK

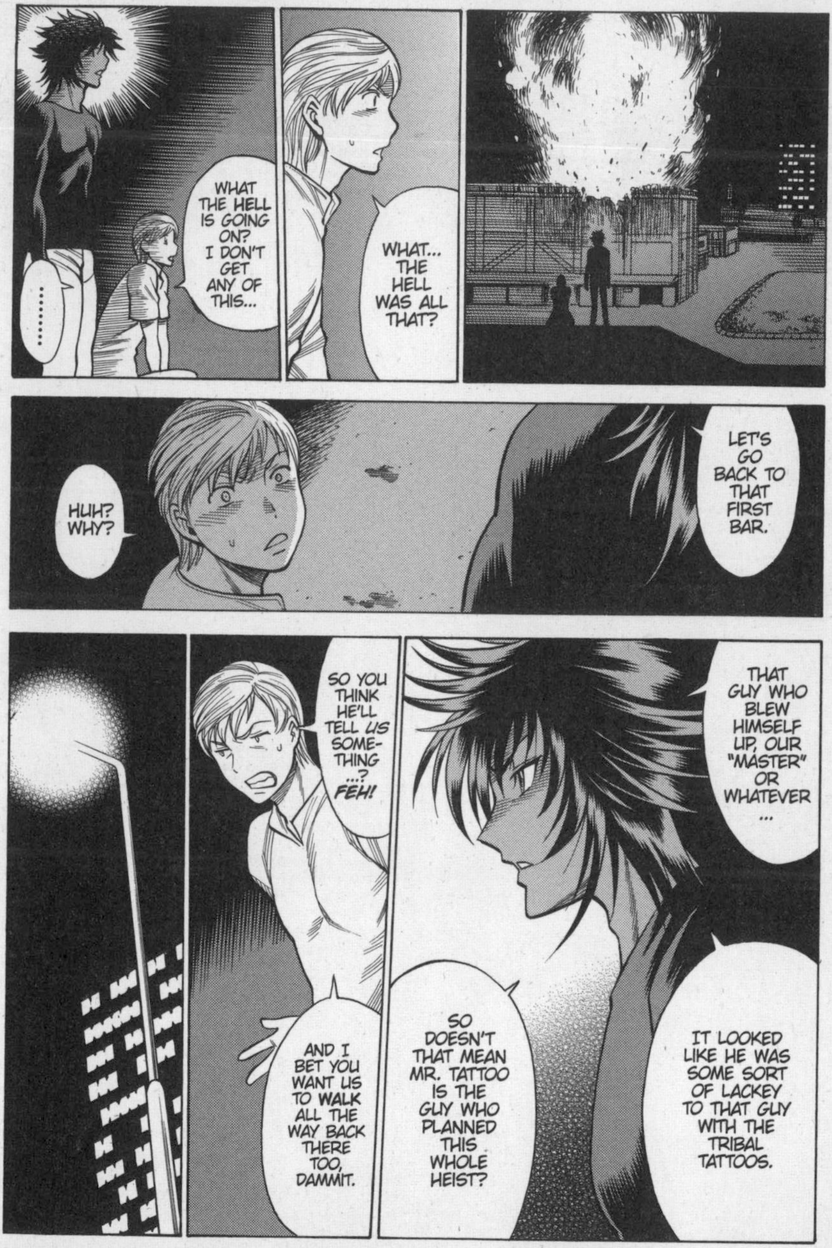
WHAT... THE HELL WAS ALL THAT?
WHAT THE HELL IS GOING ON? I DON'T GET ANY OF THIS...
......
LET'S GO BACK TO THAT FIRST BAR.
HUH? WHY?
THAT GUY WHO BLEW HIMSELF UP, OUR "MASTER" OR WHATEVER ...
IT LOOKED LIKE HE WAS SOME SORT OF LACKEY TO THAT GUY WITH THE TRIBAL TATTOOS.
SO DOESN'T THAT MEAN MR. TATTOO IS THE GUY WHO PLANNED THIS WHOLE HEIST?
SO YOU THINK HE'LL TELL *US* SOMETHING ...? ***FEH!***
AND I BET YOU WANT US TO **WALK** ALL THE WAY BACK THERE TOO, DAMMIT.

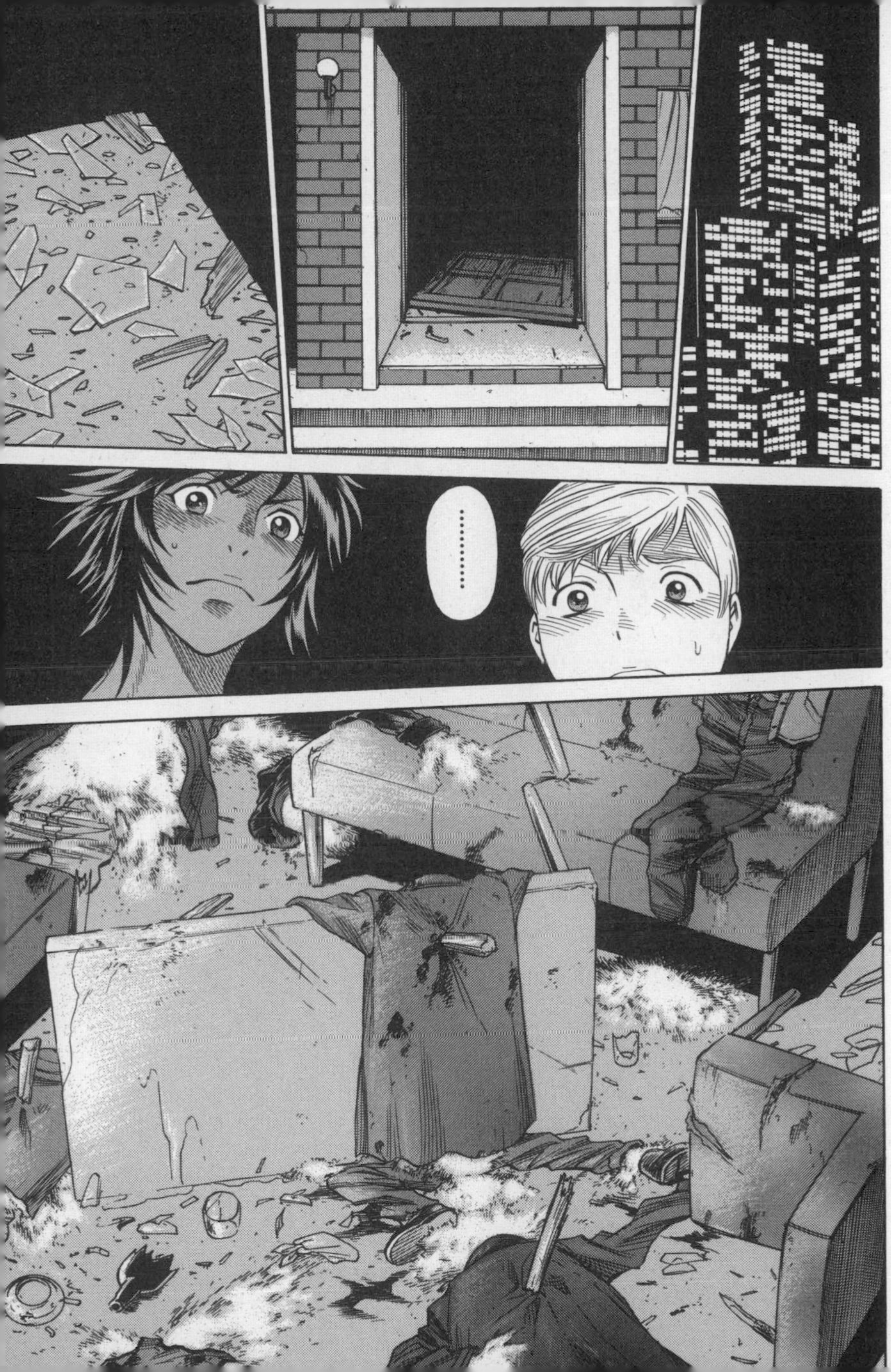
………

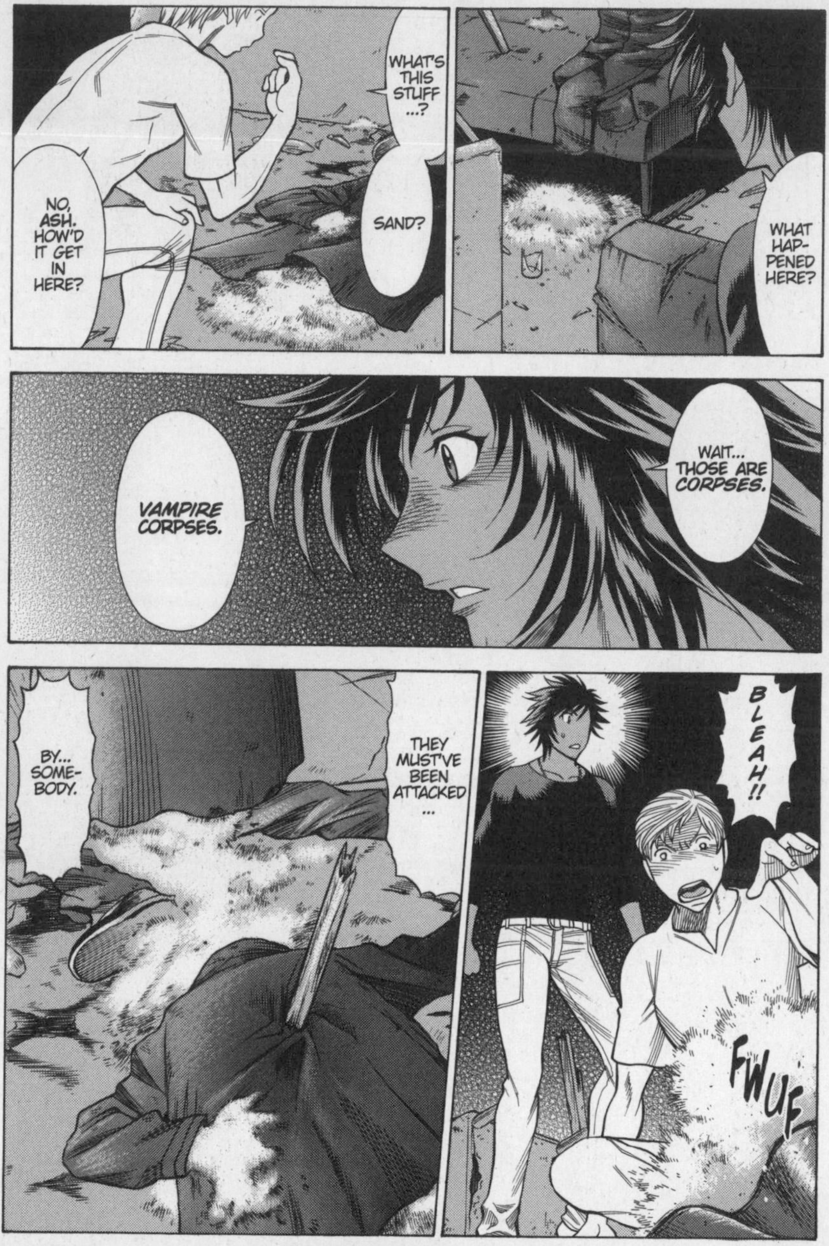
WHAT HAP-PENED HERE?
WHAT'S THIS STUFF ...?
SAND?
NO, ASH. HOW'D IT GET IN HERE?
WAIT... THOSE ARE CORPSES.
VAMPIRE CORPSES.
BLEAH!!
FWUF
THEY MUST'VE BEEN ATTACKED ...
BY... SOME-BODY.

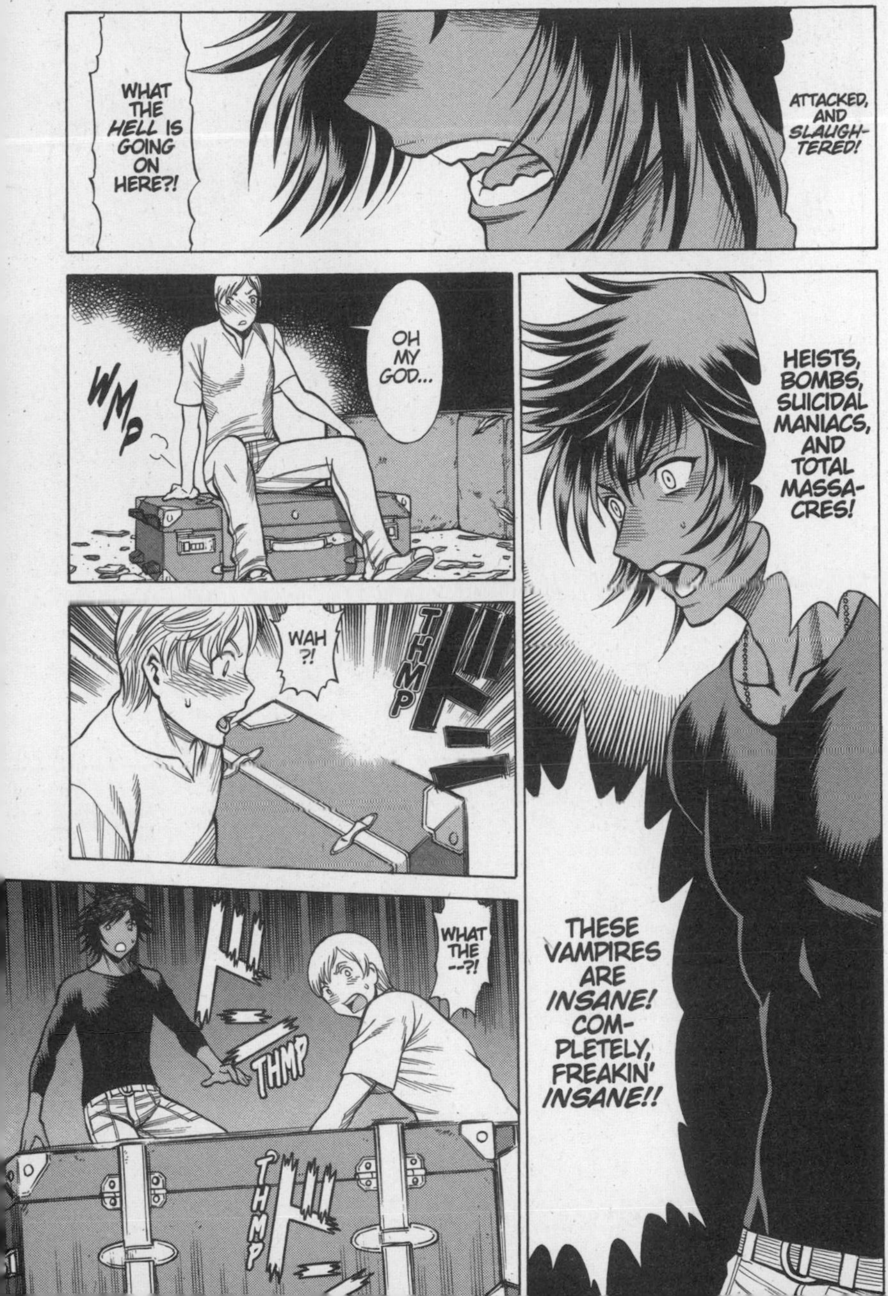
ATTACKED, AND SLAUGHTERED!
WHAT THE HELL IS GOING ON HERE?!
HEISTS, BOMBS, SUICIDAL MANIACS, AND TOTAL MASSACRES!
THESE VAMPIRES ARE INSANE! COMPLETELY, FREAKIN' INSANE!!
OH MY GOD...
WMP
WAH?!
THMP
WHAT THE--?!
THMP
THMP

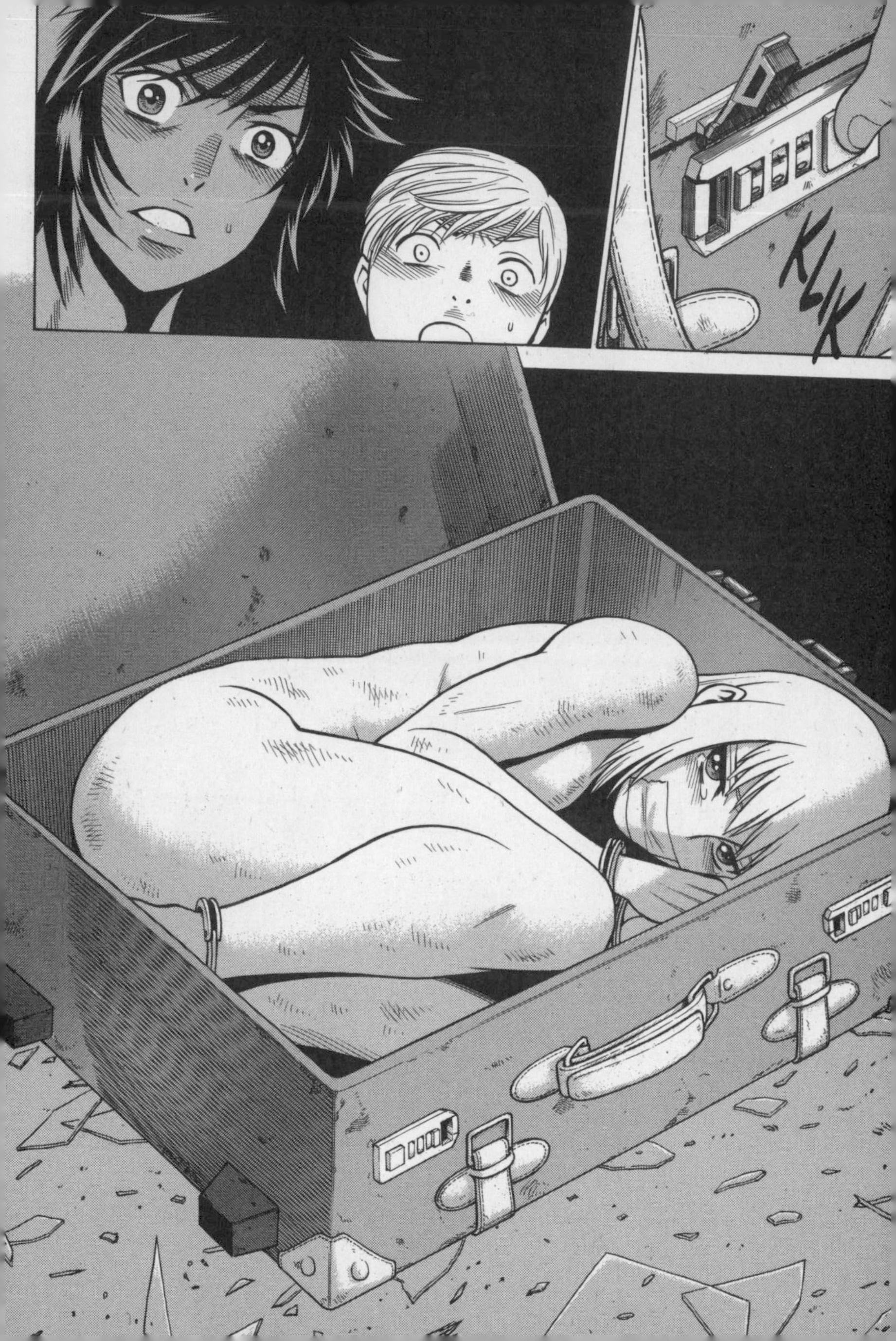
KLIK

Chapter 3: The Underground Kingdom

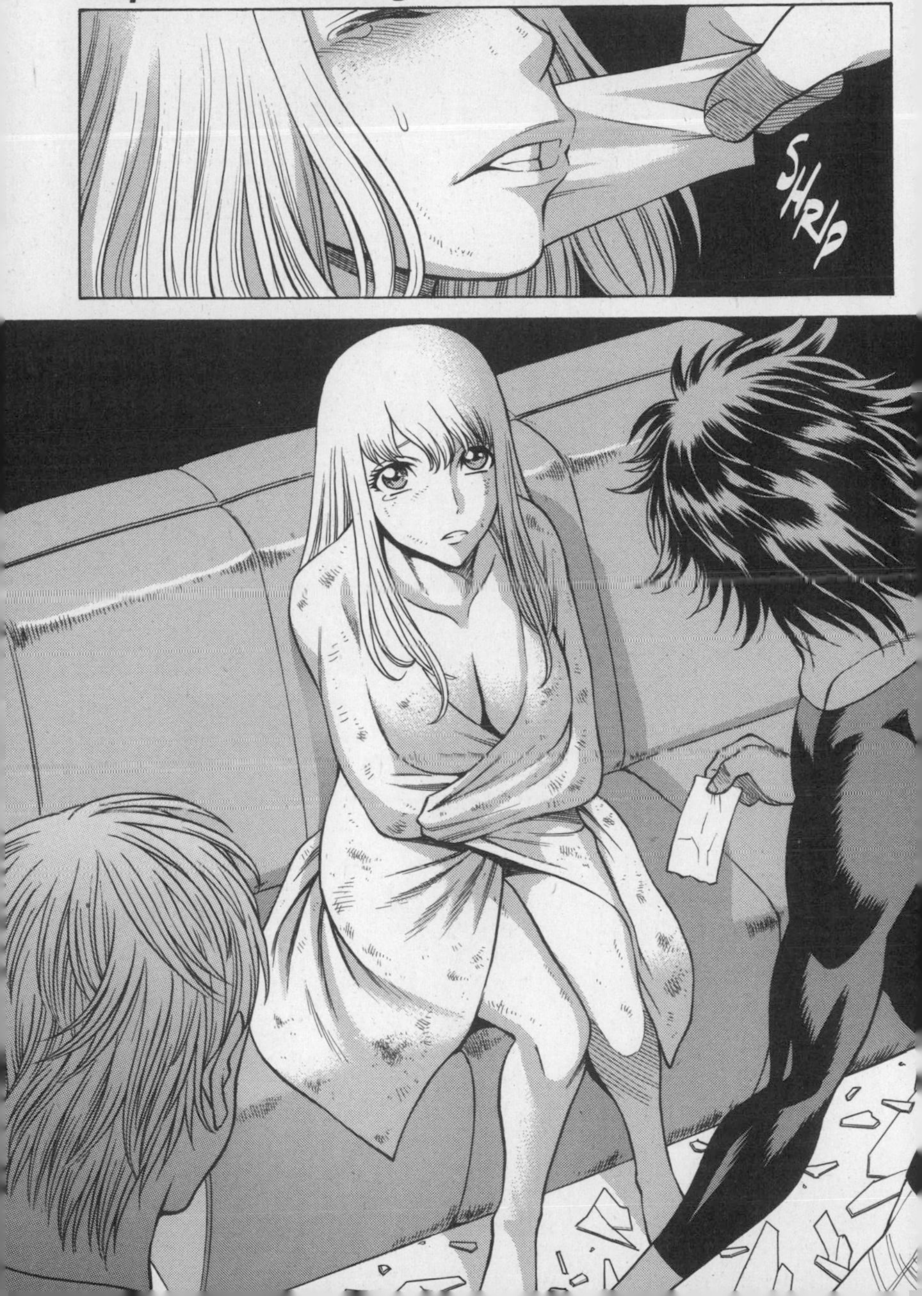
SHRIP

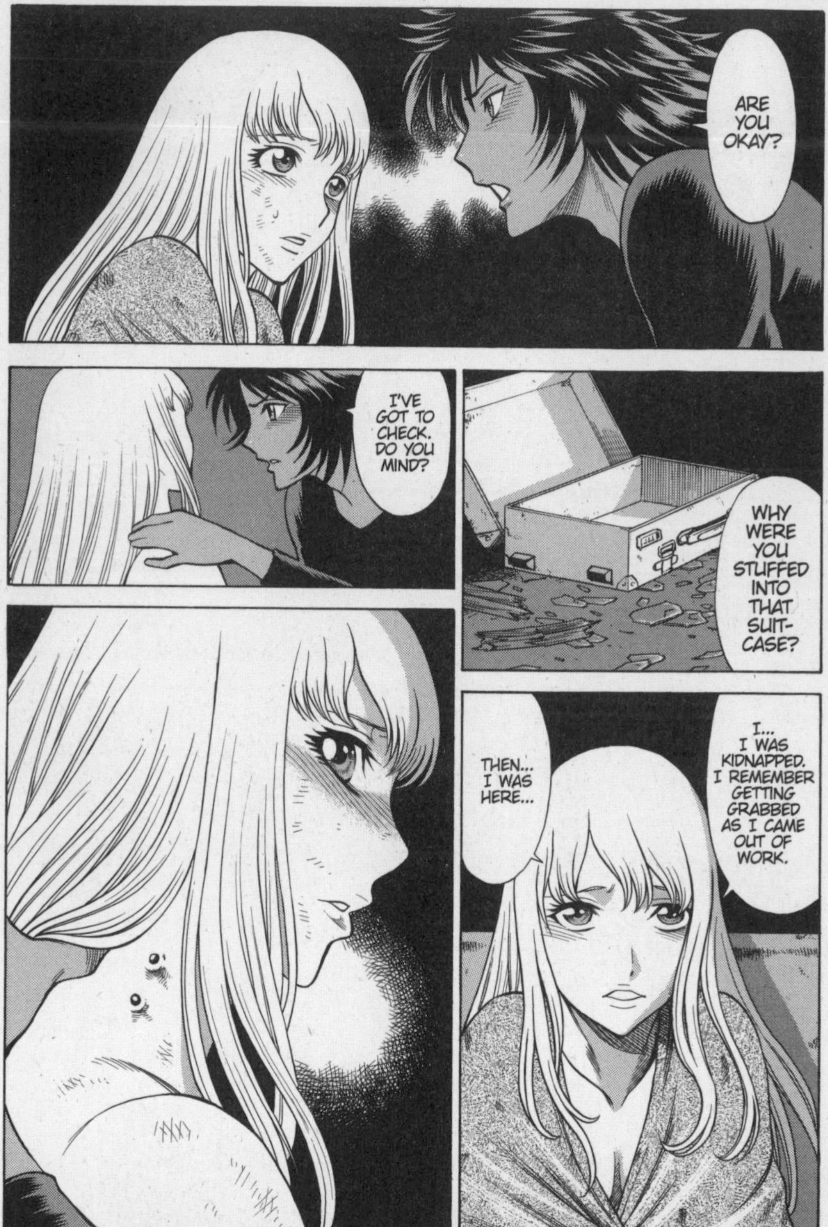
ARE YOU OKAY?
WHY WERE YOU STUFFED INTO THAT SUIT-CASE?
I'VE GOT TO CHECK. DO YOU MIND?
I... I WAS KIDNAPPED. I REMEMBER GETTING GRABBED AS I CAME OUT OF WORK.
THEN... I WAS HERE...

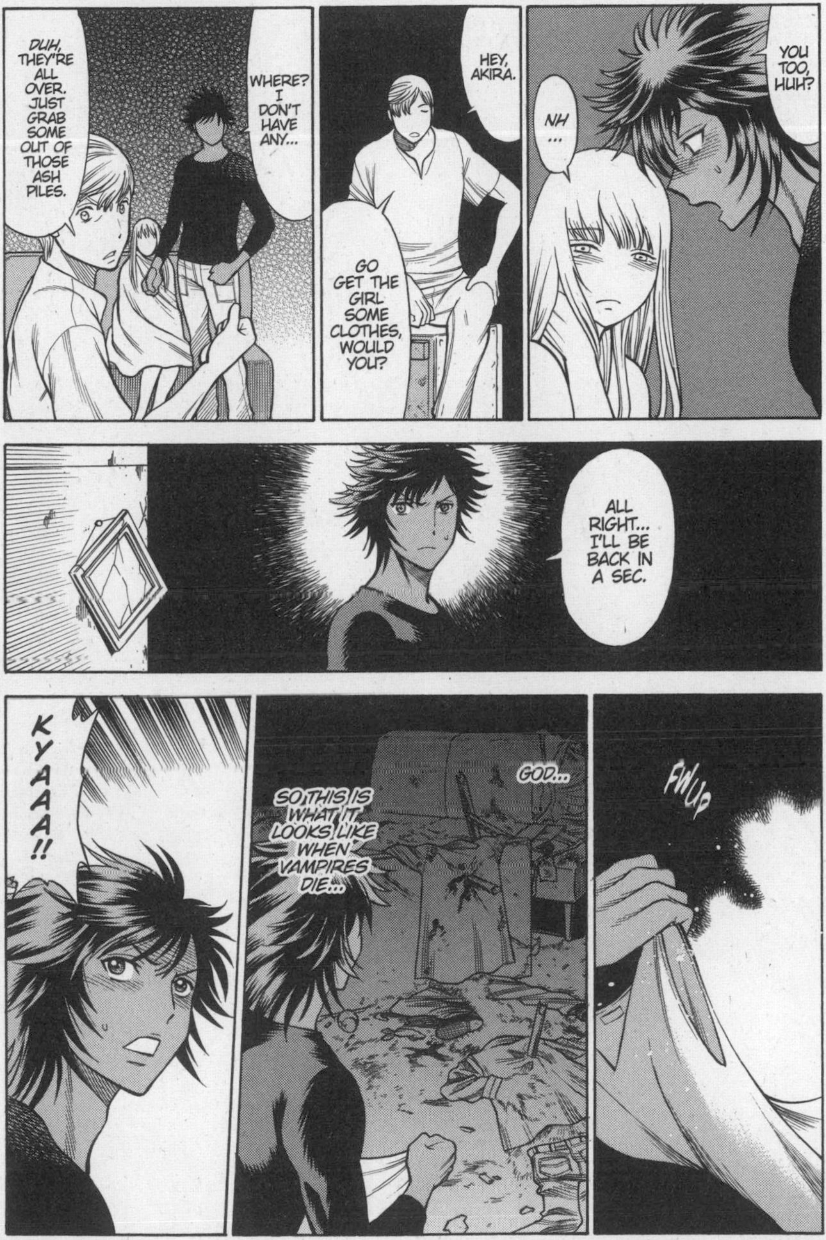
YOU TOO, HUH?
NH ...
HEY, AKIRA.
GO GET THE GIRL SOME CLOTHES, WOULD YOU?
WHERE? I DON'T HAVE ANY...
DUH, THEY'RE ALL OVER. JUST GRAB SOME OUT OF THOSE ASH PILES.
ALL RIGHT... I'LL BE BACK IN A SEC.
FWUP
GOD...
SO THIS IS WHAT IT LOOKS LIKE WHEN VAMPIRES DIE...
KYAAAA!!

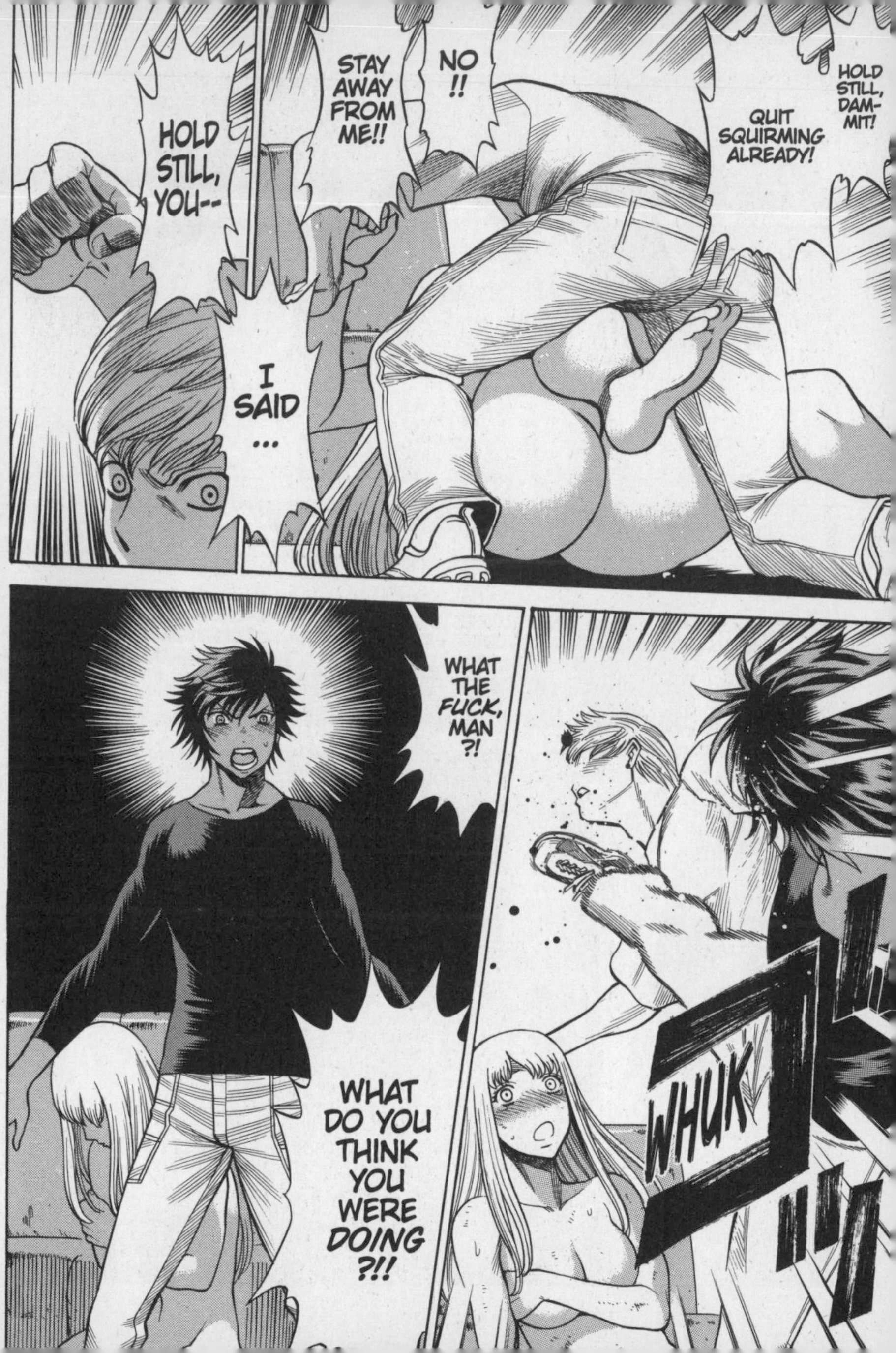
HOLD STILL, DAM-MIT!
QUIT SQUIRMING ALREADY!
NO !!
STAY AWAY FROM ME!!
HOLD STILL, YOU--
I SAID ...
WHUK
WHAT THE FUCK, MAN ?!
WHAT DO YOU THINK YOU WERE DOING ?!!

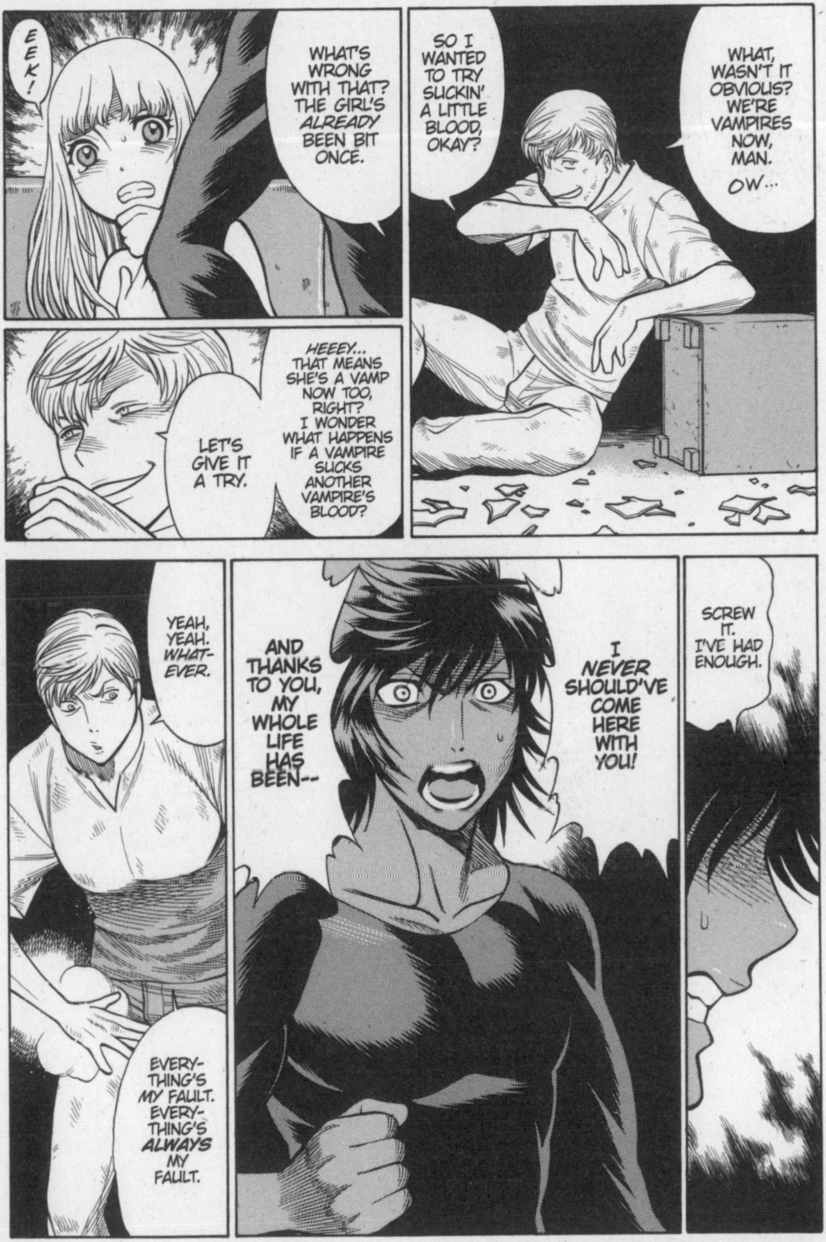
WHAT, WASN'T IT OBVIOUS? WE'RE VAMPIRES NOW, MAN.
OW...
SO I WANTED TO TRY SUCKIN' A LITTLE BLOOD, OKAY?
WHAT'S WRONG WITH THAT? THE GIRL'S ALREADY BEEN BIT ONCE.
EEK!
HEEEY... THAT MEANS SHE'S A VAMP NOW TOO, RIGHT? I WONDER WHAT HAPPENS IF A VAMPIRE SUCKS ANOTHER VAMPIRE'S BLOOD?
LET'S GIVE IT A TRY.
SCREW IT. I'VE HAD ENOUGH.
I NEVER SHOULD'VE COME HERE WITH YOU!
AND THANKS TO YOU, MY WHOLE LIFE HAS BEEN--
YEAH, YEAH. WHATEVER.
EVERYTHING'S MY FAULT. EVERYTHING'S ALWAYS MY FAULT.

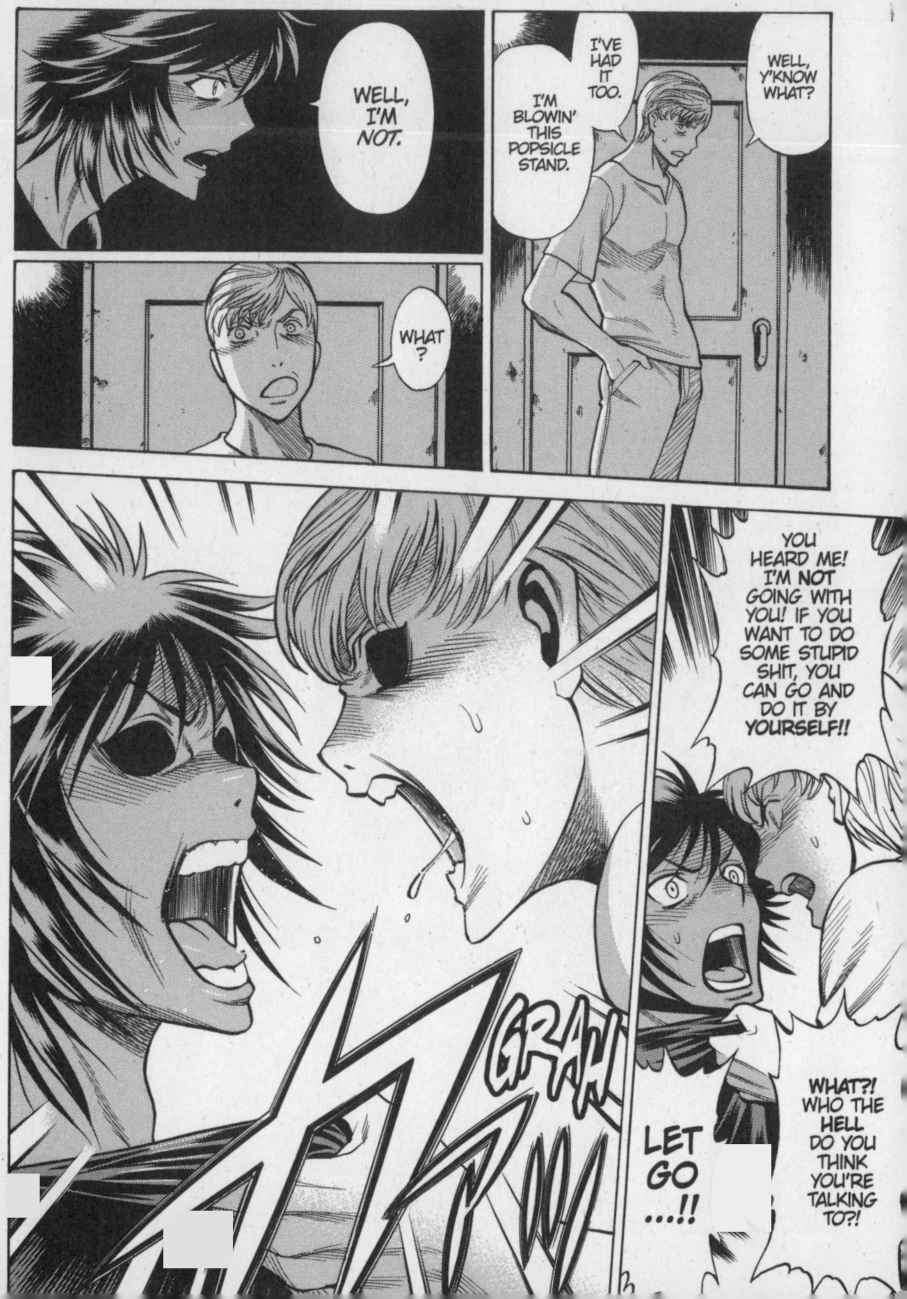
WELL, Y'KNOW WHAT?
I'VE HAD IT TOO.
I'M BLOWIN' THIS POPSICLE STAND.
WELL, I'M NOT.
WHAT?
YOU HEARD ME! I'M NOT GOING WITH YOU! IF YOU WANT TO DO SOME STUPID SHIT, YOU CAN GO AND DO IT BY YOURSELF!!
WHAT?! WHO THE HELL DO YOU THINK YOU'RE TALKING TO?!
LET GO ...!!
GRAH

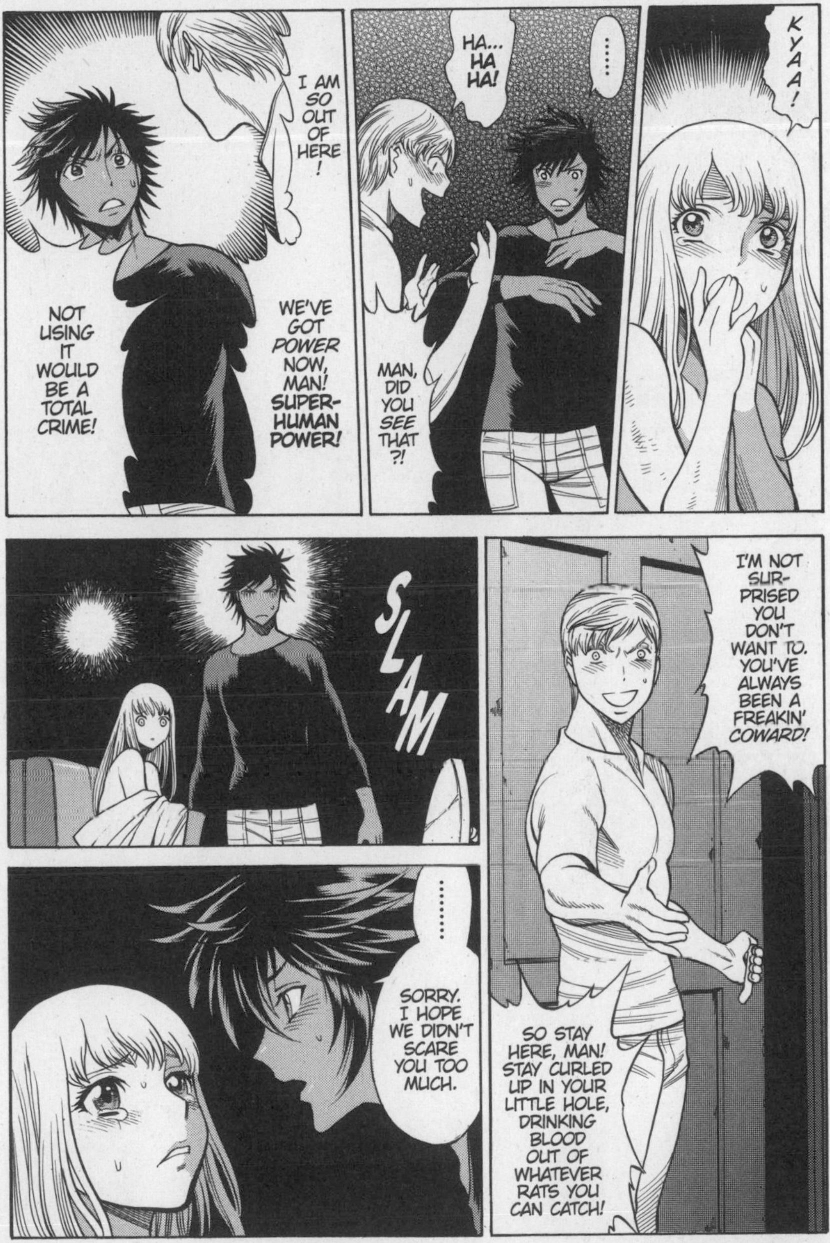
KYAA!
......
HA... HA HA!
MAN, DID YOU SEE THAT?!
I AM SO OUT OF HERE!
WE'VE GOT POWER NOW, MAN! SUPER-HUMAN POWER!
NOT USING IT WOULD BE A TOTAL CRIME!
I'M NOT SUR-PRISED YOU DON'T WANT TO. YOU'VE ALWAYS BEEN A FREAKIN' COWARD!
SO STAY HERE, MAN! STAY CURLED UP IN YOUR LITTLE HOLE, DRINKING BLOOD OUT OF WHATEVER RATS YOU CAN CATCH!
SLAM
......
SORRY. I HOPE WE DIDN'T SCARE YOU TOO MUCH.

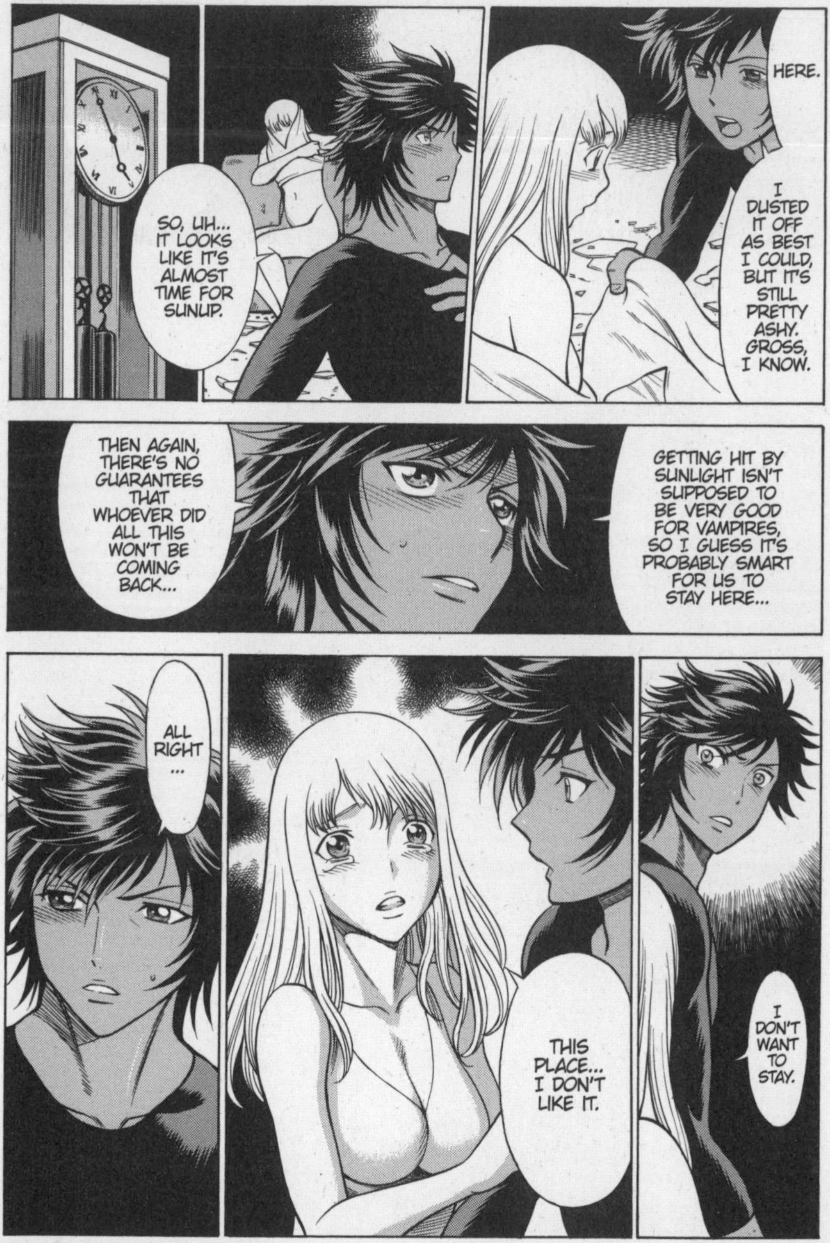
HERE.
I DUSTED IT OFF AS BEST I COULD, BUT IT'S STILL PRETTY ASHY. GROSS, I KNOW.
SO, UH... IT LOOKS LIKE IT'S ALMOST TIME FOR SUNUP.
GETTING HIT BY SUNLIGHT ISN'T SUPPOSED TO BE VERY GOOD FOR VAMPIRES, SO I GUESS IT'S PROBABLY SMART FOR US TO STAY HERE...
THEN AGAIN, THERE'S NO GUARANTEES THAT WHOEVER DID ALL THIS WON'T BE COMING BACK...
I DON'T WANT TO STAY.
THIS PLACE... I DON'T LIKE IT.
ALL RIGHT...

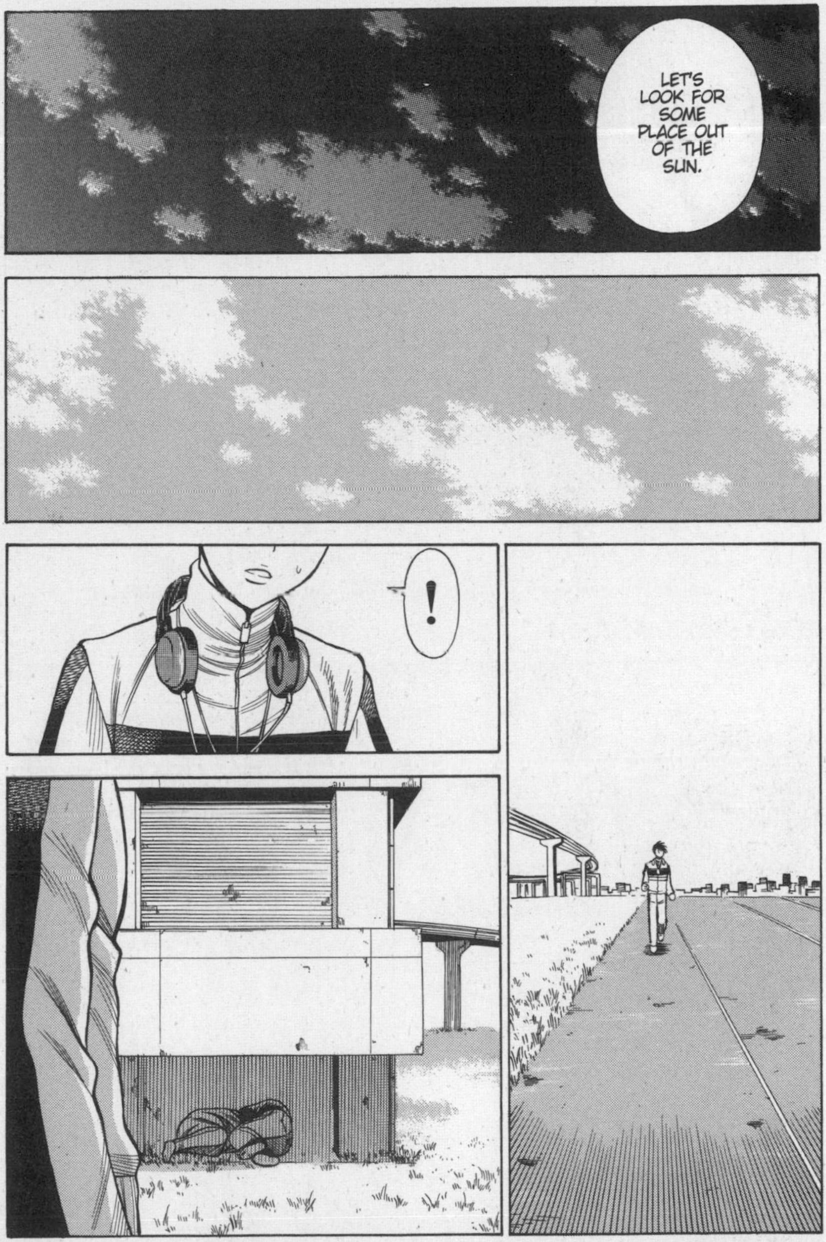
LET'S LOOK FOR SOME PLACE OUT OF THE SUN.
!

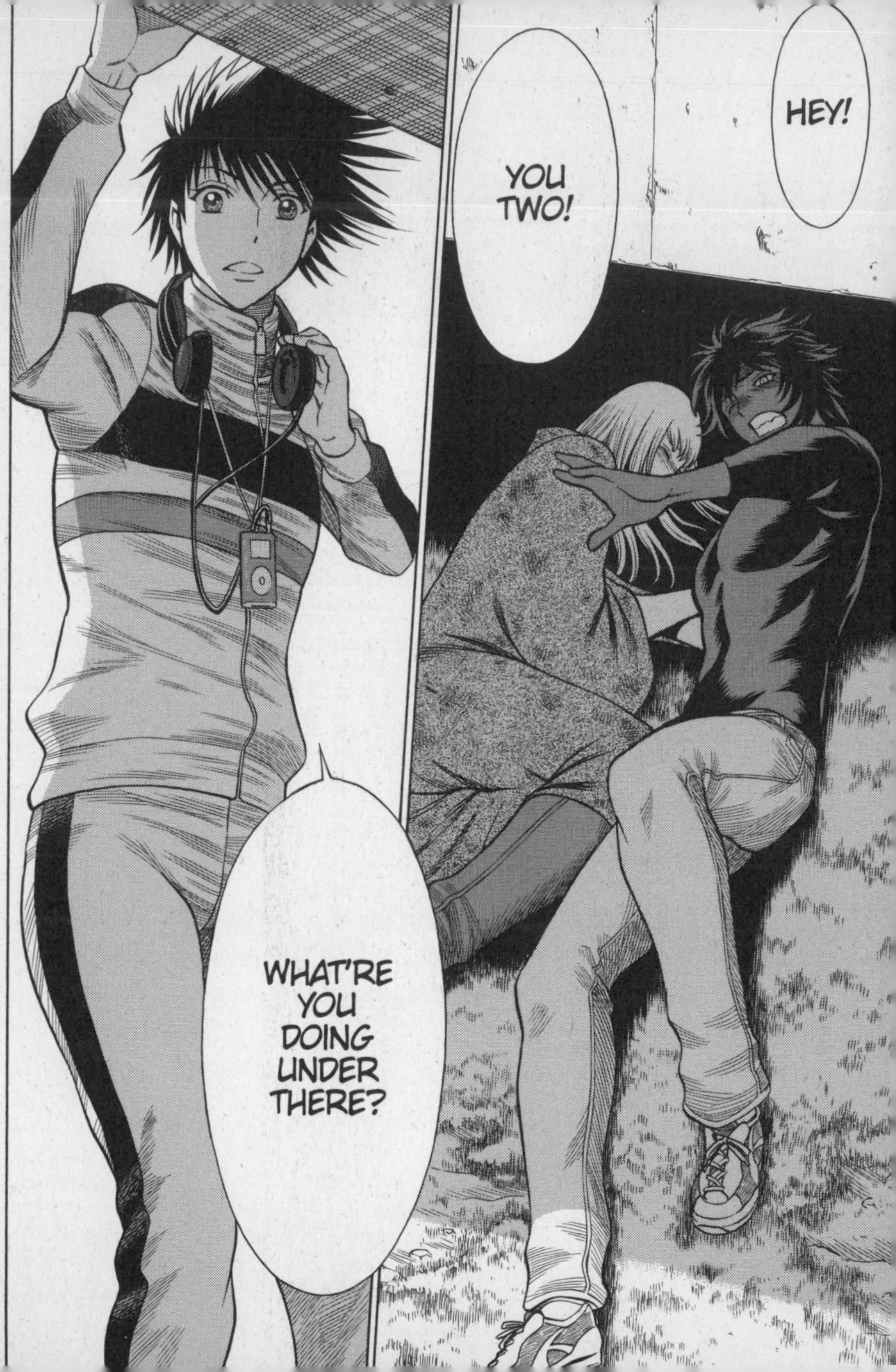
HEY!
YOU TWO!
WHAT'RE YOU DOING UNDER THERE?

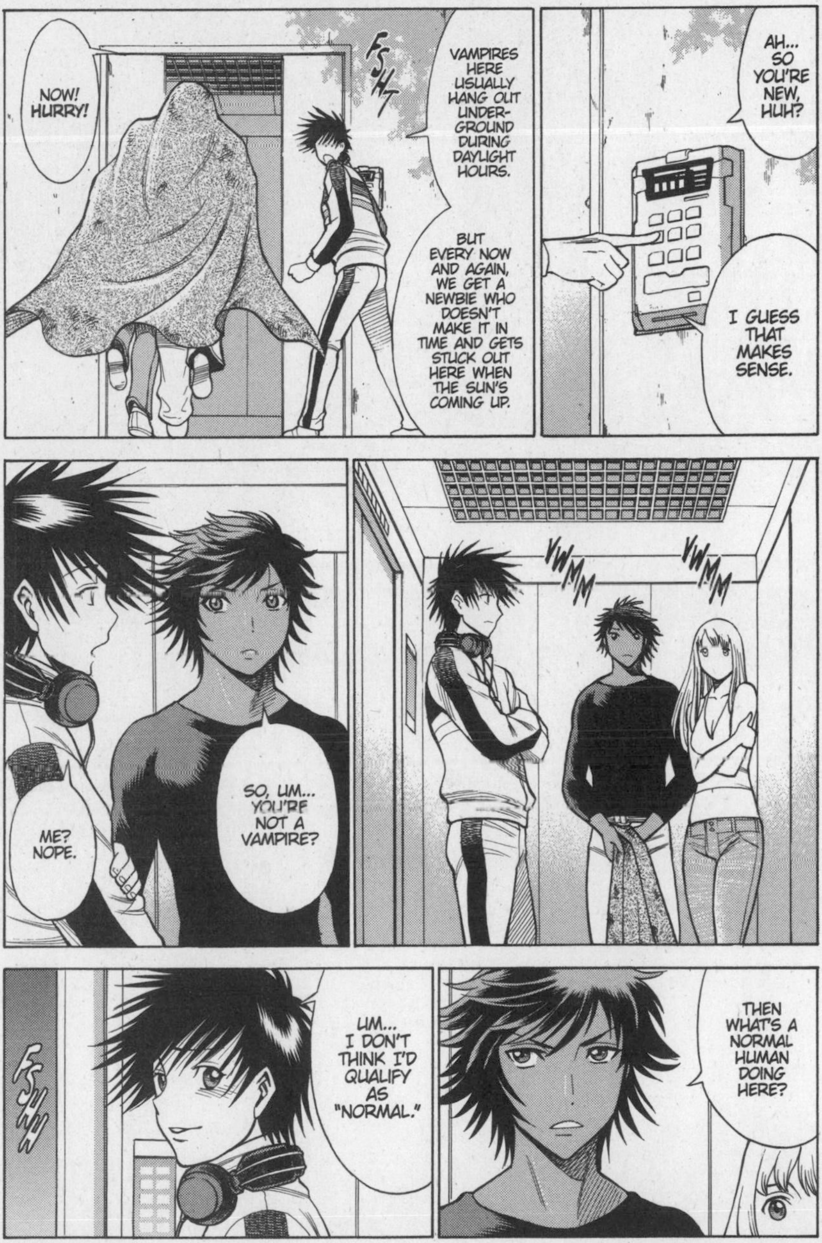
AH... SO YOU'RE NEW, HUH?
I GUESS THAT MAKES SENSE.
VAMPIRES HERE USUALLY HANG OUT UNDERGROUND DURING DAYLIGHT HOURS.
FSHT
BUT EVERY NOW AND AGAIN, WE GET A NEWBIE WHO DOESN'T MAKE IT IN TIME AND GETS STUCK OUT HERE WHEN THE SUN'S COMING UP.
NOW! HURRY!
VWMM
VWMM
SO, UM... YOU'RE NOT A VAMPIRE?
ME? NOPE.
THEN WHAT'S A NORMAL HUMAN DOING HERE?
UM... I DON'T THINK I'D QUALIFY AS "NORMAL."
FSHH

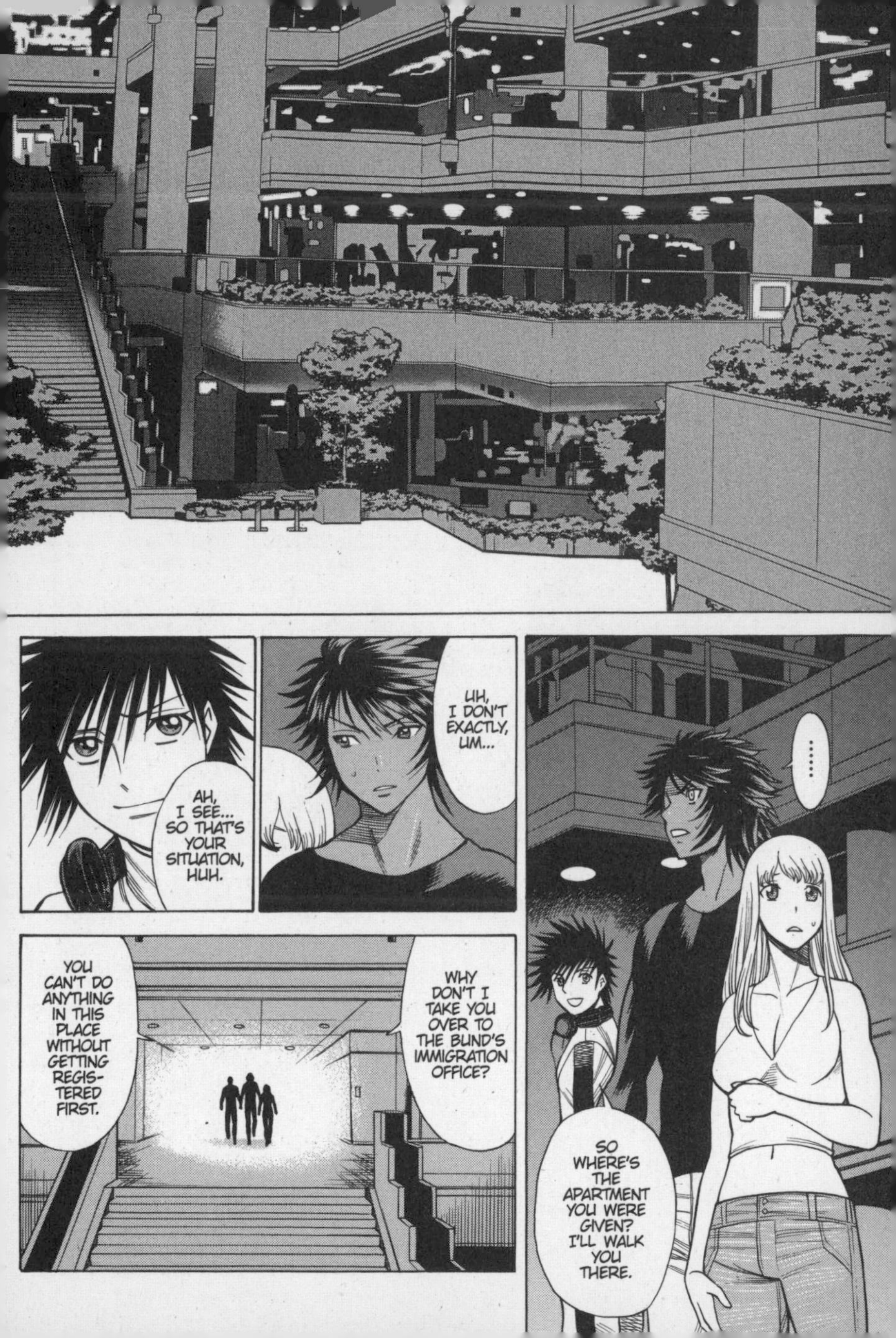
......
SO WHERE'S THE APARTMENT YOU WERE GIVEN? I'LL WALK YOU THERE.
UH, I DON'T EXACTLY, UM...
AH, I SEE... SO THAT'S YOUR SITUATION, HUH.
WHY DON'T I TAKE YOU OVER TO THE BUND'S IMMIGRATION OFFICE?
YOU CAN'T DO ANYTHING IN THIS PLACE WITHOUT GETTING REGIS-TERED FIRST.

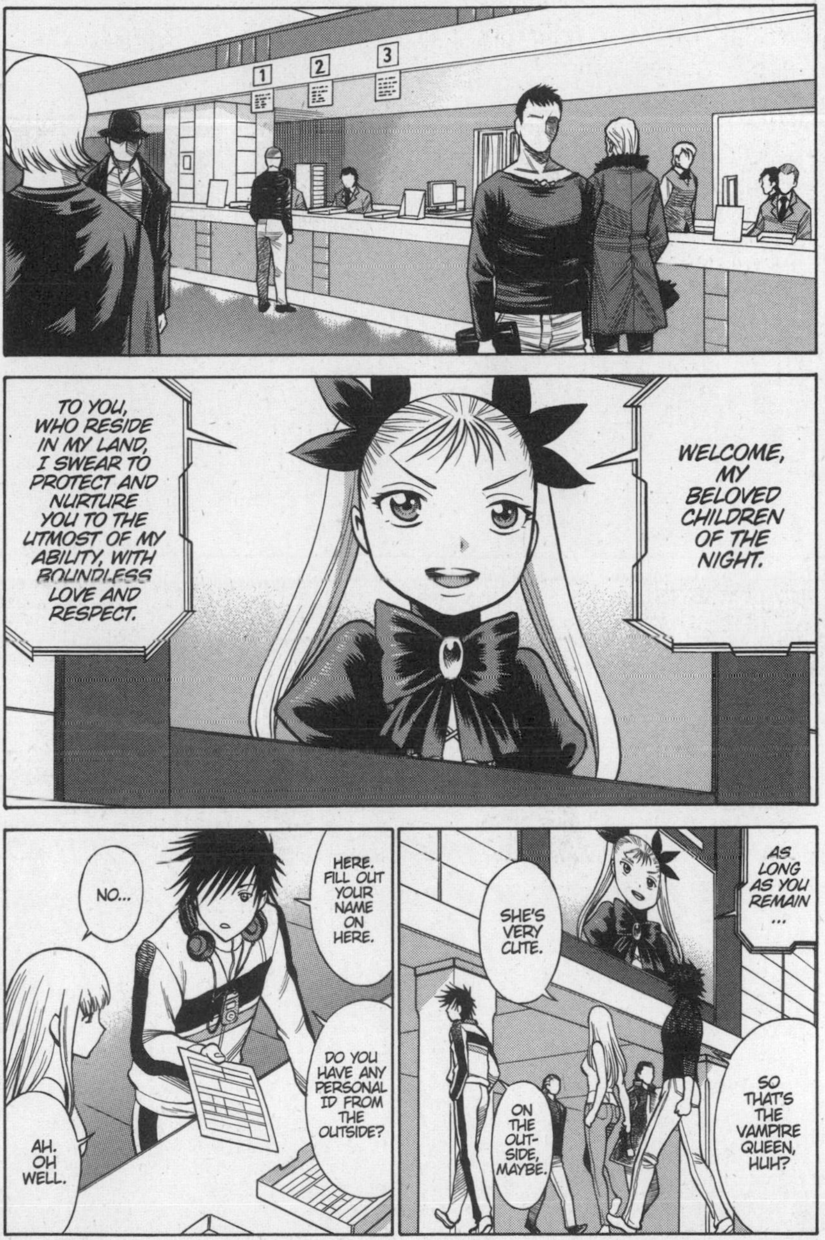
WELCOME, MY BELOVED CHILDREN OF THE NIGHT.
TO YOU, WHO RESIDE IN MY LAND, I SWEAR TO PROTECT AND NURTURE YOU TO THE UTMOST OF MY ABILITY, WITH BOUNDLESS LOVE AND RESPECT.
AS LONG AS YOU REMAIN ...
SHE'S VERY CUTE.
SO THAT'S THE VAMPIRE QUEEN, HUH?
ON THE OUT-SIDE, MAYBE.
HERE. FILL OUT YOUR NAME ON HERE.
NO...
DO YOU HAVE ANY PERSONAL ID FROM THE OUTSIDE?
AH. OH WELL.

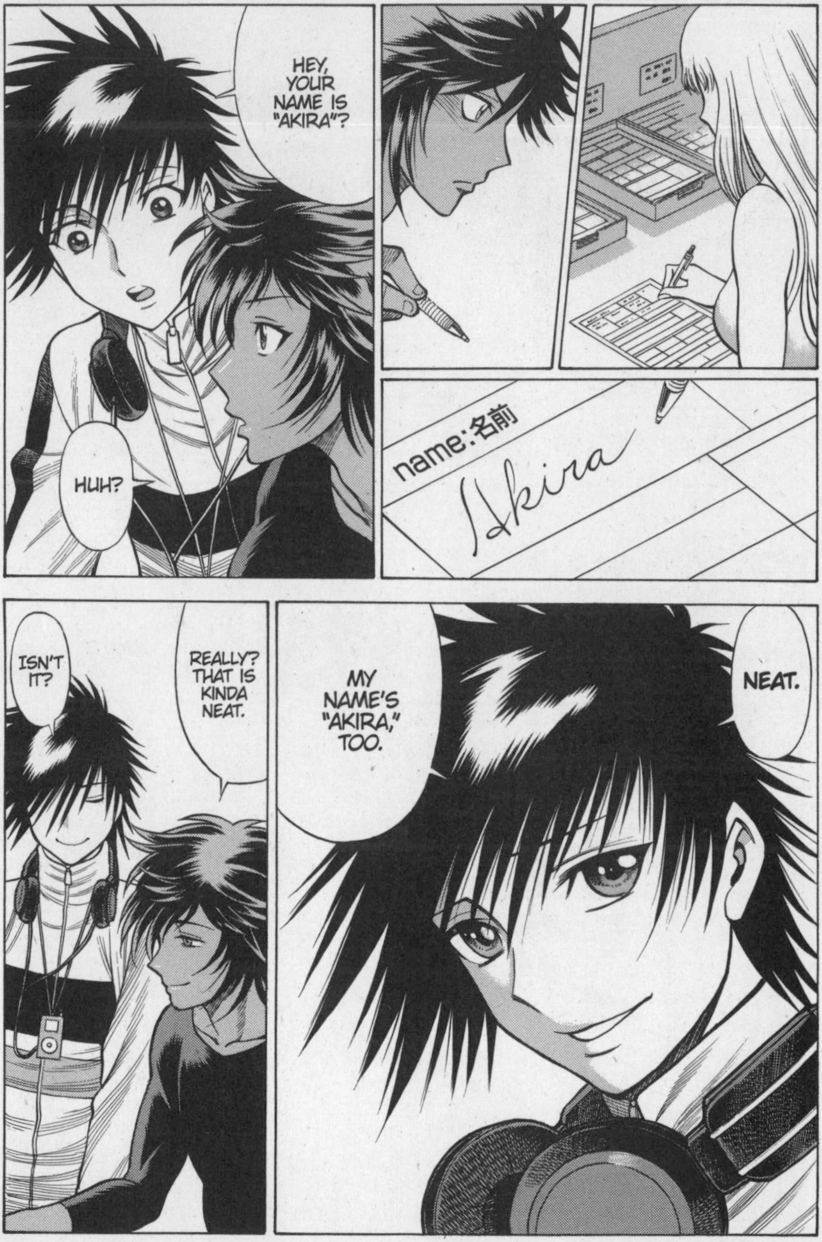
name:名前
Akira
HEY, YOUR NAME IS "AKIRA"?
HUH?
NEAT.
MY NAME'S "AKIRA," TOO.
REALLY? THAT IS KINDA NEAT.
ISN'T IT?

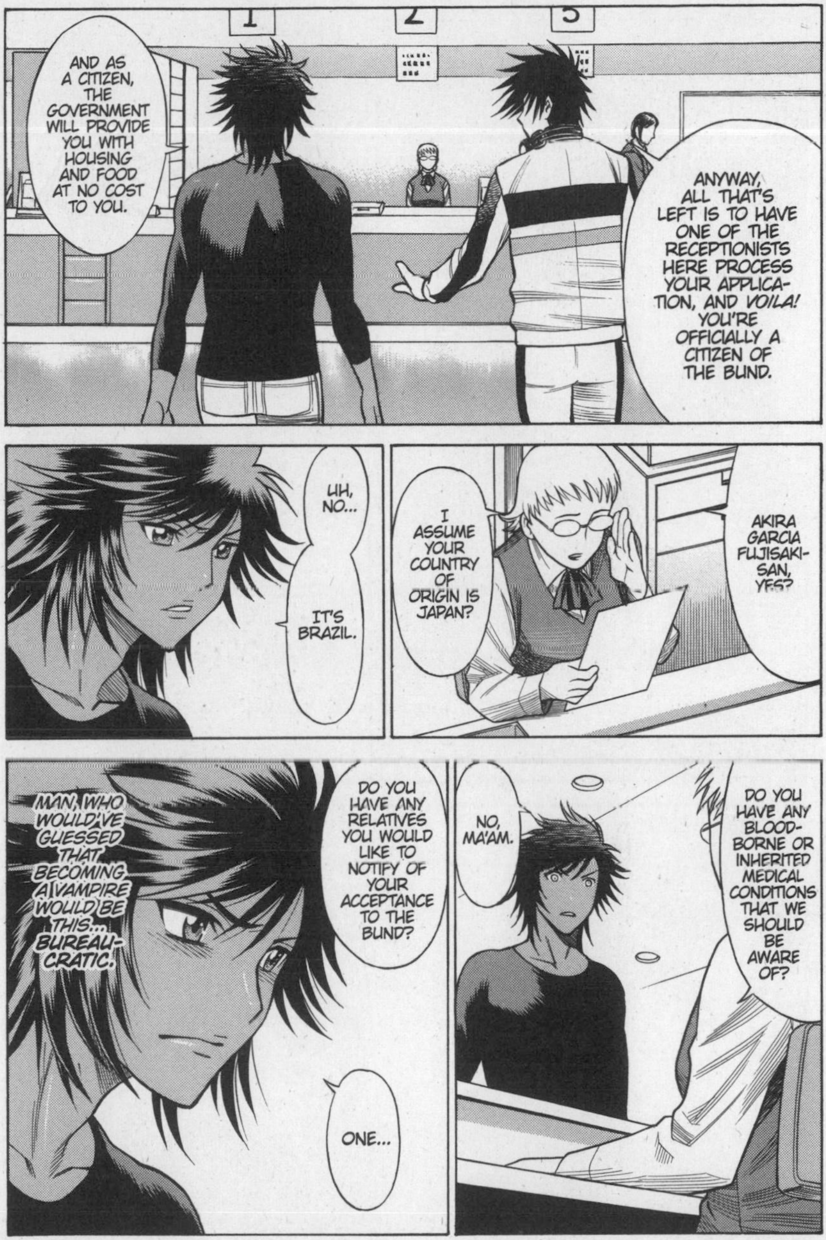
AND AS A CITIZEN, THE GOVERNMENT WILL PROVIDE YOU WITH HOUSING AND FOOD AT NO COST TO YOU.
ANYWAY, ALL THAT'S LEFT IS TO HAVE ONE OF THE RECEPTIONISTS HERE PROCESS YOUR APPLICATION, AND *VOILA!* YOU'RE OFFICIALLY A CITIZEN OF THE BUND.
AKIRA GARCIA FUJISAKI-SAN, YES?
I ASSUME YOUR COUNTRY OF ORIGIN IS JAPAN?
UH, NO...
IT'S BRAZIL.
DO YOU HAVE ANY BLOOD-BORNE OR INHERITED MEDICAL CONDITIONS THAT WE SHOULD BE AWARE OF?
NO, MA'AM.
DO YOU HAVE ANY RELATIVES YOU WOULD LIKE TO NOTIFY OF YOUR ACCEPTANCE TO THE BUND?
MAN, WHO WOULD'VE GUESSED THAT BECOMING A VAMPIRE WOULD BE THIS... BUREAUCRATIC.
ONE...

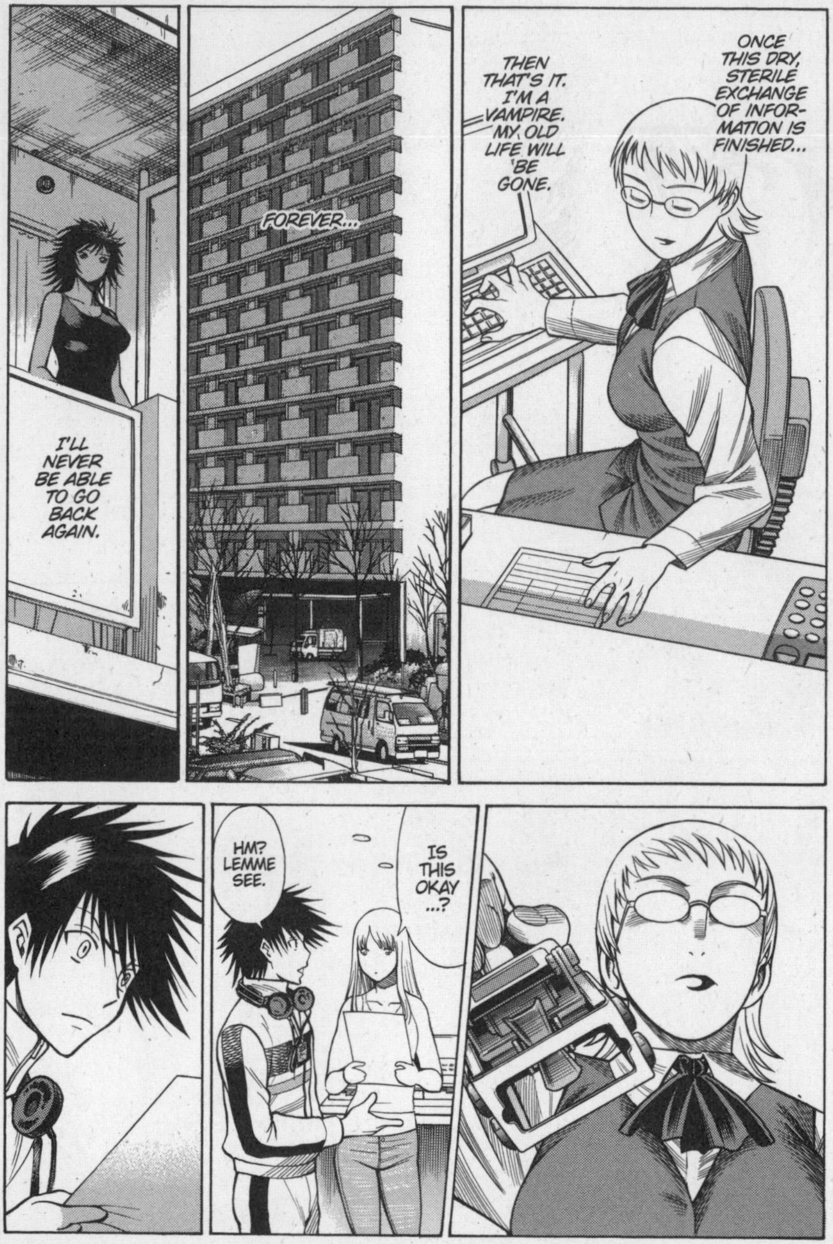
ONCE THIS DRY, STERILE EXCHANGE OF INFORMATION IS FINISHED...
THEN THAT'S IT. I'M A VAMPIRE. MY OLD LIFE WILL BE GONE.
FOREVER...
I'LL NEVER BE ABLE TO GO BACK AGAIN.
IS THIS OKAY ...?
HM? LEMME SEE.

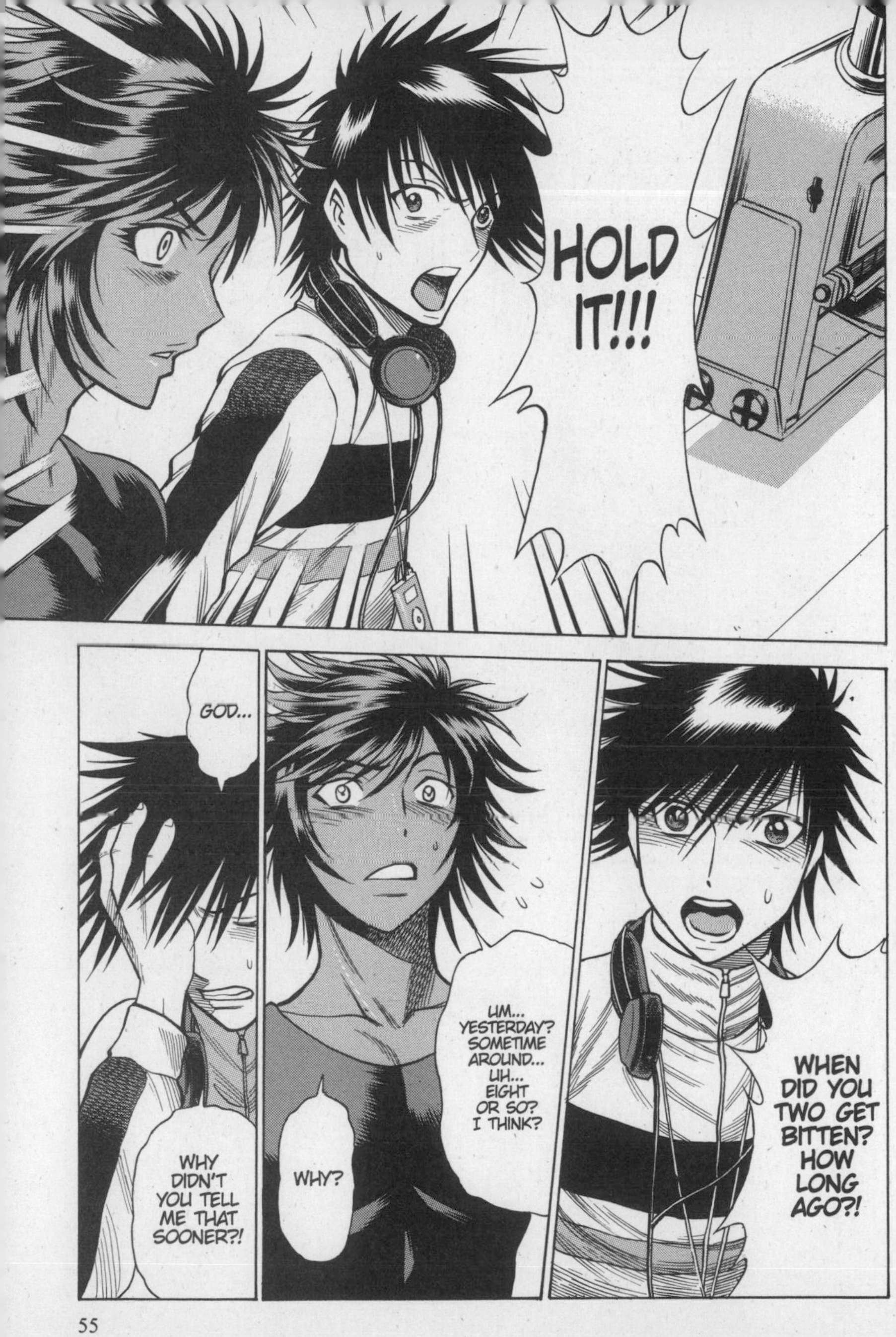
HOLD IT!!!
WHEN DID YOU TWO GET BITTEN? HOW LONG AGO?!
UM... YESTERDAY? SOMETIME AROUND... UH... EIGHT OR SO? I THINK?
WHY?
GOD...
WHY DIDN'T YOU TELL ME THAT SOONER?!

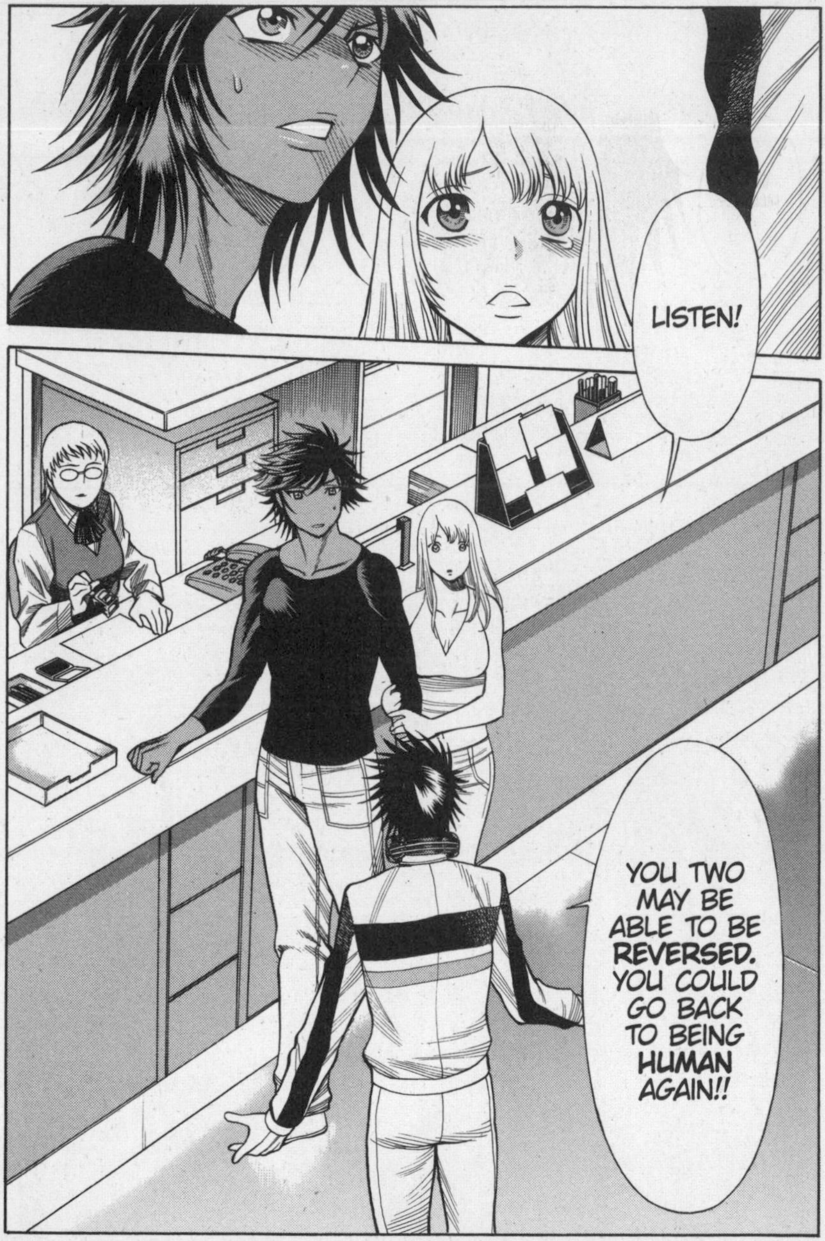
LISTEN!
YOU TWO MAY BE ABLE TO BE REVERSED. YOU COULD GO BACK TO BEING HUMAN AGAIN!!

Chapter 4: The Queen & Me

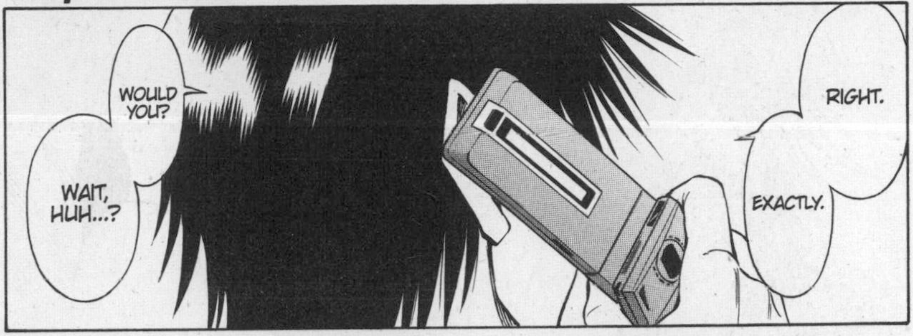
RIGHT.
EXACTLY.
WOULD YOU?
WAIT, HUH...?

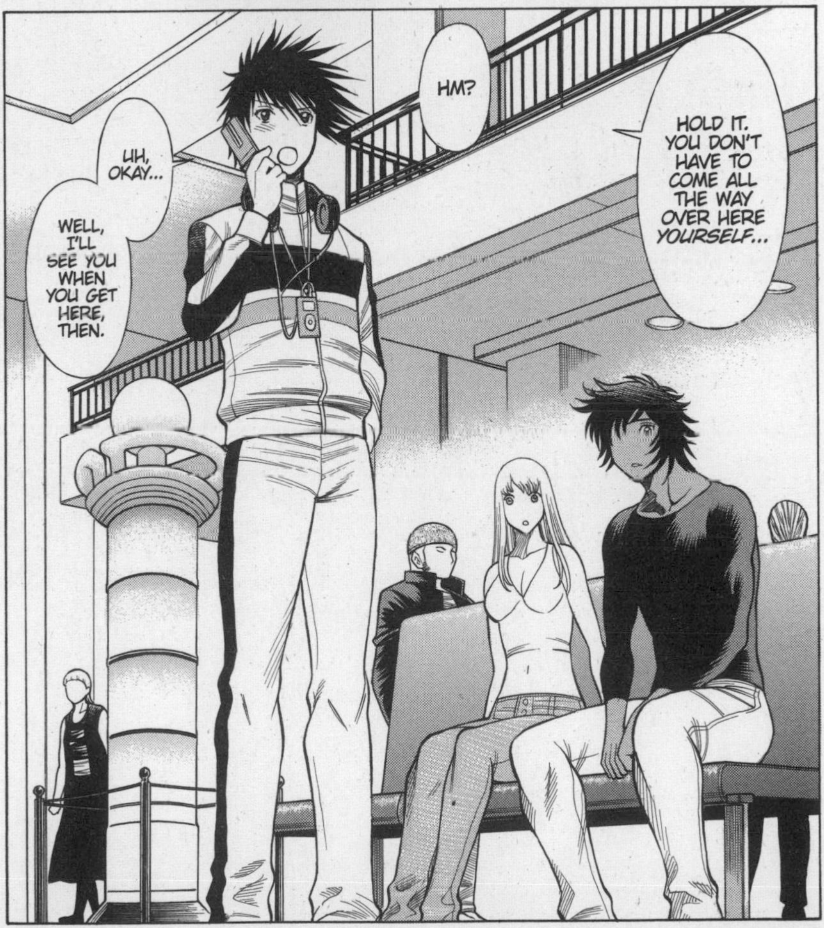
HOLD IT. YOU DON'T HAVE TO COME ALL THE WAY OVER HERE *YOURSELF*...
HM?
UH, OKAY...
WELL, I'LL SEE YOU WHEN YOU GET HERE, THEN.

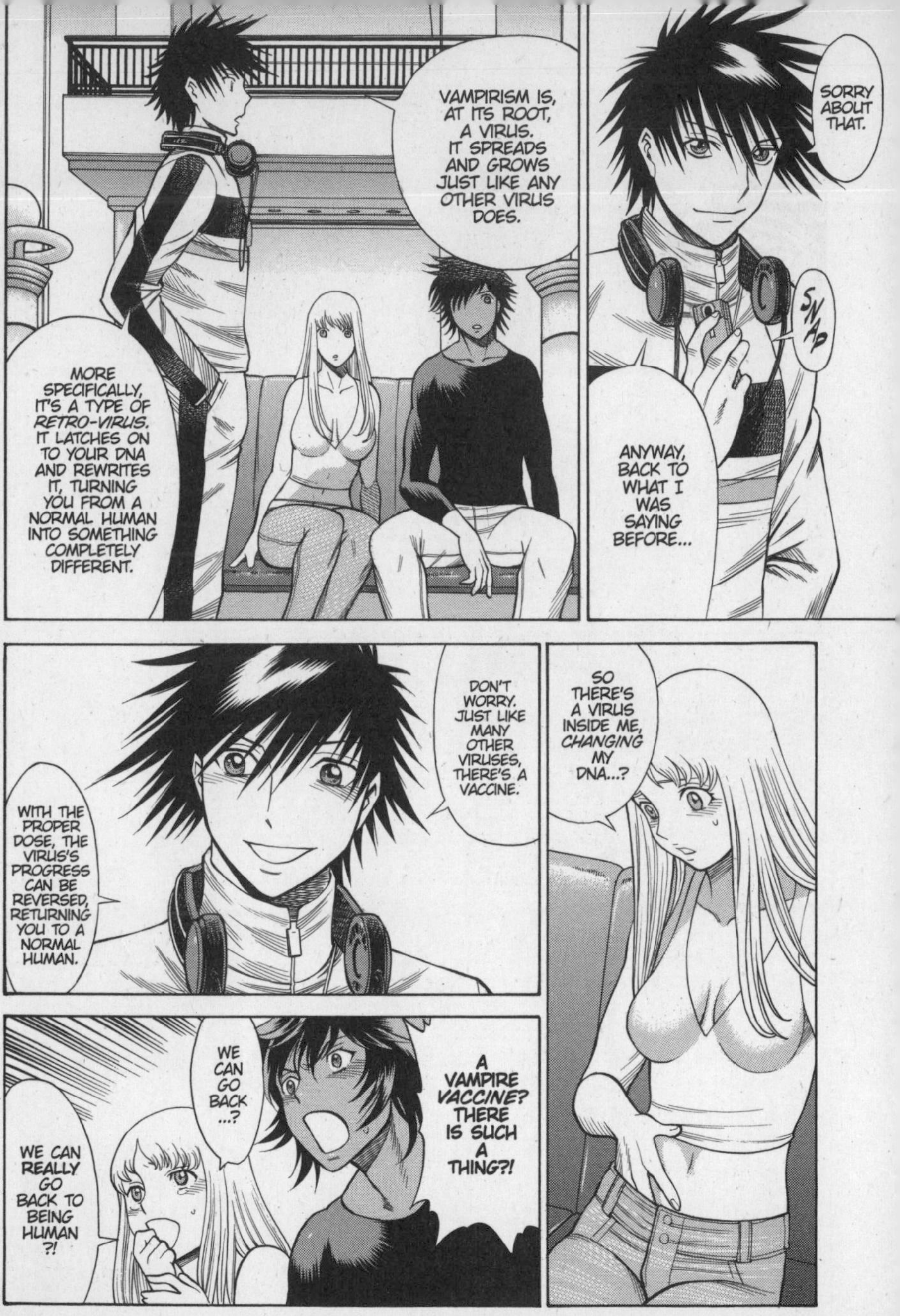
SORRY ABOUT THAT.
SNAP
ANYWAY, BACK TO WHAT I WAS SAYING BEFORE...
VAMPIRISM IS, AT ITS ROOT, A VIRUS. IT SPREADS AND GROWS JUST LIKE ANY OTHER VIRUS DOES.
MORE SPECIFICALLY, IT'S A TYPE OF *RETRO-VIRUS.* IT LATCHES ON TO YOUR DNA AND REWRITES IT, TURNING YOU FROM A NORMAL HUMAN INTO SOMETHING COMPLETELY DIFFERENT.
SO THERE'S A VIRUS INSIDE ME, *CHANGING* MY DNA...?
DON'T WORRY. JUST LIKE MANY OTHER VIRUSES, THERE'S A VACCINE.
WITH THE PROPER DOSE, THE VIRUS'S PROGRESS CAN BE REVERSED, RETURNING YOU TO A NORMAL HUMAN.
A VAMPIRE *VACCINE?* THERE IS SUCH A THING?!
WE CAN GO BACK ...?
WE CAN **REALLY** GO BACK TO BEING HUMAN ?!

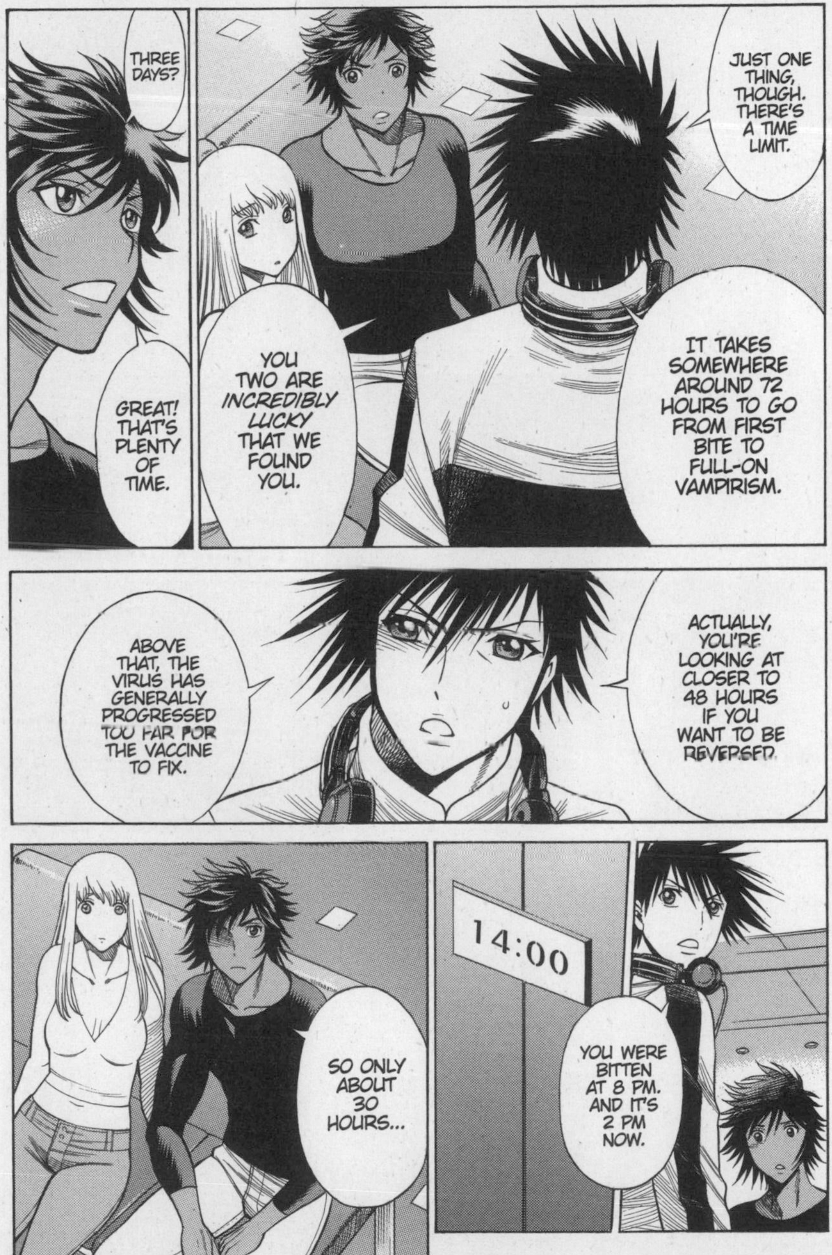
JUST ONE THING, THOUGH. THERE'S A TIME LIMIT.
IT TAKES SOMEWHERE AROUND 72 HOURS TO GO FROM FIRST BITE TO FULL-ON VAMPIRISM.
YOU TWO ARE *INCREDIBLY LUCKY* THAT WE FOUND YOU.
THREE DAYS?
GREAT! THAT'S PLENTY OF TIME.
ACTUALLY, YOU'RE LOOKING AT CLOSER TO 48 HOURS IF YOU WANT TO BE REVERSED.
ABOVE THAT, THE VIRUS HAS GENERALLY PROGRESSED TOO FAR FOR THE VACCINE TO FIX.
14:00
YOU WERE BITTEN AT 8 PM. AND IT'S 2 PM NOW.
SO ONLY ABOUT 30 HOURS...

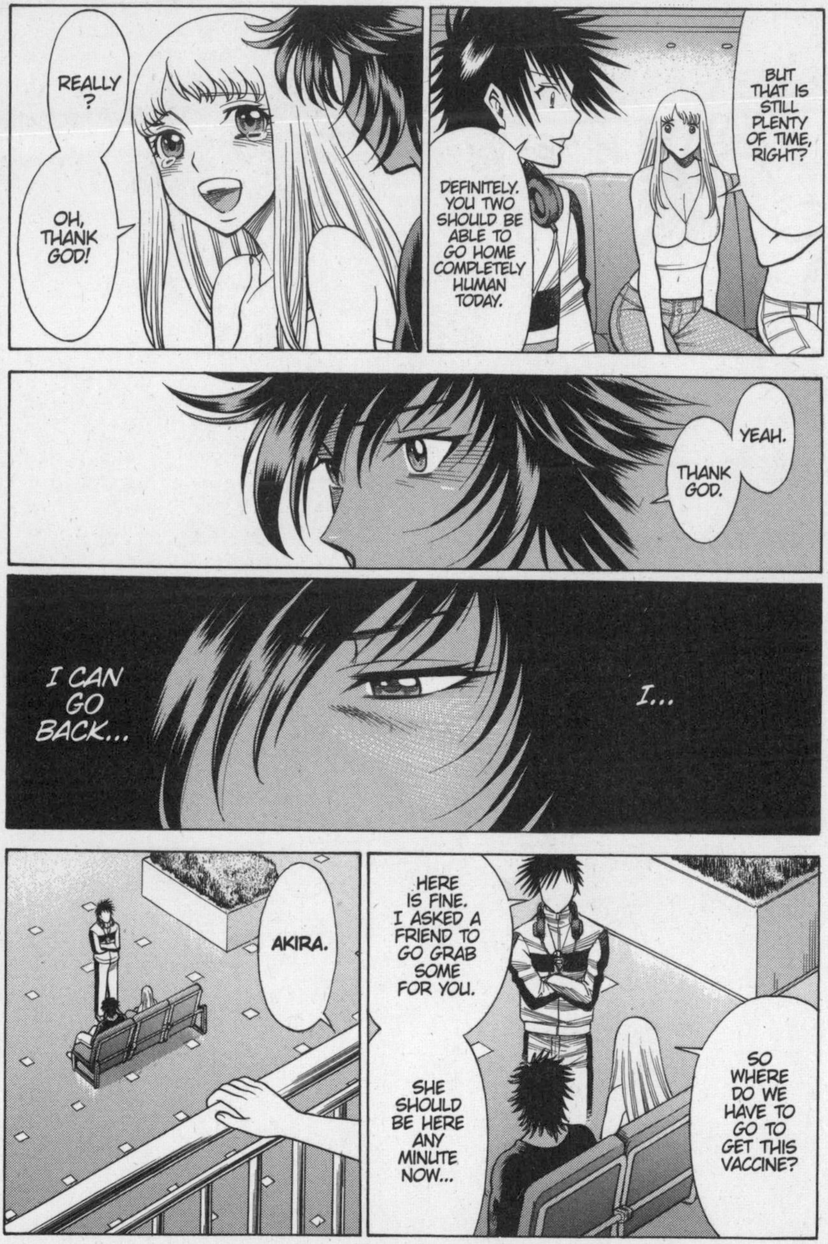
BUT THAT IS STILL PLENTY OF TIME, RIGHT?
DEFINITELY. YOU TWO SHOULD BE ABLE TO GO HOME COMPLETELY HUMAN TODAY.
REALLY?
OH, THANK GOD!
YEAH.
THANK GOD.
I...
I CAN GO BACK...
SO WHERE DO WE HAVE TO GO TO GET THIS VACCINE?
HERE IS FINE. I ASKED A FRIEND TO GO GRAB SOME FOR YOU.
SHE SHOULD BE HERE ANY MINUTE NOW...
AKIRA.

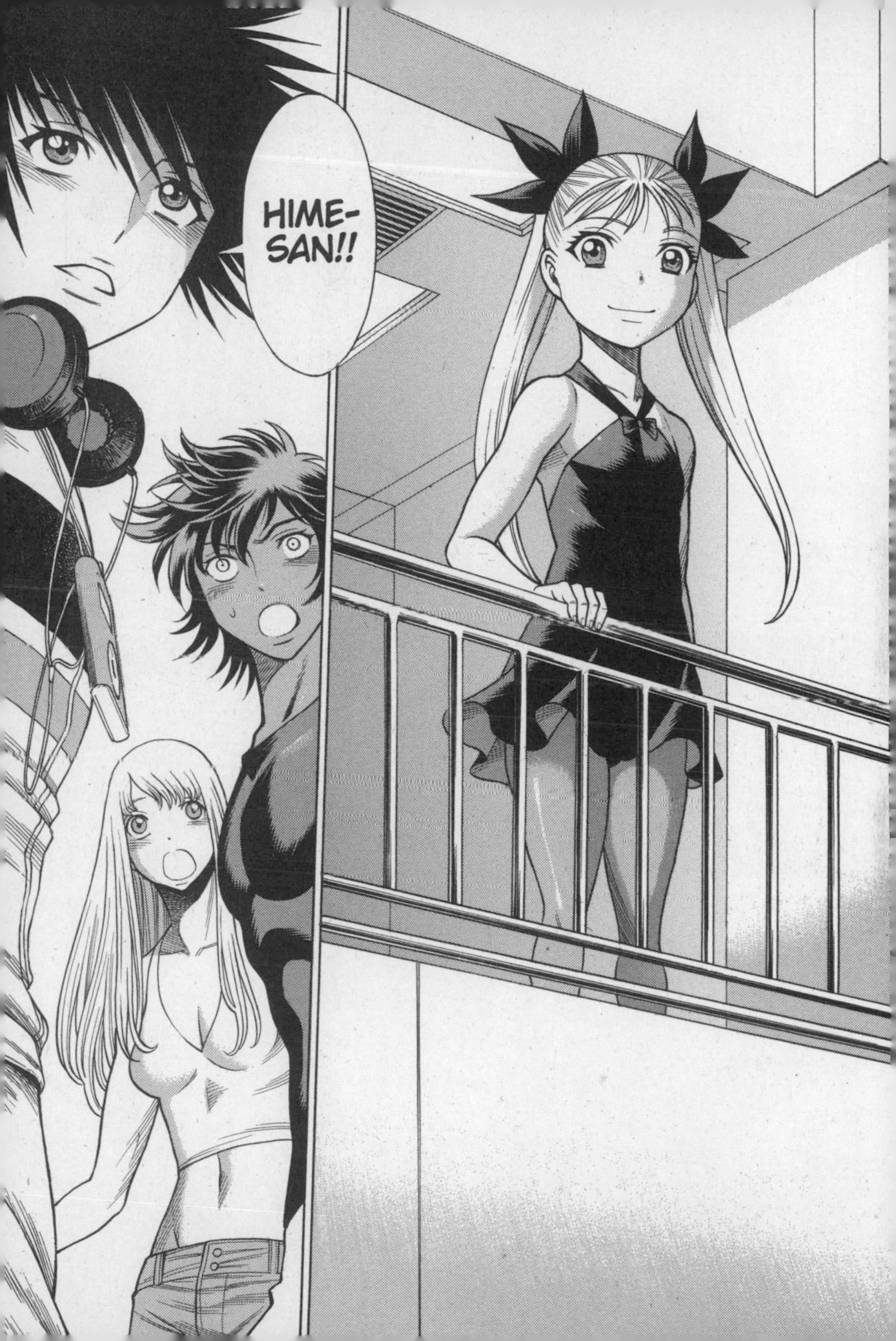
HIME-
SAN!!

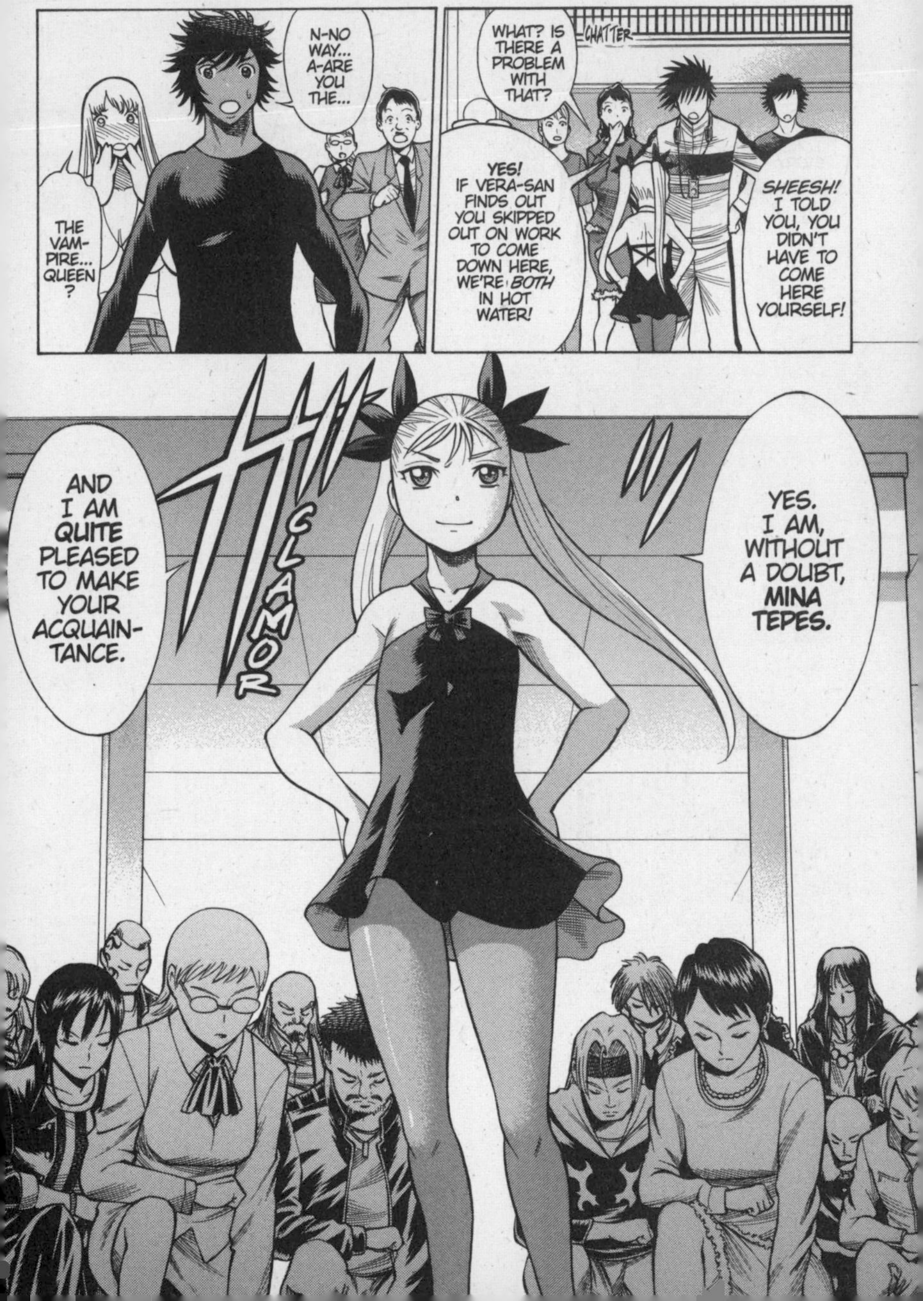
CHATTER
WHAT? IS THERE A PROBLEM WITH THAT?
SHEESH! I TOLD YOU, YOU DIDN'T HAVE TO COME HERE YOURSELF!
YES! IF VERA-SAN FINDS OUT YOU SKIPPED OUT ON WORK TO COME DOWN HERE, WE'RE BOTH IN HOT WATER!
N-NO WAY... A-ARE YOU THE...
THE VAMPIRE... QUEEN?
YES. I AM, WITHOUT A DOUBT, MINA TEPES.
CLAMOR
AND I AM QUITE PLEASED TO MAKE YOUR ACQUAINTANCE.

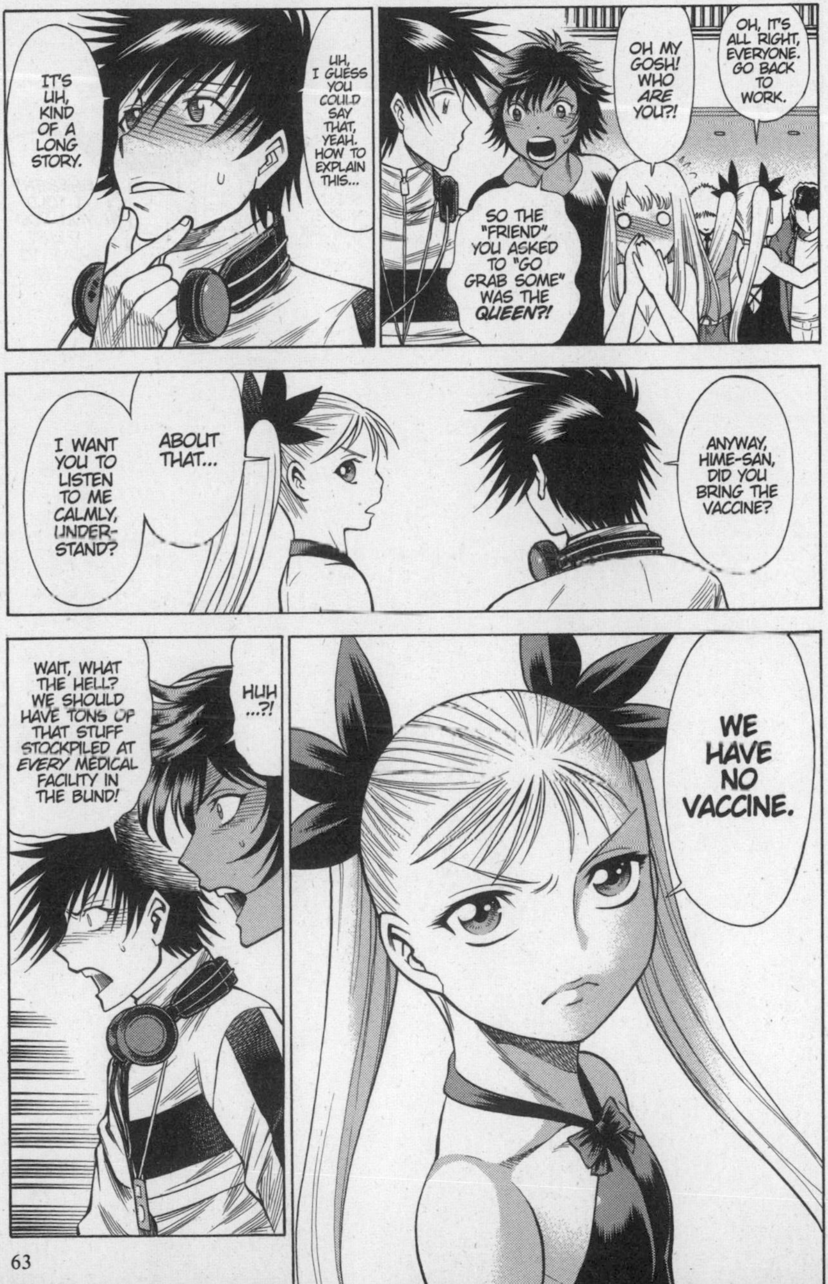
OH, IT'S ALL RIGHT, EVERYONE. GO BACK TO WORK.
OH MY GOSH! WHO *ARE* YOU?!
SO THE "FRIEND" YOU ASKED TO "GO GRAB SOME" WAS THE ***QUEEN?!***
UH, I GUESS YOU COULD SAY THAT, YEAH. HOW TO EXPLAIN THIS...
IT'S UH, KIND OF A LONG STORY.
ANYWAY, HIME-SAN, DID YOU BRING THE VACCINE?
ABOUT THAT...
I WANT YOU TO LISTEN TO ME CALMLY, UNDERSTAND?
WE HAVE NO VACCINE.
HUH ...?!
WAIT, WHAT THE HELL? WE SHOULD HAVE TONS OF THAT STUFF STOCKPILED AT *EVERY* MEDICAL FACILITY IN THE BUND!

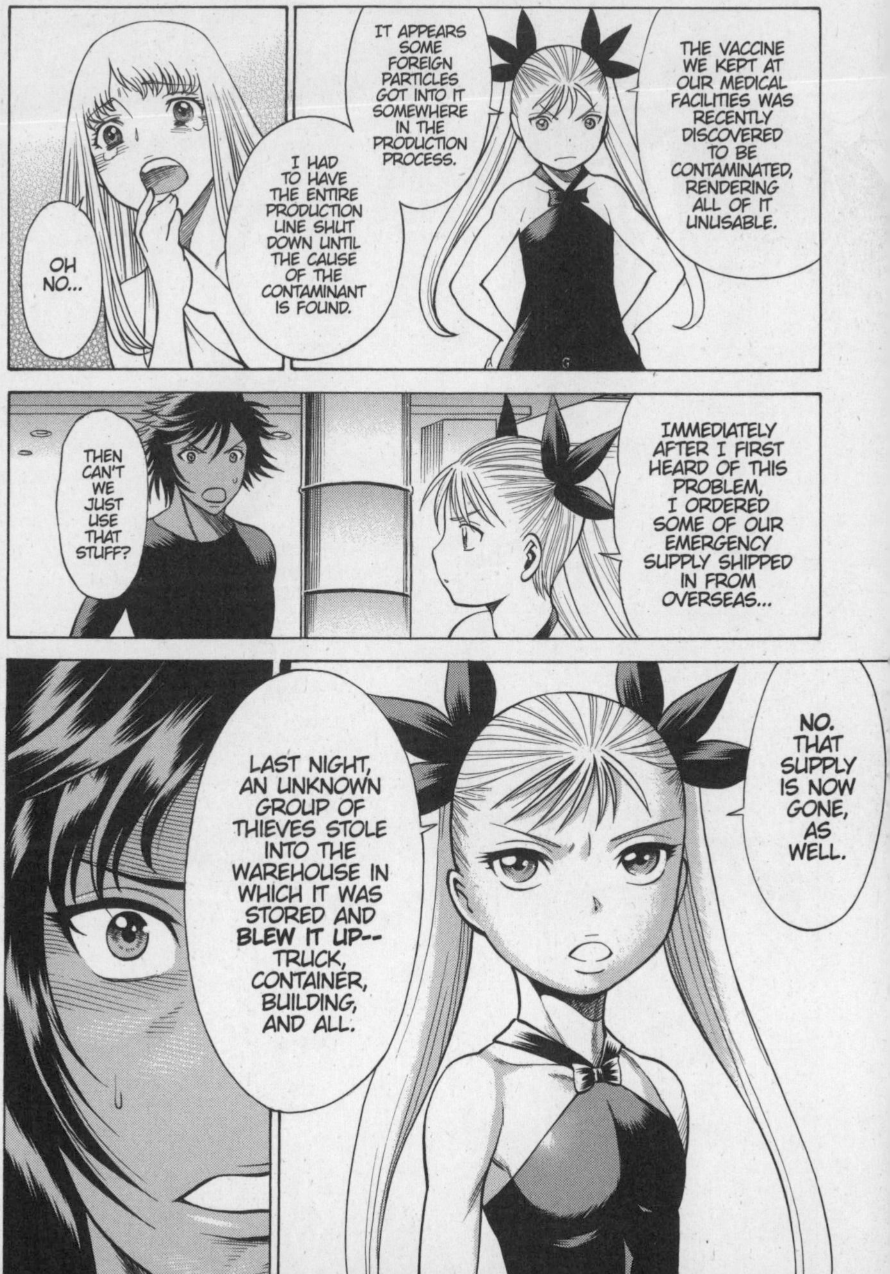
THE VACCINE WE KEPT AT OUR MEDICAL FACILITIES WAS RECENTLY DISCOVERED TO BE CONTAMINATED, RENDERING ALL OF IT UNUSABLE.
IT APPEARS SOME FOREIGN PARTICLES GOT INTO IT SOMEWHERE IN THE PRODUCTION PROCESS.
I HAD TO HAVE THE ENTIRE PRODUCTION LINE SHUT DOWN UNTIL THE CAUSE OF THE CONTAMINANT IS FOUND.
OH NO...
IMMEDIATELY AFTER I FIRST HEARD OF THIS PROBLEM, I ORDERED SOME OF OUR EMERGENCY SUPPLY SHIPPED IN FROM OVERSEAS...
THEN CAN'T WE JUST USE THAT STUFF?
NO. THAT SUPPLY IS NOW GONE, AS WELL.
LAST NIGHT, AN UNKNOWN GROUP OF THIEVES STOLE INTO THE WAREHOUSE IN WHICH IT WAS STORED AND BLEW IT UP-- TRUCK, CONTAINER, BUILDING, AND ALL.

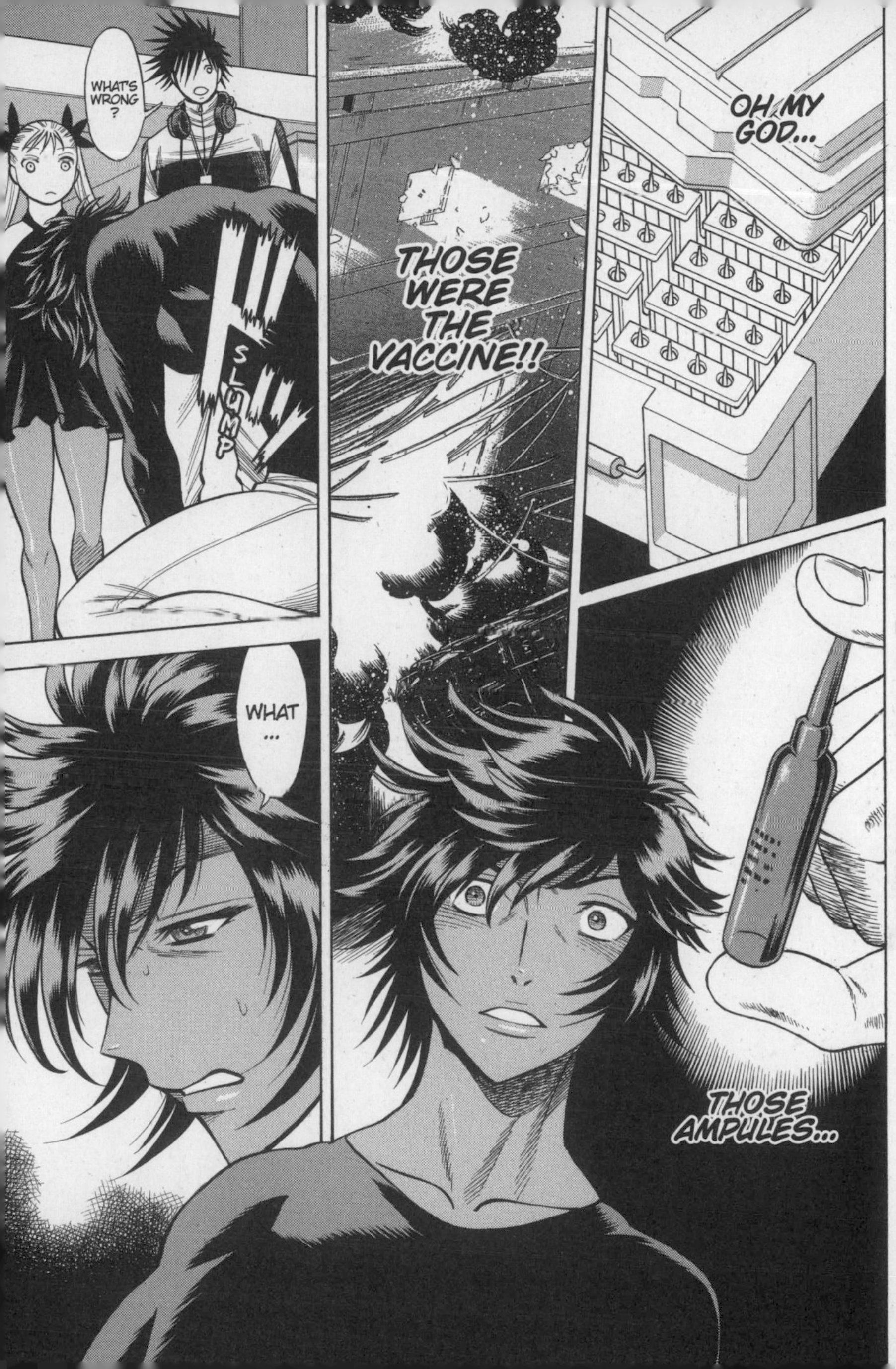
OH MY GOD...
THOSE AMPULES...
THOSE WERE THE VACCINE!!
WHAT'S WRONG ?
SLUMP
WHAT ...

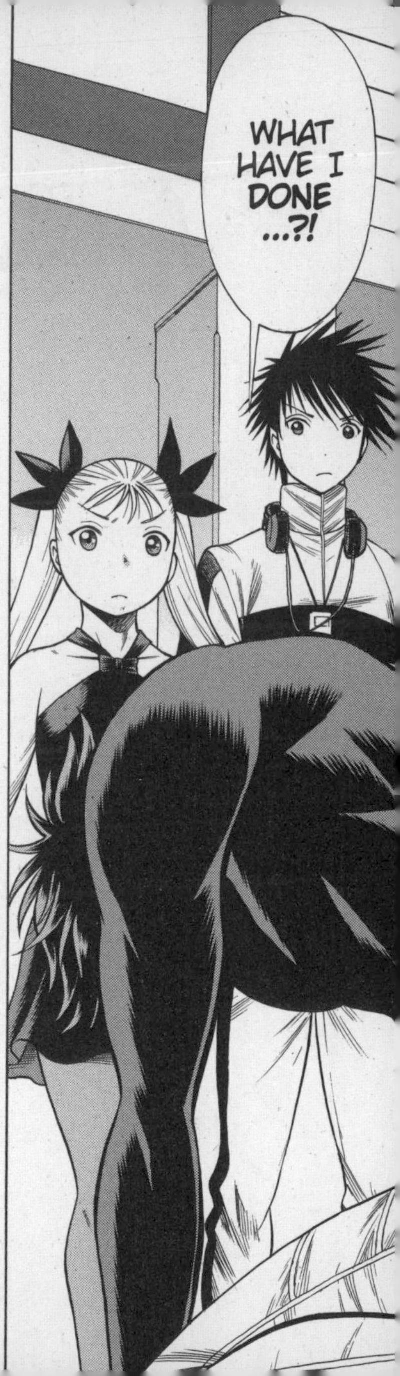
WHAT HAVE I DONE ...?!

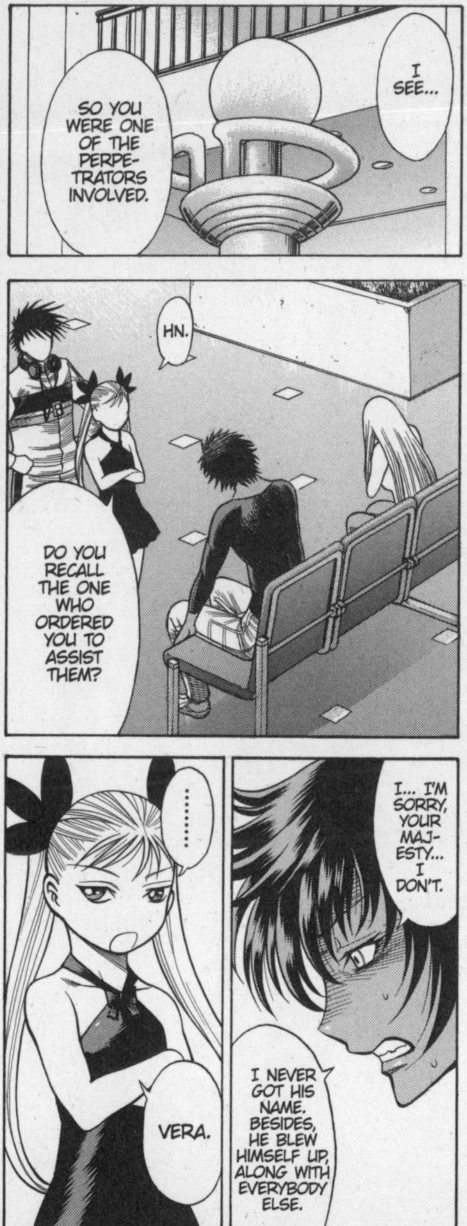
I SEE...
SO YOU WERE ONE OF THE PERPE-TRATORS INVOLVED.
HN.
DO YOU RECALL THE ONE WHO ORDERED YOU TO ASSIST THEM?
I... I'M SORRY, YOUR MAJ-ESTY... I DON'T.
I NEVER GOT HIS NAME. BESIDES, HE BLEW HIMSELF UP, ALONG WITH EVERYBODY ELSE.
....
VERA.

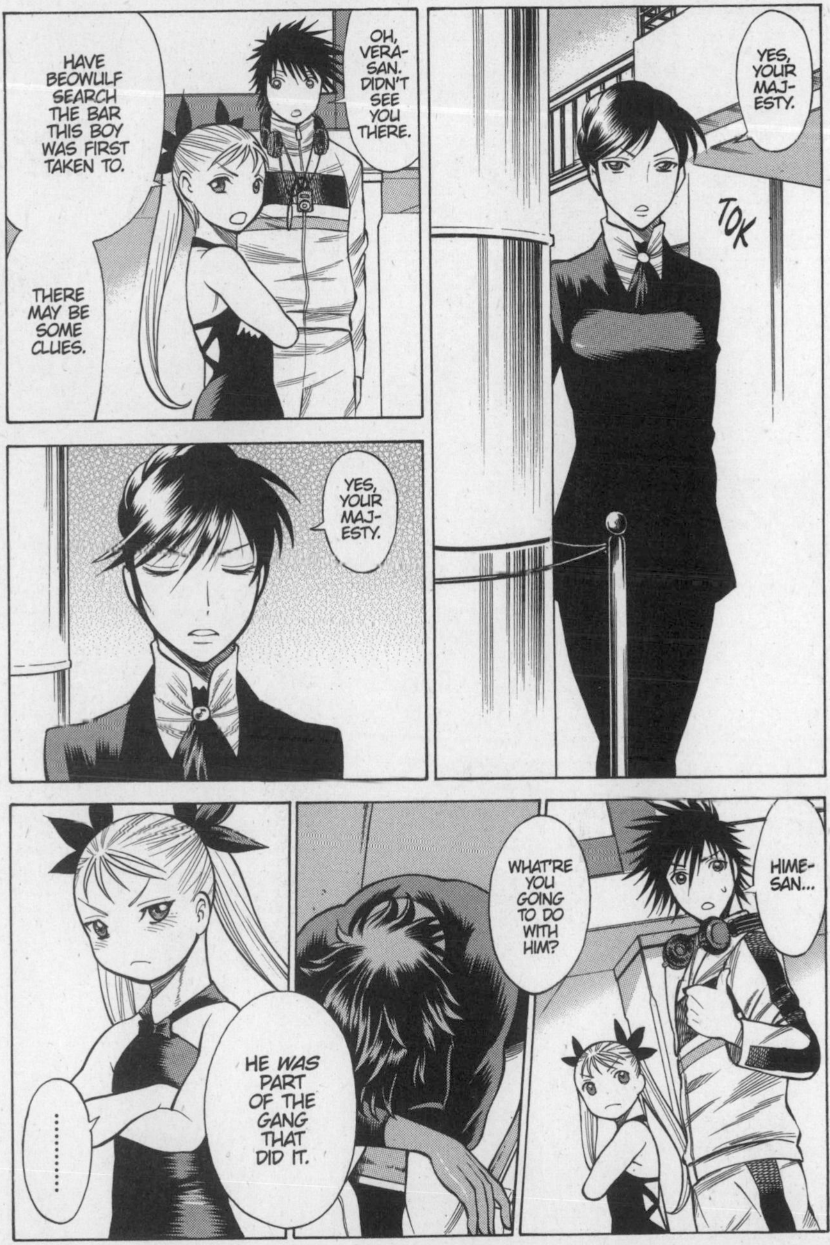
YES, YOUR MAJ-ESTY.
TOK
OH, VERA-SAN. DIDN'T SEE YOU THERE.
HAVE BEOWULF SEARCH THE BAR THIS BOY WAS FIRST TAKEN TO.
THERE MAY BE SOME CLUES.
YES, YOUR MAJ-ESTY.
HIME-SAN...
WHAT'RE YOU GOING TO DO WITH HIM?
HE *WAS* PART OF THE GANG THAT DID IT.
....

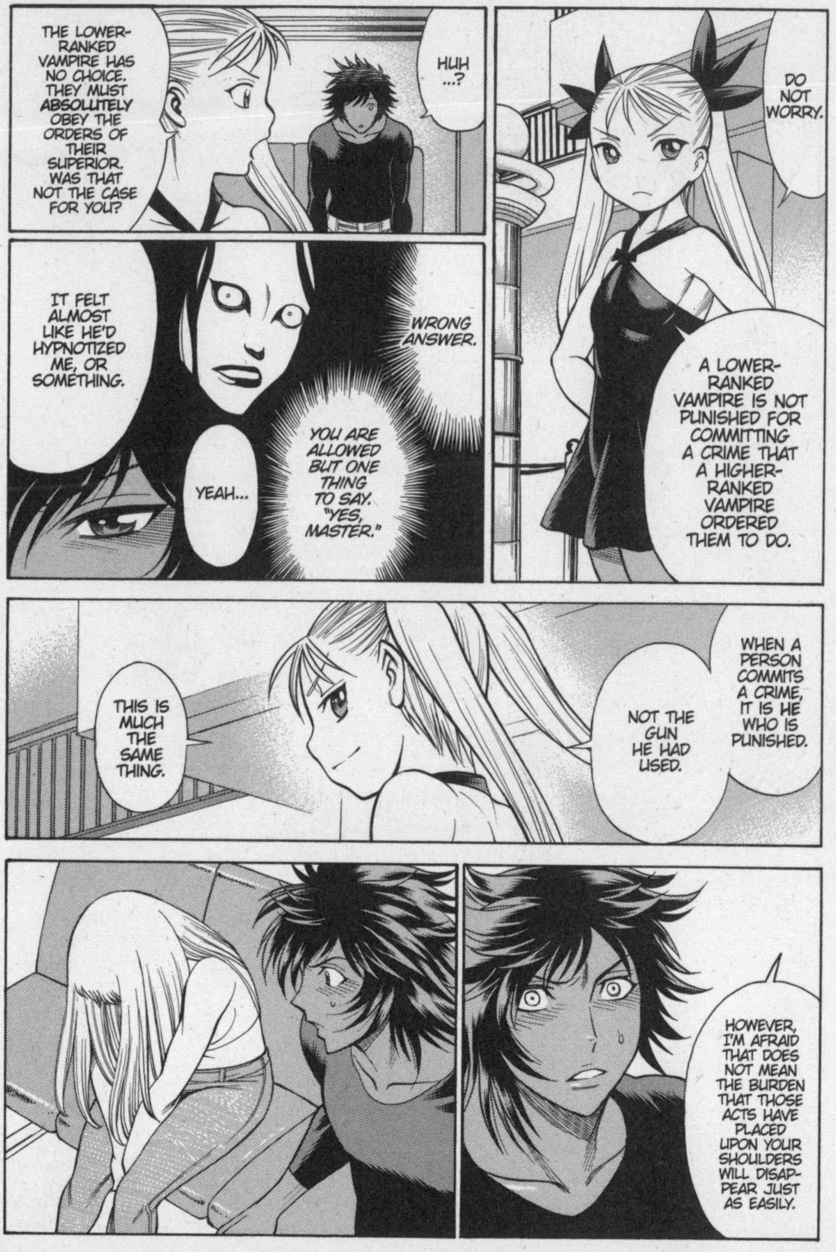
DO NOT WORRY.
A LOWER-RANKED VAMPIRE IS NOT PUNISHED FOR COMMITTING A CRIME THAT A HIGHER-RANKED VAMPIRE ORDERED THEM TO DO.
HUH ...?
THE LOWER-RANKED VAMPIRE HAS NO CHOICE. THEY MUST ABSOLUTELY OBEY THE ORDERS OF THEIR SUPERIOR. WAS THAT NOT THE CASE FOR YOU?
WRONG ANSWER.
IT FELT ALMOST LIKE HE'D HYPNOTIZED ME, OR SOMETHING.
YOU ARE ALLOWED BUT ONE THING TO SAY. "YES, MASTER."
YEAH...
WHEN A PERSON COMMITS A CRIME, IT IS HE WHO IS PUNISHED.
NOT THE GUN HE HAD USED.
THIS IS MUCH THE SAME THING.
HOWEVER, I'M AFRAID THAT DOES NOT MEAN THE BURDEN THAT THOSE ACTS HAVE PLACED UPON YOUR SHOULDERS WILL DISAPPEAR JUST AS EASILY.

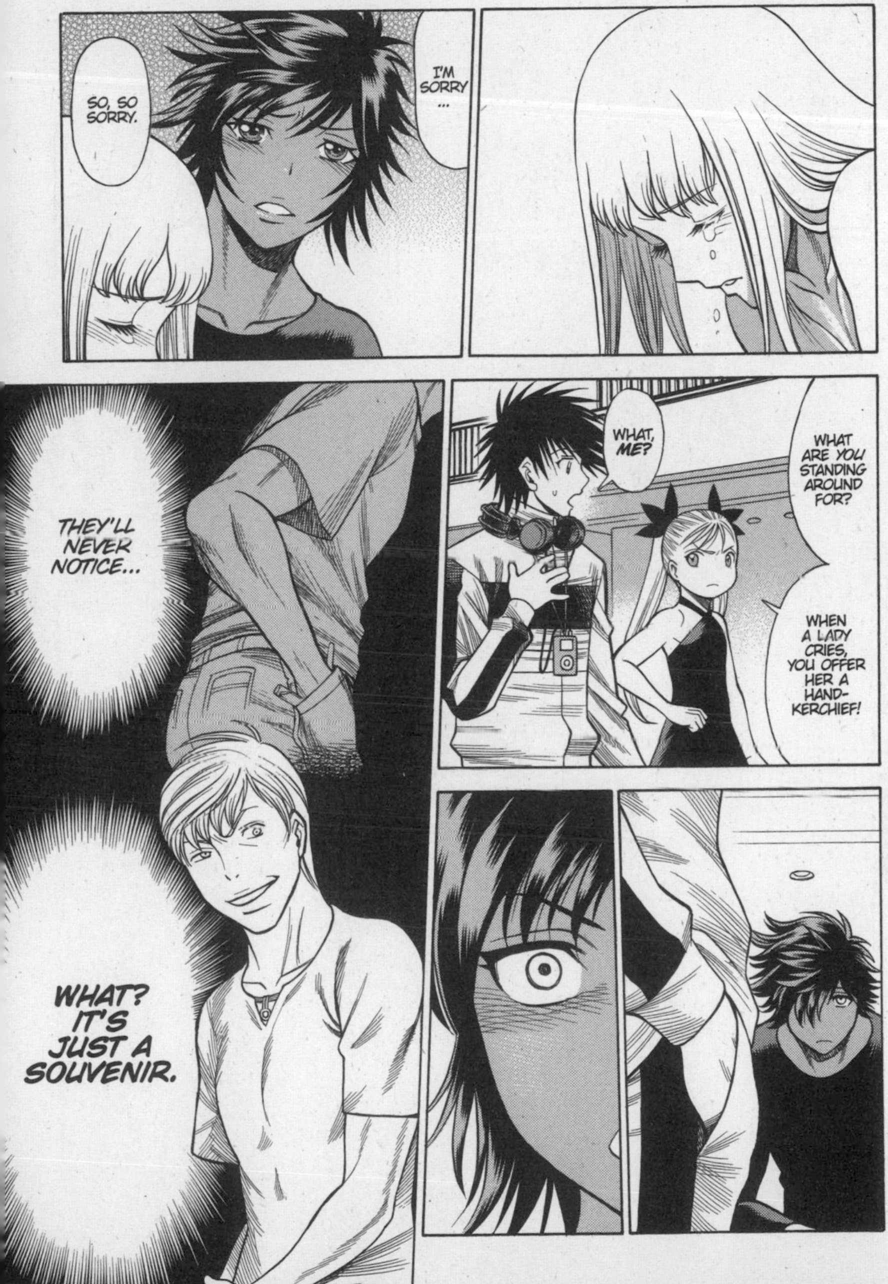
I'M SORRY ...
SO, SO SORRY.
WHAT ARE YOU STANDING AROUND FOR?
WHEN A LADY CRIES, YOU OFFER HER A HAND-KERCHIEF!
WHAT, ME?
THEY'LL NEVER NOTICE...
WHAT? IT'S JUST A SOUVENIR.

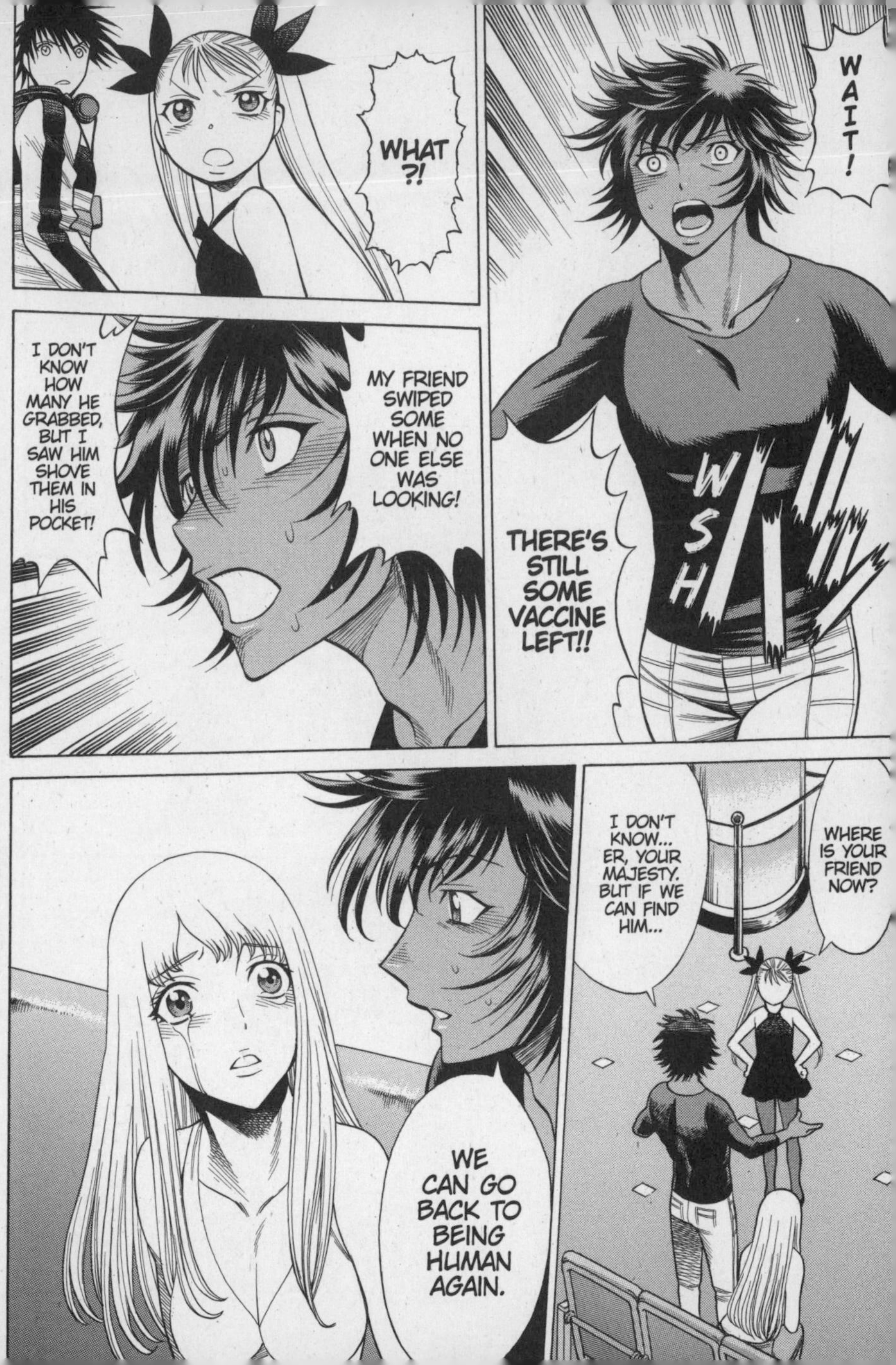
WAIT!
WSH
THERE'S STILL SOME VACCINE LEFT!!
WHAT?!
MY FRIEND SWIPED SOME WHEN NO ONE ELSE WAS LOOKING!
I DON'T KNOW HOW MANY HE GRABBED, BUT I SAW HIM SHOVE THEM IN HIS POCKET!
WHERE IS YOUR FRIEND NOW?
I DON'T KNOW... ER, YOUR MAJESTY. BUT IF WE CAN FIND HIM...
WE CAN GO BACK TO BEING HUMAN AGAIN.

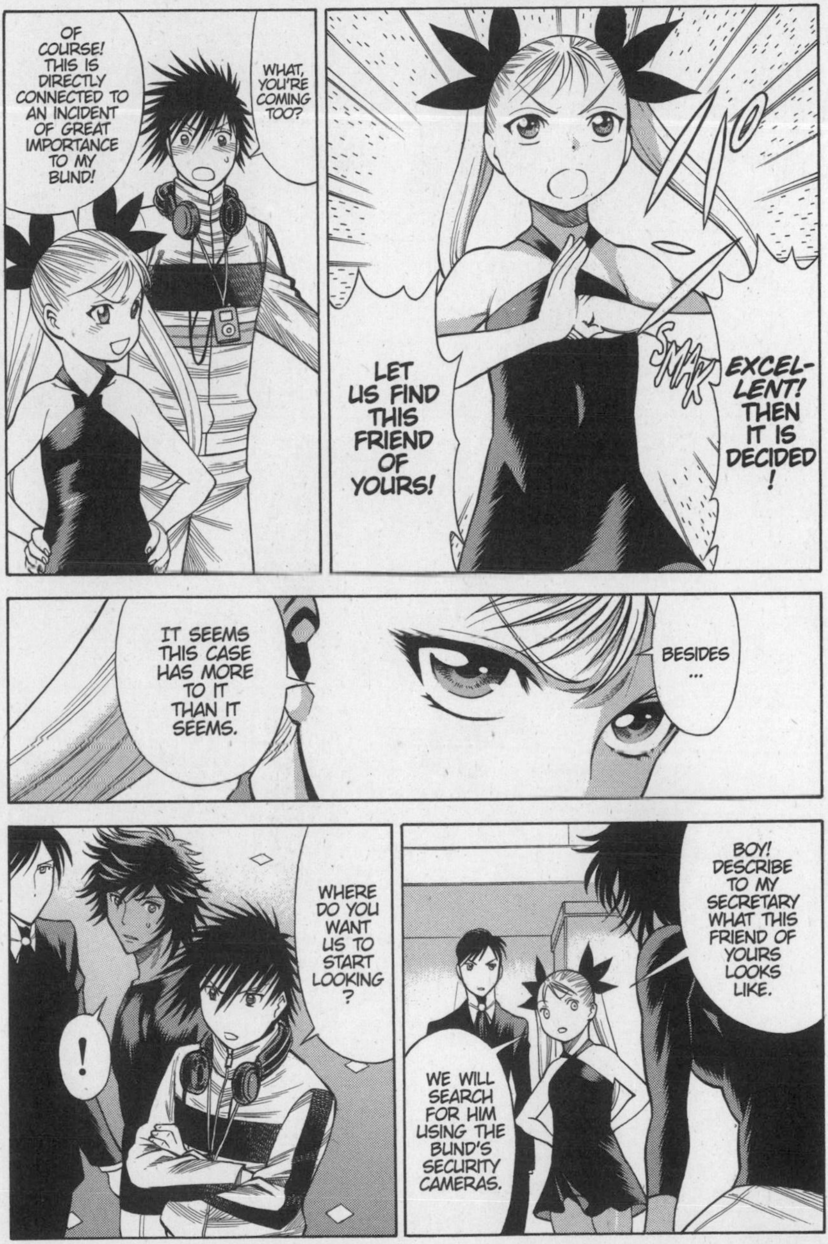
SMAK
EXCEL-LENT! THEN IT IS DECIDED!
LET US FIND THIS FRIEND OF YOURS!
WHAT, YOU'RE COMING TOO?
OF COURSE! THIS IS DIRECTLY CONNECTED TO AN INCIDENT OF GREAT IMPORTANCE TO MY BUND!
BESIDES ...
IT SEEMS THIS CASE HAS MORE TO IT THAN IT SEEMS.
BOY! DESCRIBE TO MY SECRETARY WHAT THIS FRIEND OF YOURS LOOKS LIKE.
WE WILL SEARCH FOR HIM USING THE BUND'S SECURITY CAMERAS.
WHERE DO YOU WANT US TO START LOOKING?
!

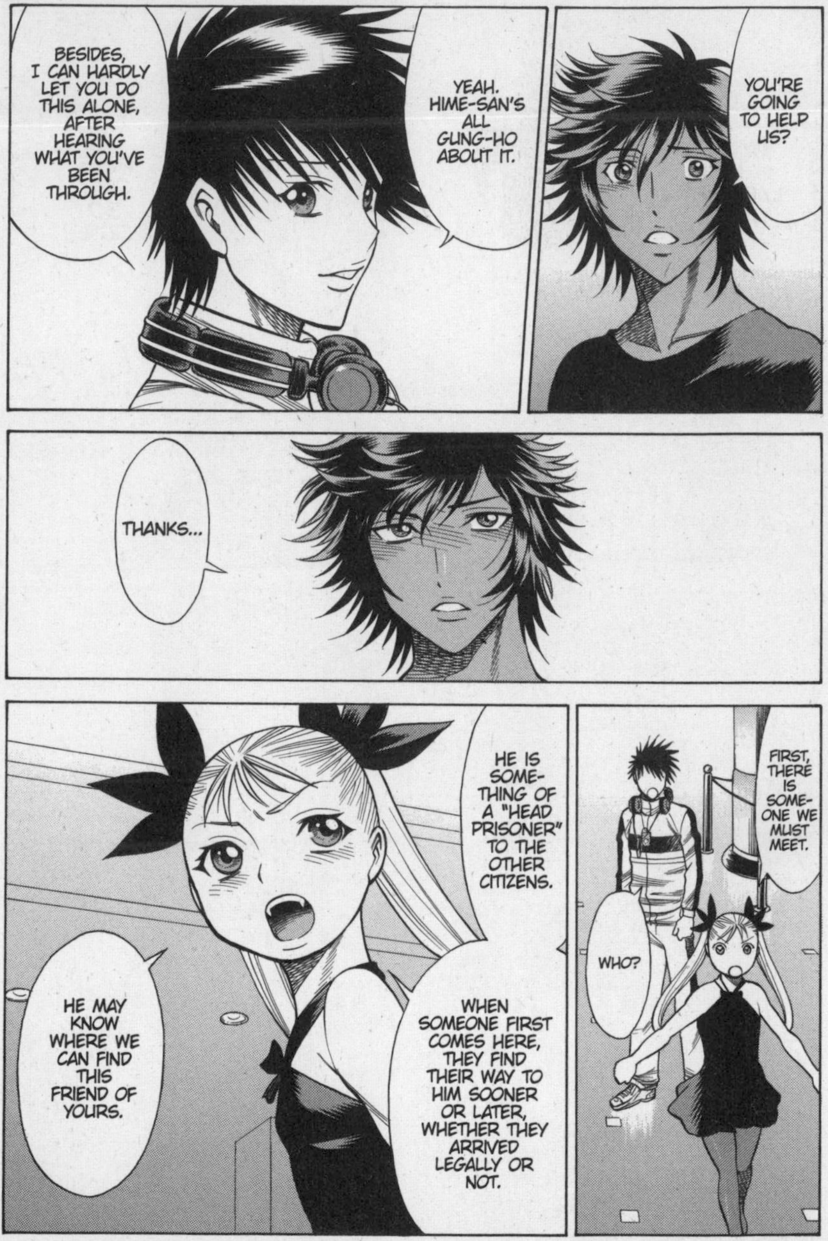

YOU'RE GOING TO HELP US?
YEAH. HIME-SAN'S ALL GUNG-HO ABOUT IT.
BESIDES, I CAN HARDLY LET YOU DO THIS ALONE, AFTER HEARING WHAT YOU'VE BEEN THROUGH.
THANKS...
FIRST, THERE IS SOME-ONE WE MUST MEET.
WHO?
HE IS SOME-THING OF A "HEAD PRISONER" TO THE OTHER CITIZENS.
WHEN SOMEONE FIRST COMES HERE, THEY FIND THEIR WAY TO HIM SOONER OR LATER, WHETHER THEY ARRIVED LEGALLY OR NOT.
HE MAY KNOW WHERE WE CAN FIND THIS FRIEND OF YOURS.

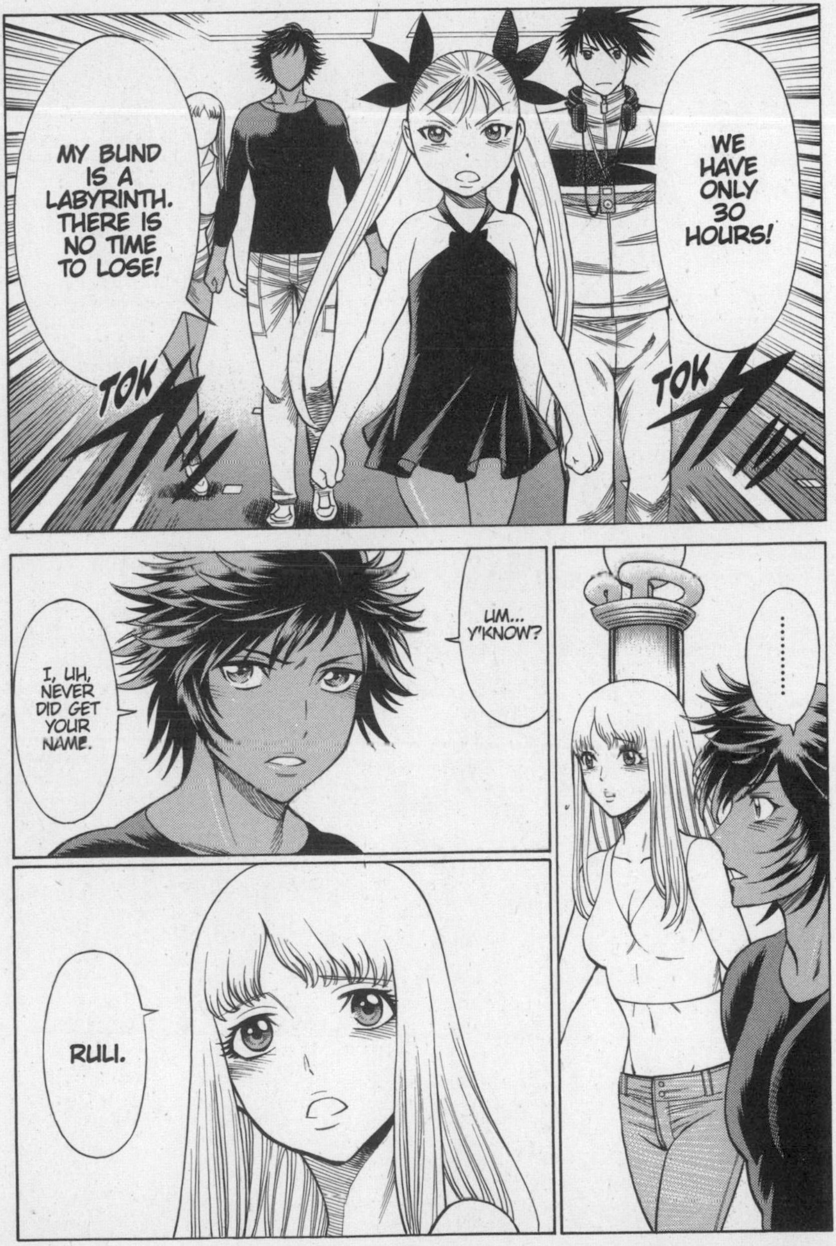
WE HAVE ONLY 30 HOURS!
TOK
MY BLIND IS A LABYRINTH. THERE IS NO TIME TO LOSE!
TOK
......
UM... Y'KNOW?
I, UH, NEVER DID GET YOUR NAME.
RULI.

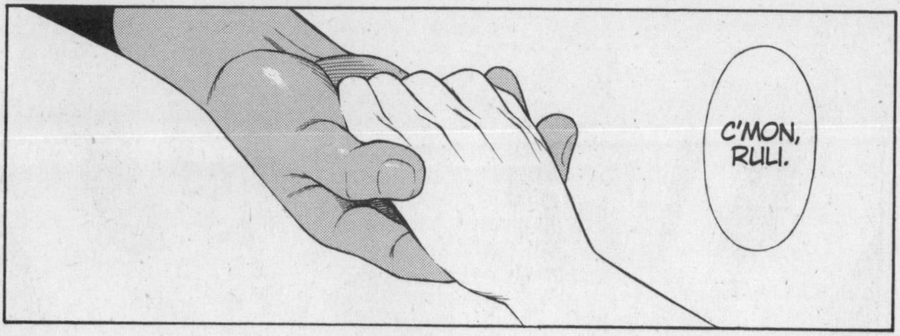
C'MON, RULI.

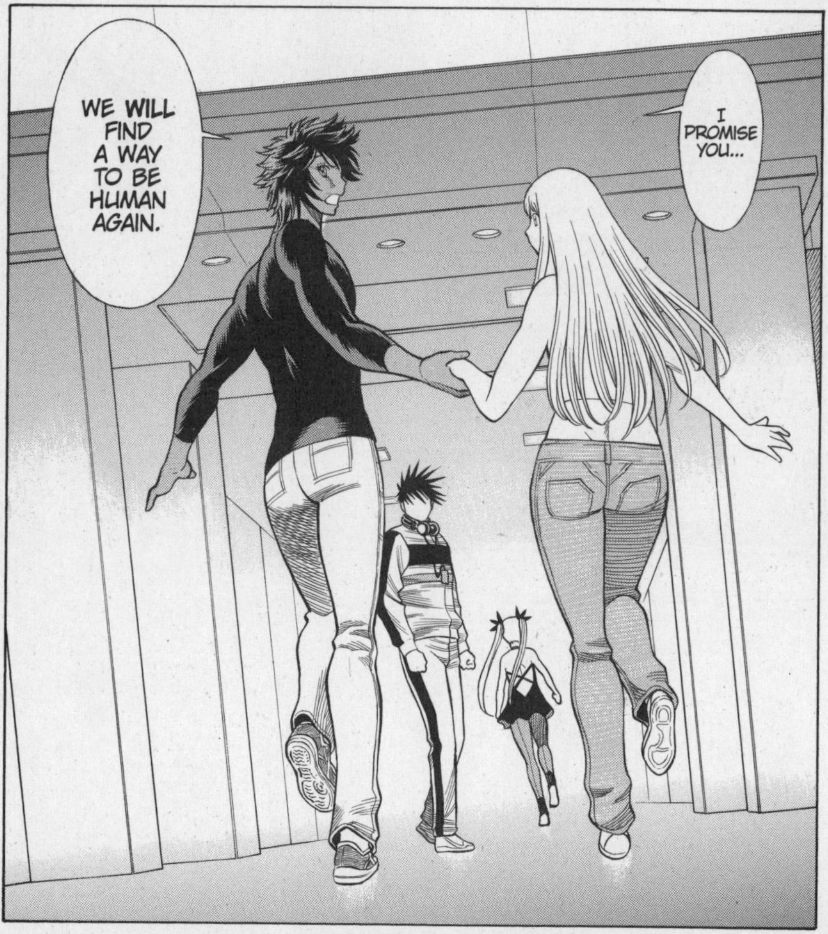
I PROMISE YOU...
WE WILL FIND A WAY TO BE HUMAN AGAIN.

Chapter 5: The Child

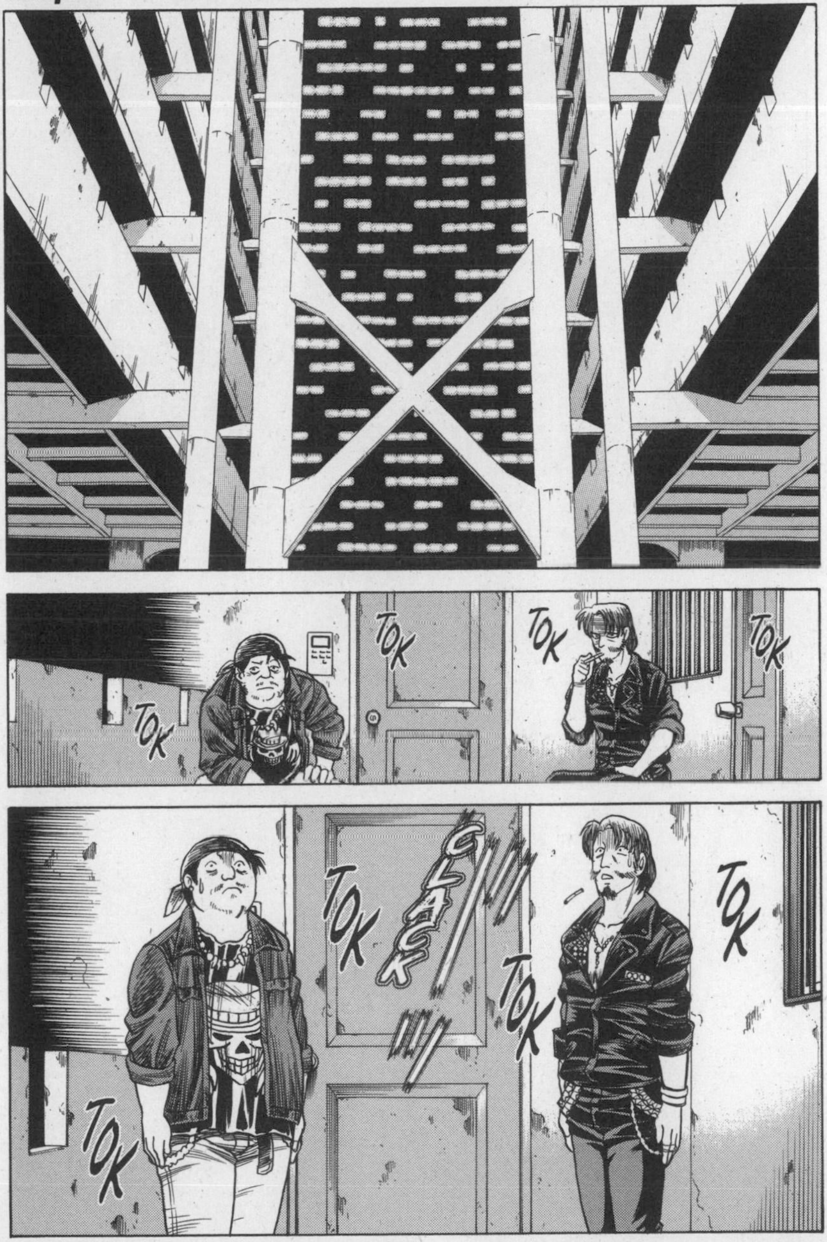
TOK
TOK
TOK
TOK
TOK
TOK
CLACK
TOK
TOK

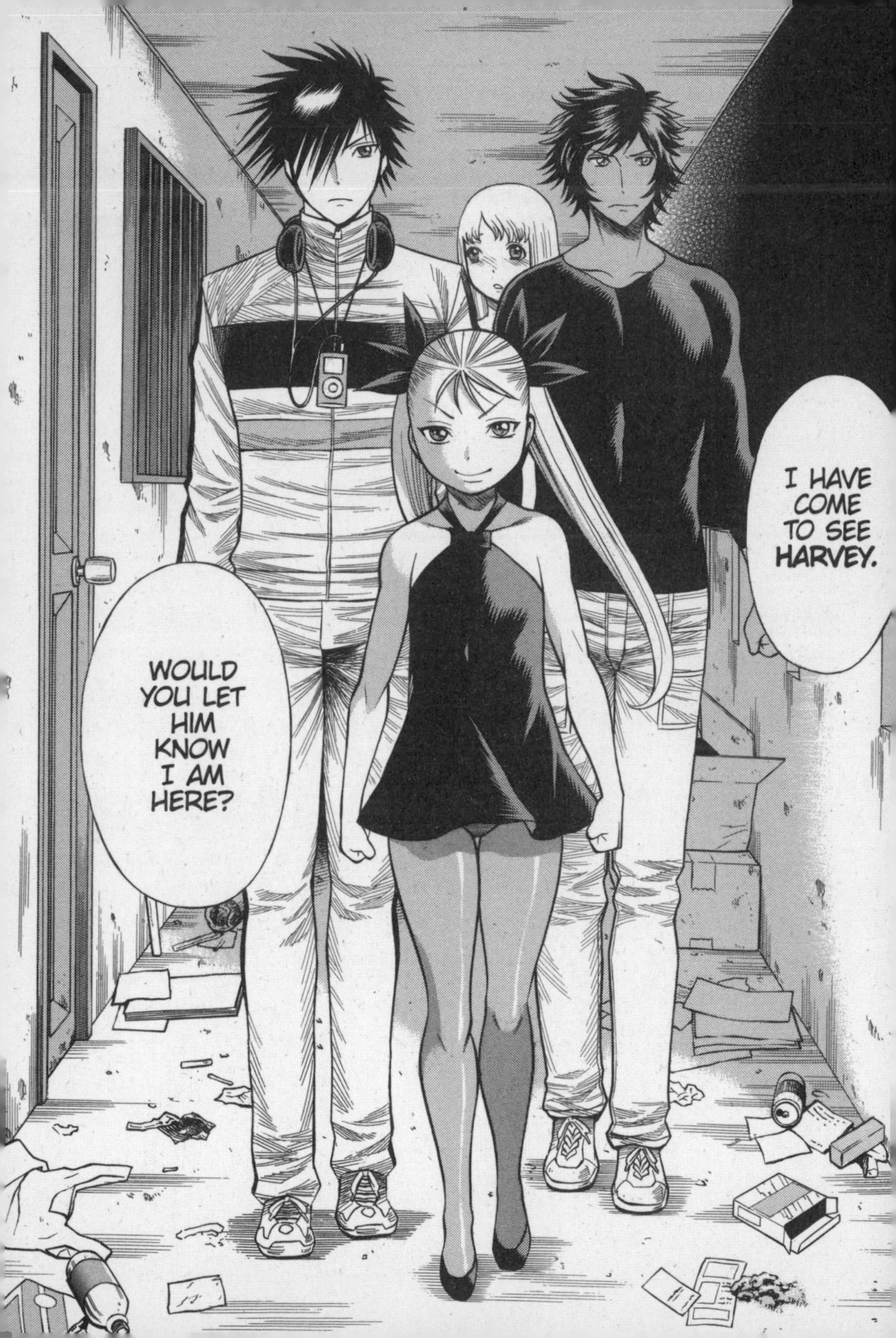
I HAVE COME TO SEE HARVEY.
WOULD YOU LET HIM KNOW I AM HERE?

HARVEY.

OKAY, EVERY-BODY... OUT.

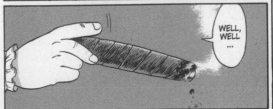

WELL, WELL...

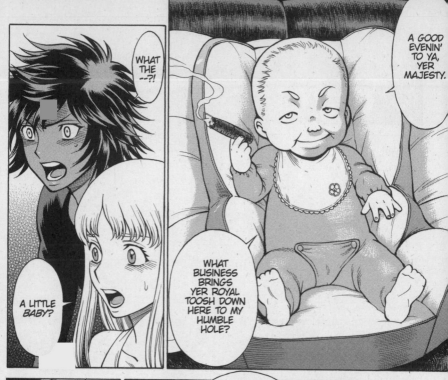

A GOOD EVENIN' TO YA, YER MAJESTY.
WHAT BUSINESS BRINGS YER ROYAL TOOSH DOWN HERE TO MY HUMBLE HOLE?
WHAT THE --?!
A LITTLE *BABY?*
YES. EVERYONE, THIS IS HARVEY, THE UNOFFICIAL CARETAKER OF MY BUND'S RESIDENTS.
DO NOT LET HIS **LOOKS** FOOL YOU. HE MAY LOOK LIKE A SWEET, INNOCENT CHILD, BUT IN ACTUALITY, HE IS OVER A **HUNDRED** YEARS OLD, AND AS SLY AS THEY COME. NOT TO MENTION, HE IS *QUITE* TWISTED.
OUCH. YOU WOUND ME, YER MAJESTY.
ANYWAY, WHAT BUSINESS BRINGS YER ROY-ALNESS DOWN HERE?
YOU DIDN'T COME HERE JUST TO POKE AT MY REPUTATION, I'M SURE.

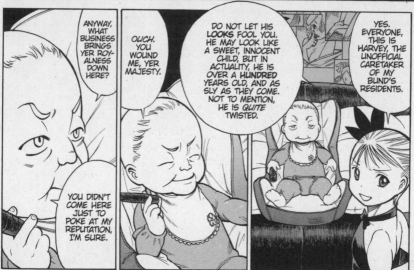

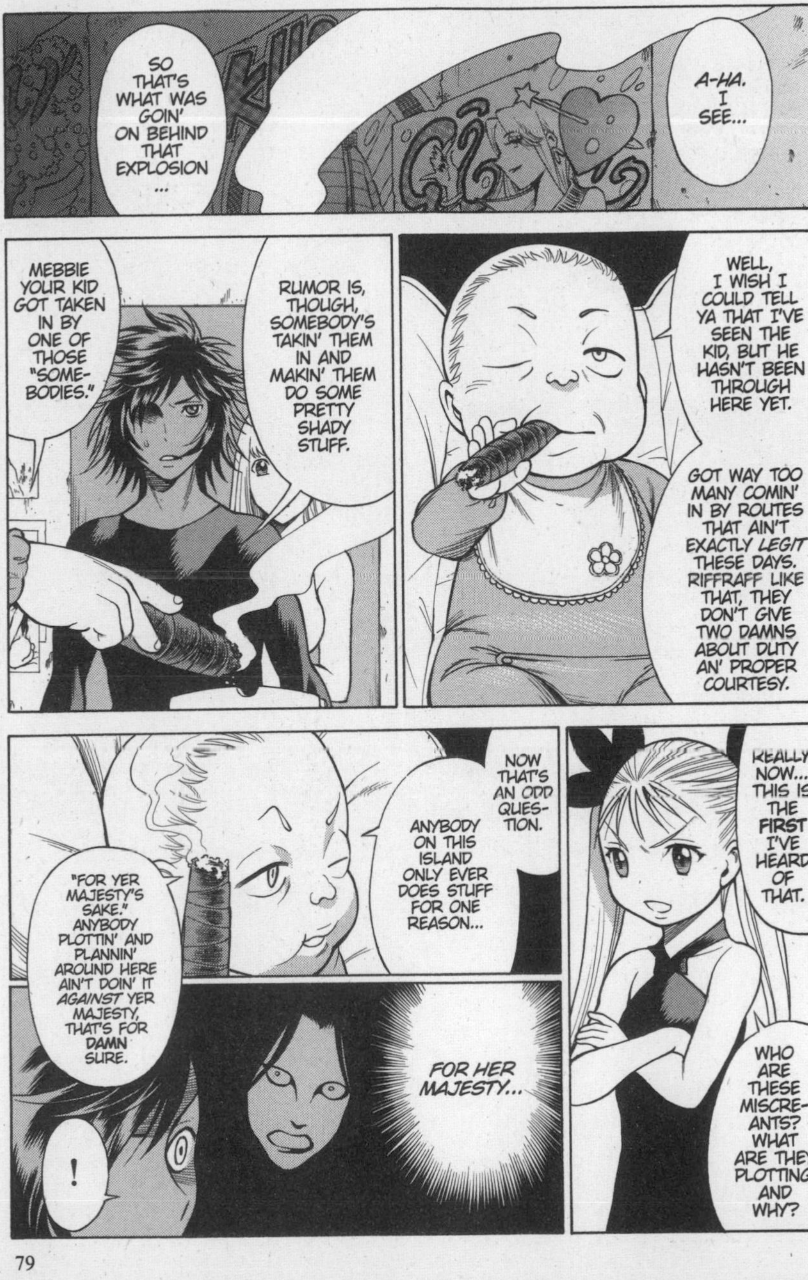
A-HA. I SEE...
SO THAT'S WHAT WAS GOIN' ON BEHIND THAT EXPLOSION ...
WELL, I WISH I COULD TELL YA THAT I'VE SEEN THE KID, BUT HE HASN'T BEEN THROUGH HERE YET.
GOT WAY TOO MANY COMIN' IN BY ROUTES THAT AIN'T EXACTLY *LEGIT* THESE DAYS. RIFFRAFF LIKE THAT, THEY DON'T GIVE TWO DAMNS ABOUT DUTY AN' PROPER COURTESY.
RUMOR IS, THOUGH, SOMEBODY'S TAKIN' THEM IN AND MAKIN' THEM DO SOME PRETTY SHADY STUFF.
MEBBIE YOUR KID GOT TAKEN IN BY ONE OF THOSE "SOME-BODIES."
REALLY, NOW... THIS IS THE **FIRST** I'VE HEARD OF THAT.
WHO ARE THESE MISCRE-ANTS? WHAT ARE THEY PLOTTING, AND WHY?
NOW THAT'S AN ODD QUES-TION.
ANYBODY ON THIS ISLAND ONLY EVER DOES STUFF FOR ONE REASON...
"FOR YER MAJESTY'S SAKE." ANYBODY PLOTTIN' AND PLANNIN' AROUND HERE AIN'T DOIN' IT *AGAINST* YER MAJESTY, THAT'S FOR DAMN SURE.
FOR HER MAJESTY...
!

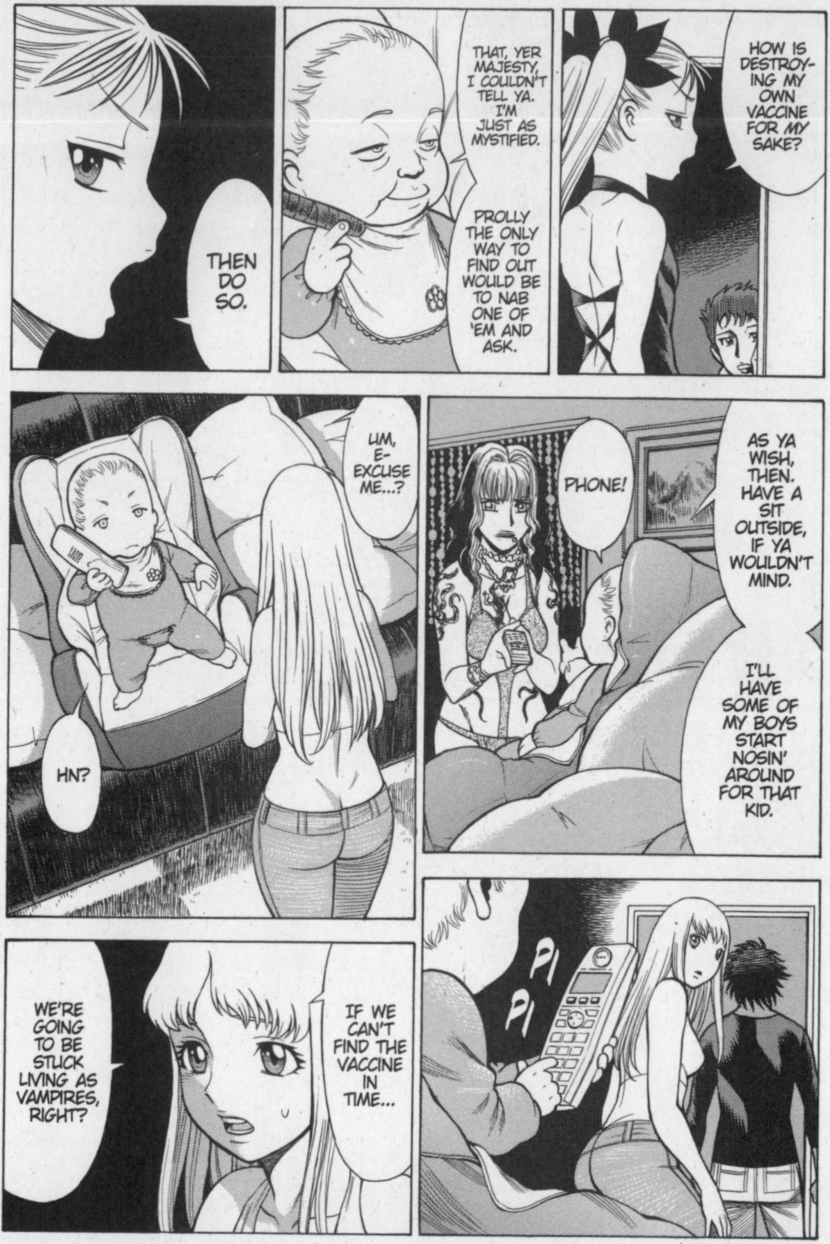
HOW IS DESTROYING MY OWN VACCINE FOR MY SAKE?
THAT, YER MAJESTY, I COULDN'T TELL YA. I'M JUST AS MYSTIFIED.
PROLLY THE ONLY WAY TO FIND OUT WOULD BE TO NAB ONE OF 'EM AND ASK.
THEN DO SO.
AS YA WISH, THEN. HAVE A SIT OUTSIDE, IF YA WOULDN'T MIND.
I'LL HAVE SOME OF MY BOYS START NOSIN' AROUND FOR THAT KID.
PHONE!
UM, E-EXCUSE ME...?
HN?
PI
PI
IF WE CAN'T FIND THE VACCINE IN TIME...
WE'RE GOING TO BE STUCK LIVING AS VAMPIRES, RIGHT?

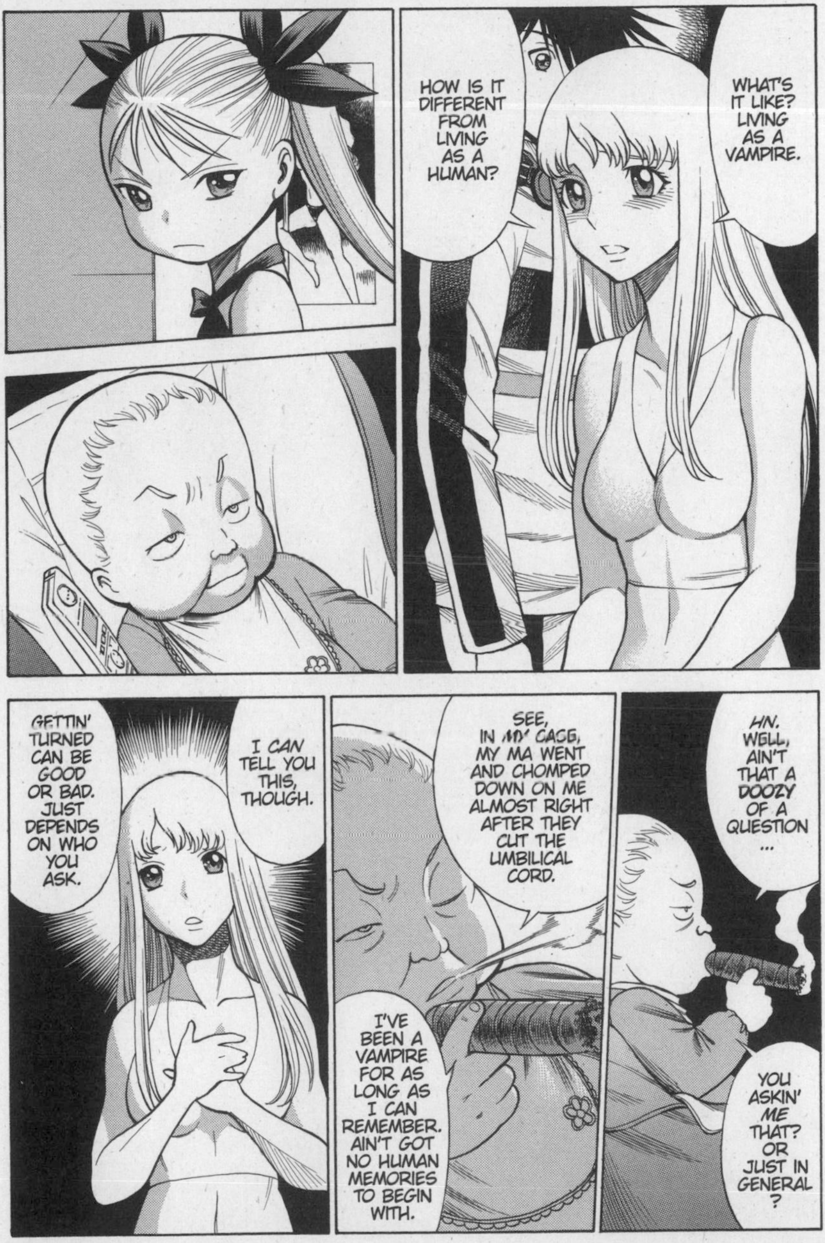
WHAT'S IT LIKE? LIVING AS A VAMPIRE.
HOW IS IT DIFFERENT FROM LIVING AS A HUMAN?
HN. WELL, AIN'T THAT A DOOZY OF A QUESTION ...
YOU ASKIN' ME THAT? OR JUST IN GENERAL?
SEE, IN MY CASE, MY MA WENT AND CHOMPED DOWN ON ME ALMOST RIGHT AFTER THEY CUT THE UMBILICAL CORD.
I'VE BEEN A VAMPIRE FOR AS LONG AS I CAN REMEMBER. AIN'T GOT NO HUMAN MEMORIES TO BEGIN WITH.
I CAN TELL YOU THIS, THOUGH.
GETTIN' TURNED CAN BE GOOD OR BAD. JUST DEPENDS ON WHO YOU ASK.

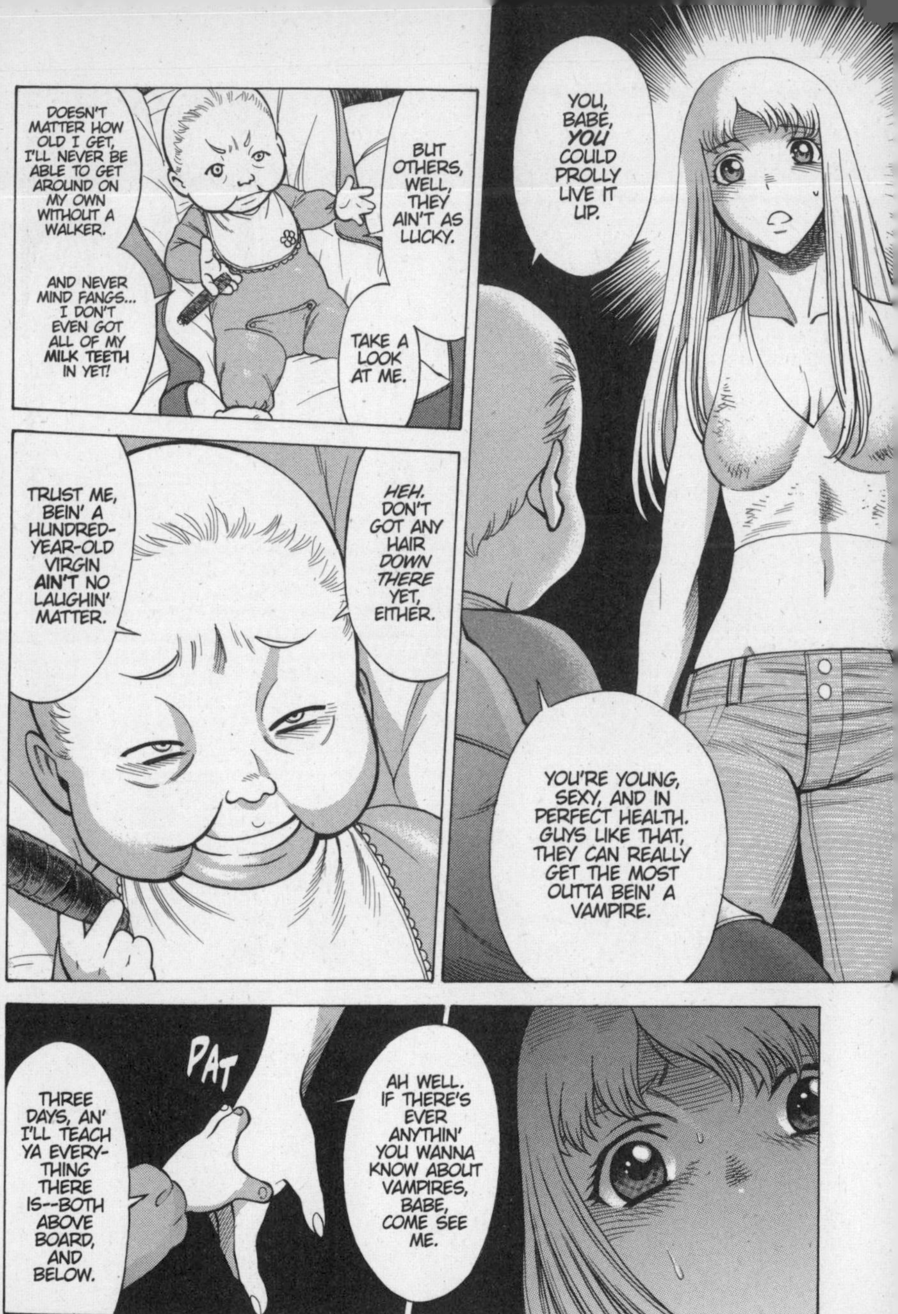
YOU, BABE, YOU COULD PROLLY LIVE IT UP.
YOU'RE YOUNG, SEXY, AND IN PERFECT HEALTH. GUYS LIKE THAT, THEY CAN REALLY GET THE MOST OUTTA BEIN' A VAMPIRE.
BUT OTHERS, WELL, THEY AIN'T AS LUCKY.
TAKE A LOOK AT ME.
DOESN'T MATTER HOW OLD I GET, I'LL NEVER BE ABLE TO GET AROUND ON MY OWN WITHOUT A WALKER.
AND NEVER MIND FANGS... I DON'T EVEN GOT ALL OF MY MILK TEETH IN YET!
HEH. DON'T GOT ANY HAIR DOWN THERE YET, EITHER.
TRUST ME, BEIN' A HUNDRED-YEAR-OLD VIRGIN AIN'T NO LAUGHIN' MATTER.
PAT
AH WELL. IF THERE'S EVER ANYTHIN' YOU WANNA KNOW ABOUT VAMPIRES, BABE, COME SEE ME.
THREE DAYS, AN' I'LL TEACH YA EVERYTHING THERE IS--BOTH ABOVE BOARD, AND BELOW.

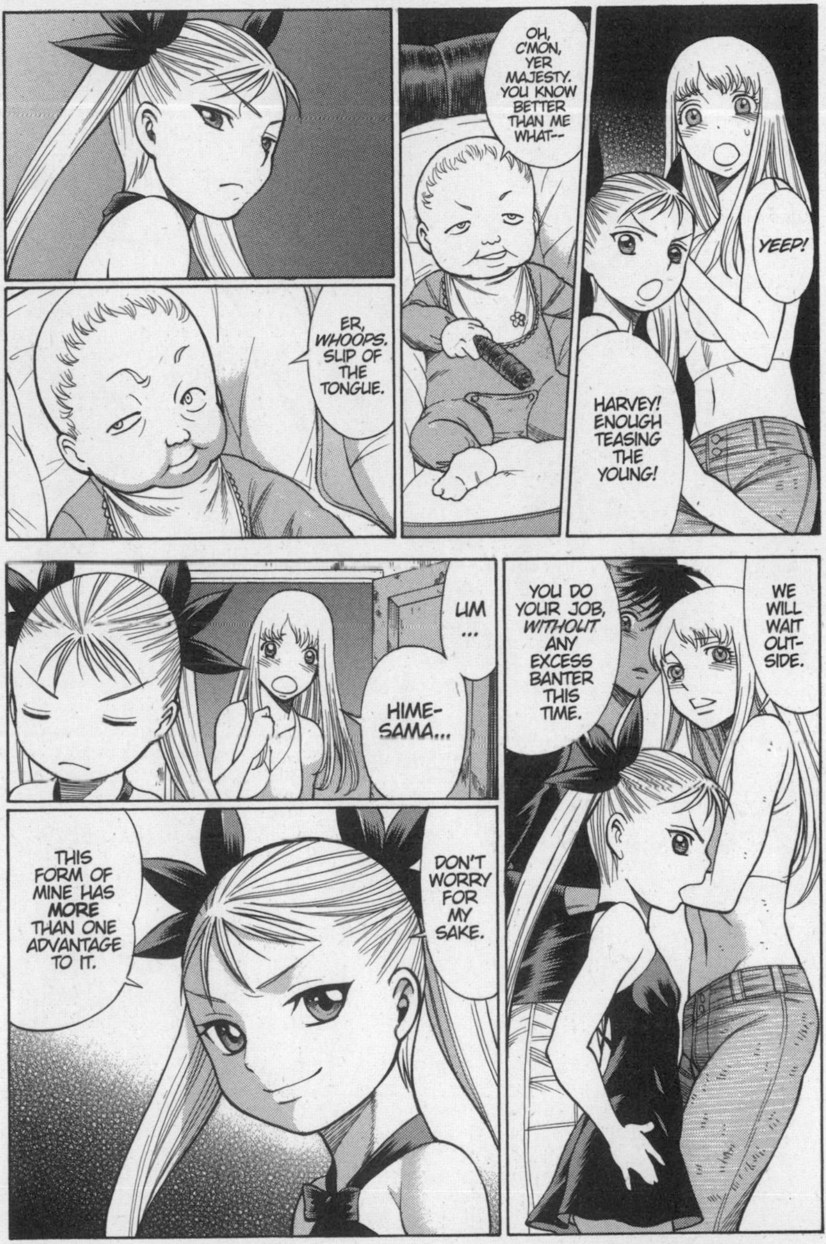
YEEP!
HARVEY! ENOUGH TEASING THE YOUNG!
OH, C'MON, YER MAJESTY. YOU KNOW BETTER THAN ME WHAT--
ER, *WHOOPS.* SLIP OF THE TONGUE.
WE WILL WAIT OUT-SIDE.
YOU DO YOUR JOB, *WITHOUT* ANY EXCESS BANTER THIS TIME.
UM ...
HIME-SAMA...
DON'T WORRY FOR MY SAKE.
THIS FORM OF MINE HAS **MORE** THAN ONE ADVANTAGE TO IT.

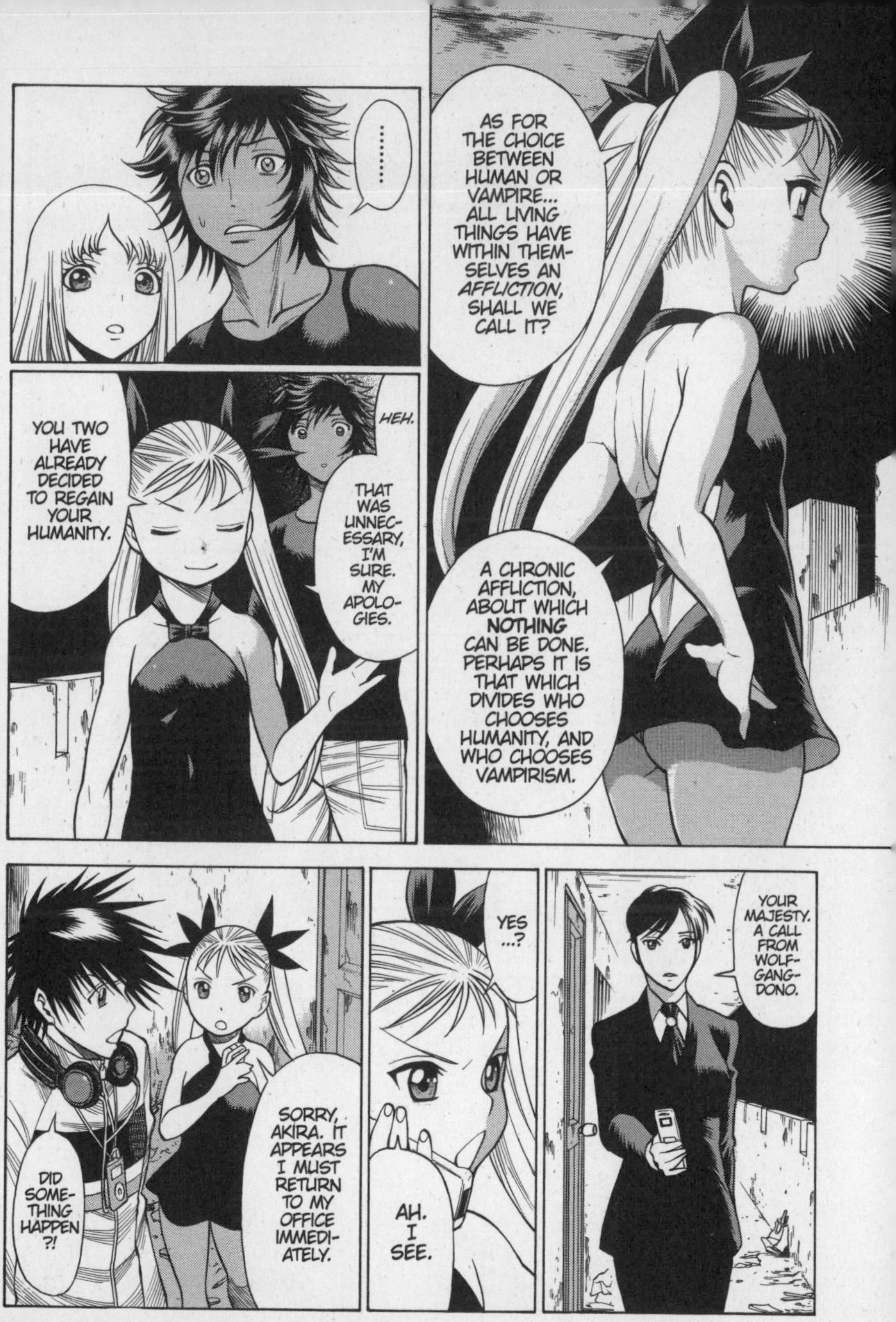
AS FOR THE CHOICE BETWEEN HUMAN OR VAMPIRE... ALL LIVING THINGS HAVE WITHIN THEMSELVES AN *AFFLICTION*, SHALL WE CALL IT?
A CHRONIC AFFLICTION, ABOUT WHICH **NOTHING** CAN BE DONE. PERHAPS IT IS THAT WHICH DIVIDES WHO CHOOSES HUMANITY, AND WHO CHOOSES VAMPIRISM.
......
YOU TWO HAVE ALREADY DECIDED TO REGAIN YOUR HUMANITY.
HEH.
THAT WAS UNNECESSARY, I'M SURE. MY APOLOGIES.
YOUR MAJESTY. A CALL FROM WOLFGANG-DONO.
YES ...?
AH. I SEE.
SORRY, AKIRA. IT APPEARS I MUST RETURN TO MY OFFICE IMMEDIATELY.
DID SOMETHING HAPPEN ?!

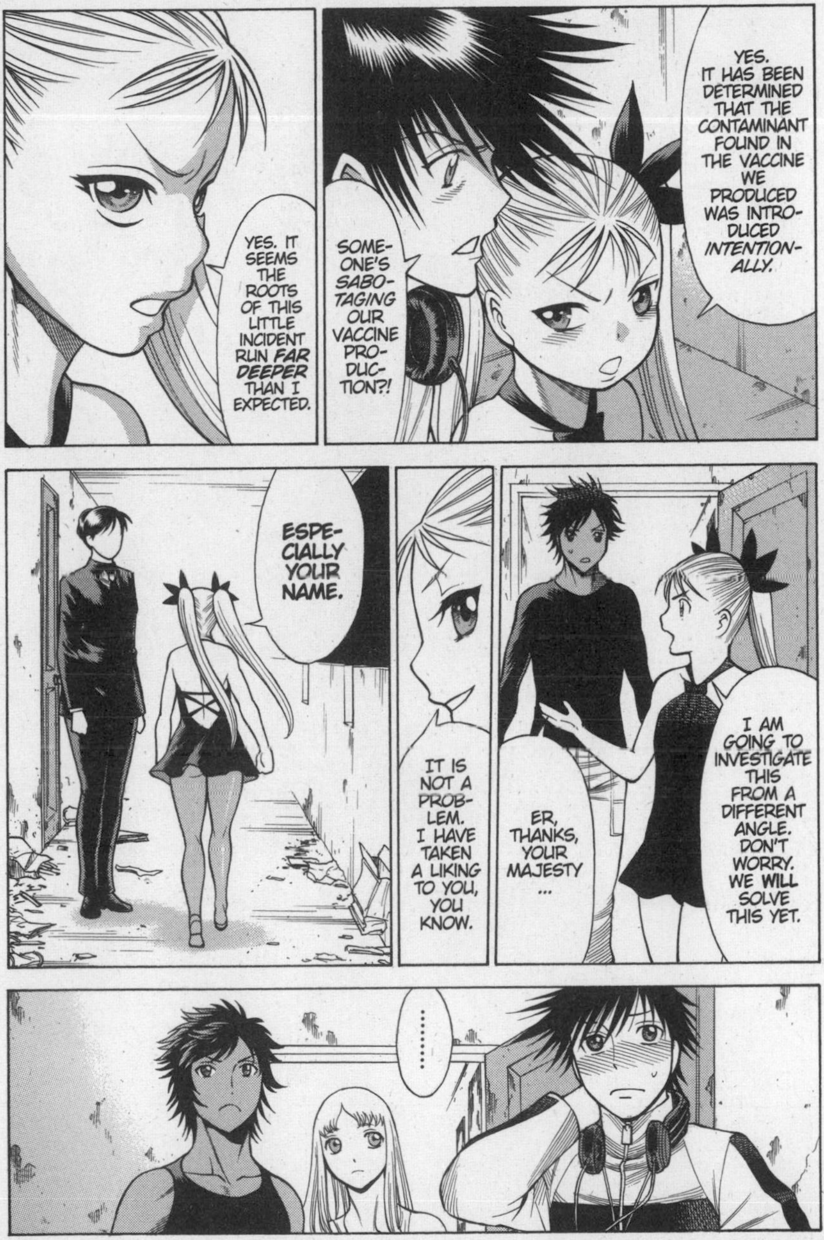
YES. IT HAS BEEN DETERMINED THAT THE CONTAMINANT FOUND IN THE VACCINE WE PRODUCED WAS INTRODUCED *INTENTIONALLY*.
SOMEONE'S *SABOTAGING* OUR VACCINE PRODUCTION?!
YES. IT SEEMS THE ROOTS OF THIS LITTLE INCIDENT RUN ***FAR DEEPER*** THAN I EXPECTED.
I AM GOING TO INVESTIGATE THIS FROM A DIFFERENT ANGLE. DON'T WORRY. WE WILL SOLVE THIS YET.
ER, THANKS, YOUR MAJESTY ...
IT IS NOT A PROBLEM. I HAVE TAKEN A LIKING TO YOU, YOU KNOW.
ESPECIALLY YOUR NAME.
......

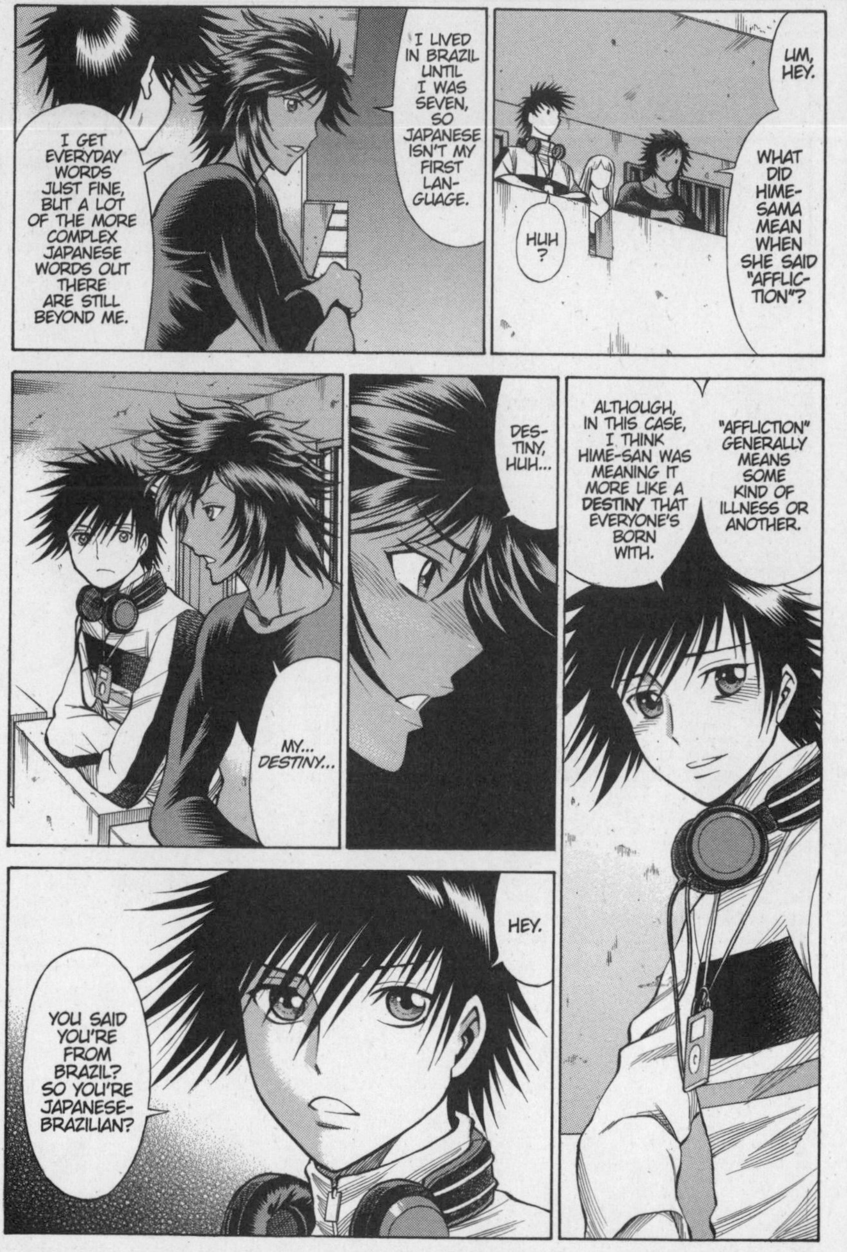
UM, HEY.
WHAT DID HIME-SAMA MEAN WHEN SHE SAID "AFFLICTION"?
HUH?
I LIVED IN BRAZIL UNTIL I WAS SEVEN, SO JAPANESE ISN'T MY FIRST LAN-GUAGE.
I GET EVERYDAY WORDS JUST FINE, BUT A LOT OF THE MORE COMPLEX JAPANESE WORDS OUT THERE ARE STILL BEYOND ME.
"AFFLICTION" GENERALLY MEANS SOME KIND OF ILLNESS OR ANOTHER.
ALTHOUGH, IN THIS CASE, I THINK HIME-SAN WAS MEANING IT MORE LIKE A DESTINY THAT EVERYONE'S BORN WITH.
DES-TINY, HUH...
MY... DESTINY...
HEY.
YOU SAID YOU'RE FROM BRAZIL? SO YOU'RE JAPANESE-BRAZILIAN?

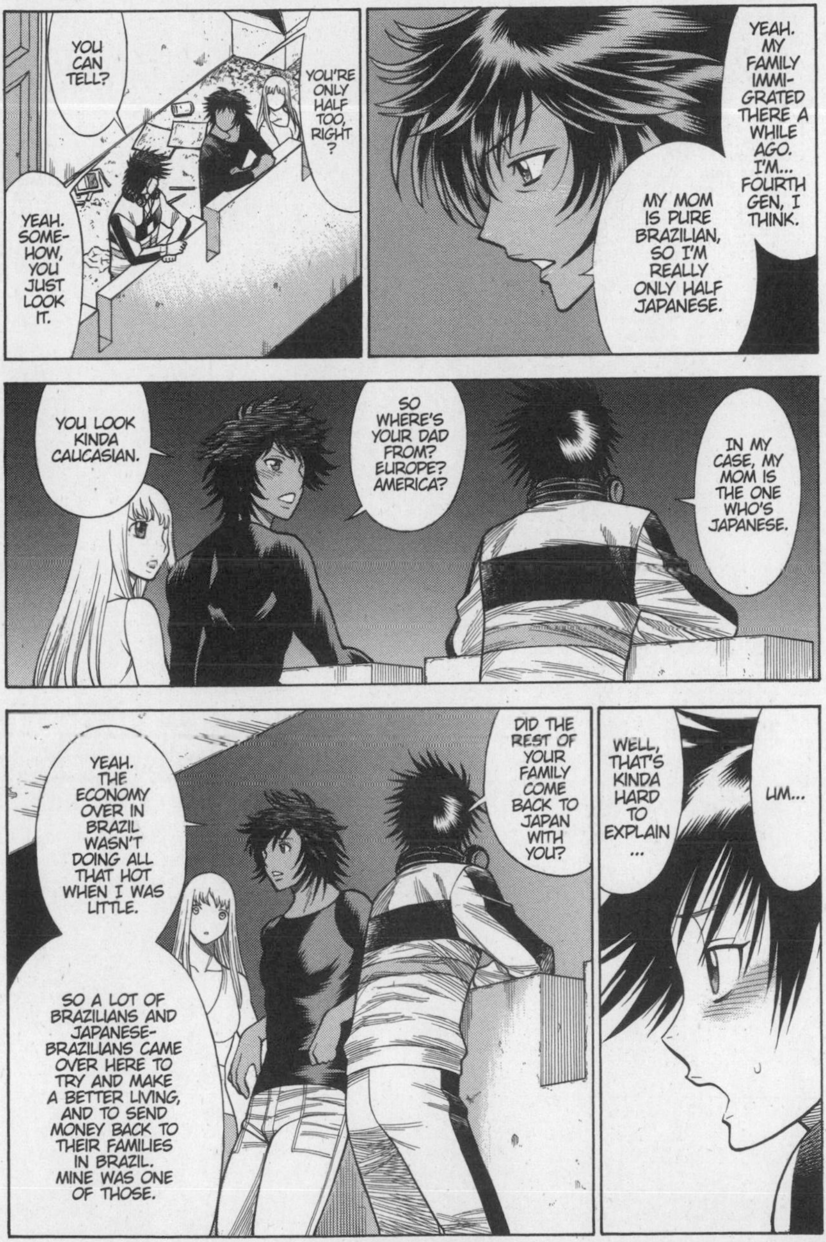
YEAH. MY FAMILY IMMI-GRATED THERE A WHILE AGO. I'M... FOURTH GEN, I THINK.
MY MOM IS PURE BRAZILIAN, SO I'M REALLY ONLY HALF JAPANESE.
YOU'RE ONLY HALF TOO, RIGHT?
YOU CAN TELL?
YEAH. SOME-HOW, YOU JUST LOOK IT.
IN MY CASE, MY MOM IS THE ONE WHO'S JAPANESE.
SO WHERE'S YOUR DAD FROM? EUROPE? AMERICA?
YOU LOOK KINDA CAUCASIAN.
UM...
WELL, THAT'S KINDA HARD TO EXPLAIN ...
DID THE REST OF YOUR FAMILY COME BACK TO JAPAN WITH YOU?
YEAH. THE ECONOMY OVER IN BRAZIL WASN'T DOING ALL THAT HOT WHEN I WAS LITTLE.
SO A LOT OF BRAZILIANS AND JAPANESE-BRAZILIANS CAME OVER HERE TO TRY AND MAKE A BETTER LIVING, AND TO SEND MONEY BACK TO THEIR FAMILIES IN BRAZIL. MINE WAS ONE OF THOSE.

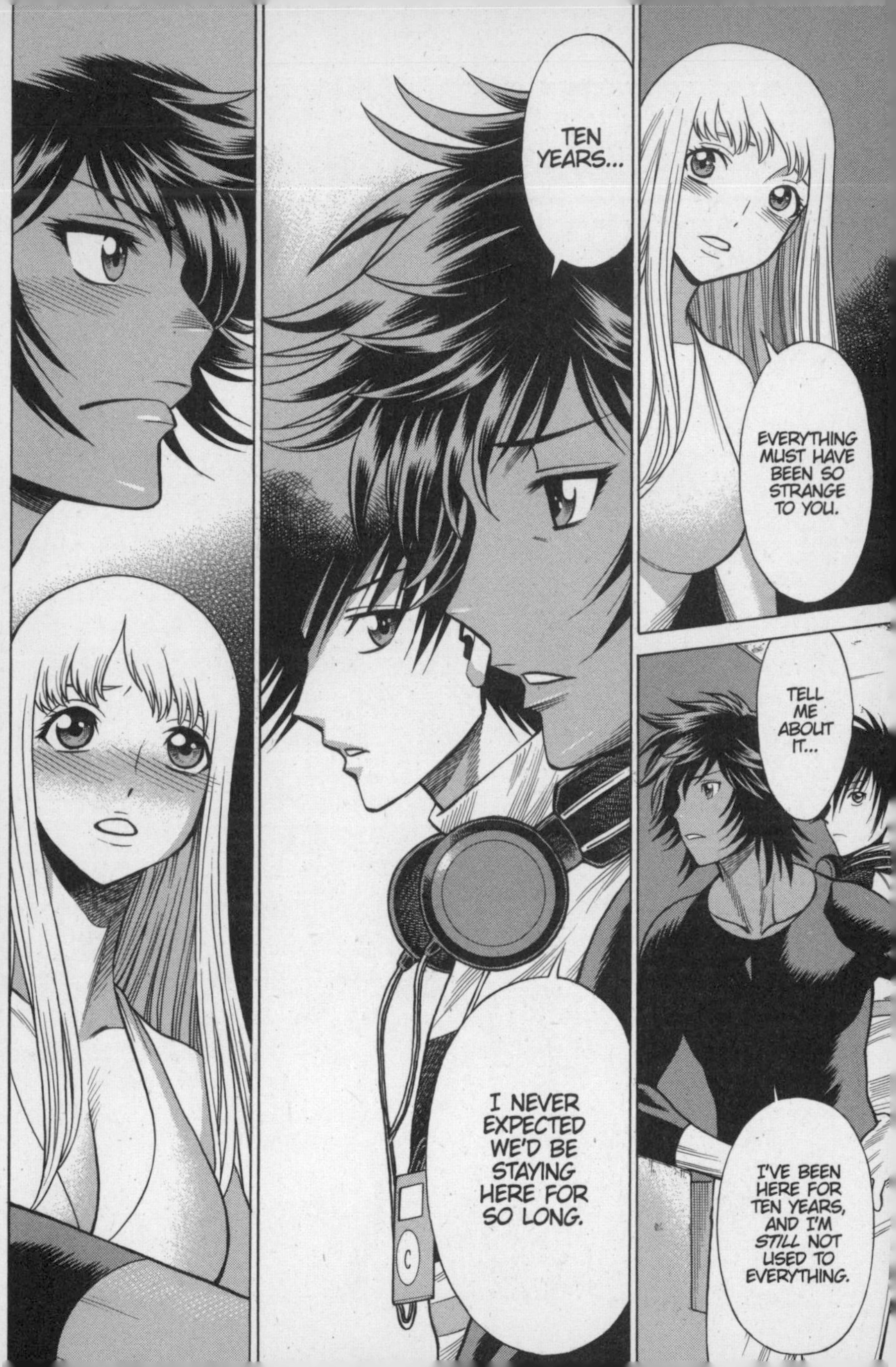
EVERYTHING MUST HAVE BEEN SO STRANGE TO YOU.
TELL ME ABOUT IT...
I'VE BEEN HERE FOR TEN YEARS, AND I'M *STILL* NOT USED TO EVERYTHING.
TEN YEARS...
I NEVER EXPECTED WE'D BE STAYING HERE FOR SO LONG.

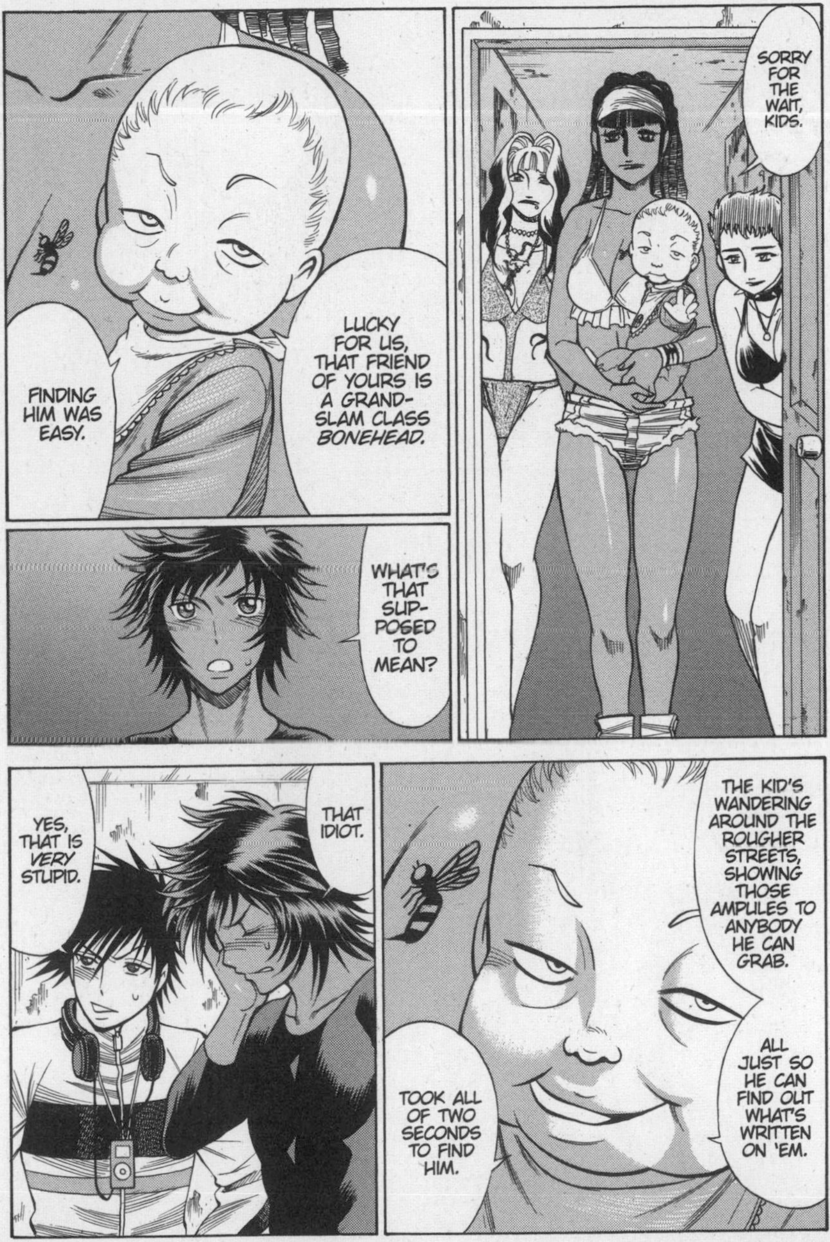
SORRY FOR THE WAIT, KIDS.
LUCKY FOR US, THAT FRIEND OF YOURS IS A GRAND-SLAM CLASS *BONEHEAD.*
FINDING HIM WAS EASY.
WHAT'S THAT SUP-POSED TO MEAN?
THE KID'S WANDERING AROUND THE ROUGHER STREETS, SHOWING THOSE AMPULES TO ANYBODY HE CAN GRAB.
ALL JUST SO HE CAN FIND OUT WHAT'S WRITTEN ON 'EM.
TOOK ALL OF TWO SECONDS TO FIND HIM.
THAT IDIOT.
YES, THAT IS *VERY* STUPID.

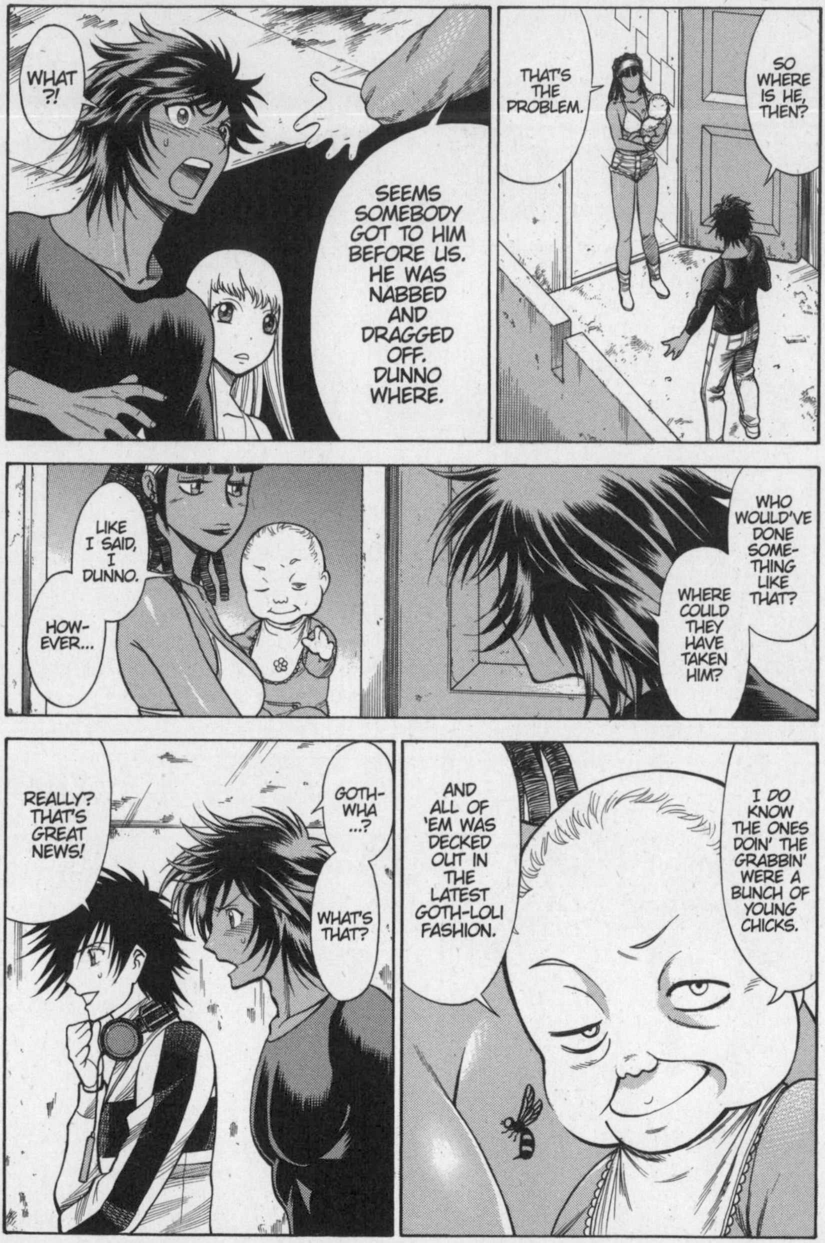
SO WHERE IS HE, THEN?
THAT'S THE PROBLEM.
SEEMS SOMEBODY GOT TO HIM BEFORE US. HE WAS NABBED AND DRAGGED OFF. DUNNO WHERE.
WHAT ?!
WHO WOULD'VE DONE SOME-THING LIKE THAT?
WHERE COULD THEY HAVE TAKEN HIM?
LIKE I SAID, I DUNNO.
HOW-EVER...
I DO KNOW THE ONES DOIN' THE GRABBIN' WERE A BUNCH OF YOUNG CHICKS.
AND ALL OF 'EM WAS DECKED OUT IN THE LATEST GOTH-LOLI FASHION.
GOTH-WHA ...?
WHAT'S THAT?
REALLY? THAT'S GREAT NEWS!

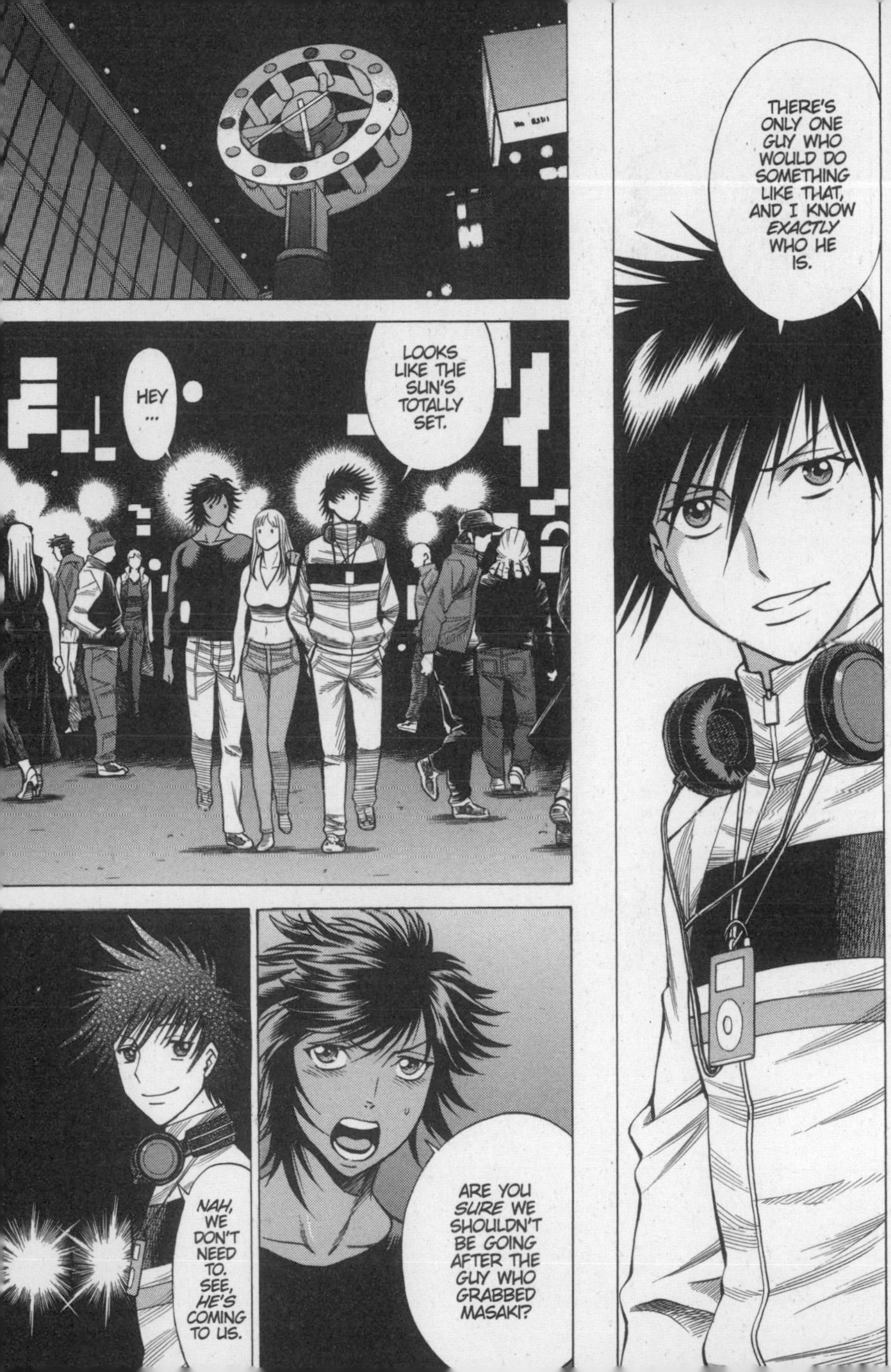
THERE'S ONLY ONE GUY WHO WOULD DO SOMETHING LIKE THAT, AND I KNOW EXACTLY WHO HE IS.
LOOKS LIKE THE SUN'S TOTALLY SET.
HEY ...
ARE YOU SURE WE SHOULDN'T BE GOING AFTER THE GUY WHO GRABBED MASAKI?
NAH, WE DON'T NEED TO. SEE, HE'S COMING TO US.

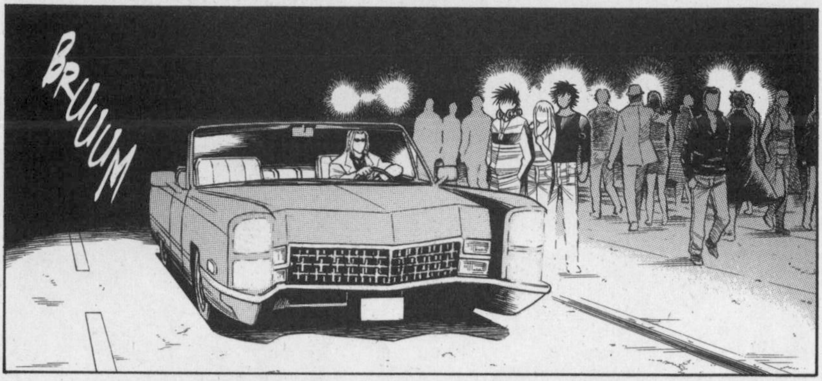
BRUUUM

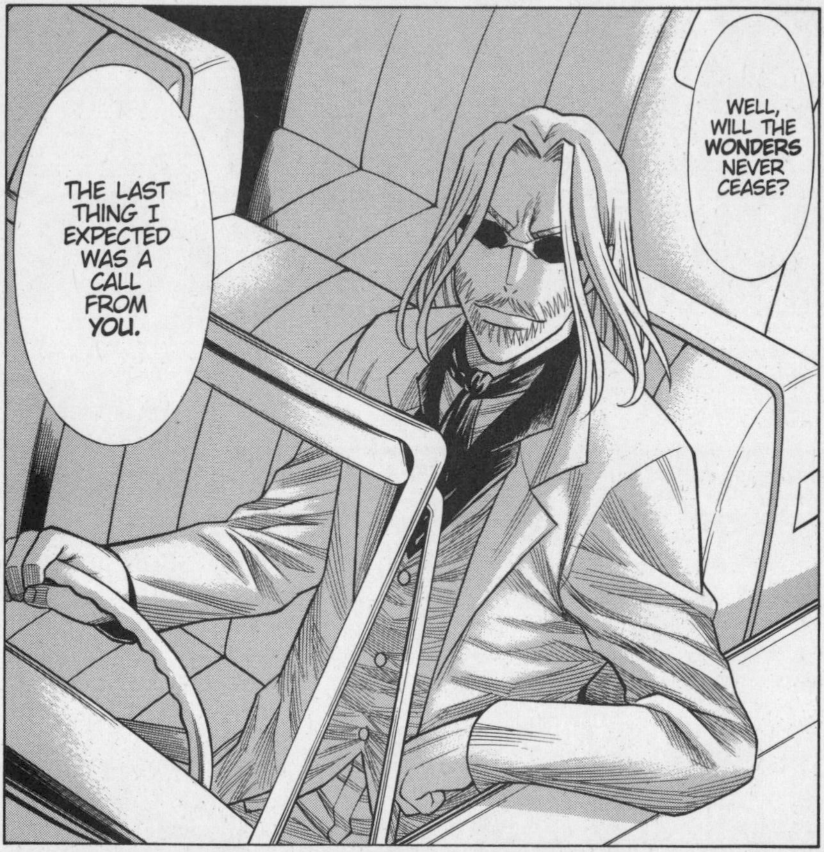
WELL, WILL THE WONDERS NEVER CEASE?
THE LAST THING I EXPECTED WAS A CALL FROM YOU.

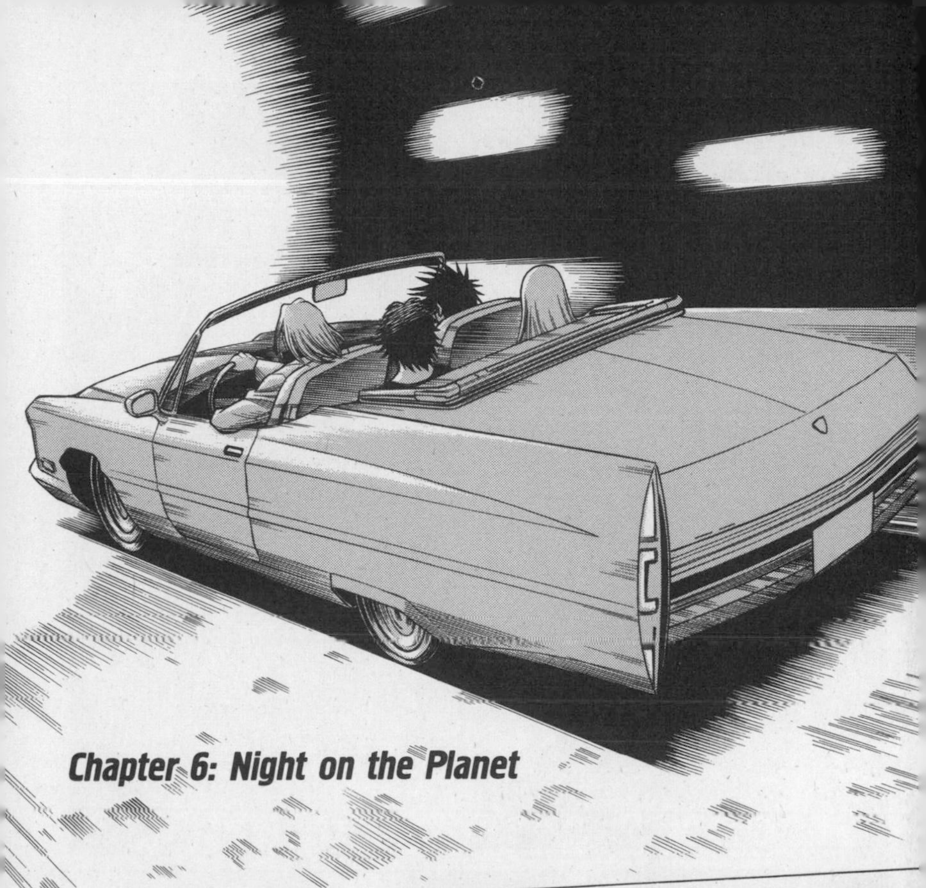

Chapter 6: Night on the Planet

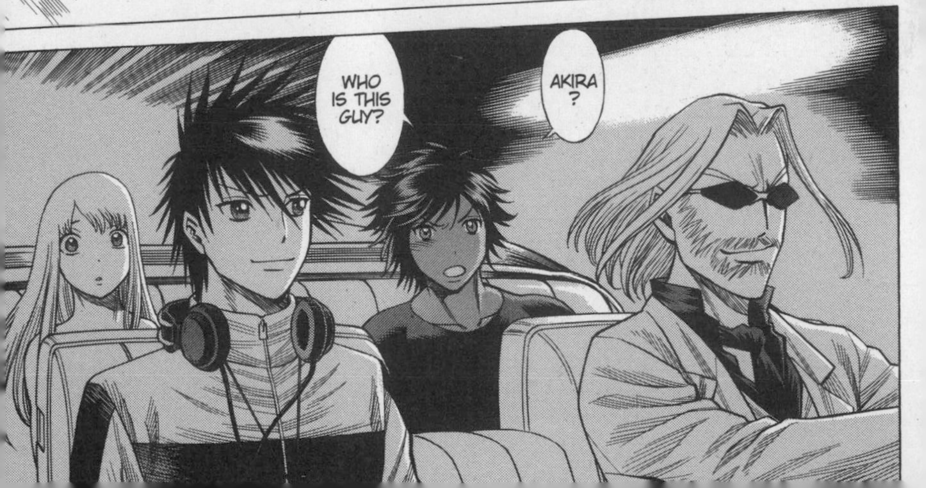
AKIRA ?
WHO IS THIS GUY?

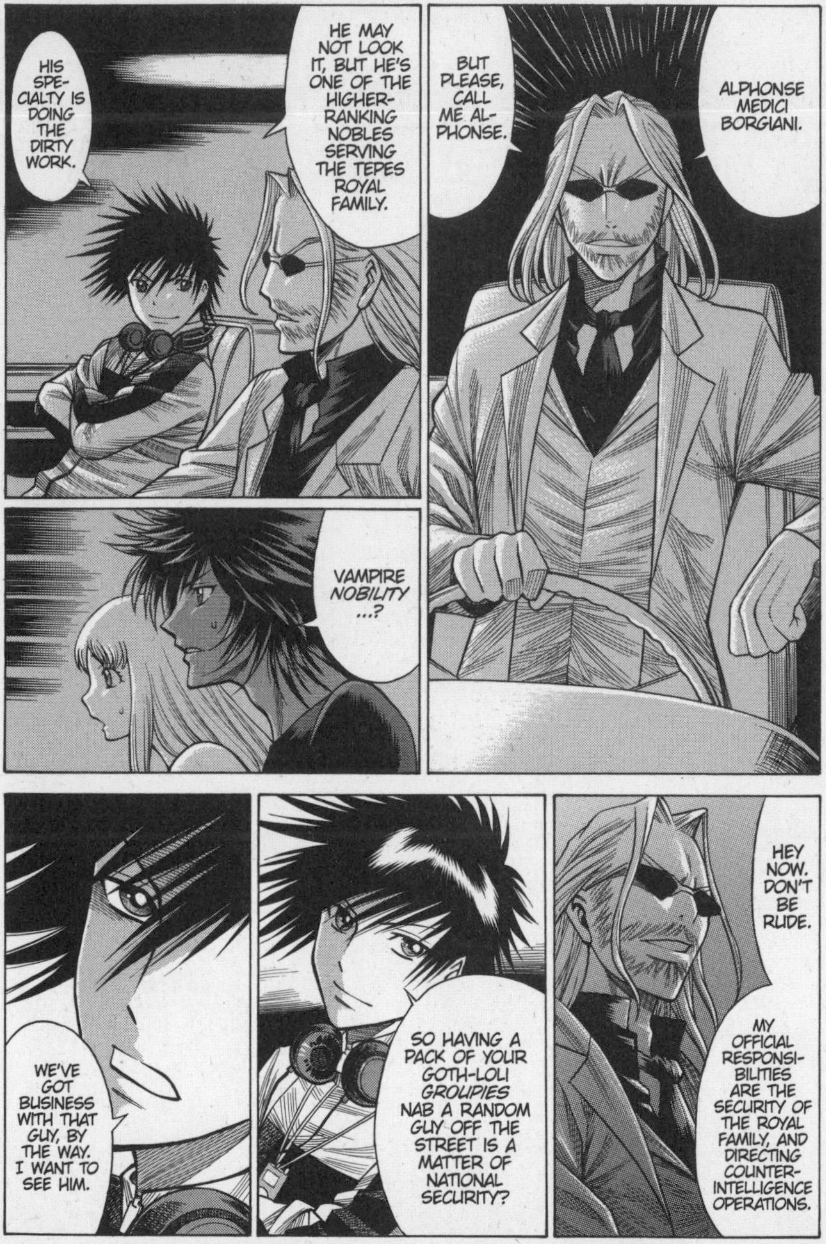
ALPHONSE MEDICI BORGIANI.
BUT PLEASE, CALL ME ALPHONSE.
HE MAY NOT LOOK IT, BUT HE'S ONE OF THE HIGHER-RANKING NOBLES SERVING THE TEPES ROYAL FAMILY.
HIS SPECIALTY IS DOING THE DIRTY WORK.
VAMPIRE *NOBILITY* ...?
HEY NOW. DON'T BE RUDE.
MY OFFICIAL RESPONSIBILITIES ARE THE SECURITY OF THE ROYAL FAMILY, AND DIRECTING COUNTER-INTELLIGENCE OPERATIONS.
SO HAVING A PACK OF YOUR GOTH-LOLI *GROUPIES* NAB A RANDOM GUY OFF THE STREET IS A MATTER OF NATIONAL SECURITY?
WE'VE GOT BUSINESS WITH THAT GUY, BY THE WAY. I WANT TO SEE HIM.

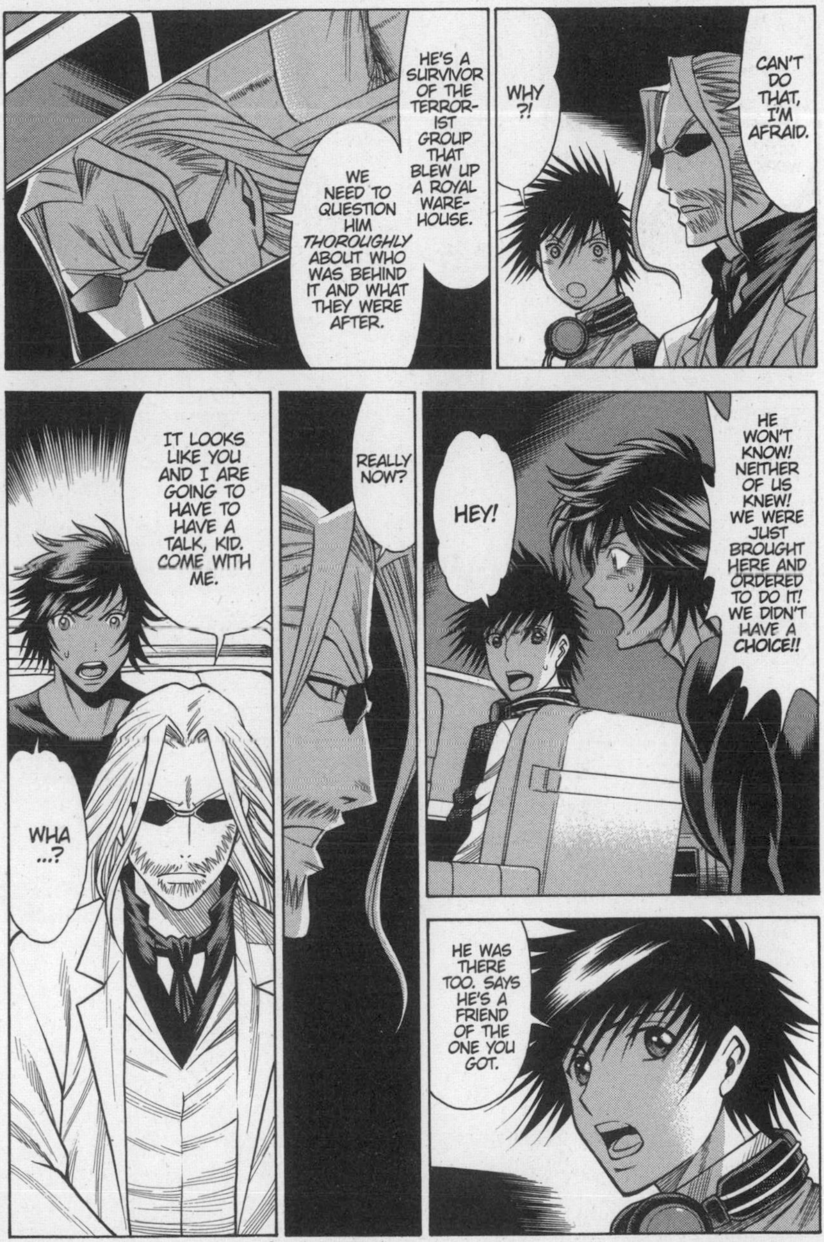
CAN'T DO THAT, I'M AFRAID.
WHY?!
HE'S A SURVIVOR OF THE TERRORIST GROUP THAT BLEW UP A ROYAL WAREHOUSE.
WE NEED TO QUESTION HIM *THOROUGHLY* ABOUT WHO WAS BEHIND IT AND WHAT THEY WERE AFTER.
HE WON'T KNOW! NEITHER OF US KNEW! WE WERE JUST BROUGHT HERE AND ORDERED TO DO IT! WE DIDN'T HAVE A **CHOICE!!**
HEY!
HE WAS THERE TOO. SAYS HE'S A FRIEND OF THE ONE YOU GOT.
REALLY NOW?
IT LOOKS LIKE YOU AND I ARE GOING TO HAVE TO HAVE A TALK, KID. COME WITH ME.
WHA...?

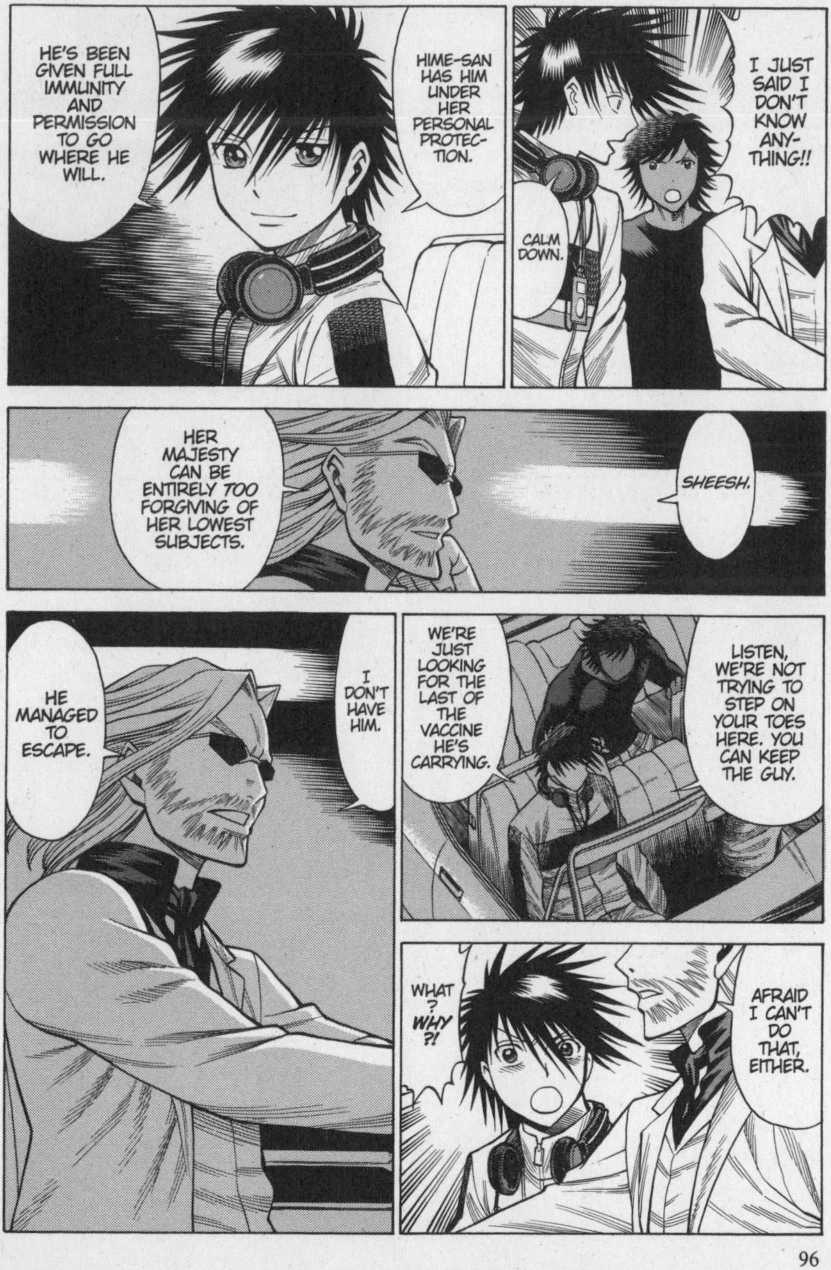
I JUST SAID I DON'T KNOW ANYTHING!!
CALM DOWN.
HIME-SAN HAS HIM UNDER HER PERSONAL PROTECTION.
HE'S BEEN GIVEN FULL IMMUNITY AND PERMISSION TO GO WHERE HE WILL.
SHEESH.
HER MAJESTY CAN BE ENTIRELY *TOO* FORGIVING OF HER LOWEST SUBJECTS.
LISTEN, WE'RE NOT TRYING TO STEP ON YOUR TOES HERE. YOU CAN KEEP THE GUY.
WE'RE JUST LOOKING FOR THE LAST OF THE VACCINE HE'S CARRYING.
AFRAID I CAN'T DO THAT, EITHER.
WHAT? ***WHY?!***
I DON'T HAVE HIM.
HE MANAGED TO ESCAPE.

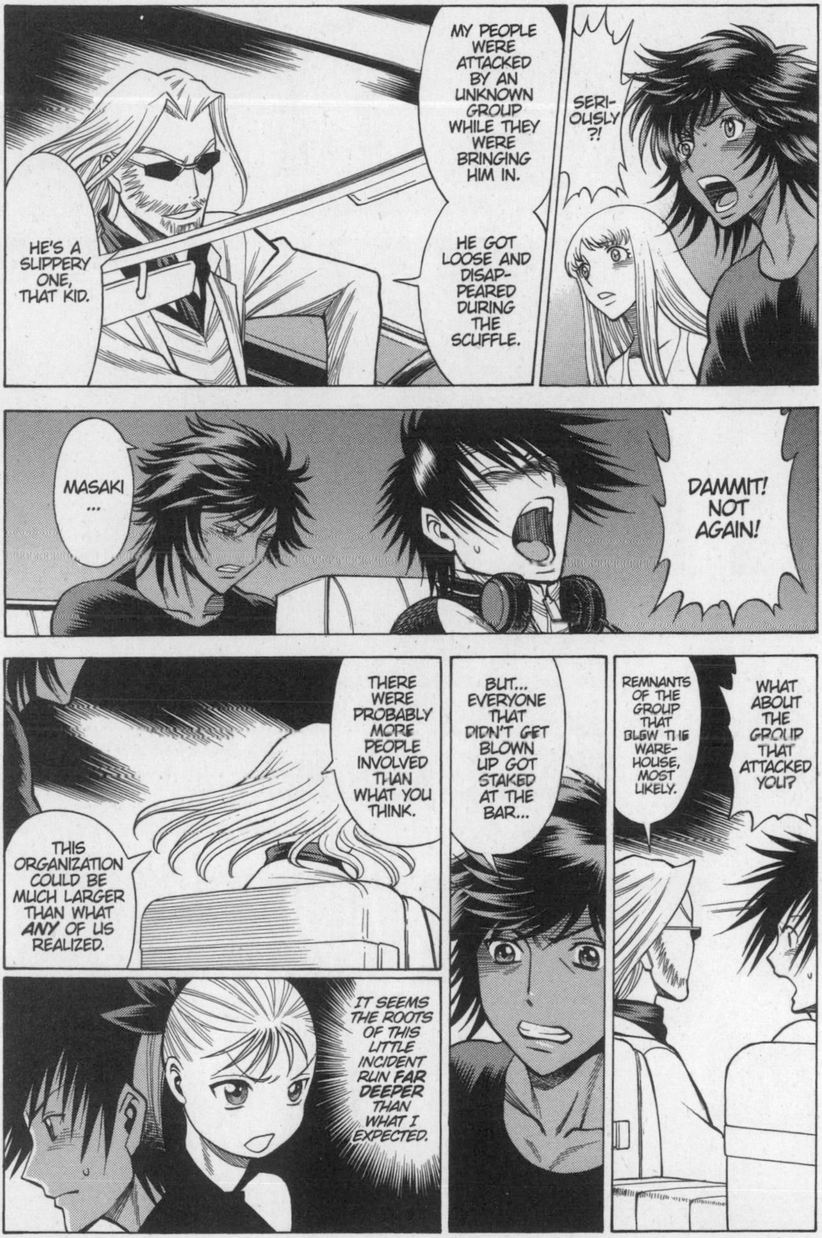
SERIOUSLY?!
MY PEOPLE WERE ATTACKED BY AN UNKNOWN GROUP WHILE THEY WERE BRINGING HIM IN.
HE GOT LOOSE AND DISAPPEARED DURING THE SCUFFLE.
HE'S A SLIPPERY ONE, THAT KID.
DAMMIT! NOT AGAIN!
MASAKI...
WHAT ABOUT THE GROUP THAT ATTACKED YOU?
REMNANTS OF THE GROUP THAT BLEW THE WAREHOUSE, MOST LIKELY.
BUT... EVERYONE THAT DIDN'T GET BLOWN UP GOT STAKED AT THE BAR...
THERE WERE PROBABLY MORE PEOPLE INVOLVED THAN WHAT YOU THINK.
THIS ORGANIZATION COULD BE MUCH LARGER THAN WHAT ANY OF US REALIZED.
IT SEEMS THE ROOTS OF THIS LITTLE INCIDENT RUN FAR DEEPER THAN WHAT I EXPECTED.

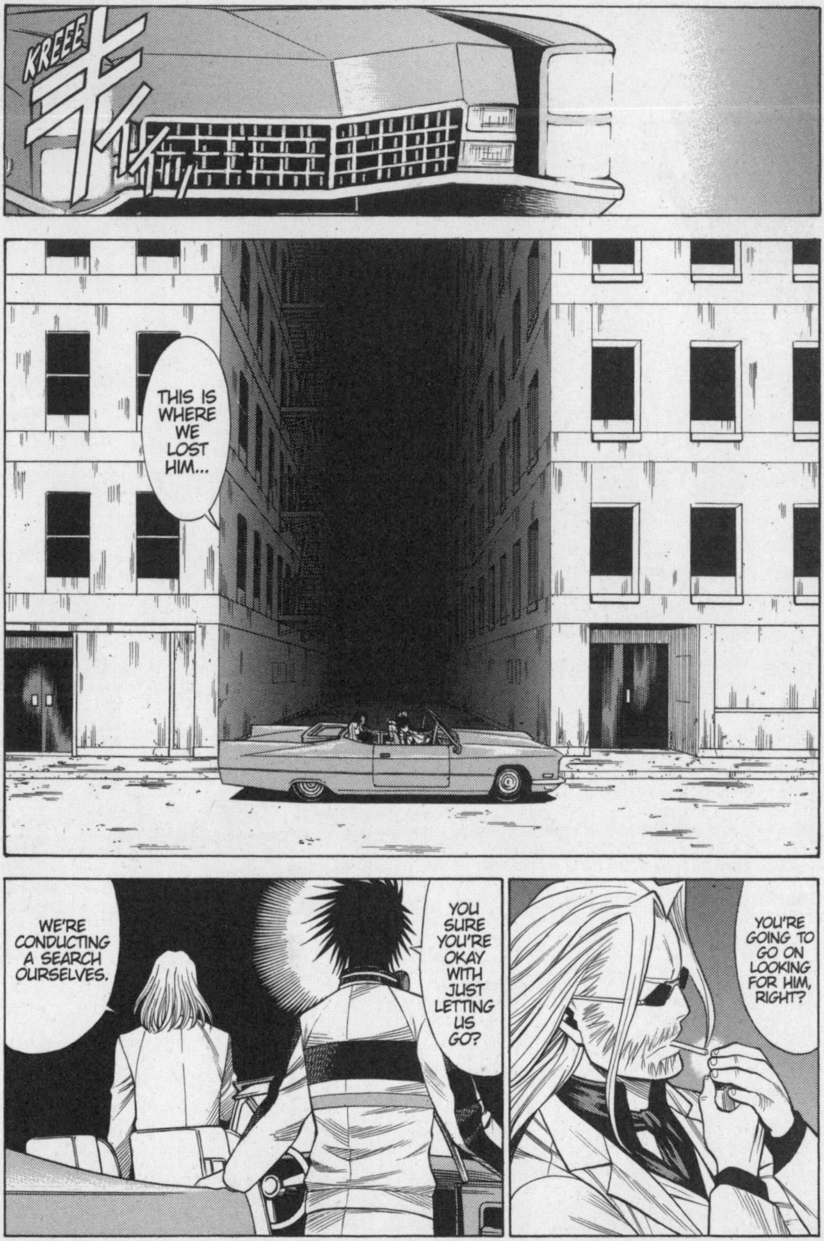
KREEE
THIS IS WHERE WE LOST HIM...
YOU'RE GOING TO GO ON LOOKING FOR HIM, RIGHT?
YOU SURE YOU'RE OKAY WITH JUST LETTING US GO?
WE'RE CONDUCTING A SEARCH OURSELVES.

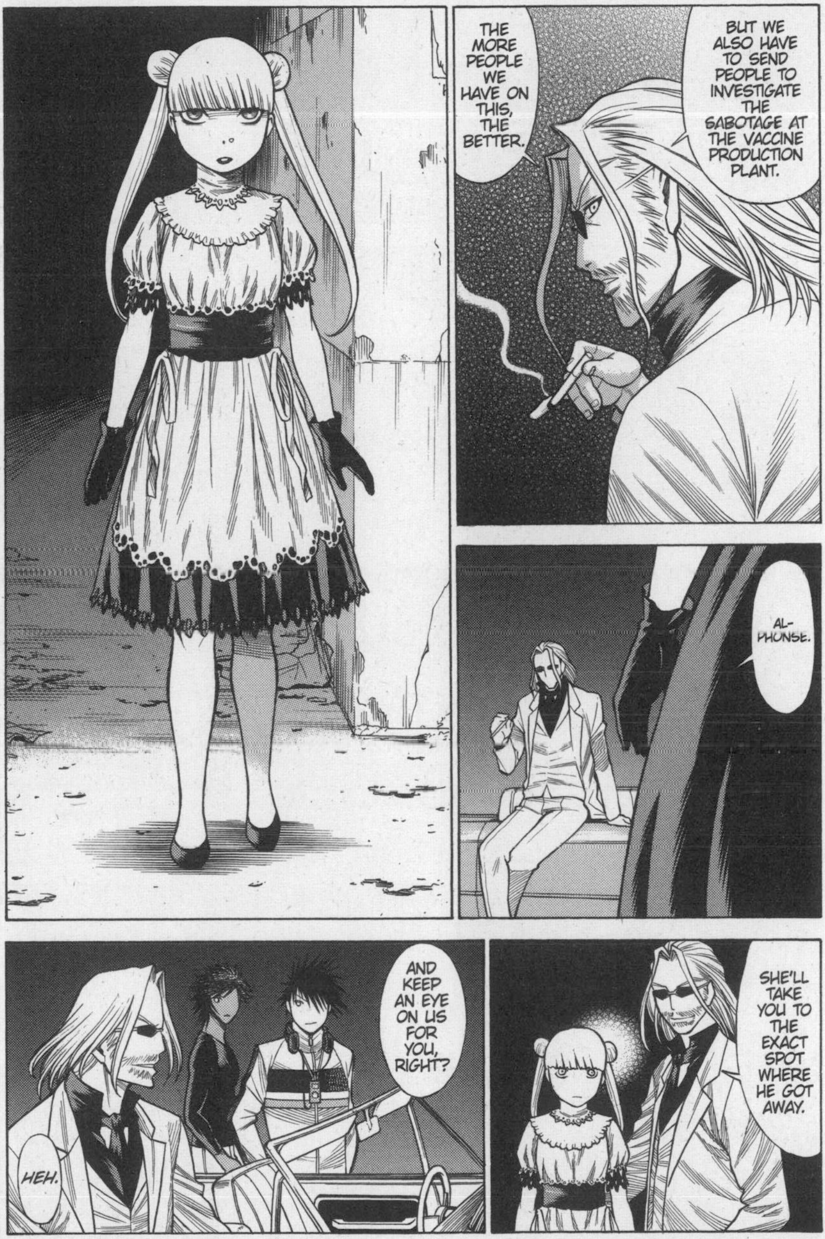
BUT WE ALSO HAVE TO SEND PEOPLE TO INVESTIGATE THE SABOTAGE AT THE VACCINE PRODUCTION PLANT.
THE MORE PEOPLE WE HAVE ON THIS, THE BETTER.
AL-PHONSE.
SHE'LL TAKE YOU TO THE EXACT SPOT WHERE HE GOT AWAY.
AND KEEP AN EYE ON US FOR YOU, RIGHT?
HEH.

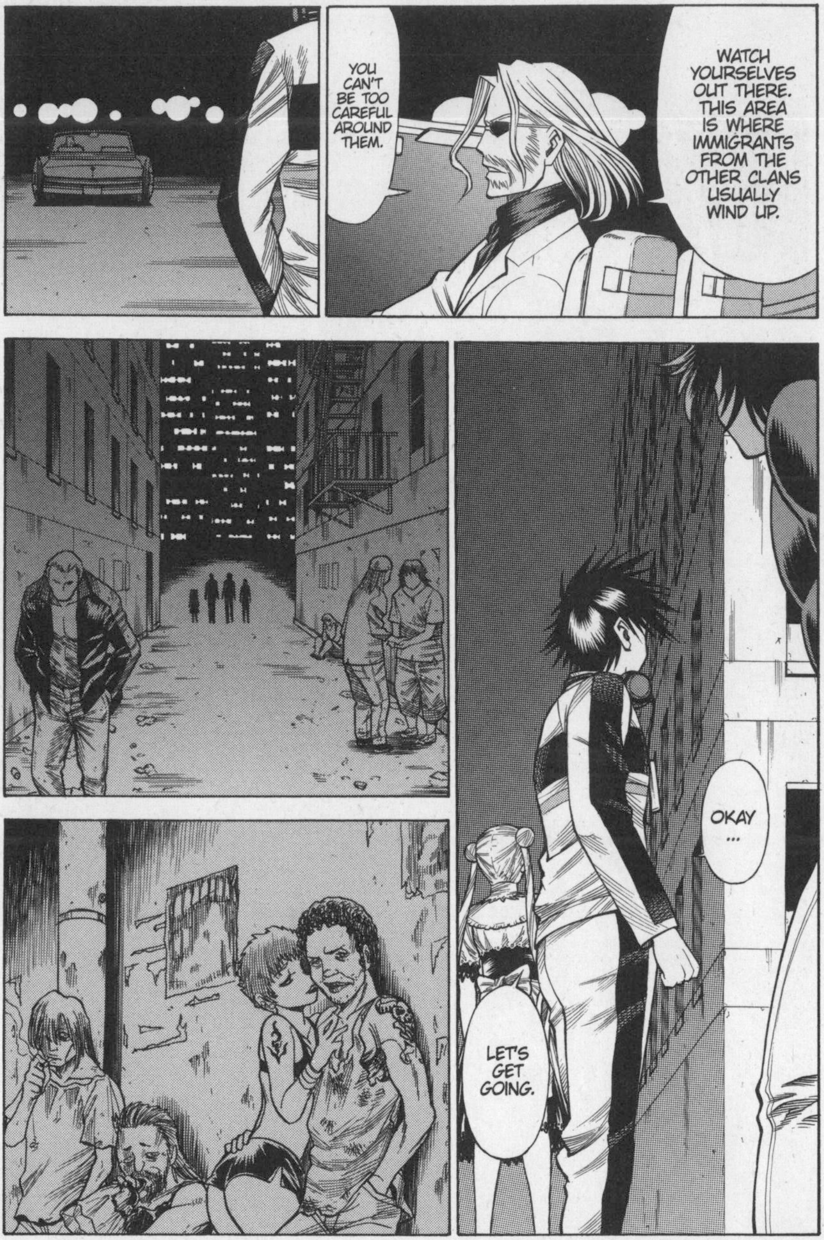
WATCH YOURSELVES OUT THERE. THIS AREA IS WHERE IMMIGRANTS FROM THE OTHER CLANS USUALLY WIND UP.
YOU CAN'T BE TOO CAREFUL AROUND THEM.
OKAY ...
LET'S GET GOING.

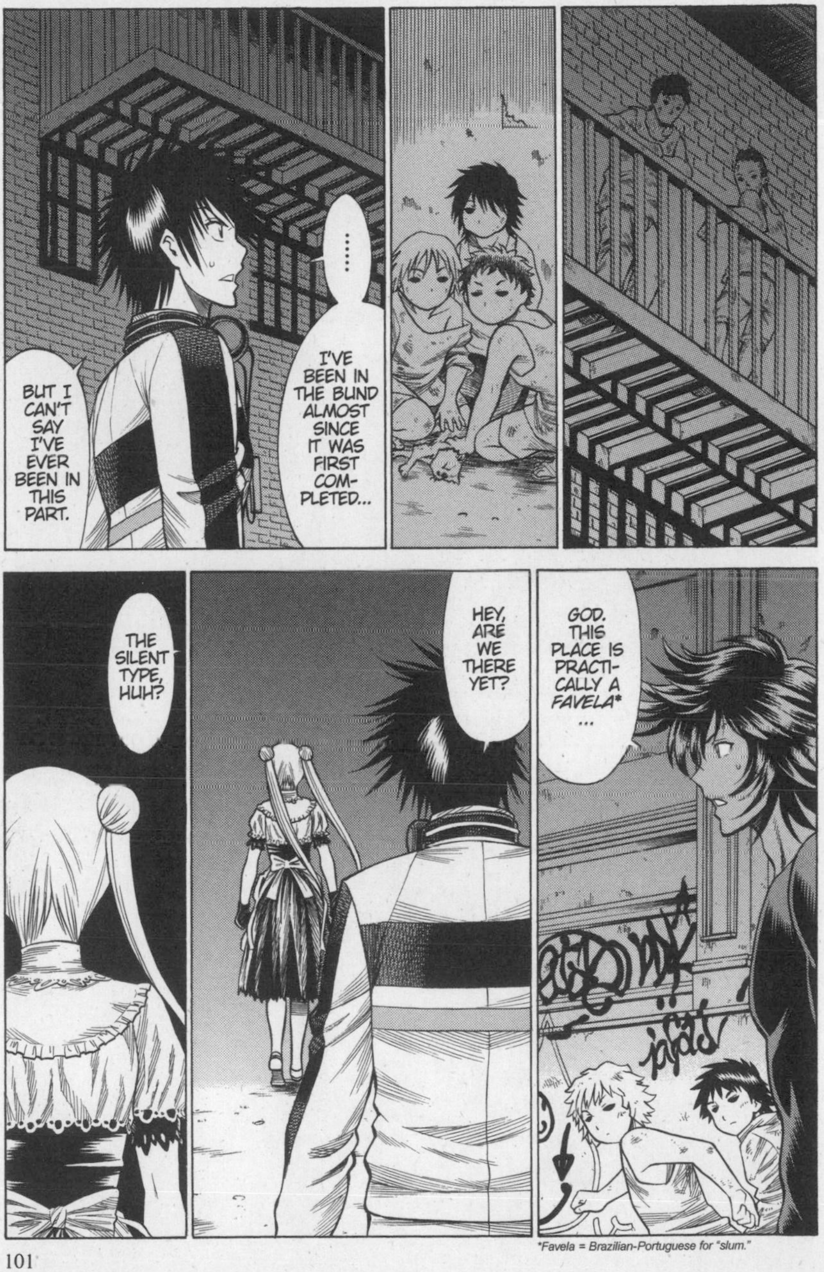
......
I'VE BEEN IN THE BUND ALMOST SINCE IT WAS FIRST COMPLETED...
BUT I CAN'T SAY I'VE EVER BEEN IN THIS PART.
GOD. THIS PLACE IS PRACTICALLY A *FAVELA**...
HEY, ARE WE THERE YET?
THE SILENT TYPE, HUH?

**Favela = Brazilian-Portuguese for "slum."*

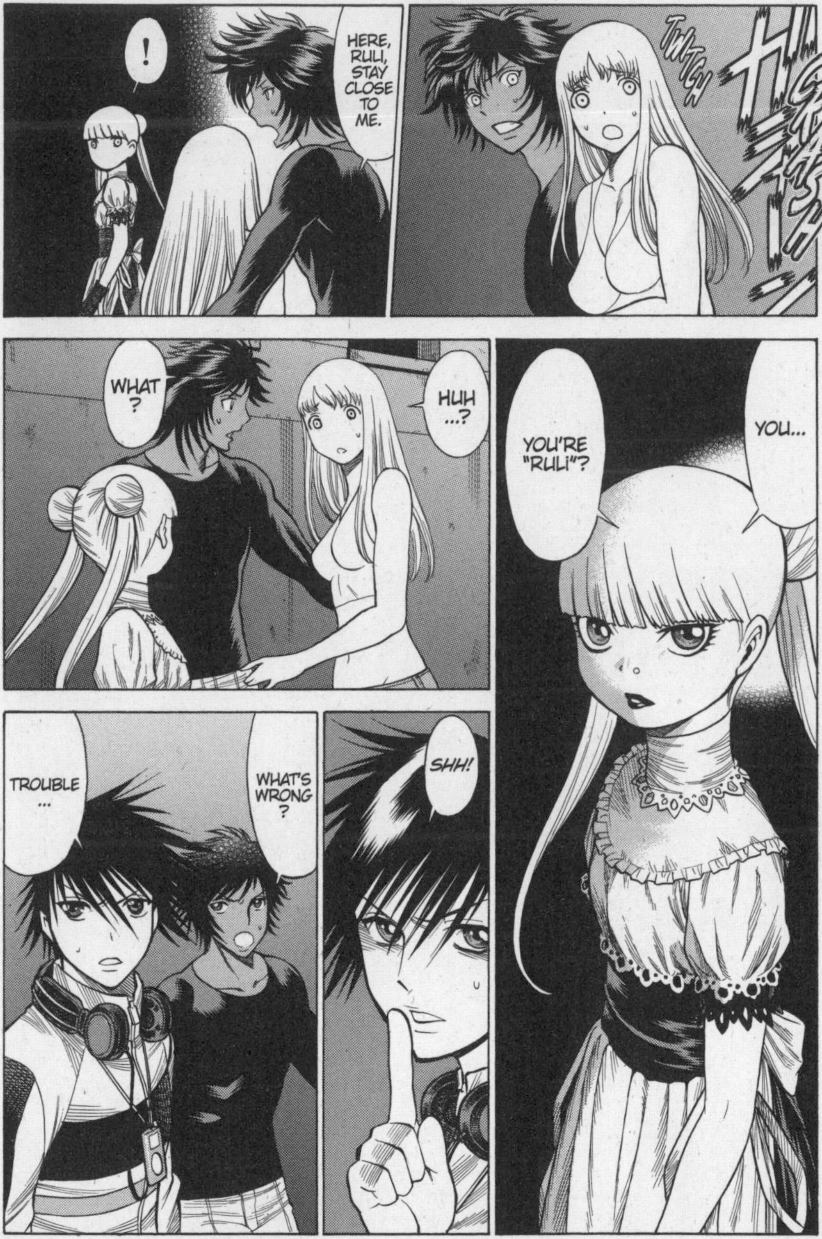
TWITCH
GRASH
!
HERE, RULI, STAY CLOSE TO ME.
YOU...
YOU'RE "RULI"?
HUH ...?
WHAT ?
SHH!
WHAT'S WRONG ?
TROUBLE ...

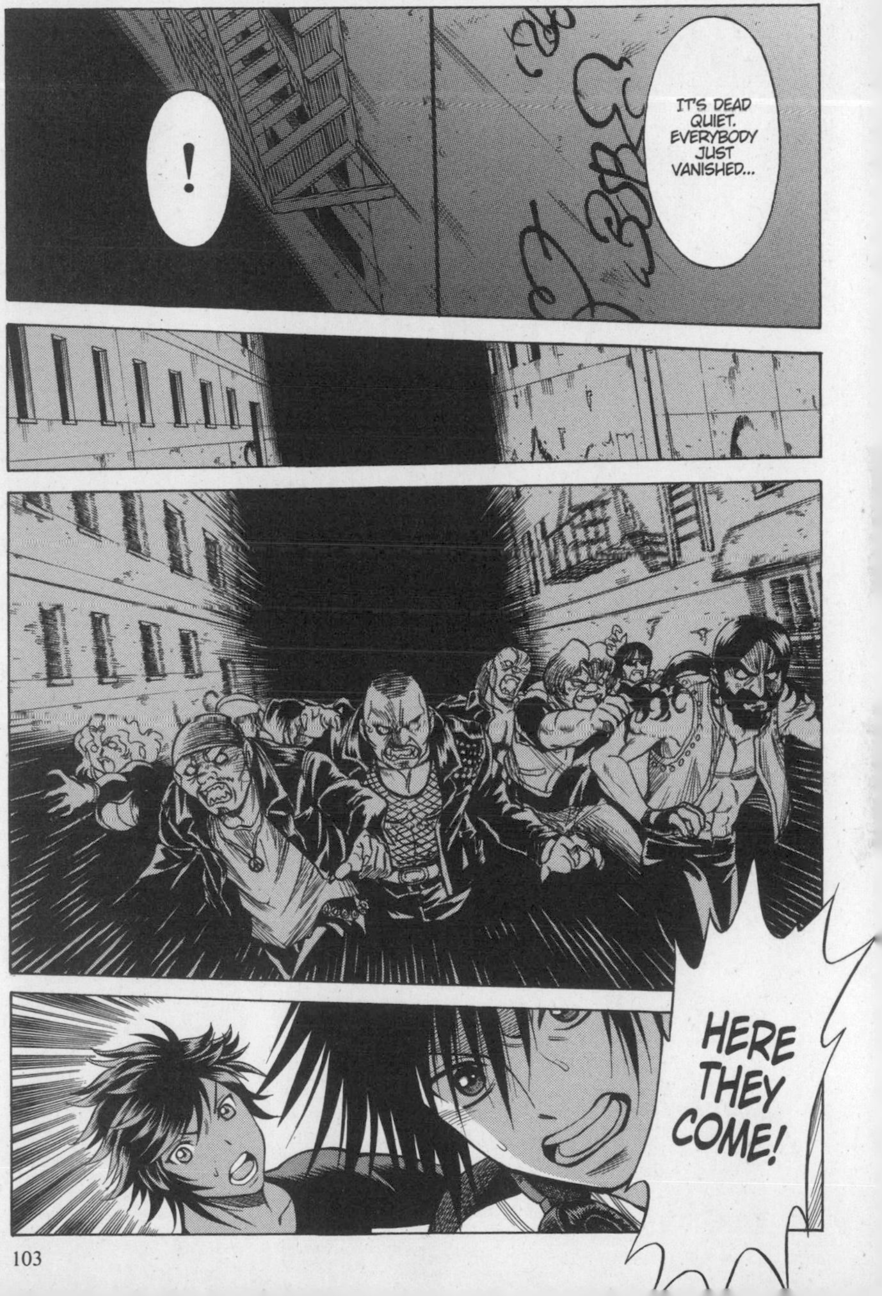
IT'S DEAD QUIET. EVERYBODY JUST VANISHED...
!
HERE THEY COME!

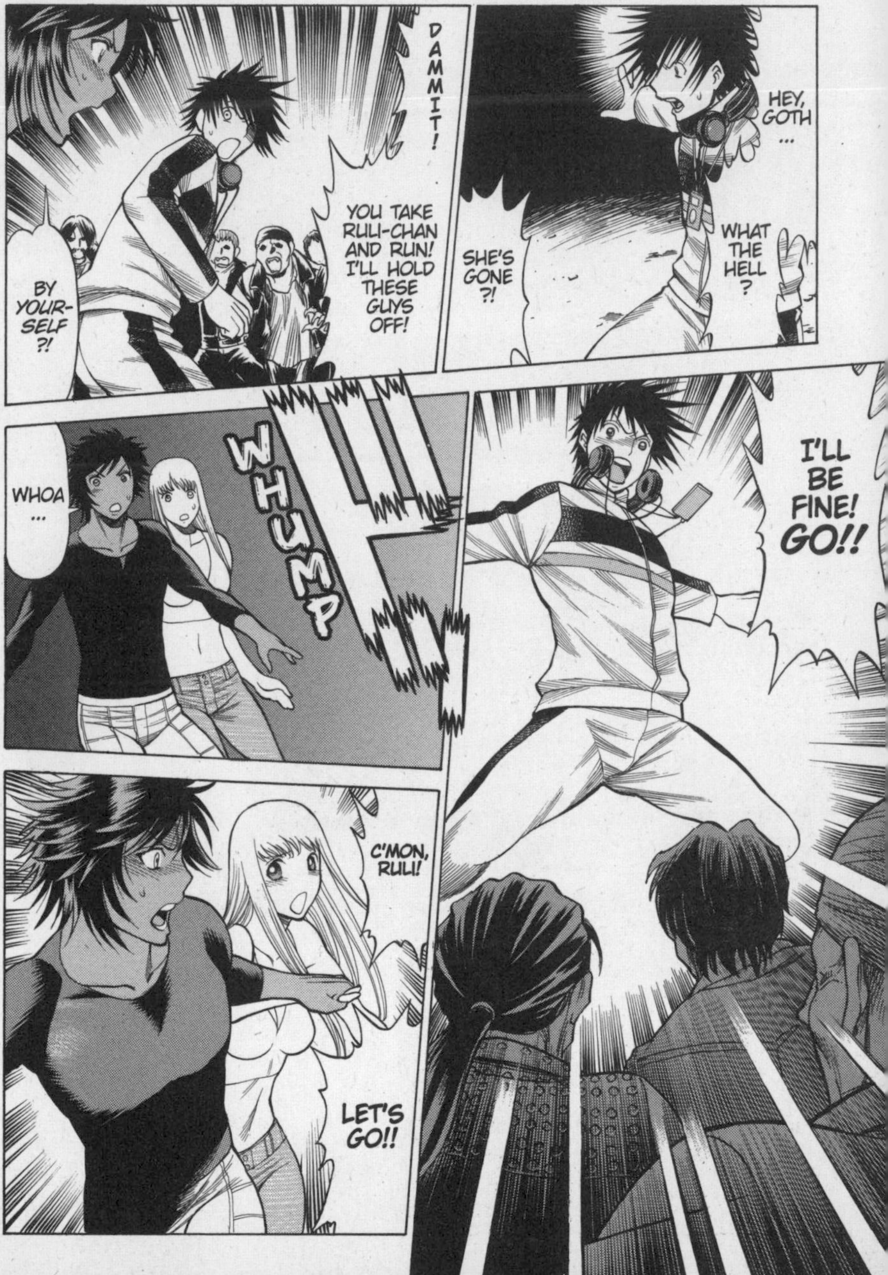
HEY, GOTH ...
WHAT THE HELL ?
SHE'S GONE ?!
DAMMIT!
YOU TAKE RULI-CHAN AND RUN! I'LL HOLD THESE GUYS OFF!
BY YOURSELF ?!
I'LL BE FINE! GO!!
WHUMP
WHOA ...
C'MON, RULI!
LET'S GO!!

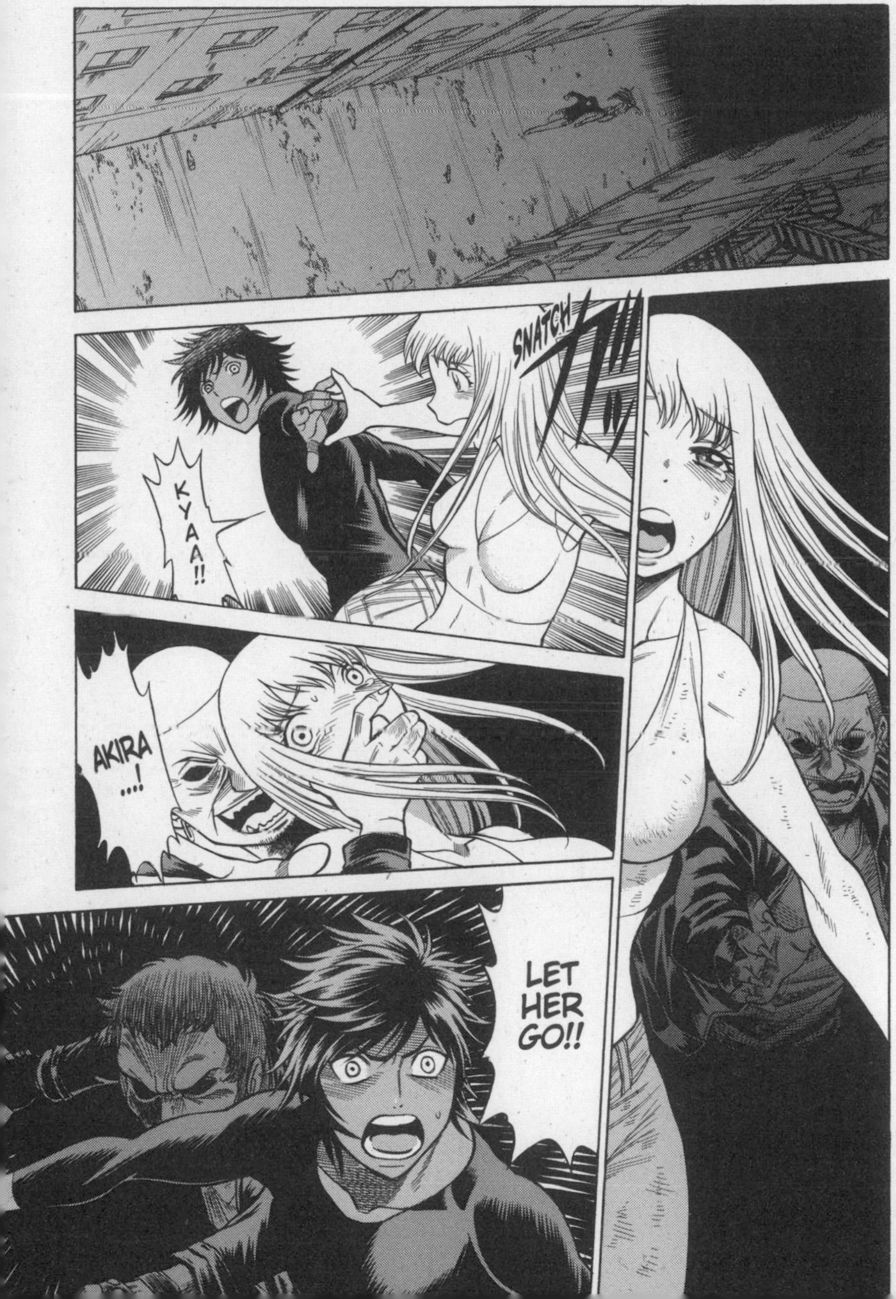
SNATCH
KYAA!!
AKIRA ...!
LET HER GO!!

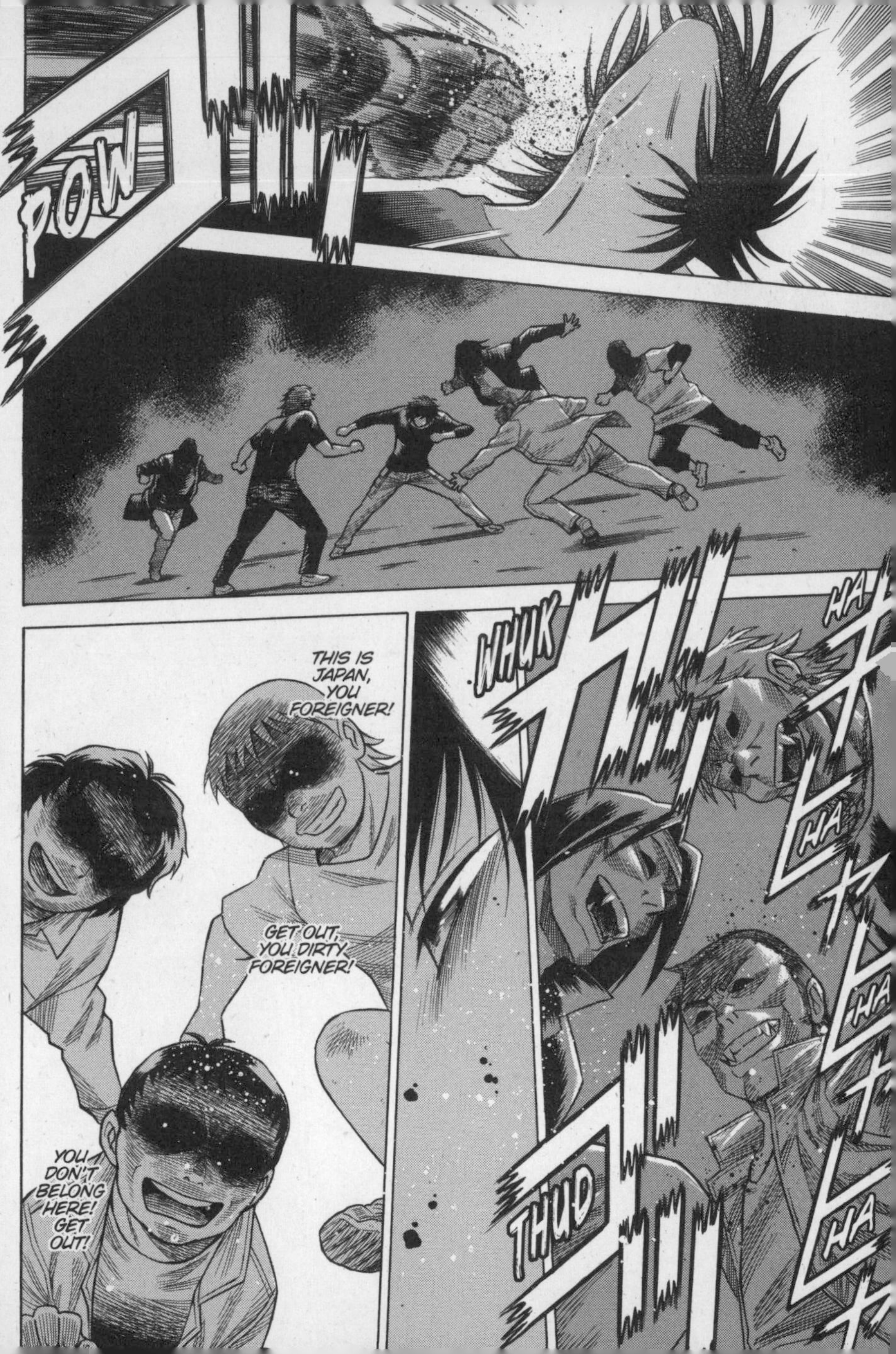
POW
WHUK
HA
HA
HA
HA
THUD
THIS IS JAPAN, YOU FOREIGNER!
GET OUT, YOU DIRTY FOREIGNER!
YOU DON'T BELONG HERE! GET OUT!

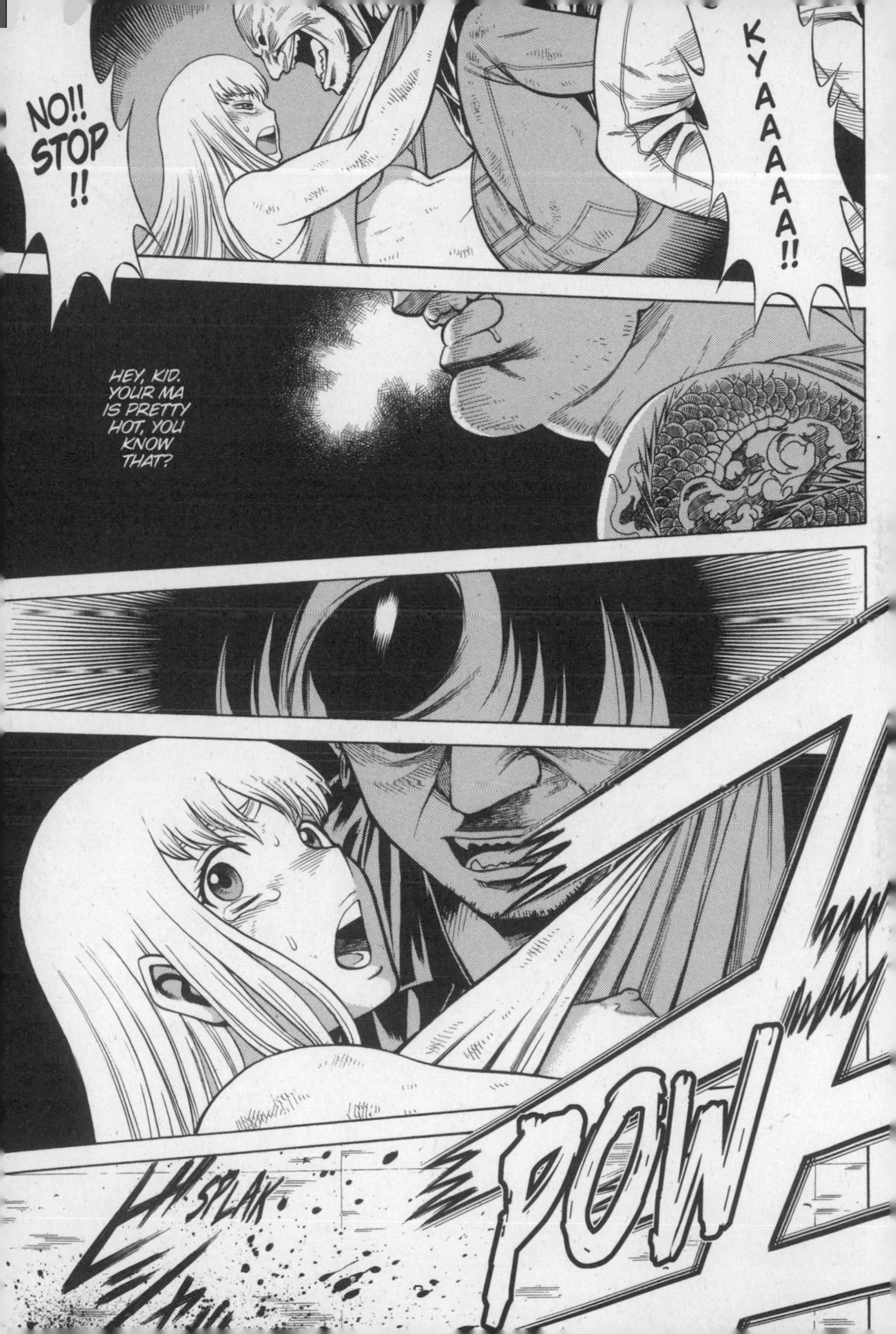
KYAAAAA!!
NO!! STOP!!
HEY, KID. YOUR MA IS PRETTY HOT, YOU KNOW THAT?
POW
SPLAK

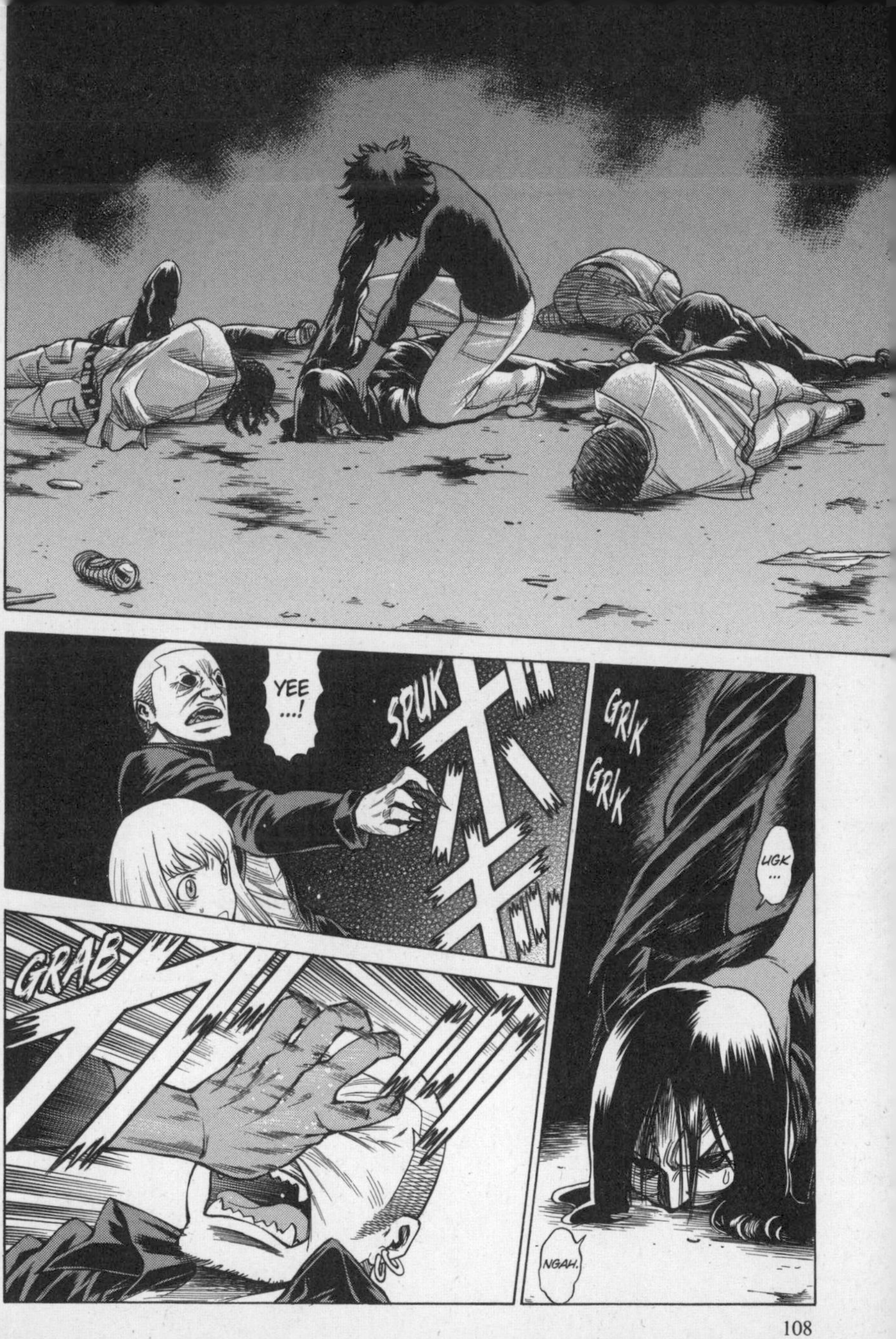
GRIK
GRIK
UGK ...
NGAH.
YEE ...!
SPUK
GRAB

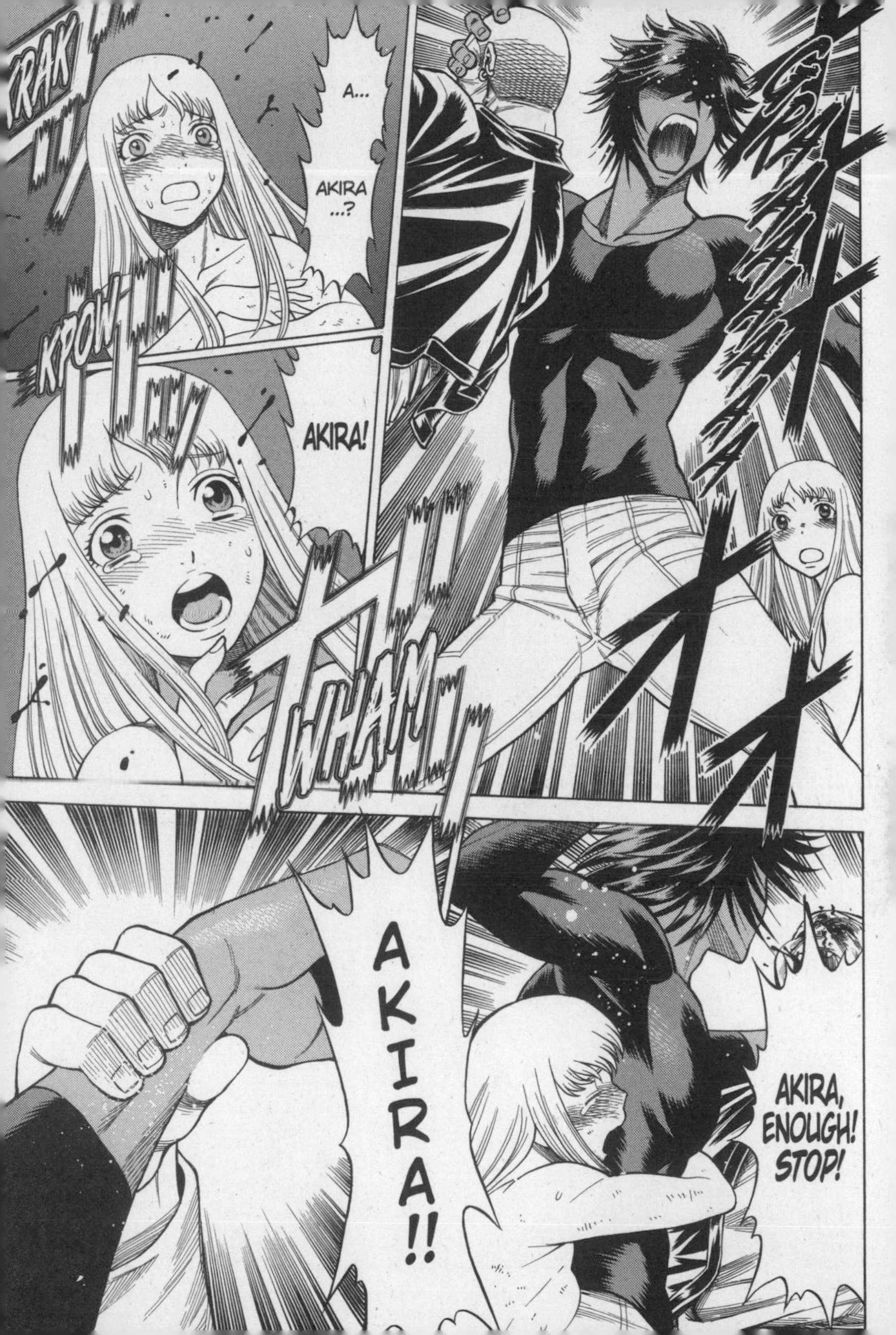
KRAK
A...
AKIRA ...?
KPOW!!
AKIRA!
WHAM
AKIRA, ENOUGH! STOP!
AKIRA!!

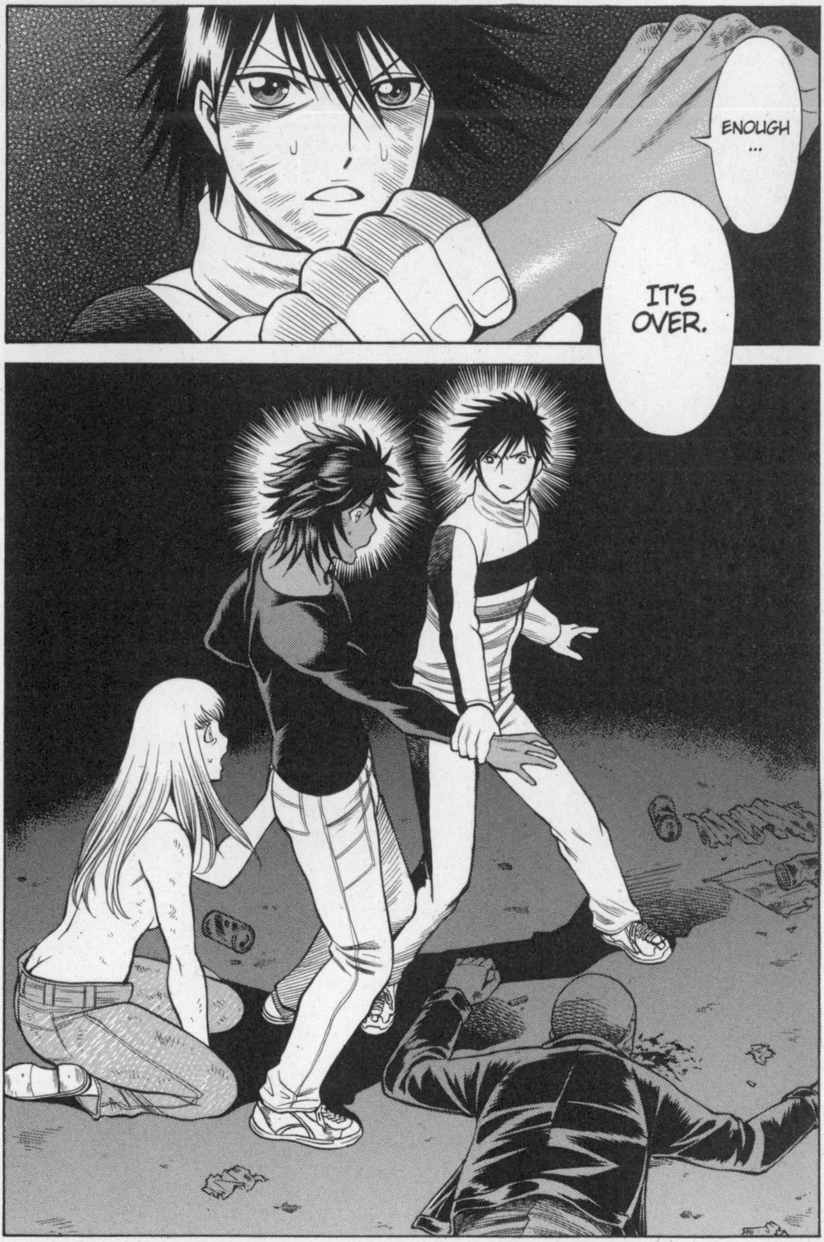

ENOUGH ...
IT'S OVER.

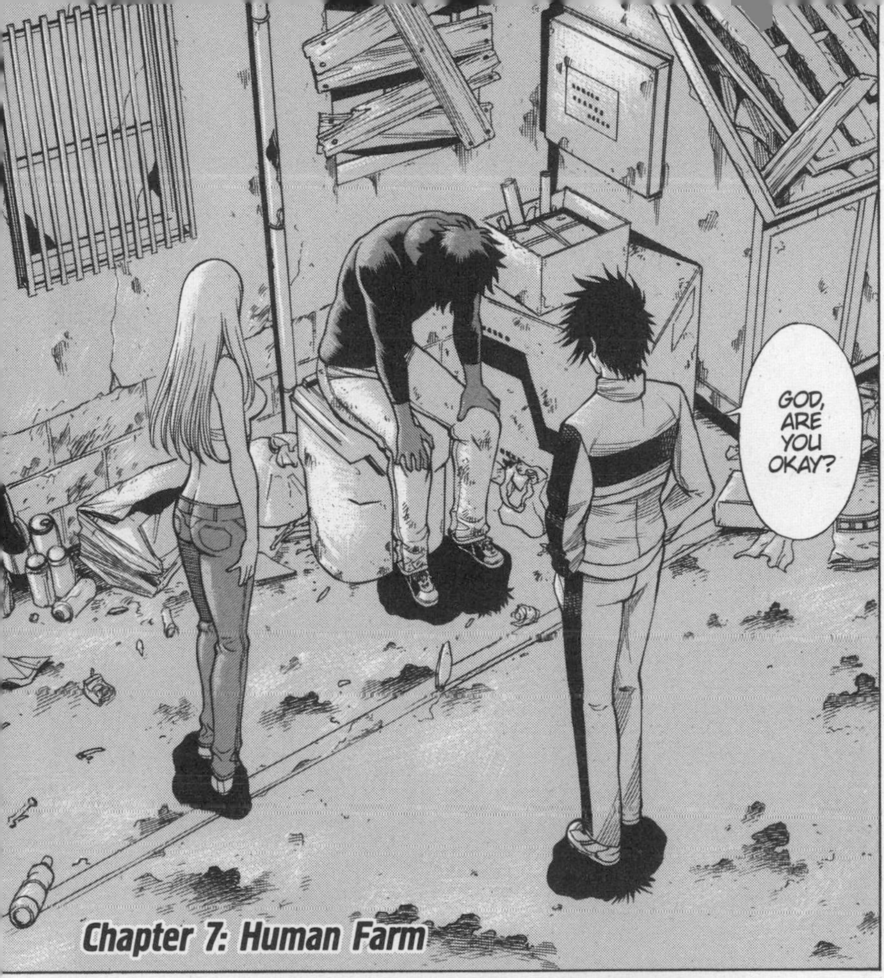
GOD, ARE YOU OKAY?
Chapter 7: Human Farm

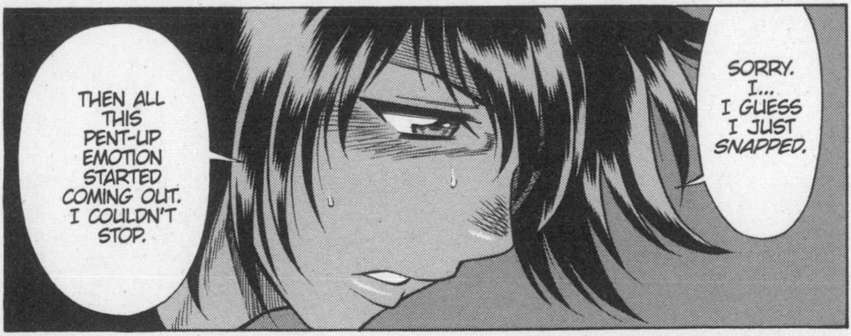
SORRY. I... I GUESS I JUST SNAPPED.
THEN ALL THIS PENT-UP EMOTION STARTED COMING OUT. I COULDN'T STOP.

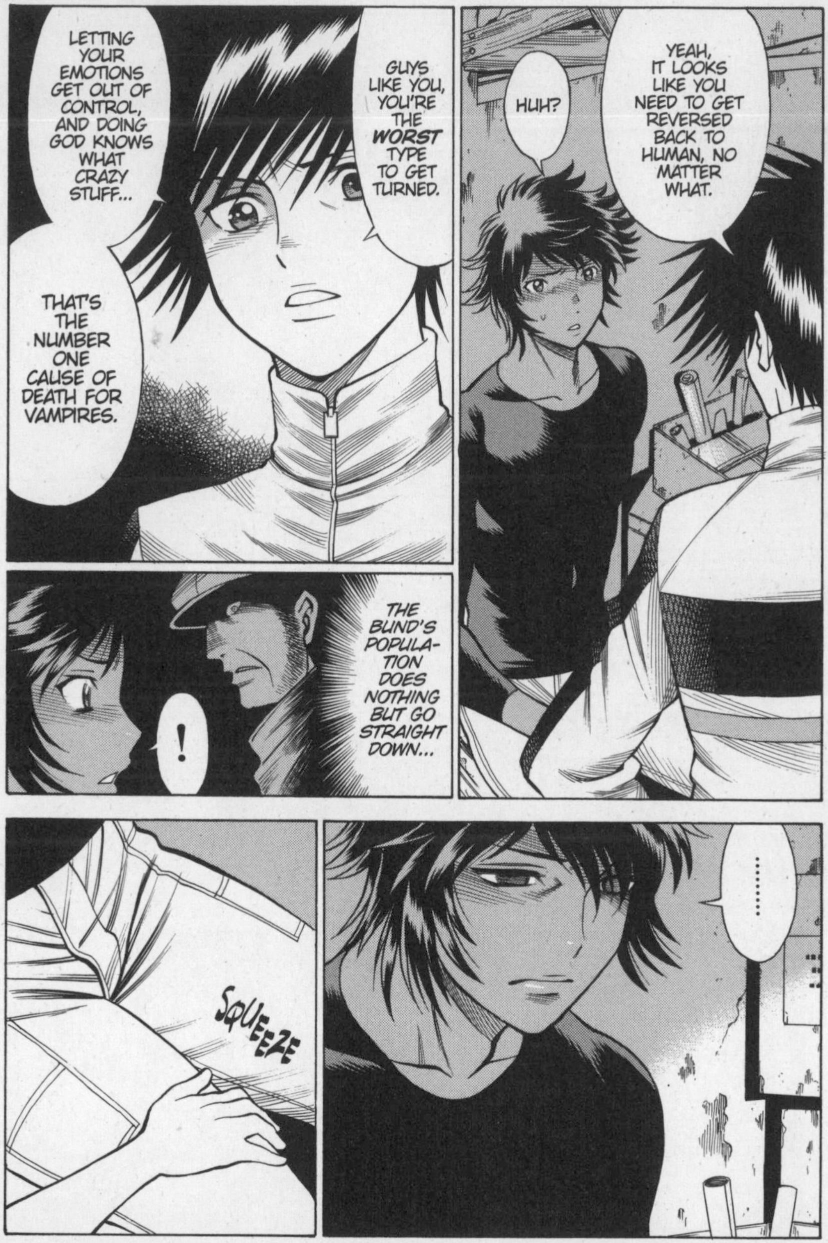

YEAH, IT LOOKS LIKE YOU NEED TO GET REVERSED BACK TO HUMAN, NO MATTER WHAT.
HUH?
GUYS LIKE YOU, YOU'RE THE ***WORST*** TYPE TO GET TURNED.
LETTING YOUR EMOTIONS GET OUT OF CONTROL, AND DOING GOD KNOWS WHAT CRAZY STUFF...
THAT'S THE NUMBER ONE CAUSE OF DEATH FOR VAMPIRES.
THE BUND'S POPULATION DOES NOTHING BUT GO STRAIGHT DOWN...
!
......
SQUEEZE

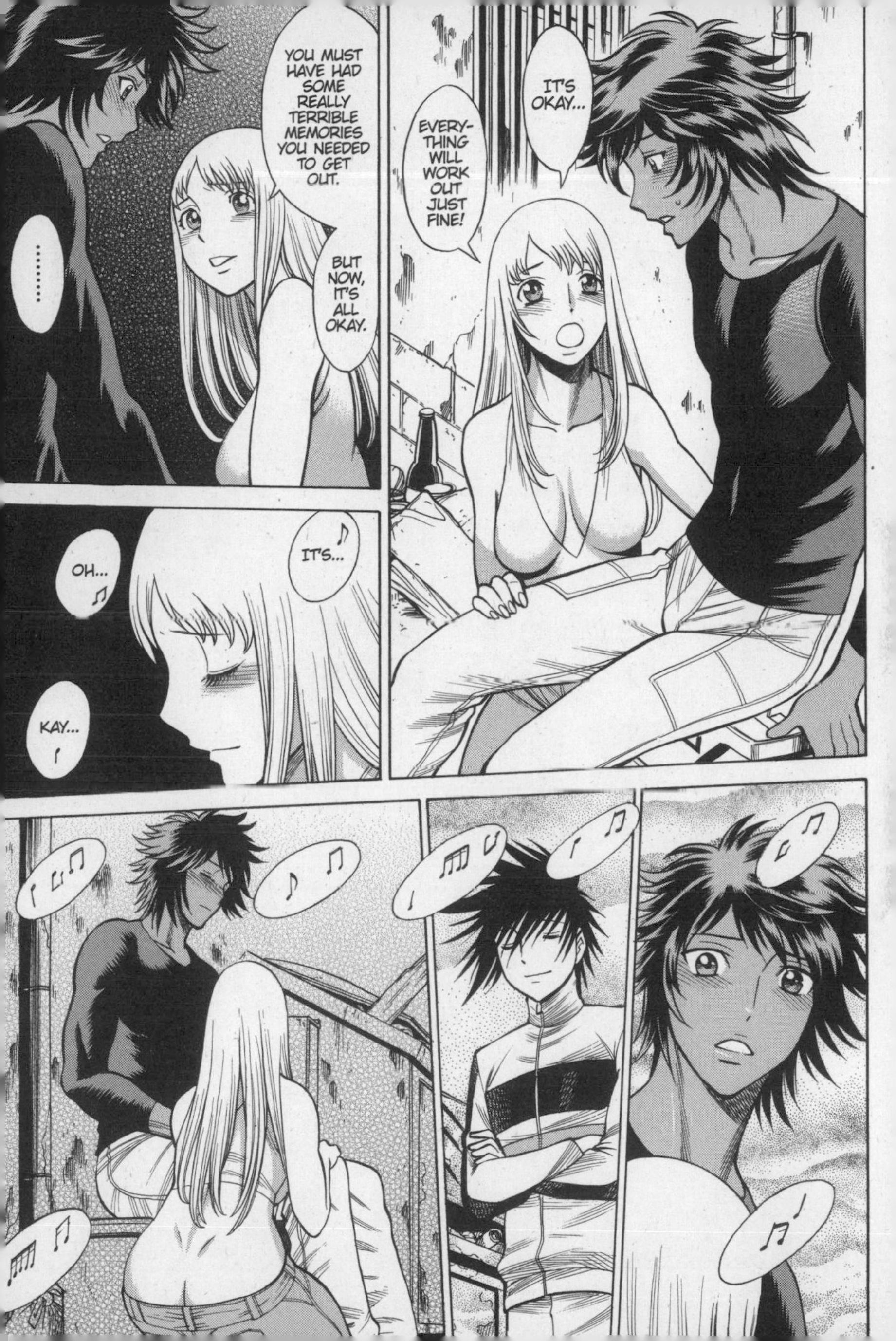
IT'S OKAY...
EVERY-THING WILL WORK OUT JUST FINE!
YOU MUST HAVE HAD SOME REALLY TERRIBLE MEMORIES YOU NEEDED TO GET OUT.
BUT NOW, IT'S ALL OKAY.
......
IT'S... ♪
OH... ♫
KAY...

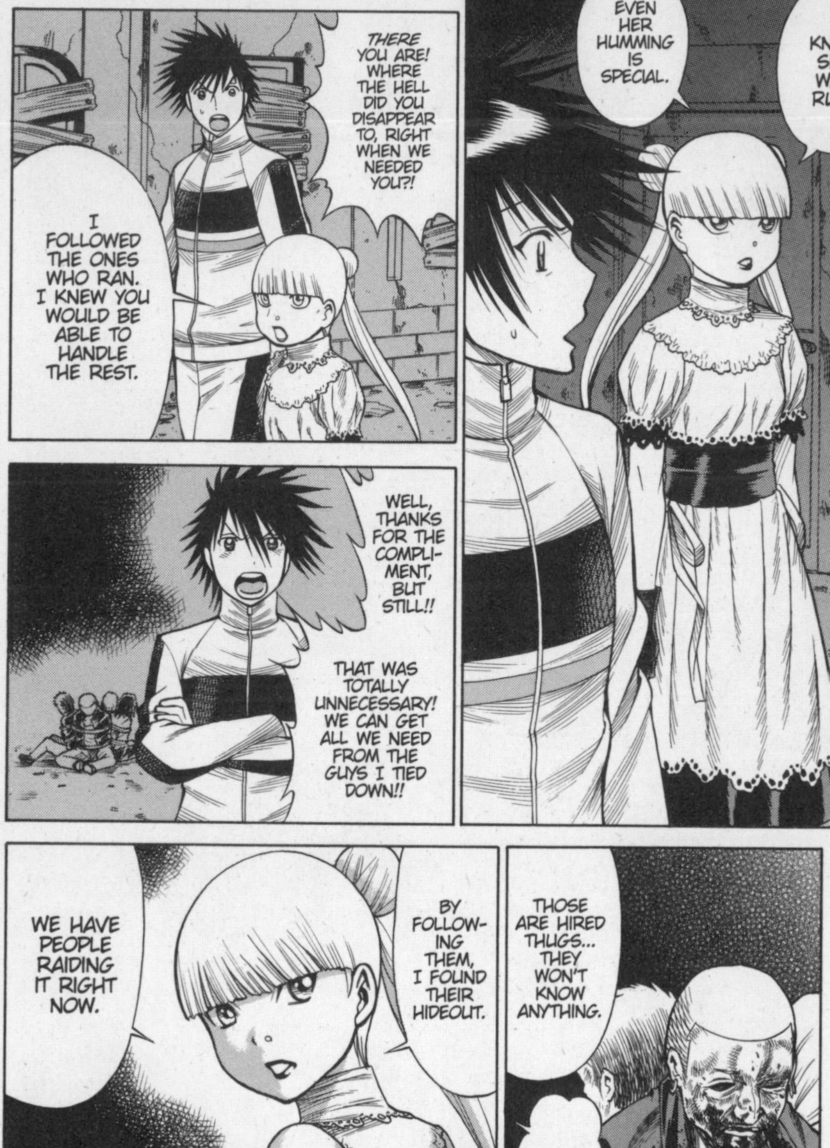
I KNEW SHE WAS RULi.
EVEN HER HUMMING IS SPECIAL.
THERE YOU ARE! WHERE THE HELL DID YOU DISAPPEAR TO, RIGHT WHEN WE NEEDED YOU?!
I FOLLOWED THE ONES WHO RAN. I KNEW YOU WOULD BE ABLE TO HANDLE THE REST.
WELL, THANKS FOR THE COMPLI-MENT, BUT STILL!!
THAT WAS TOTALLY UNNECESSARY! WE CAN GET ALL WE NEED FROM THE GUYS I TIED DOWN!!
THOSE ARE HIRED THUGS... THEY WON'T KNOW ANYTHING.
WHA ?!
BY FOLLOW-ING THEM, I FOUND THEIR HIDEOUT.
WE HAVE PEOPLE RAIDING IT RIGHT NOW.

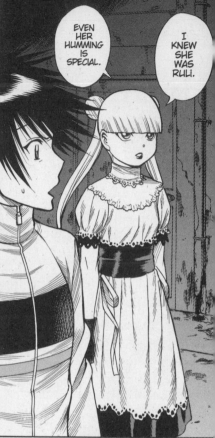

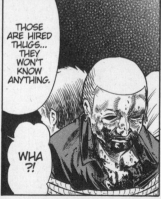

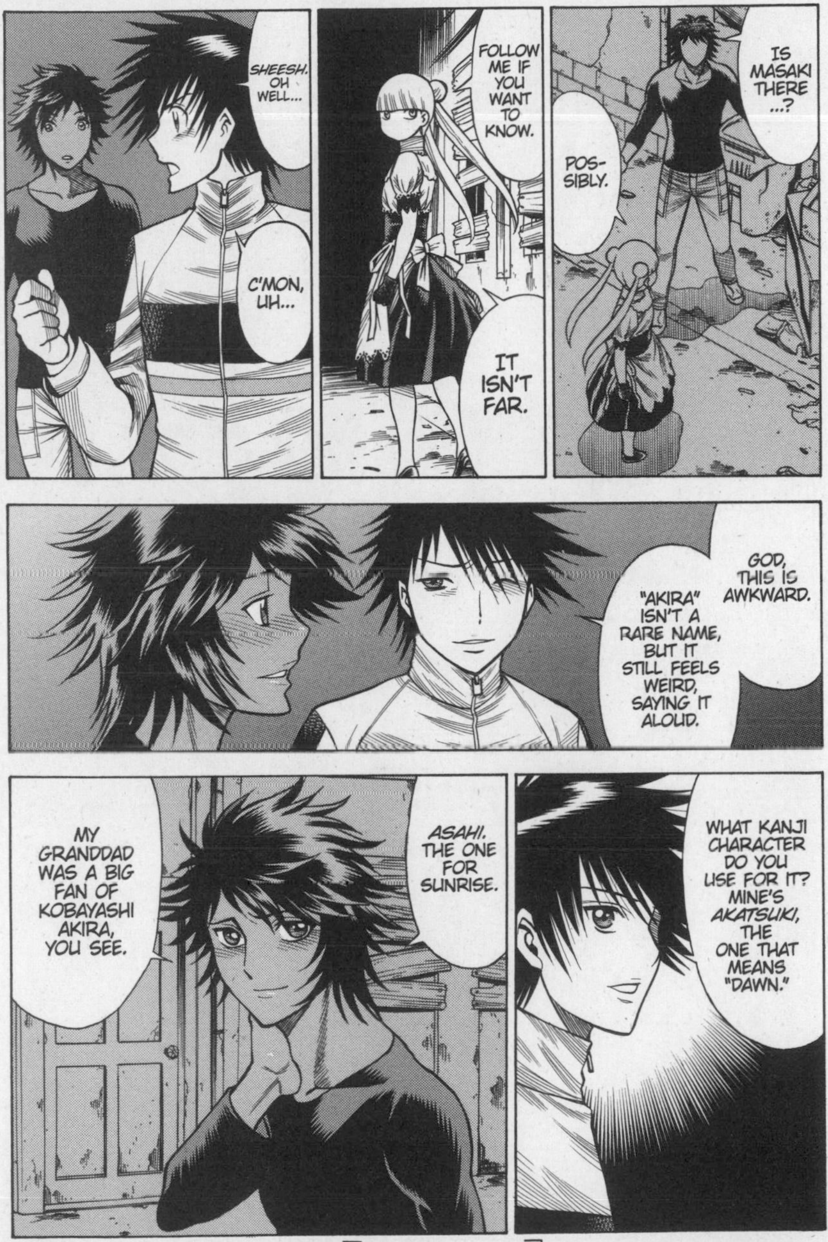
IS MASAKI THERE ...?
POS-SIBLY.
FOLLOW ME IF YOU WANT TO KNOW.
IT ISN'T FAR.
SHEESH. OH WELL...
C'MON, UH...
GOD, THIS IS AWKWARD.
"AKIRA" ISN'T A RARE NAME, BUT IT STILL FEELS WEIRD, SAYING IT ALOUD.
WHAT KANJI CHARACTER DO YOU USE FOR IT? MINE'S *AKATSUKI*, THE ONE THAT MEANS "DAWN."
ASAHI. THE ONE FOR SUNRISE.
MY GRANDDAD WAS A BIG FAN OF KOBAYASHI AKIRA, YOU SEE.

「旭」(あさひ) = asashi 「暁」(あかつき) = akatsuki

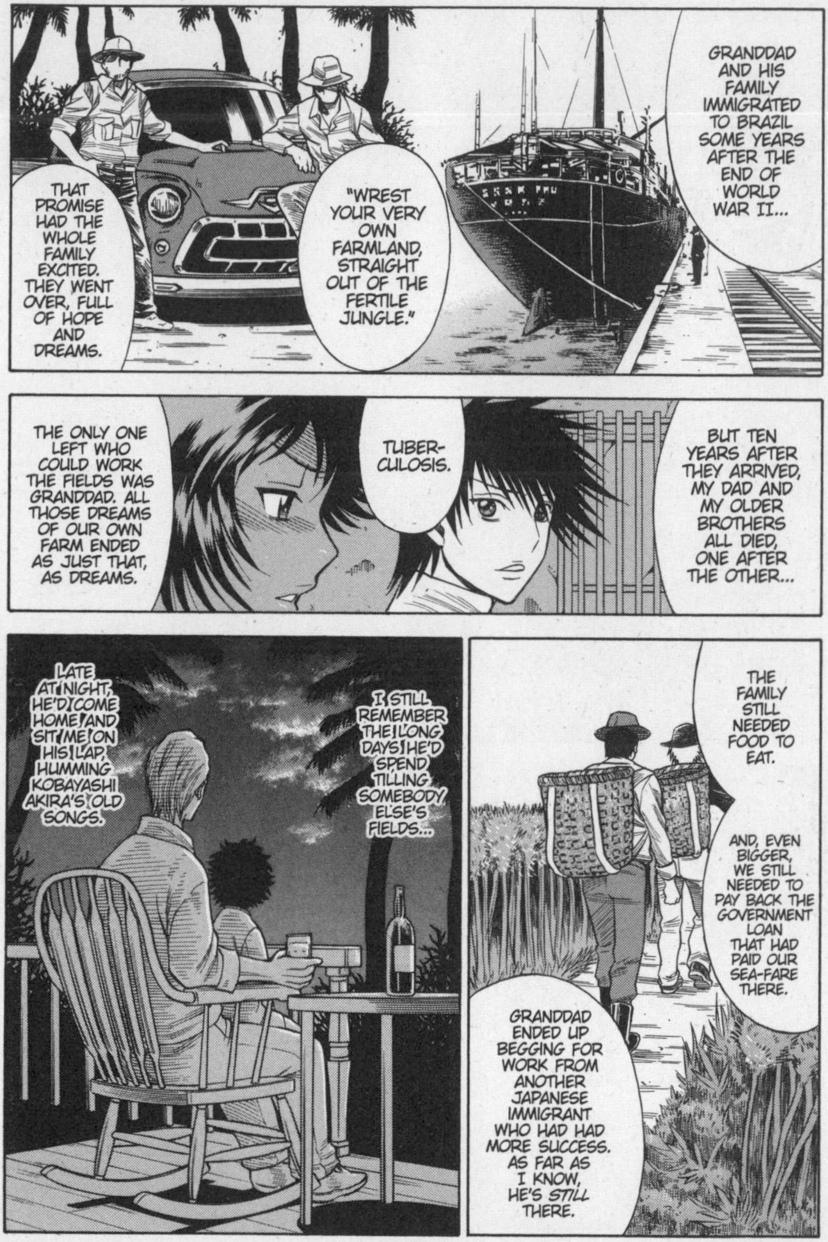
GRANDDAD AND HIS FAMILY IMMIGRATED TO BRAZIL SOME YEARS AFTER THE END OF WORLD WAR II...
"WREST YOUR VERY OWN FARMLAND, STRAIGHT OUT OF THE FERTILE JUNGLE."
THAT PROMISE HAD THE WHOLE FAMILY EXCITED. THEY WENT OVER, FULL OF HOPE AND DREAMS.
BUT TEN YEARS AFTER THEY ARRIVED, MY DAD AND MY OLDER BROTHERS ALL DIED, ONE AFTER THE OTHER...
TUBER-CULOSIS.
THE ONLY ONE LEFT WHO COULD WORK THE FIELDS WAS GRANDDAD. ALL THOSE DREAMS OF OUR OWN FARM ENDED AS JUST THAT, AS DREAMS.
THE FAMILY STILL NEEDED FOOD TO EAT.
AND, EVEN BIGGER, WE STILL NEEDED TO PAY BACK THE GOVERNMENT LOAN THAT HAD PAID OUR SEA-FARE THERE.
GRANDDAD ENDED UP BEGGING FOR WORK FROM ANOTHER JAPANESE IMMIGRANT WHO HAD HAD MORE SUCCESS. AS FAR AS I KNOW, HE'S *STILL* THERE.
I STILL REMEMBER THE LONG DAYS HE'D SPEND TILLING SOMEBODY ELSE'S FIELDS...
LATE AT NIGHT, HE'D COME HOME AND SIT ME ON HIS LAP, HUMMING KOBAYASHI AKIRA'S OLD SONGS.

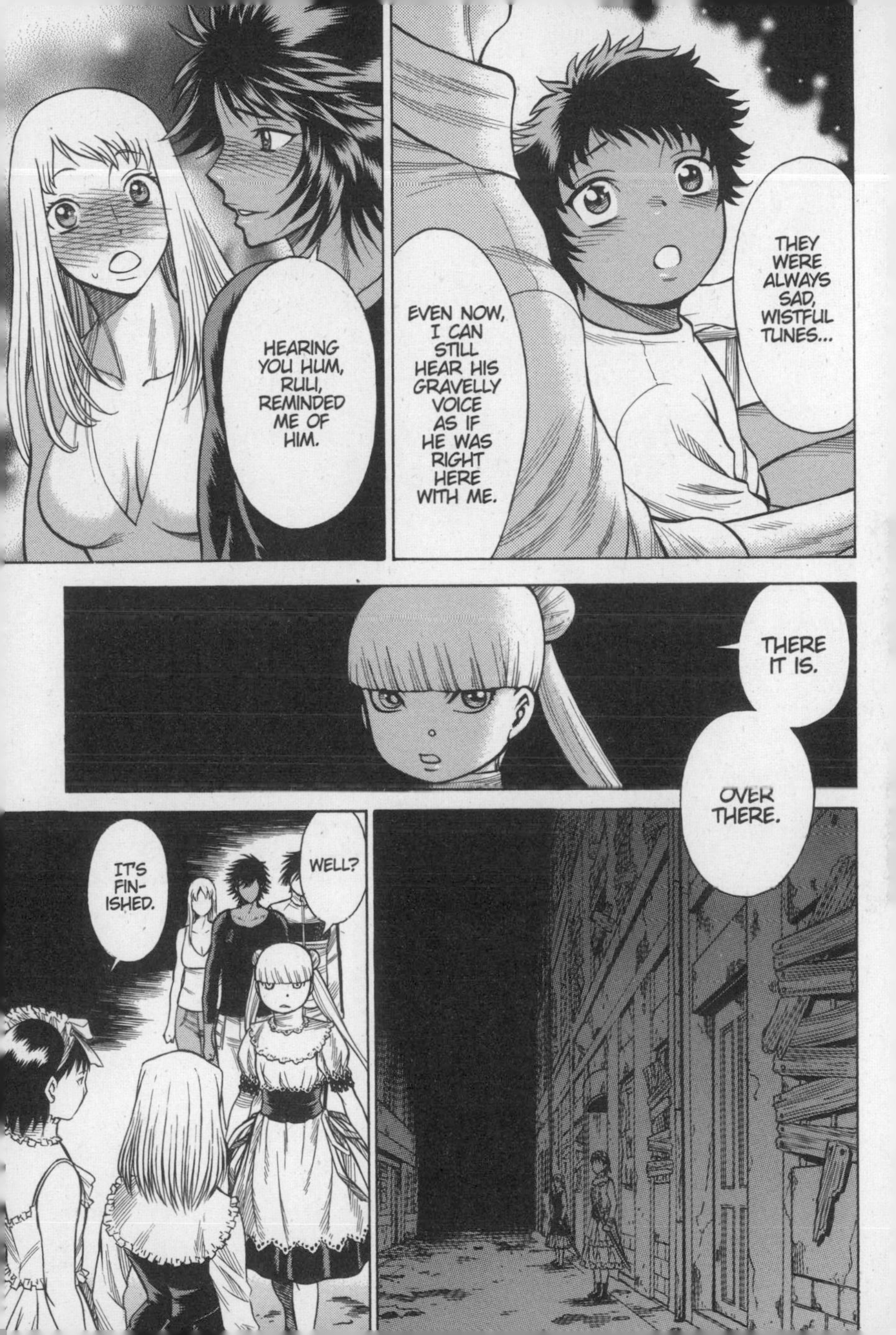
THEY WERE ALWAYS SAD, WISTFUL TUNES...
EVEN NOW, I CAN STILL HEAR HIS GRAVELLY VOICE AS IF HE WAS RIGHT HERE WITH ME.
HEARING YOU HUM, RULI, REMINDED ME OF HIM.
THERE IT IS.
OVER THERE.
WELL?
IT'S FIN-ISHED.

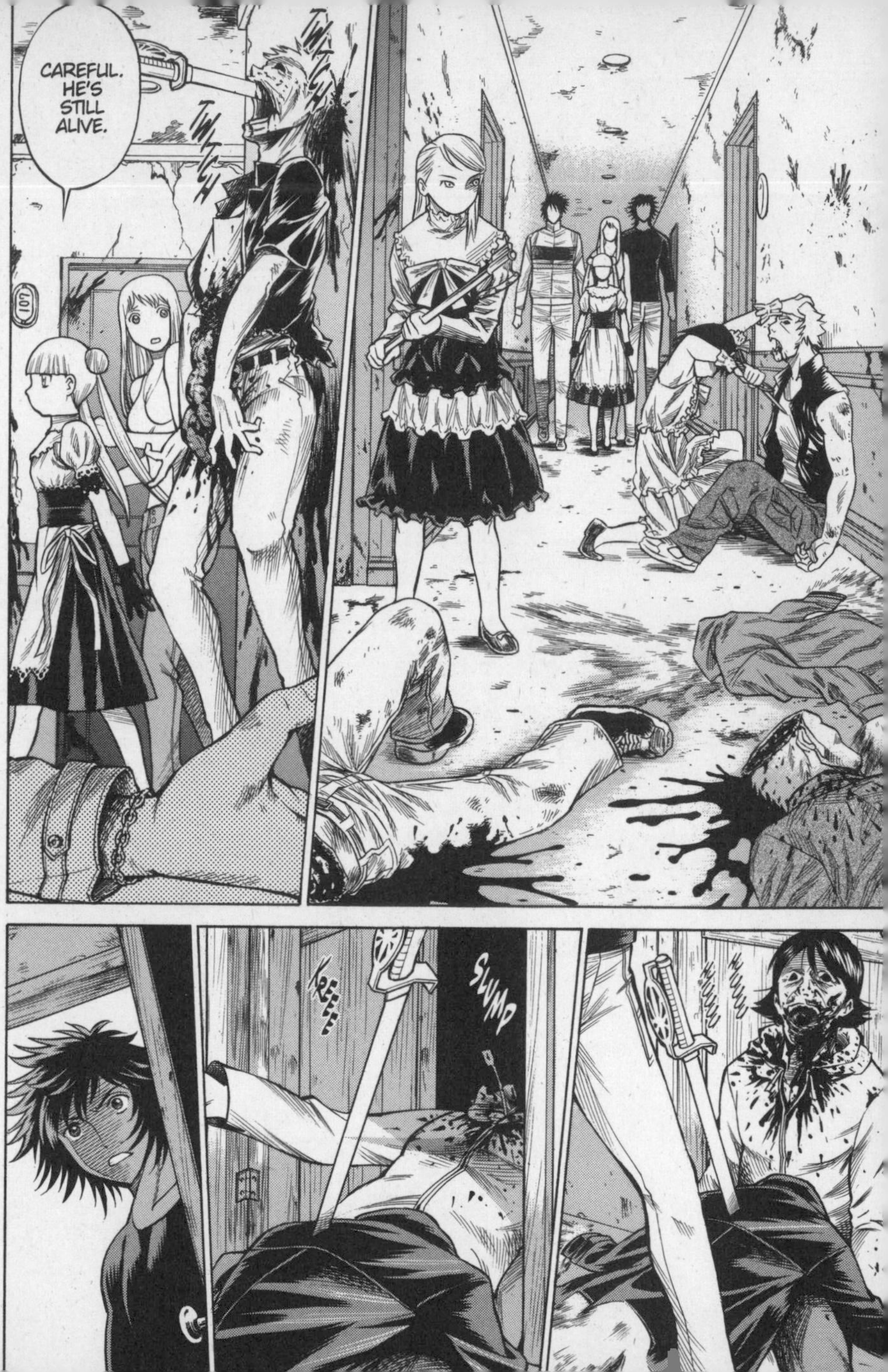
CAREFUL. HE'S STILL ALIVE.
TWITCH
TWITCH
HUUUU
HUUUUU
KREEE
SLUMP

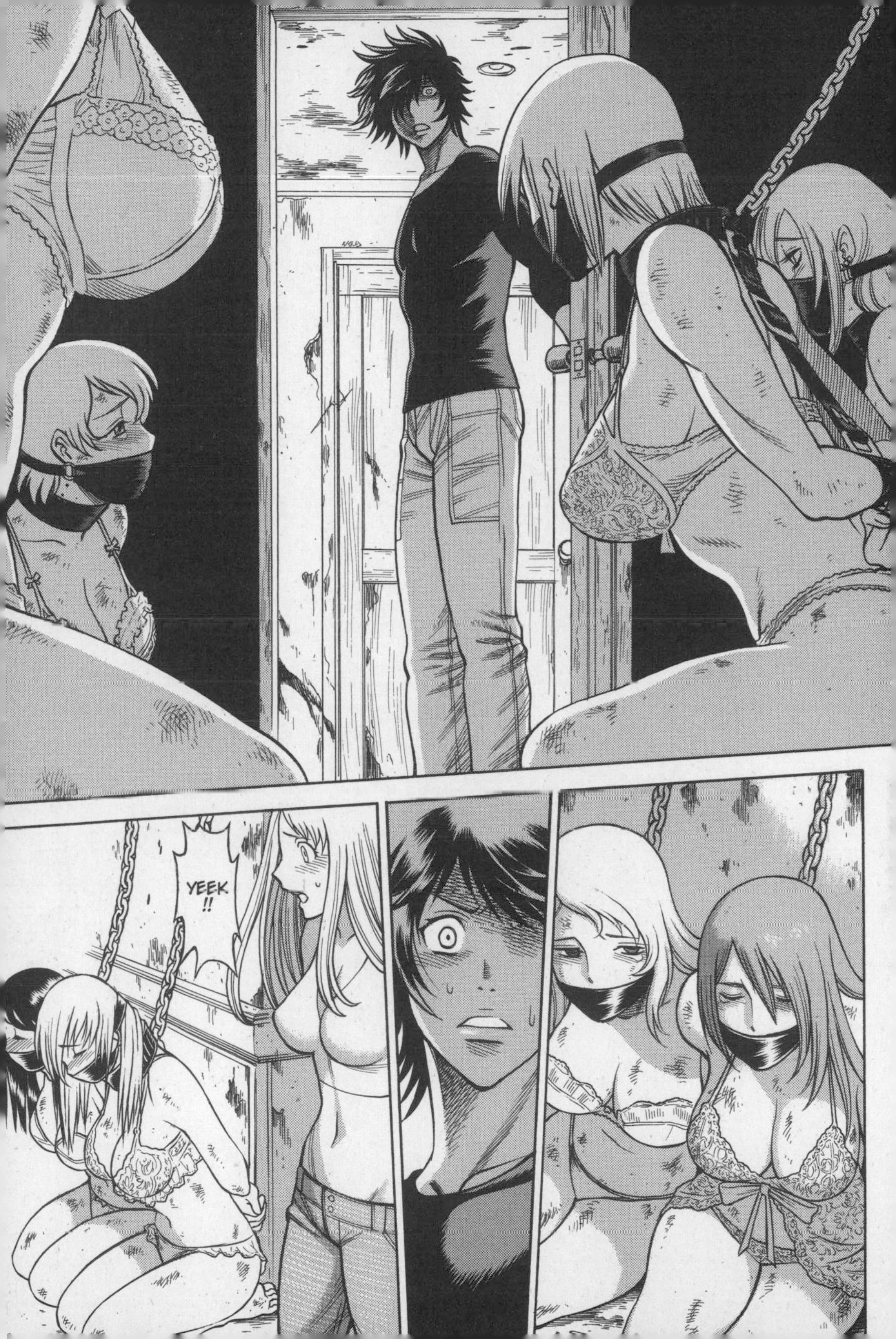
YEEK
!!

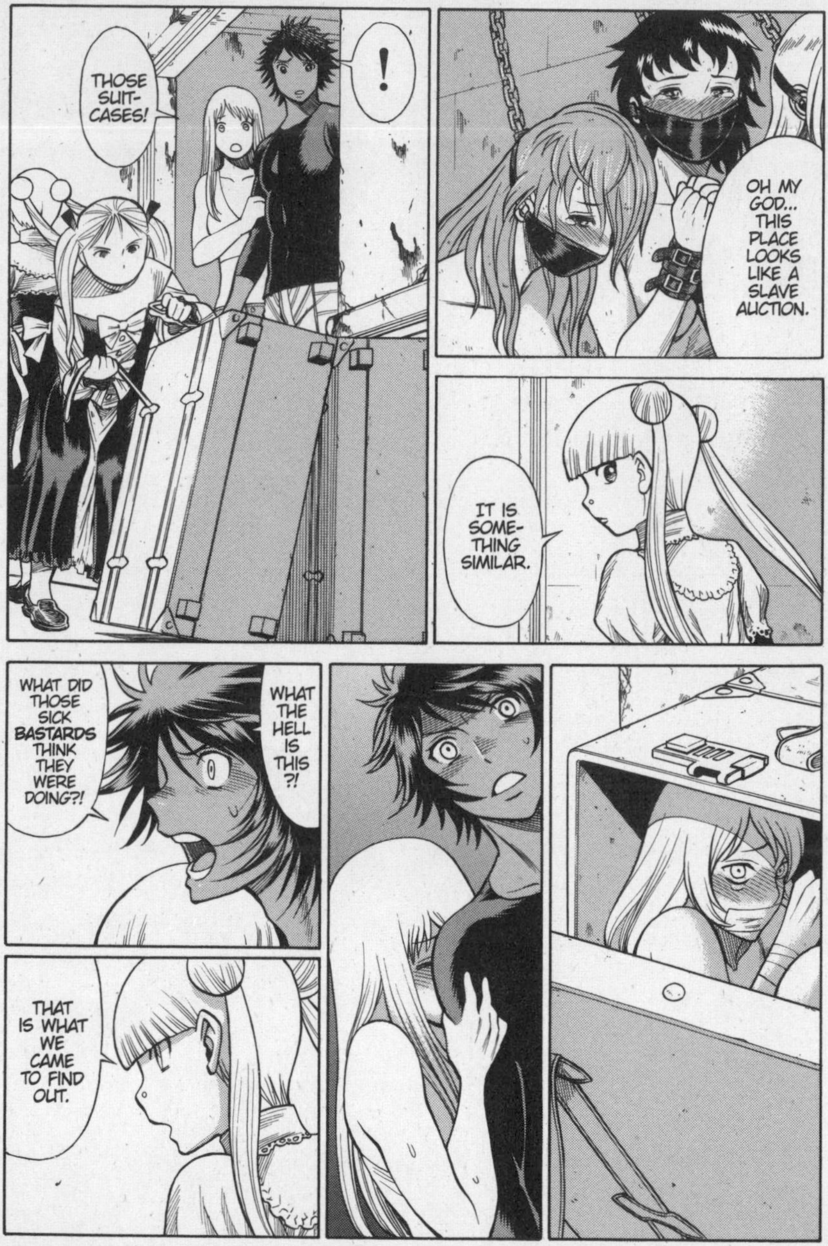
OH MY GOD... THIS PLACE LOOKS LIKE A SLAVE AUCTION.
IT IS SOME-THING SIMILAR.
!
THOSE SUIT-CASES!
WHAT THE HELL IS THIS?!
WHAT DID THOSE SICK BASTARDS THINK THEY WERE DOING?!
THAT IS WHAT WE CAME TO FIND OUT.

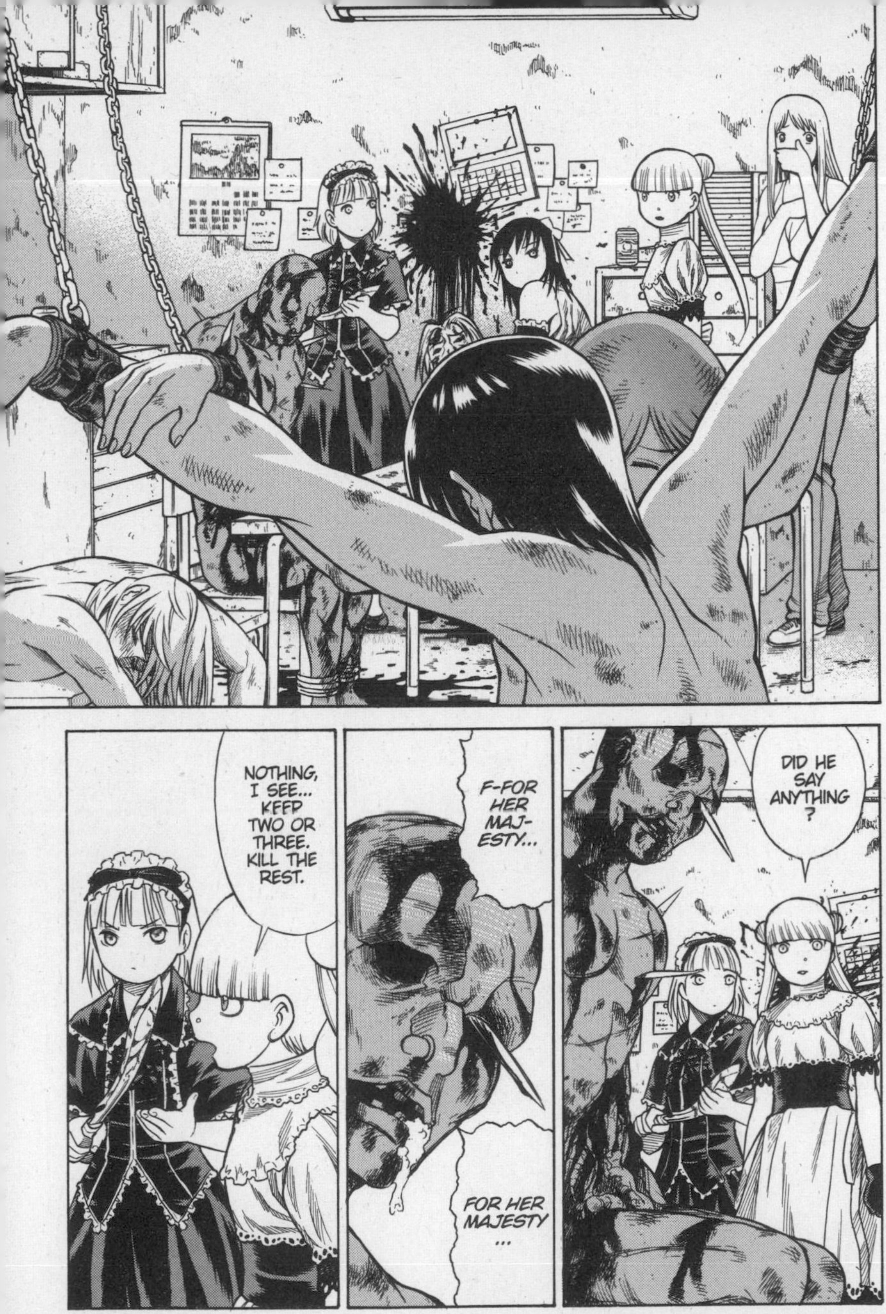
DID HE SAY ANYTHING ?
F-FOR HER MAJ-ESTY...
FOR HER MAJESTY ...
NOTHING, I SEE... KEEP TWO OR THREE. KILL THE REST.

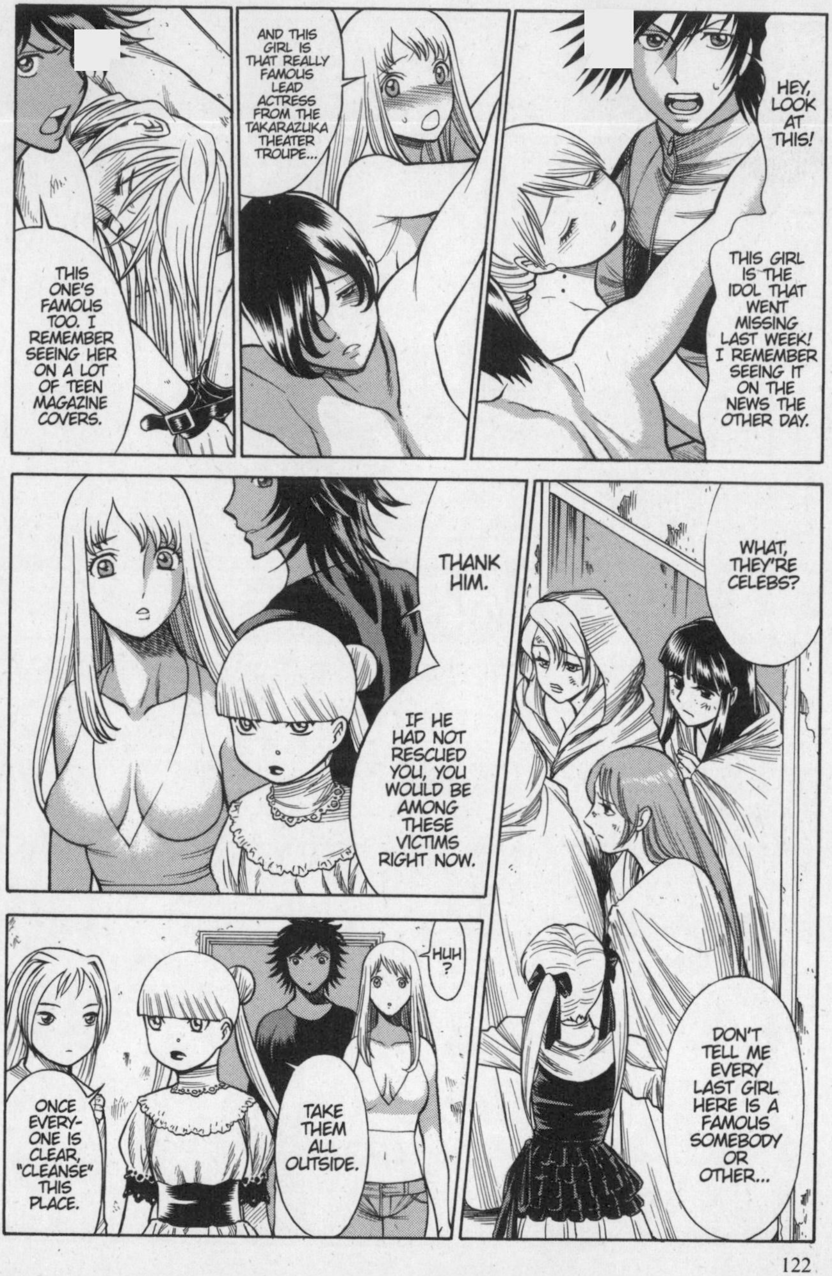
HEY, LOOK AT THIS!
THIS GIRL IS THE IDOL THAT WENT MISSING LAST WEEK! I REMEMBER SEEING IT ON THE NEWS THE OTHER DAY.
AND THIS GIRL IS THAT REALLY FAMOUS LEAD ACTRESS FROM THE TAKARAZUKA THEATER TROUPE...
THIS ONE'S FAMOUS TOO. I REMEMBER SEEING HER ON A LOT OF TEEN MAGAZINE COVERS.
WHAT, THEY'RE CELEBS?
DON'T TELL ME EVERY LAST GIRL HERE IS A FAMOUS SOMEBODY OR OTHER...
THANK HIM.
IF HE HAD NOT RESCUED YOU, YOU WOULD BE AMONG THESE VICTIMS RIGHT NOW.
HUH?
TAKE THEM ALL OUTSIDE.
ONCE EVERY-ONE IS CLEAR, "CLEANSE" THIS PLACE.

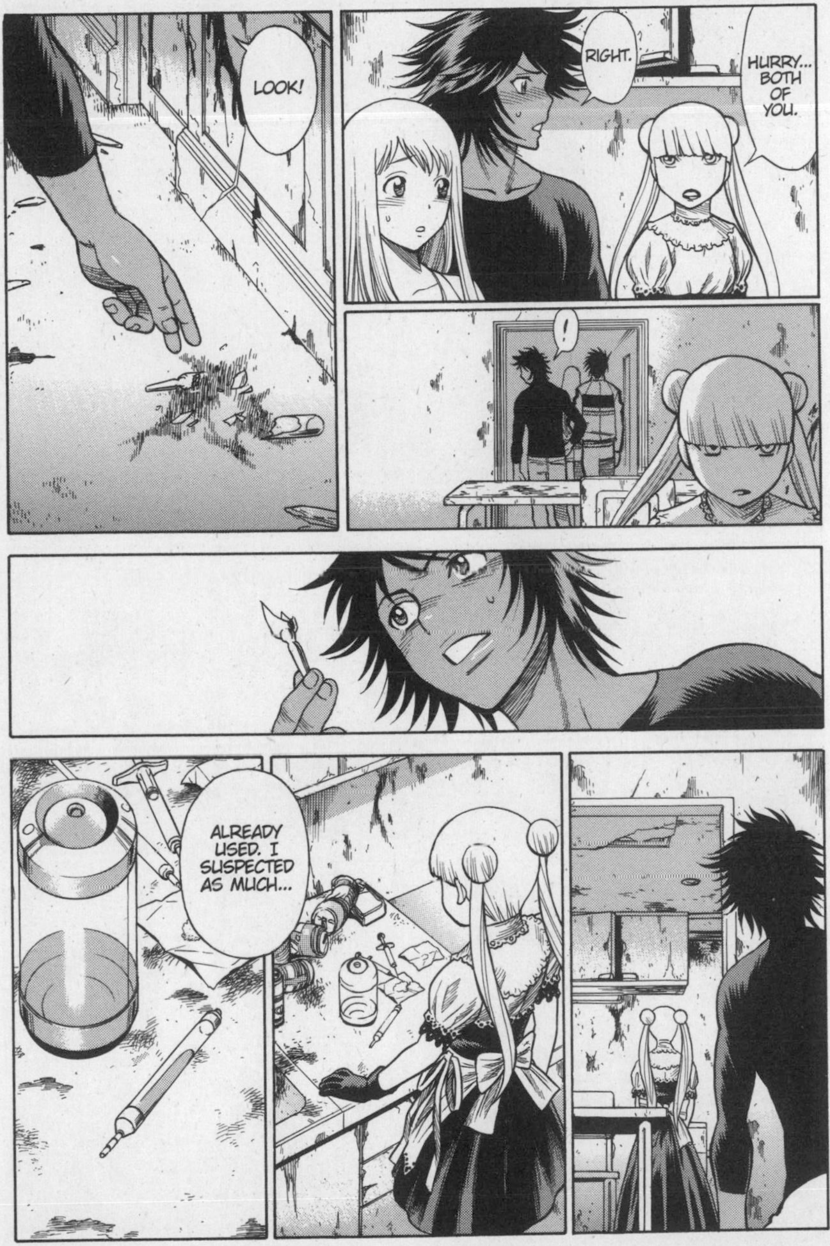
HURRY... BOTH OF YOU.
RIGHT.
!
LOOK!
ALREADY USED. I SUSPECTED AS MUCH...

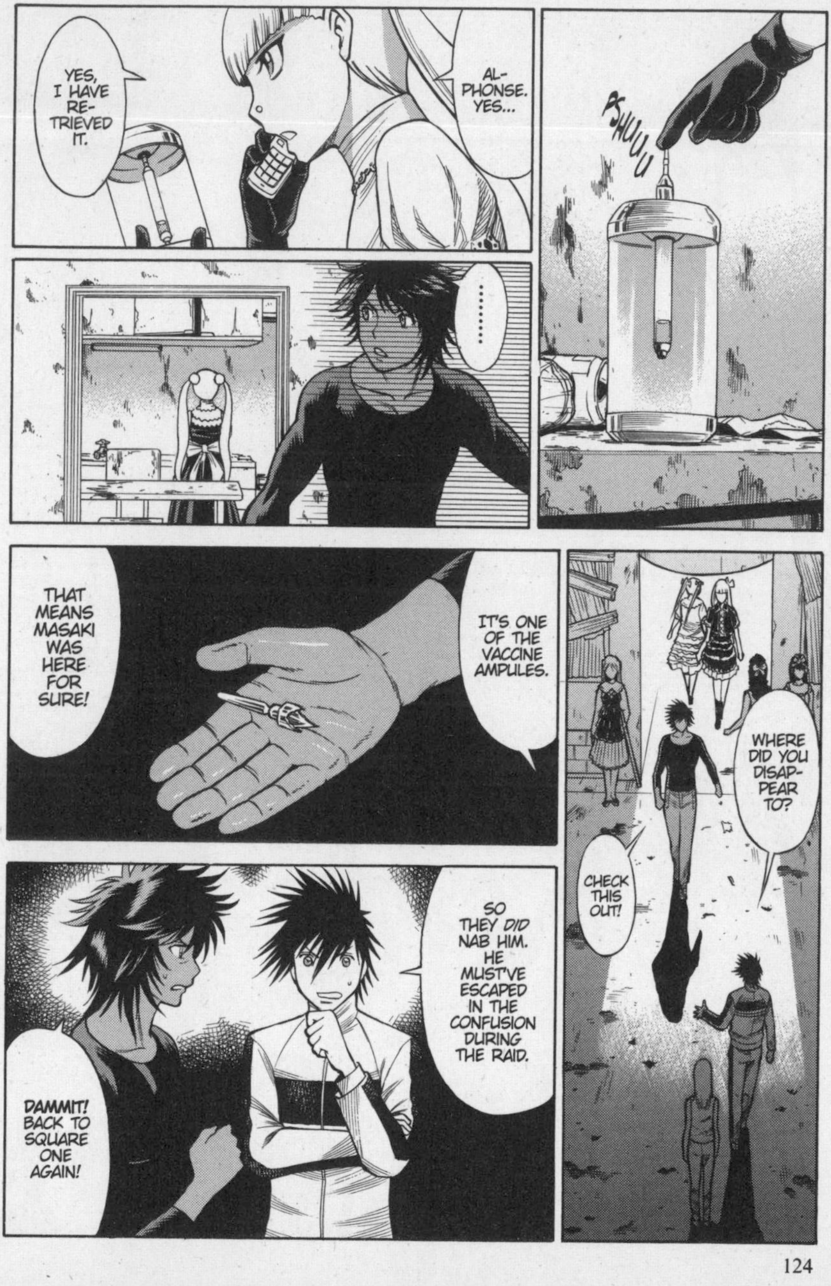
PSHUUU
AL-PHONSE. YES...
YES, I HAVE RE-TRIEVED IT.
......
WHERE DID YOU DISAP-PEAR TO?
CHECK THIS OUT!
IT'S ONE OF THE VACCINE AMPULES.
THAT MEANS MASAKI WAS HERE FOR SURE!
SO THEY *DID* NAB HIM. HE MUST'VE ESCAPED IN THE CONFUSION DURING THE RAID.
DAMMIT! BACK TO SQUARE ONE AGAIN!

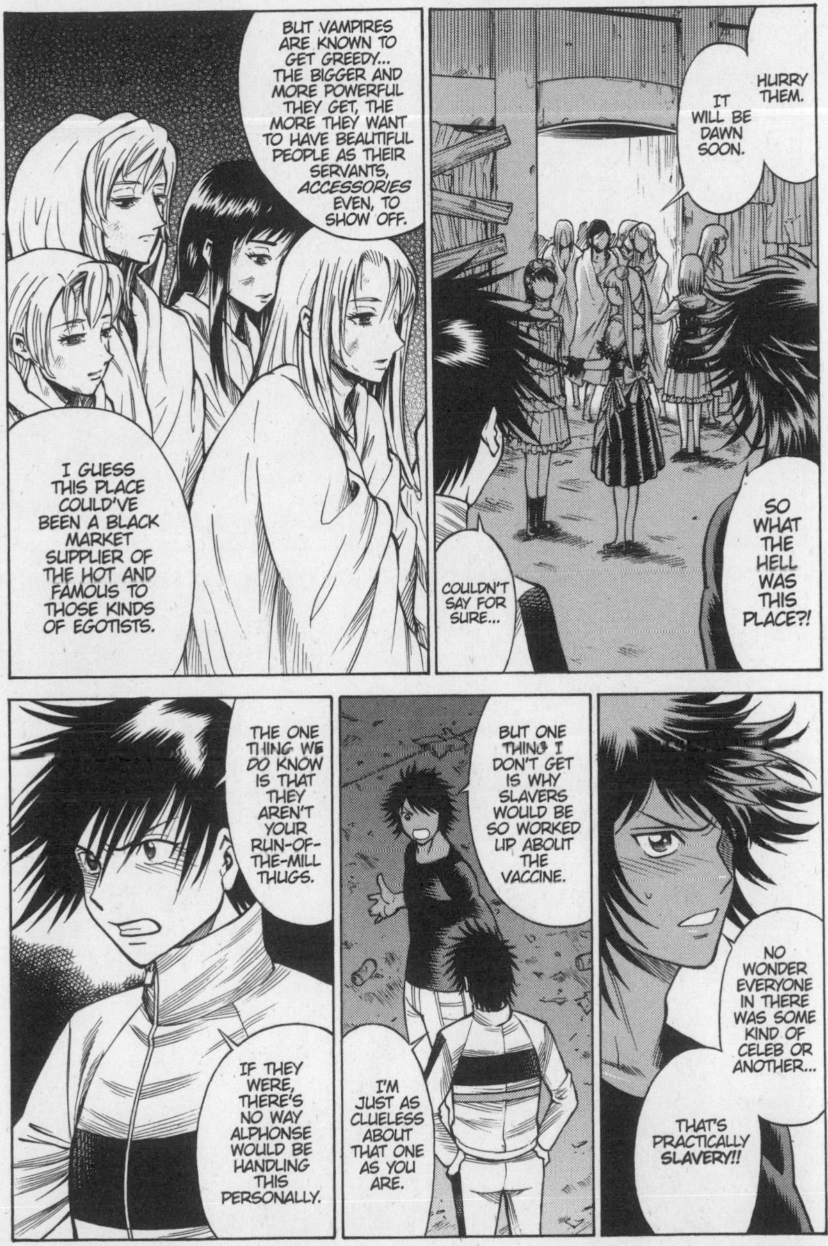
HURRY THEM.
IT WILL BE DAWN SOON.
SO WHAT THE HELL WAS THIS PLACE?!
COULDN'T SAY FOR SURE...
BUT VAMPIRES ARE KNOWN TO GET GREEDY... THE BIGGER AND MORE POWERFUL THEY GET, THE MORE THEY WANT TO HAVE BEAUTIFUL PEOPLE AS THEIR SERVANTS, *ACCESSORIES* EVEN, TO SHOW OFF.
I GUESS THIS PLACE COULD'VE BEEN A BLACK MARKET SUPPLIER OF THE HOT AND FAMOUS TO THOSE KINDS OF EGOTISTS.
NO WONDER EVERYONE IN THERE WAS SOME KIND OF CELEB OR ANOTHER...
THAT'S PRACTICALLY SLAVERY!!
BUT ONE THING I DON'T GET IS WHY SLAVERS WOULD BE SO WORKED UP ABOUT THE VACCINE.
I'M JUST AS CLUELESS ABOUT THAT ONE AS YOU ARE.
THE ONE THING WE *DO* KNOW IS THAT THEY AREN'T YOUR RUN-OF-THE-MILL THUGS.
IF THEY WERE, THERE'S NO WAY ALPHONSE WOULD BE HANDLING THIS PERSONALLY.

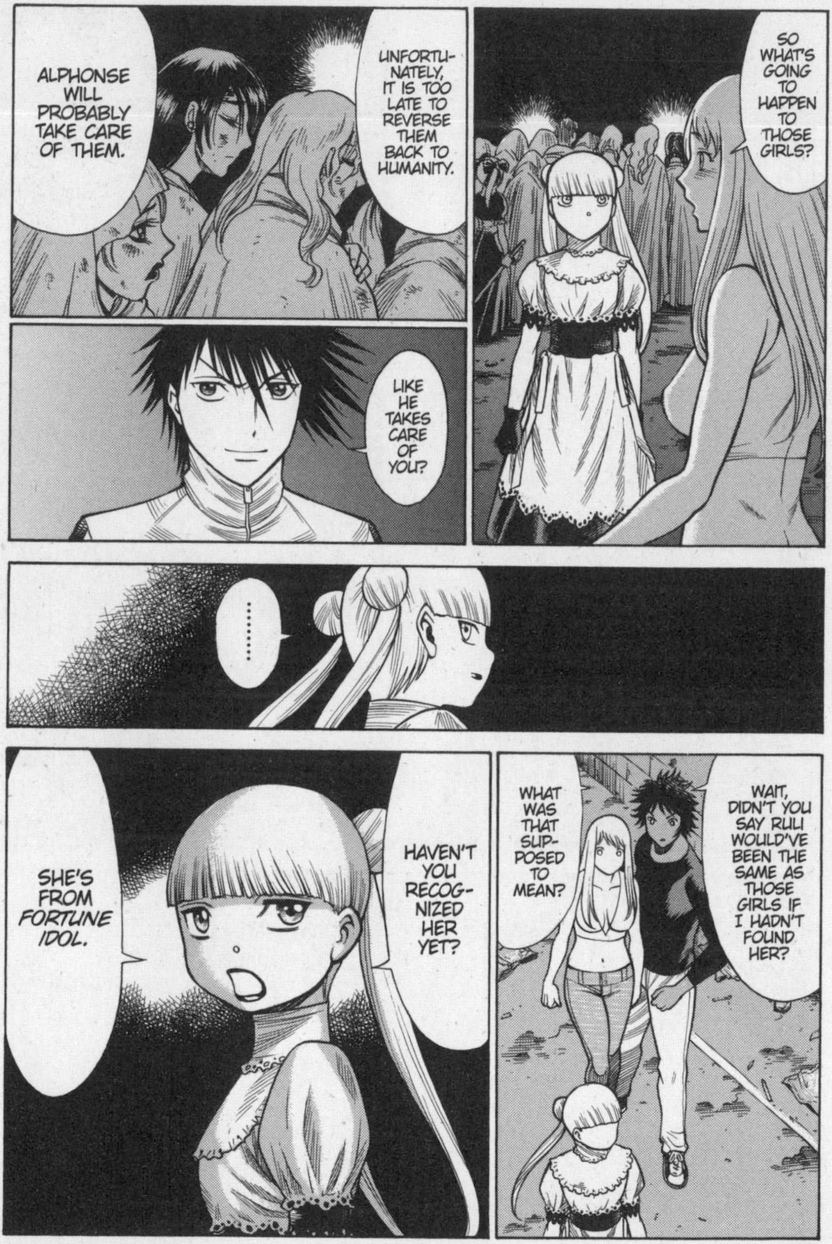
SO WHAT'S GOING TO HAPPEN TO THOSE GIRLS?
UNFORTUNATELY, IT IS TOO LATE TO REVERSE THEM BACK TO HUMANITY.
ALPHONSE WILL PROBABLY TAKE CARE OF THEM.
LIKE HE TAKES CARE OF YOU?
......
WAIT, DIDN'T YOU SAY RULI WOULD'VE BEEN THE SAME AS THOSE GIRLS IF I HADN'T FOUND HER?
WHAT WAS THAT SUPPOSED TO MEAN?
HAVEN'T YOU RECOGNIZED HER YET?
SHE'S FROM FORTUNE IDOL.

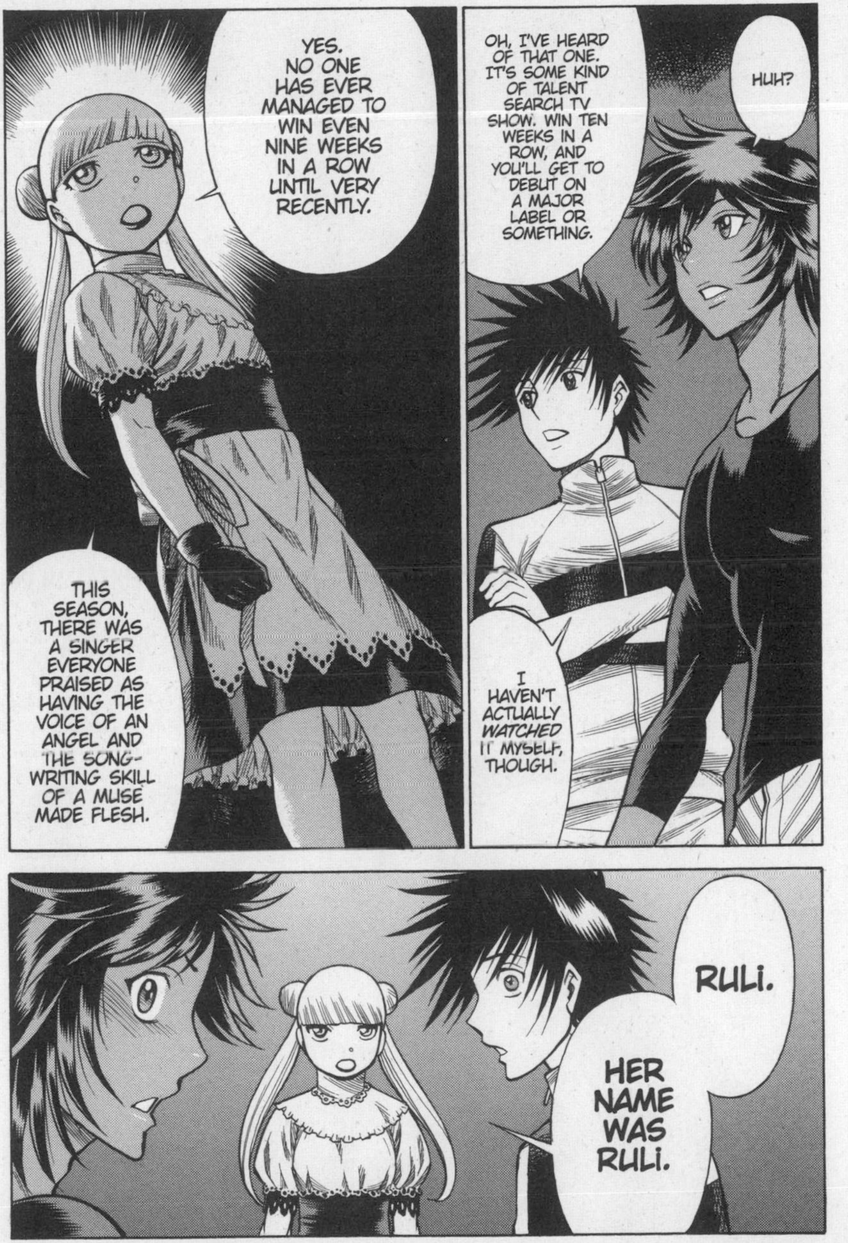
HUH?
OH, I'VE HEARD OF THAT ONE. IT'S SOME KIND OF TALENT SEARCH TV SHOW. WIN TEN WEEKS IN A ROW, AND YOU'LL GET TO DEBUT ON A MAJOR LABEL OR SOMETHING.
I HAVEN'T ACTUALLY *WATCHED* IT MYSELF, THOUGH.
YES. NO ONE HAS EVER MANAGED TO WIN EVEN NINE WEEKS IN A ROW UNTIL VERY RECENTLY.
THIS SEASON, THERE WAS A SINGER EVERYONE PRAISED AS HAVING THE VOICE OF AN ANGEL AND THE SONG-WRITING SKILL OF A MUSE MADE FLESH.
RULi.
HER NAME WAS RULi.

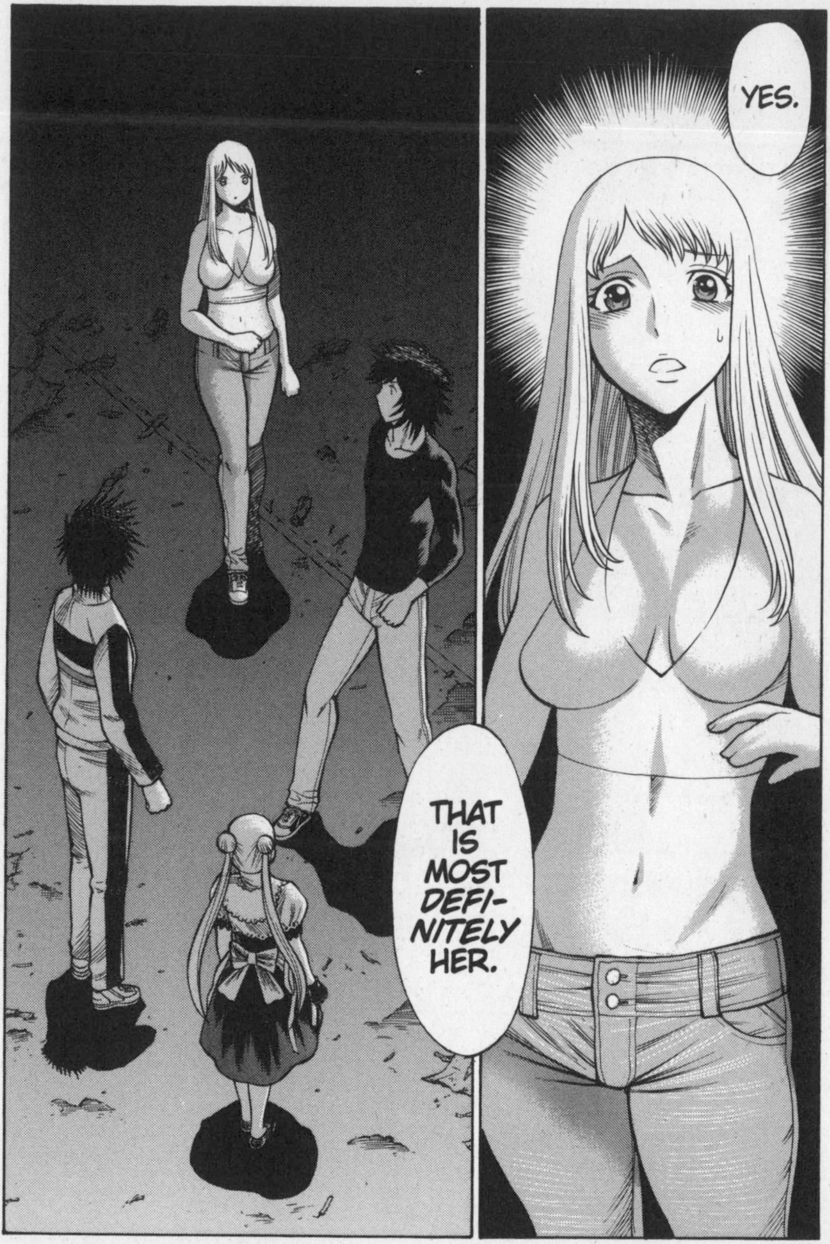
YES.
THAT IS MOST DEFI-NITELY HER.

Chapter 8: Labyrinth

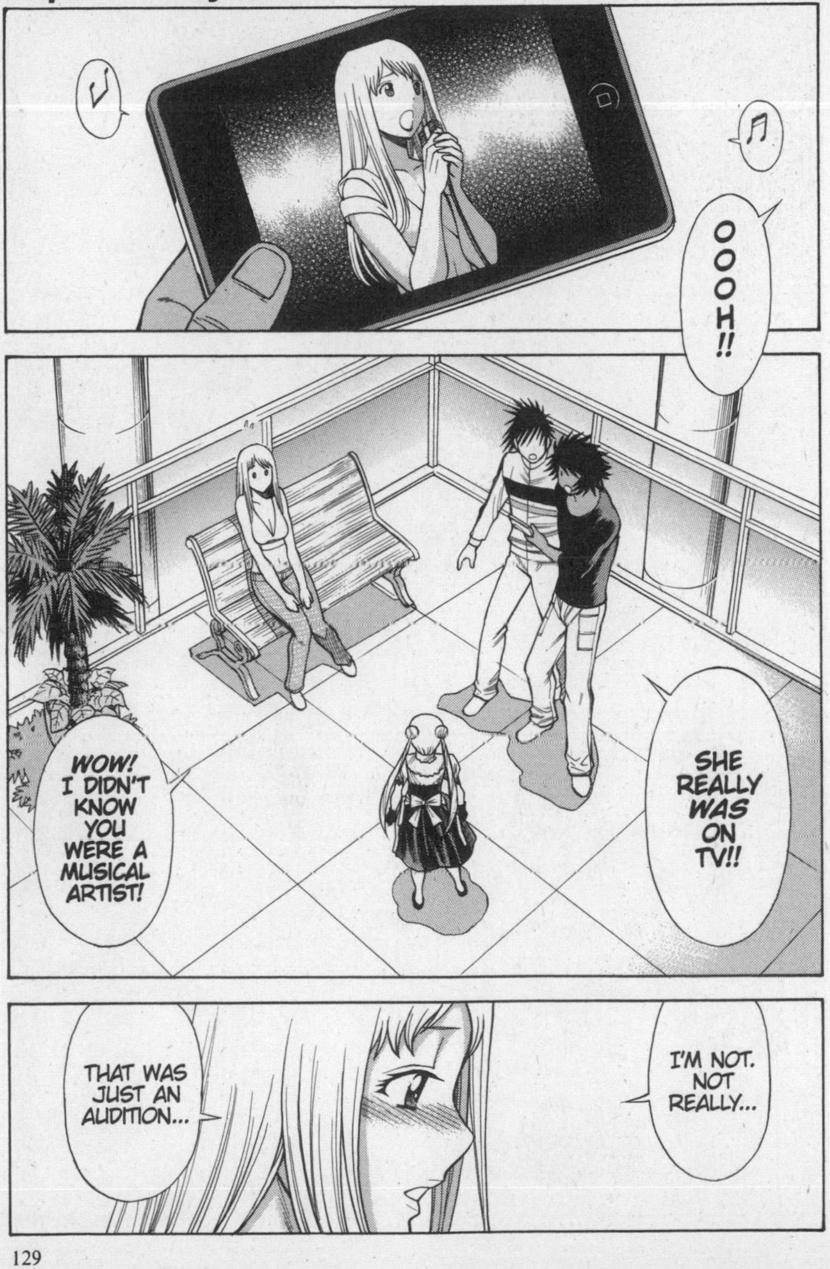
OOOH!!
SHE REALLY WAS ON TV!!
WOW! I DIDN'T KNOW YOU WERE A MUSICAL ARTIST!
I'M NOT. NOT REALLY...
THAT WAS JUST AN AUDITION...

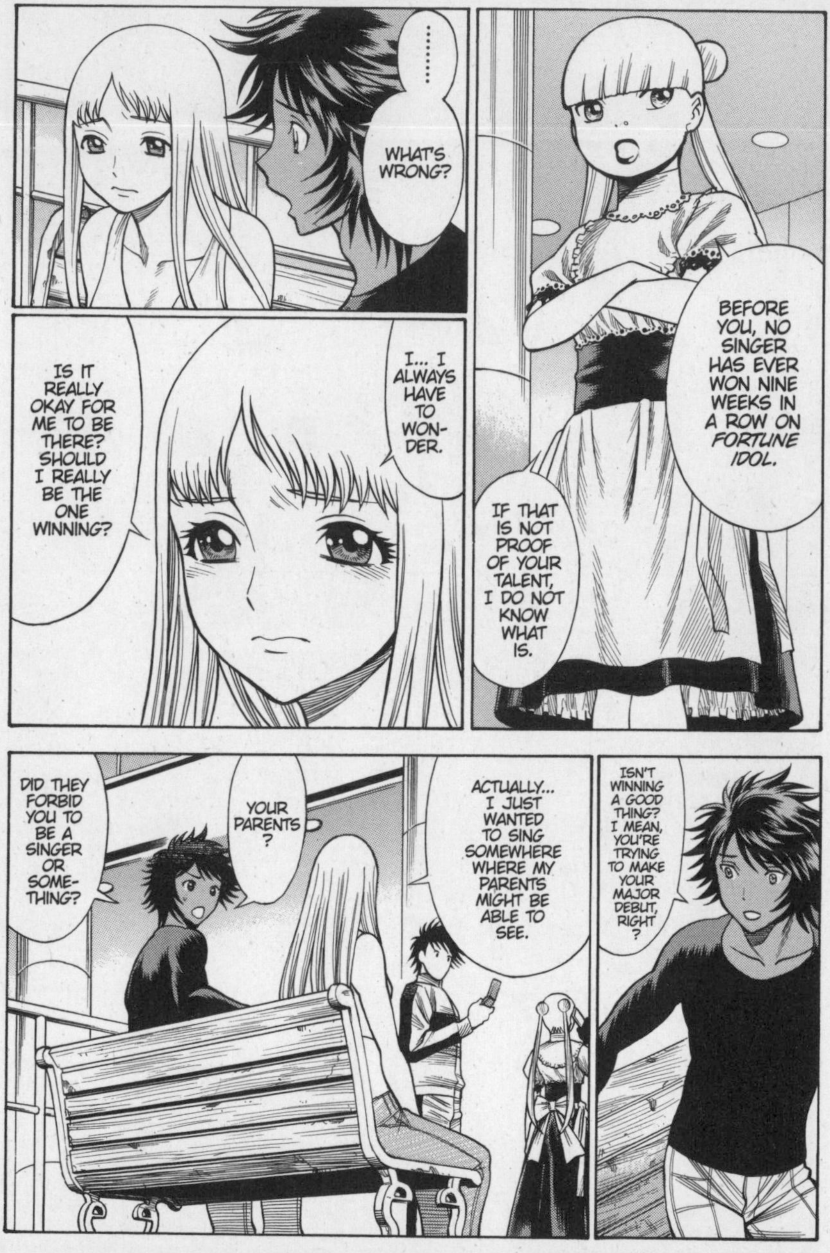
BEFORE YOU, NO SINGER HAS EVER WON NINE WEEKS IN A ROW ON *FORTUNE IDOL.*
IF THAT IS NOT PROOF OF YOUR TALENT, I DO NOT KNOW WHAT IS.
......
WHAT'S WRONG?
I... I ALWAYS HAVE TO WON-DER.
IS IT REALLY OKAY FOR ME TO BE THERE? SHOULD I REALLY BE THE ONE WINNING?
ISN'T WINNING A GOOD THING? I MEAN, YOU'RE TRYING TO MAKE YOUR MAJOR DEBUT, RIGHT?
ACTUALLY... I JUST WANTED TO SING SOMEWHERE WHERE MY PARENTS MIGHT BE ABLE TO SEE.
YOUR PARENTS?
DID THEY FORBID YOU TO BE A SINGER OR SOME-THING?

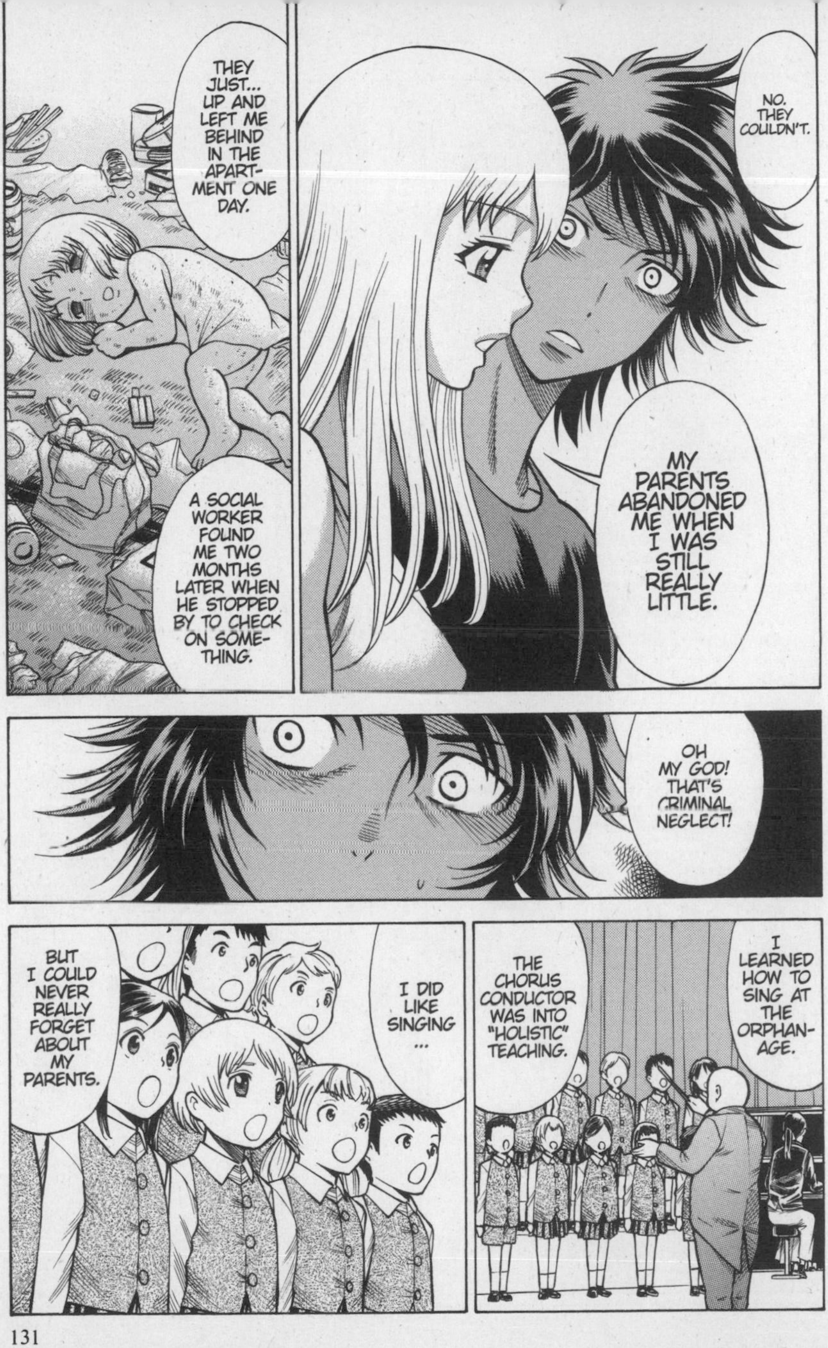
NO. THEY COULDN'T.
MY PARENTS ABANDONED ME WHEN I WAS STILL REALLY LITTLE.
THEY JUST... UP AND LEFT ME BEHIND IN THE APARTMENT ONE DAY.
A SOCIAL WORKER FOUND ME TWO MONTHS LATER WHEN HE STOPPED BY TO CHECK ON SOMETHING.
OH MY GOD! THAT'S CRIMINAL NEGLECT!
I LEARNED HOW TO SING AT THE ORPHANAGE.
THE CHORUS CONDUCTOR WAS INTO "HOLISTIC" TEACHING.
I DID LIKE SINGING ...
BUT I COULD NEVER REALLY FORGET ABOUT MY PARENTS.

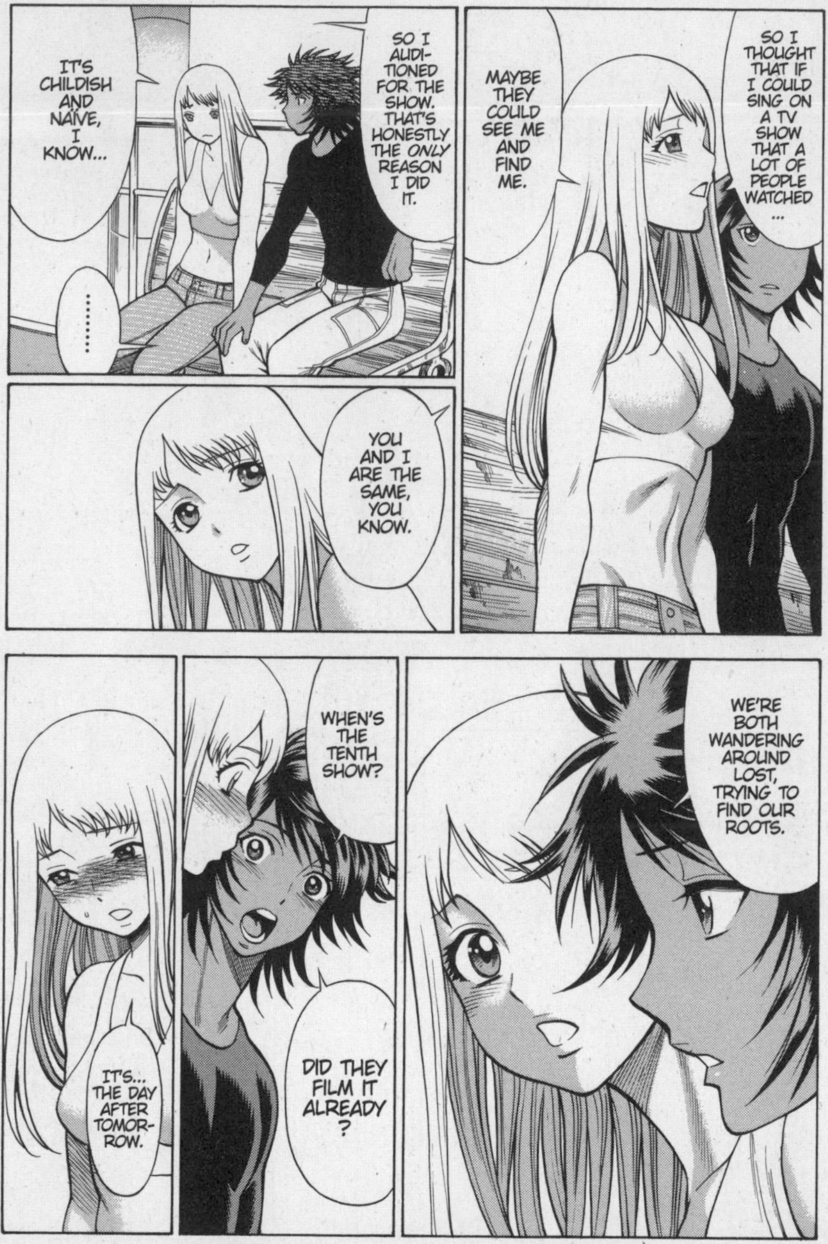
SO I THOUGHT THAT IF I COULD SING ON A TV SHOW THAT A LOT OF PEOPLE WATCHED ...
MAYBE THEY COULD SEE ME AND FIND ME.
SO I AUDITIONED FOR THE SHOW. THAT'S HONESTLY THE *ONLY* REASON I DID IT.
IT'S CHILDISH AND NAÏVE, I KNOW...
....
YOU AND I ARE THE SAME, YOU KNOW.
WE'RE BOTH WANDERING AROUND LOST, TRYING TO FIND OUR ROOTS.
WHEN'S THE TENTH SHOW?
DID THEY FILM IT ALREADY ?
IT'S... THE DAY AFTER TOMORROW.

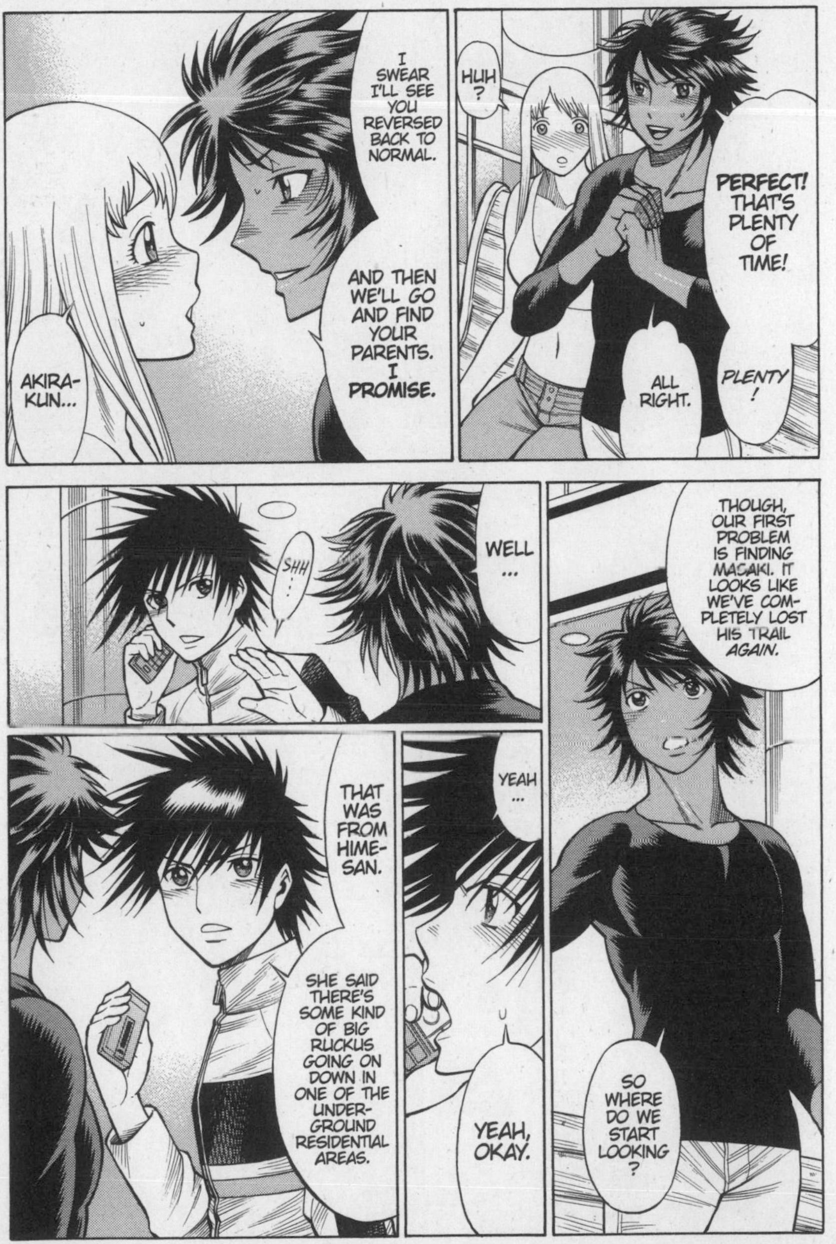
HUH?
PERFECT! THAT'S PLENTY OF TIME!
PLENTY!
ALL RIGHT.
I SWEAR I'LL SEE YOU REVERSED BACK TO NORMAL.
AND THEN WE'LL GO AND FIND YOUR PARENTS. I PROMISE.
AKIRA-KUN...
THOUGH, OUR FIRST PROBLEM IS FINDING MASAKI. IT LOOKS LIKE WE'VE COM-PLETELY LOST HIS TRAIL AGAIN.
SO WHERE DO WE START LOOKING?
WELL...
SHH...
YEAH...
YEAH, OKAY.
THAT WAS FROM HIME-SAN.
SHE SAID THERE'S SOME KIND OF BIG RUCKUS GOING ON DOWN IN ONE OF THE UNDER-GROUND RESIDENTIAL AREAS.

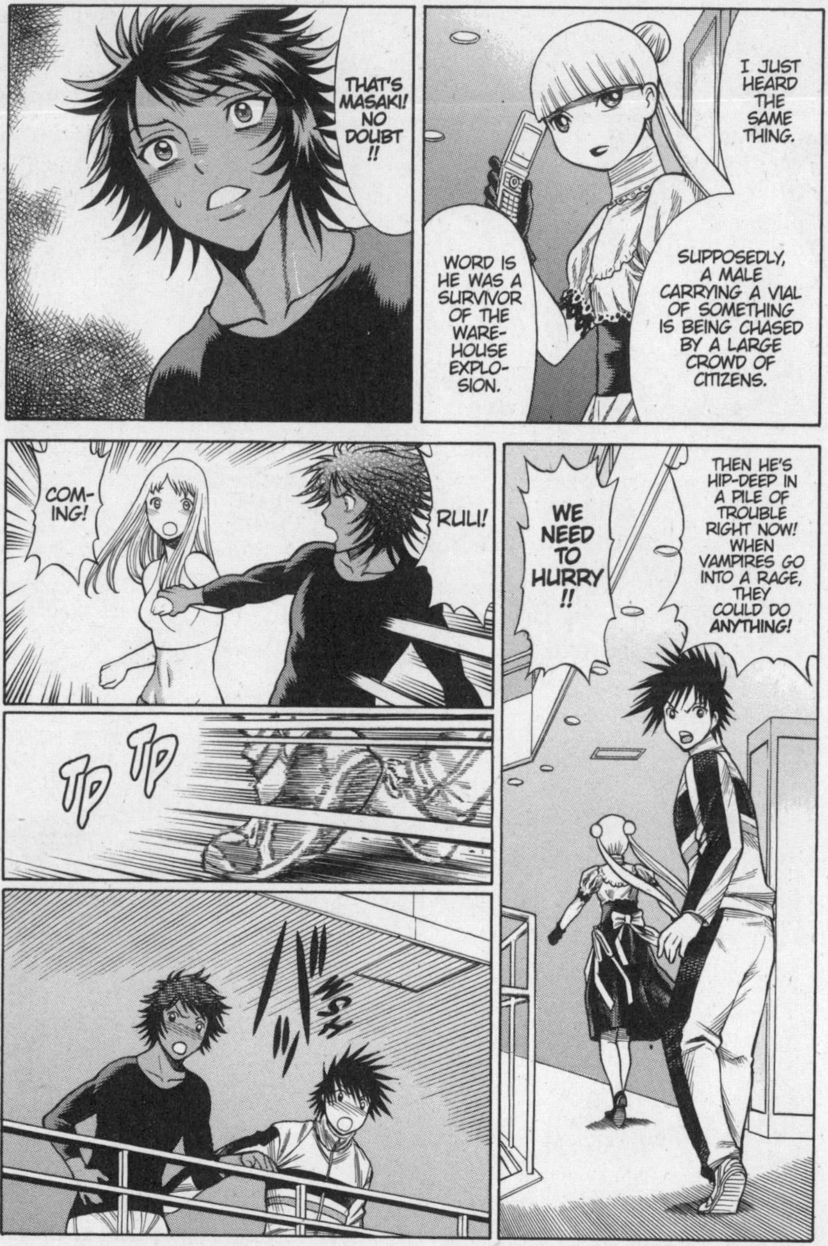

I JUST HEARD THE SAME THING.
SUPPOSEDLY, A MALE CARRYING A VIAL OF SOMETHING IS BEING CHASED BY A LARGE CROWD OF CITIZENS.
WORD IS HE WAS A SURVIVOR OF THE WARE-HOUSE EXPLO-SION.
THAT'S MASAKI! NO DOUBT !!
THEN HE'S HIP-DEEP IN A PILE OF TROUBLE RIGHT NOW! WHEN VAMPIRES GO INTO A RAGE, THEY COULD DO ANYTHING!
WE NEED TO HURRY !!
RULI!
COM-ING!
TP TP
WSH

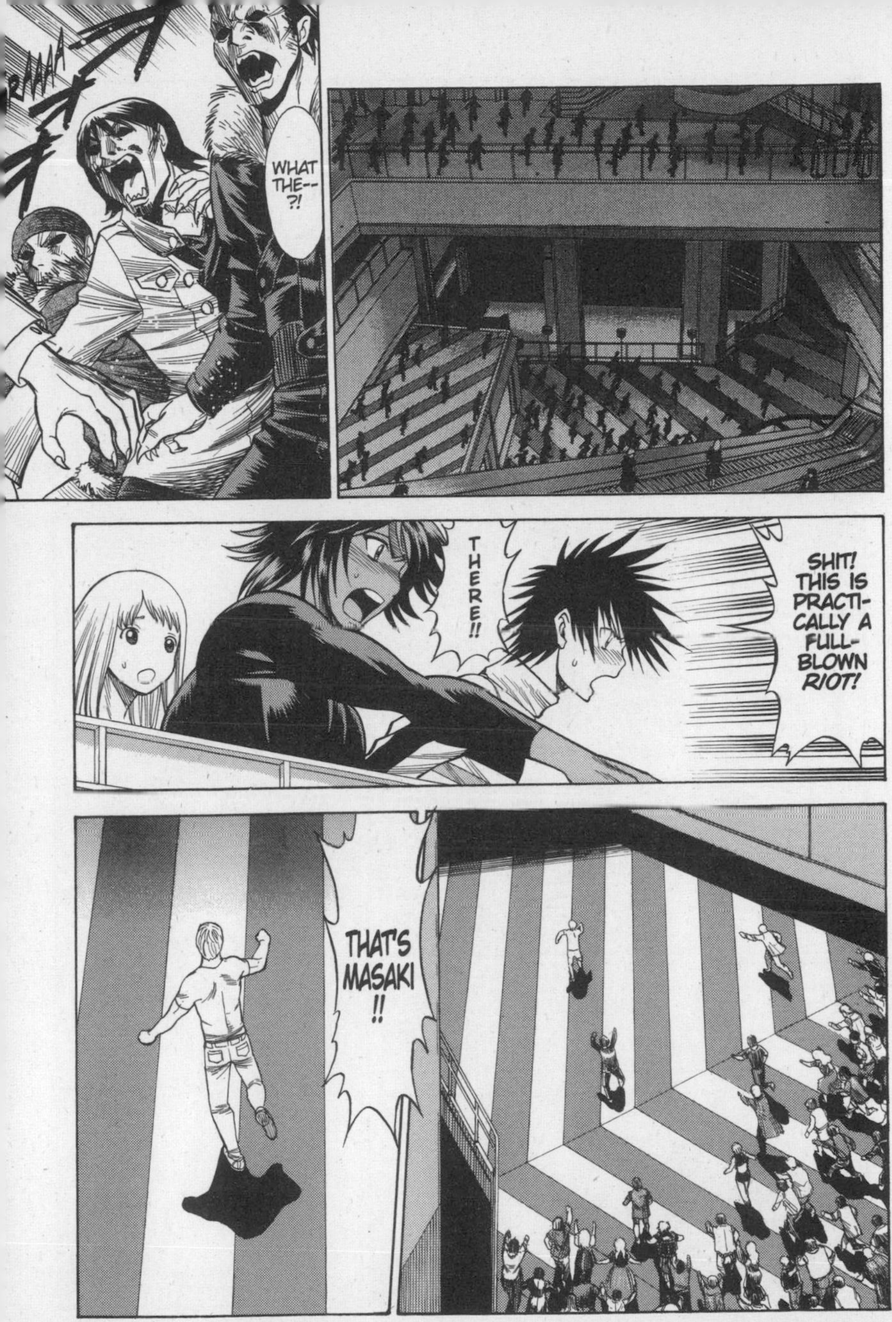
RAAAA
WHAT THE--?!
SHIT! THIS IS PRACTI-CALLY A FULL-BLOWN RIOT!
THERE!!
THAT'S MASAKI!!

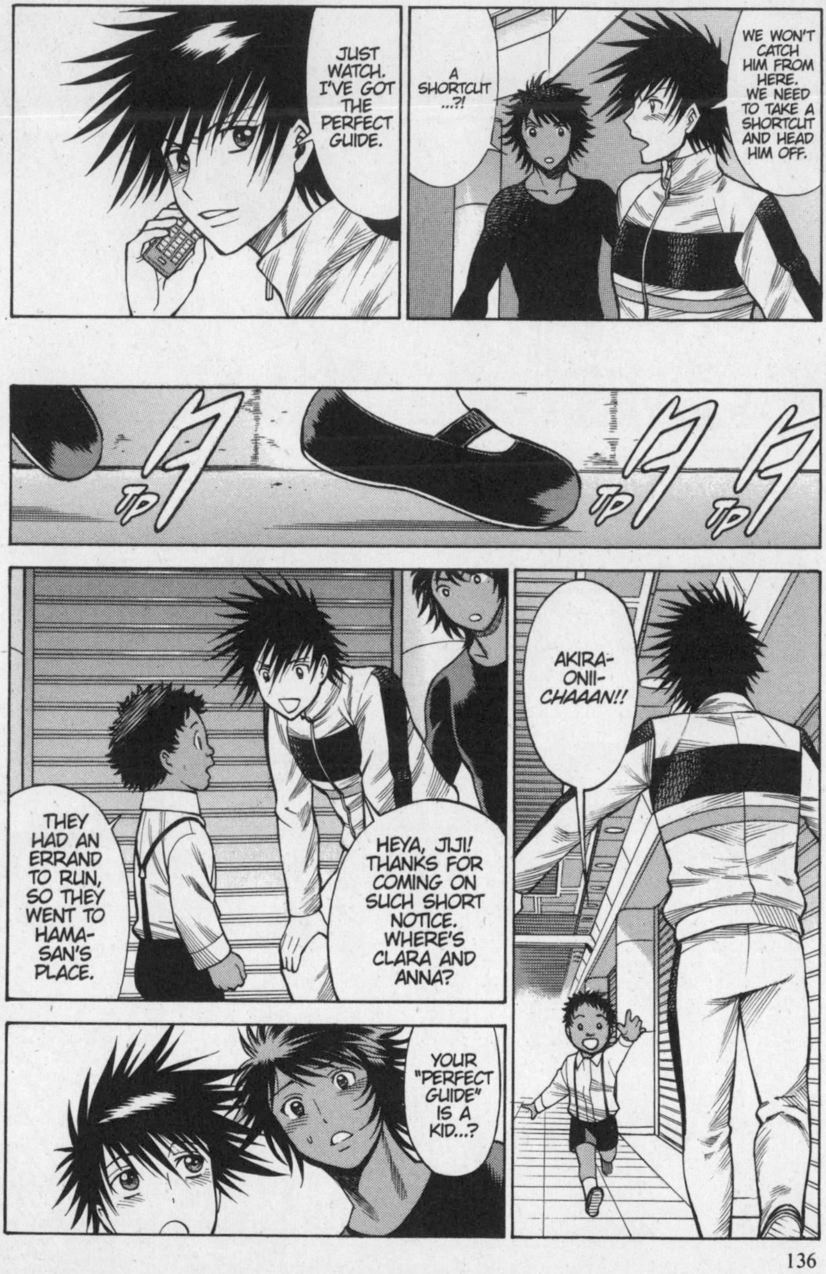
WE WON'T CATCH HIM FROM HERE. WE NEED TO TAKE A SHORTCUT AND HEAD HIM OFF.
A SHORTCUT ...?!
JUST WATCH. I'VE GOT THE PERFECT GUIDE.
TP
TP
TP
AKIRA-ONII-CHAAAN!!
HEYA, JIJI! THANKS FOR COMING ON SUCH SHORT NOTICE. WHERE'S CLARA AND ANNA?
THEY HAD AN ERRAND TO RUN, SO THEY WENT TO HAMA-SAN'S PLACE.
YOUR "PERFECT GUIDE" IS A KID...?

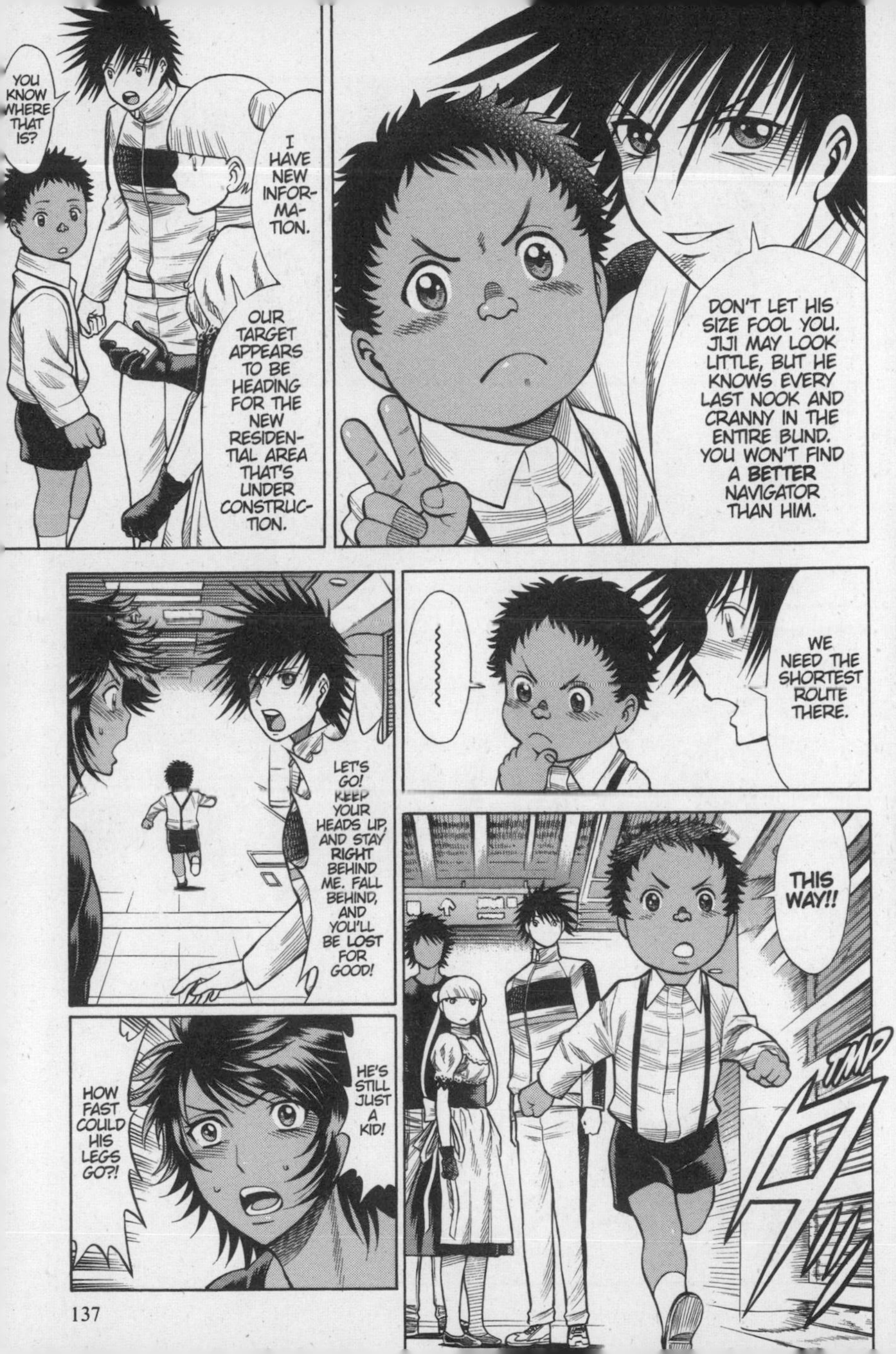
DON'T LET HIS SIZE FOOL YOU. JIJI MAY LOOK LITTLE, BUT HE KNOWS EVERY LAST NOOK AND CRANNY IN THE ENTIRE BUND. YOU WON'T FIND A BETTER NAVIGATOR THAN HIM.
I HAVE NEW INFORMATION.
OUR TARGET APPEARS TO BE HEADING FOR THE NEW RESIDENTIAL AREA THAT'S UNDER CONSTRUCTION.
YOU KNOW WHERE THAT IS?
WE NEED THE SHORTEST ROUTE THERE.
~~~
THIS WAY!!
TMP
LET'S GO! KEEP YOUR HEADS UP, AND STAY RIGHT BEHIND ME. FALL BEHIND, AND YOU'LL BE LOST FOR GOOD!
HE'S STILL JUST A KID!
HOW FAST COULD HIS LEGS GO?!
~~~

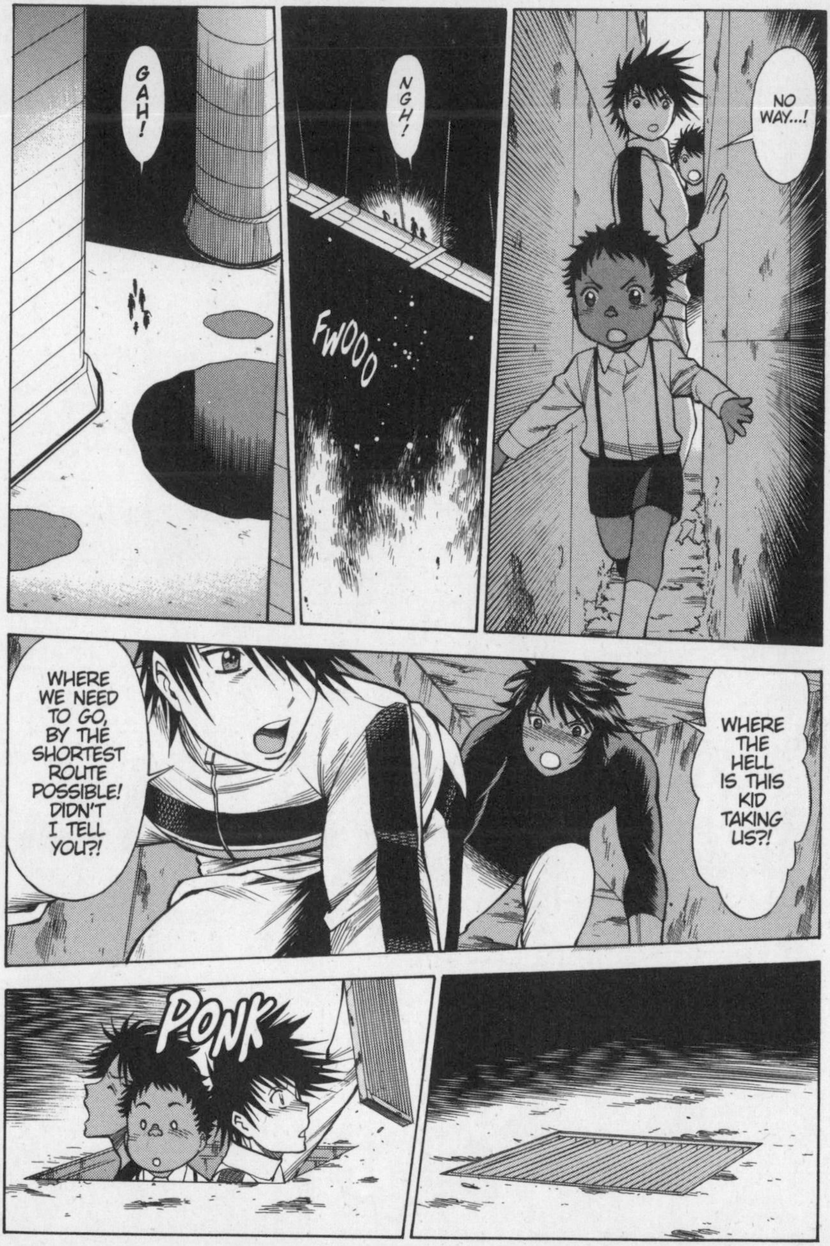
NO WAY...!
NGH!
FWOOO
GAH!
WHERE THE HELL IS THIS KID TAKING US?!
WHERE WE NEED TO GO, BY THE SHORTEST ROUTE POSSIBLE! DIDN'T I TELL YOU?!
PONK

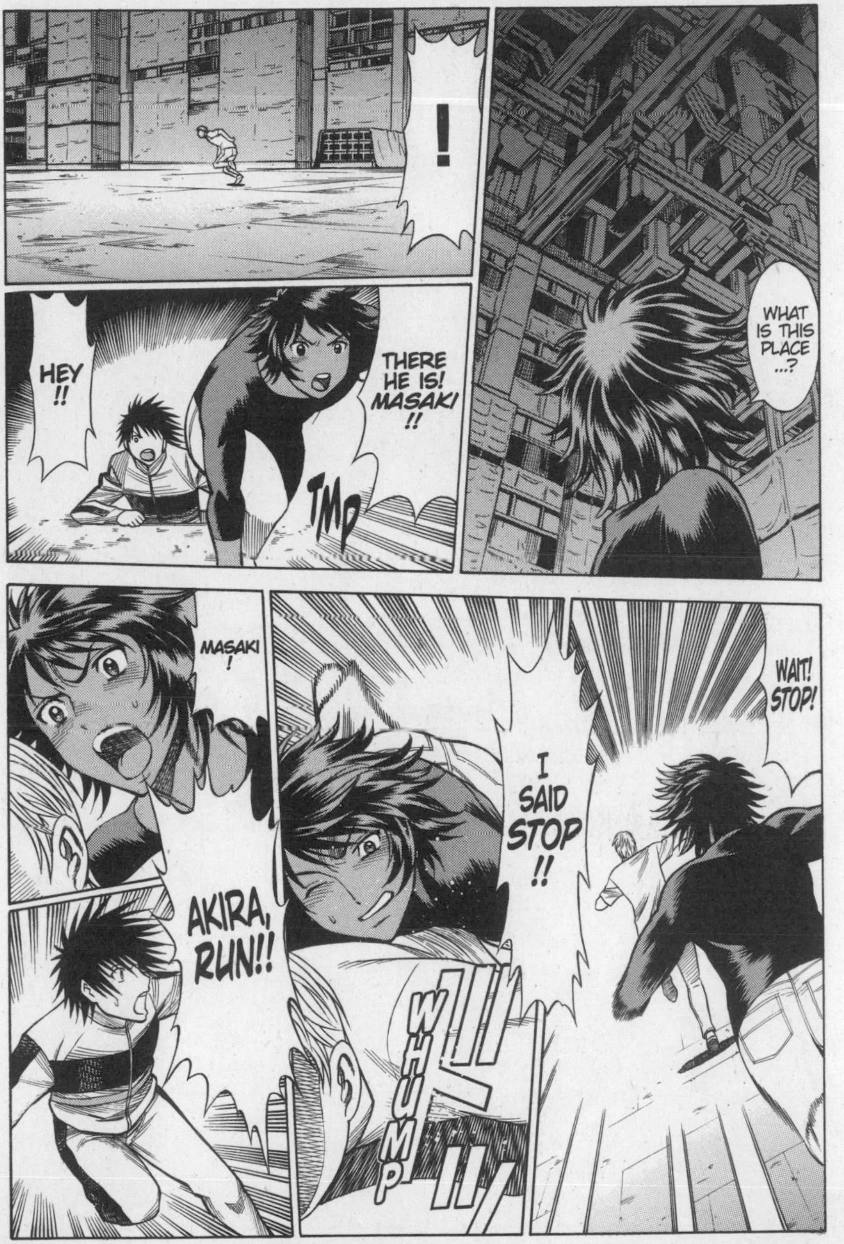
WHAT IS THIS PLACE ...?
!
THERE HE IS! MASAKI!!
HEY!!
TMP
WAIT! STOP!
I SAID STOP!!
WHUMP
MASAKI!
AKIRA, RUN!!

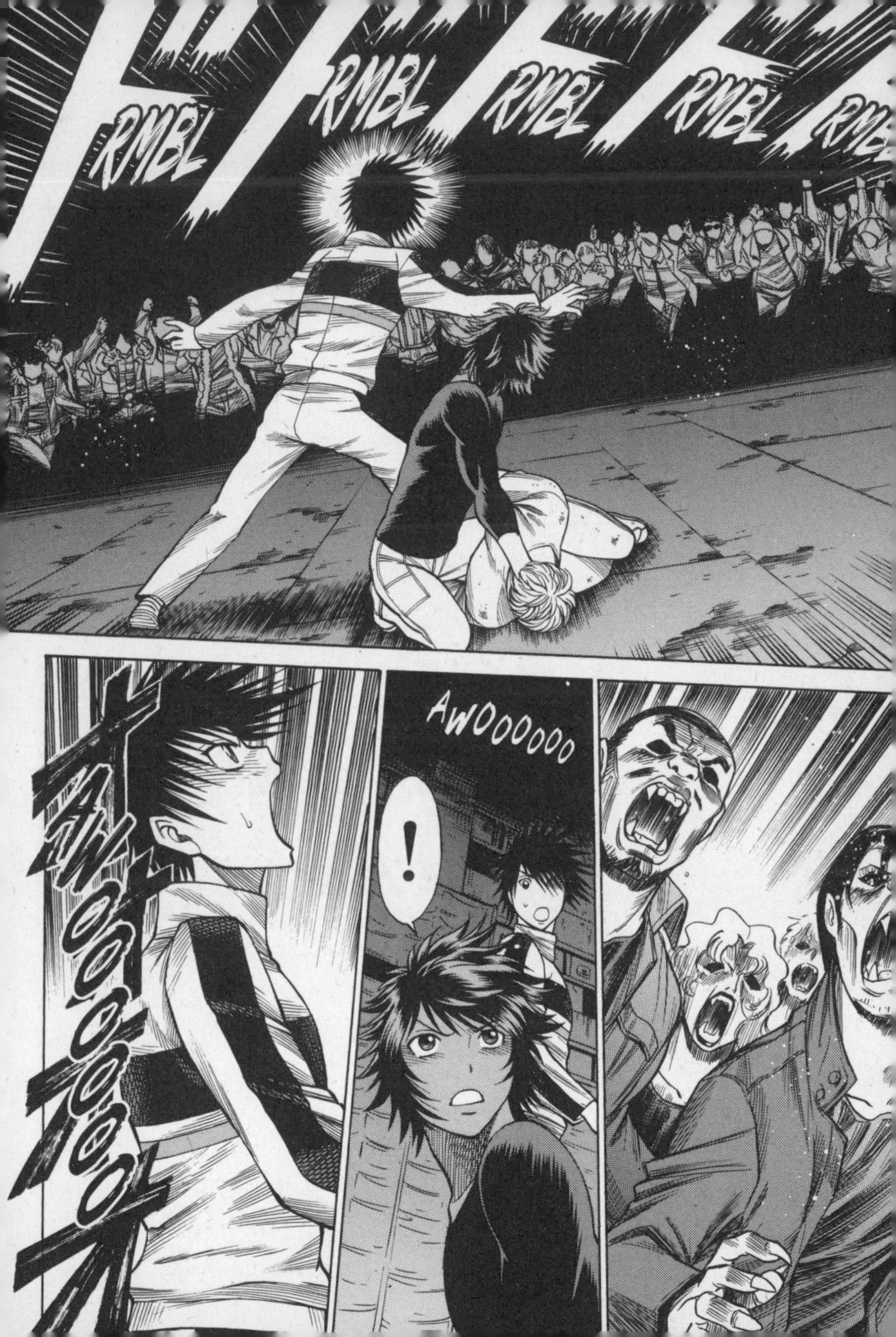
RMBL RMBL RMBL RMBL RMBL
AWOOOOOO
!
AWOOOOOOOK

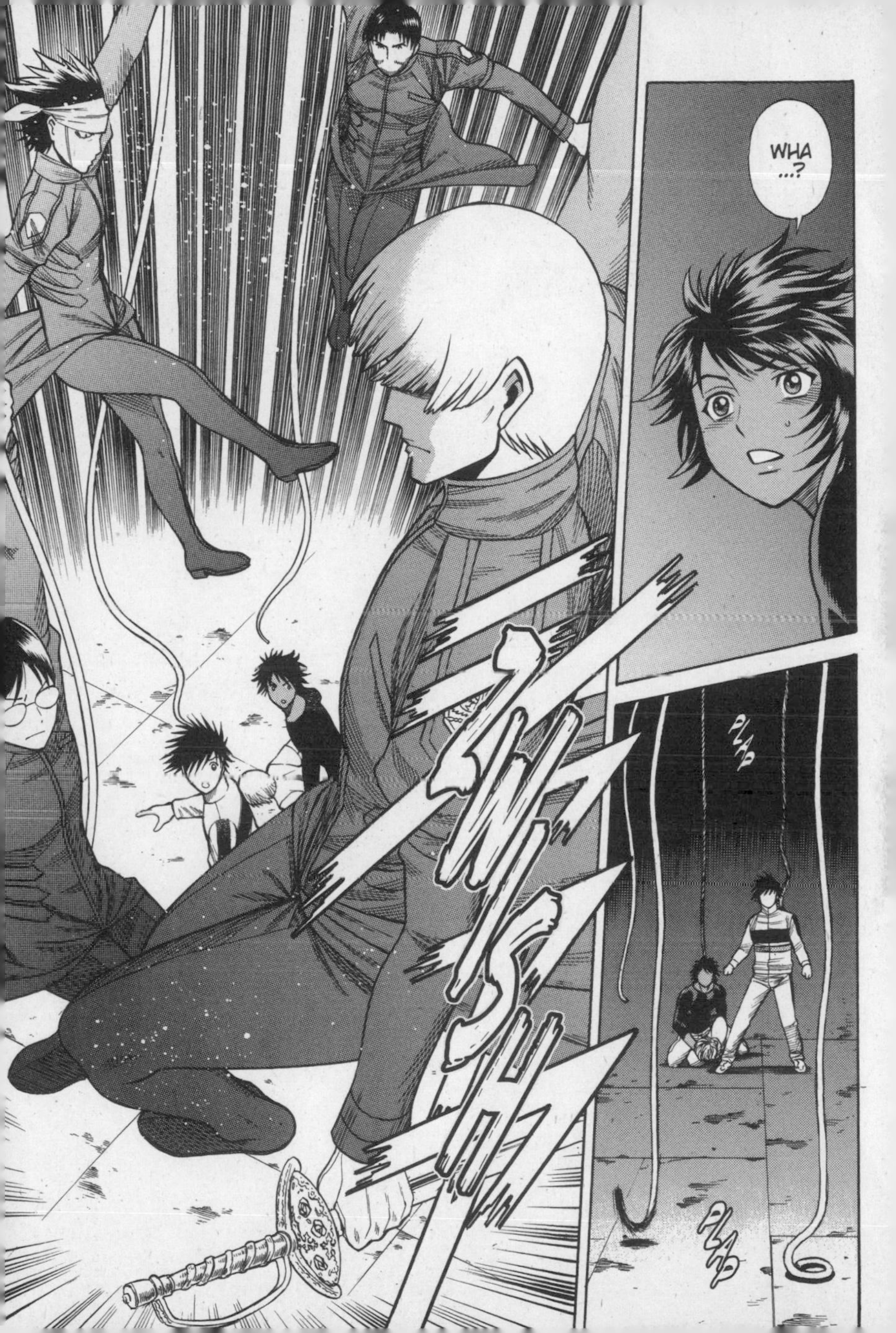
WHA ...?
PLAP
PLAP

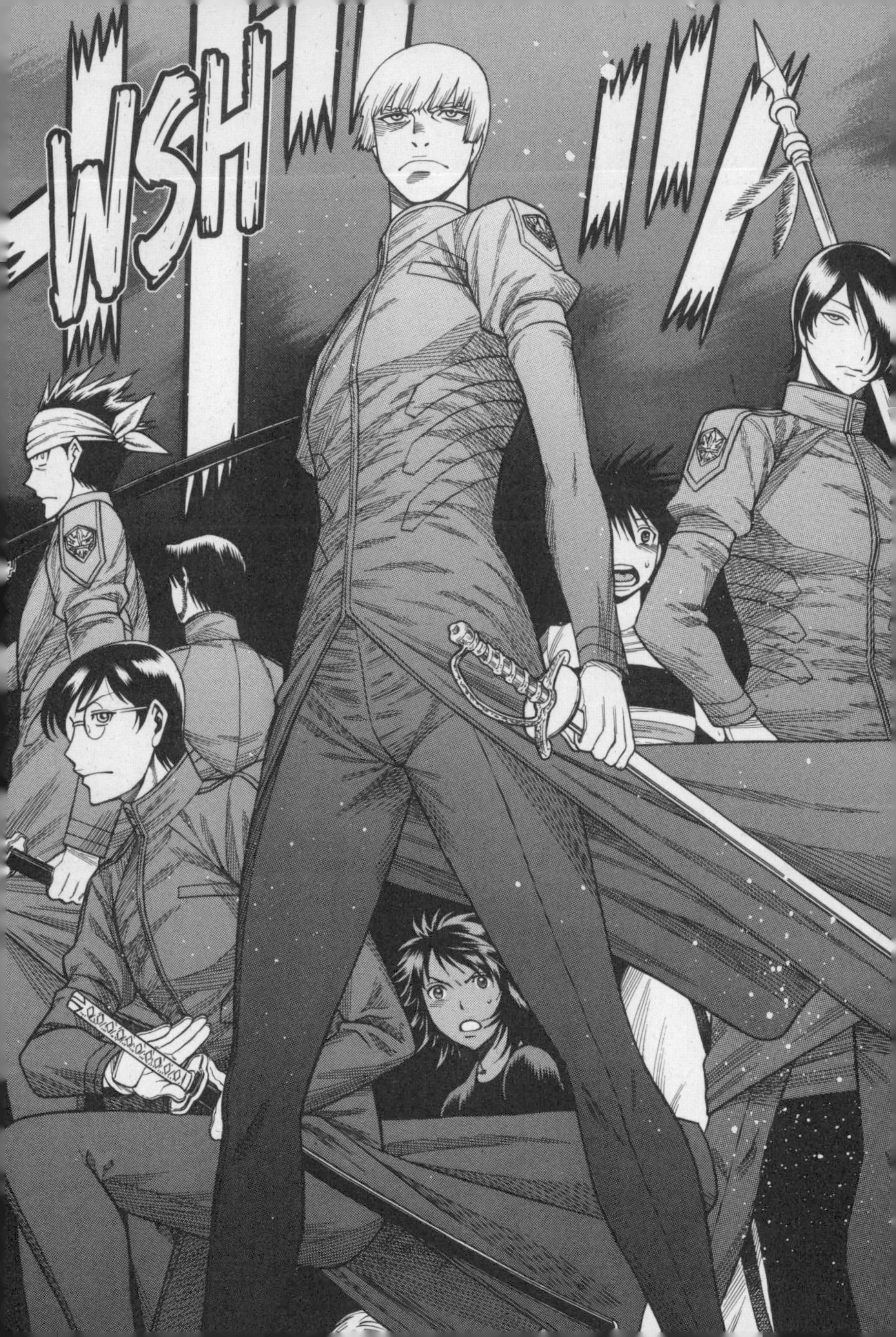
WSH

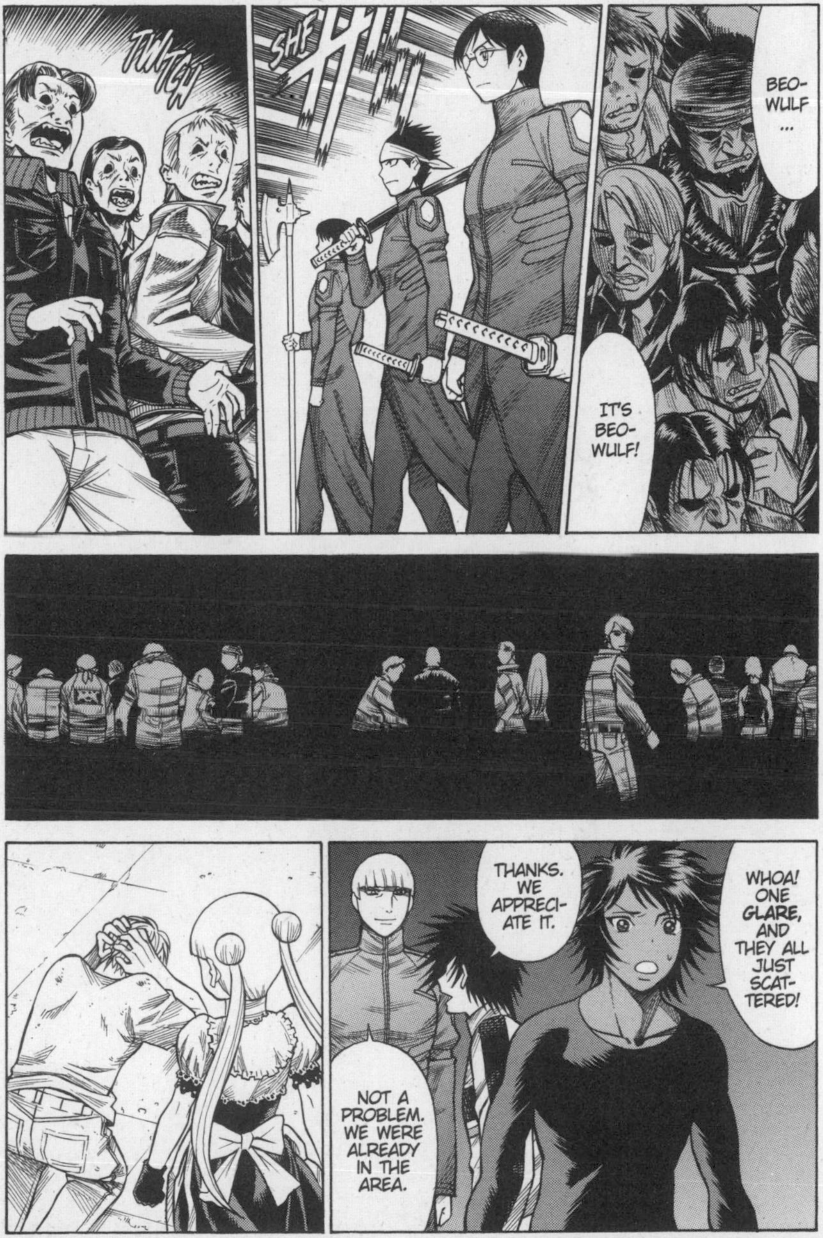
BEO-WULF ...
IT'S BEO-WULF!
SHF
TWITCH
WHOA! ONE GLARE, AND THEY ALL JUST SCAT-TERED!
THANKS. WE APPRECI-ATE IT.
NOT A PROBLEM. WE WERE ALREADY IN THE AREA.

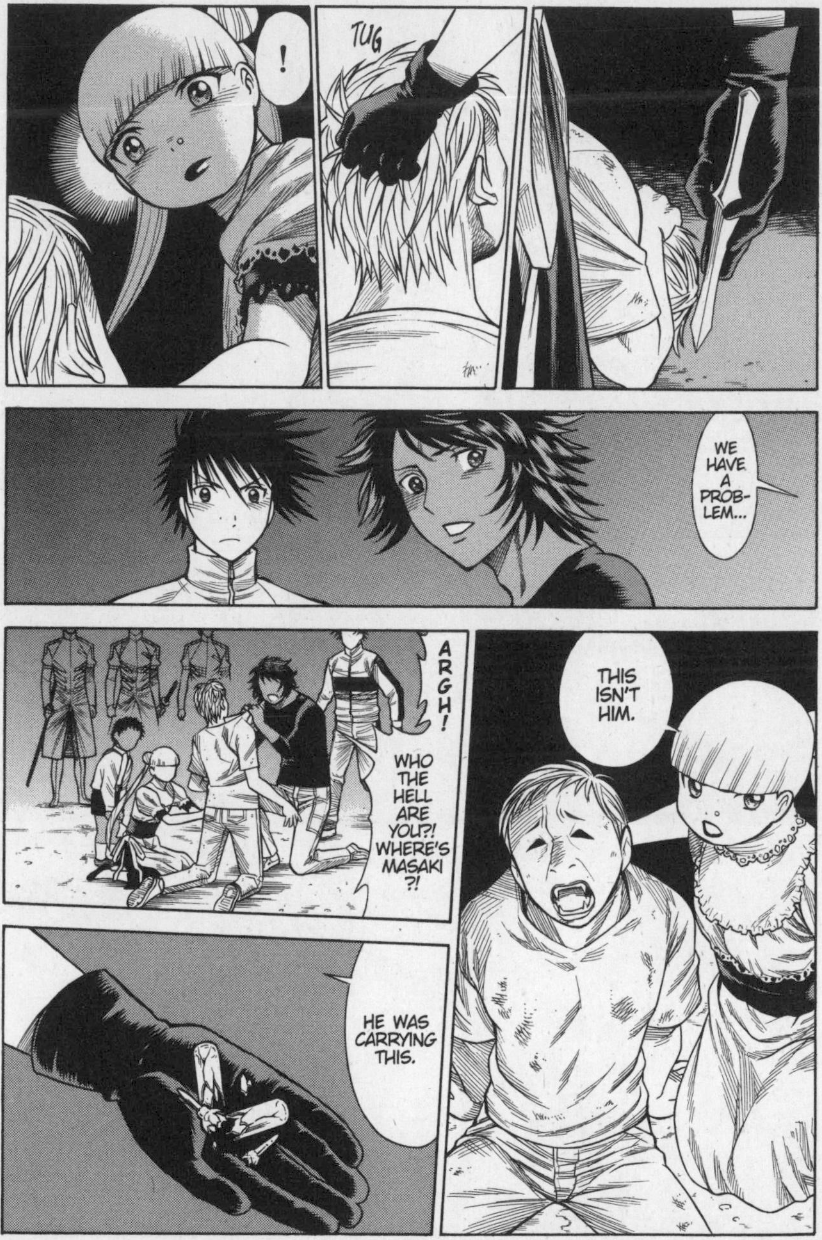
TUG
!
WE HAVE A PROB-LEM...
THIS ISN'T HIM.
ARGH!
WHO THE HELL ARE YOU?! WHERE'S MASAKI ?!
HE WAS CARRYING THIS.

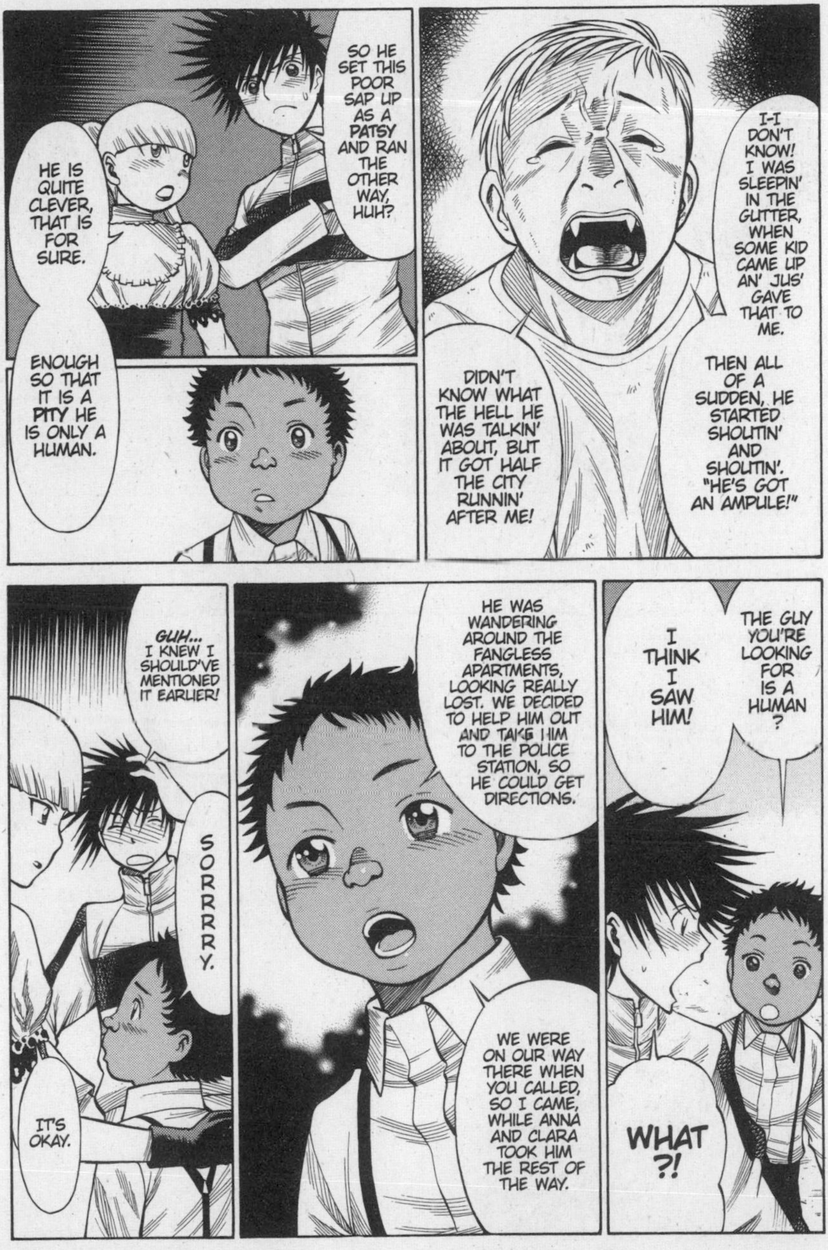
I-I DON'T KNOW! I WAS SLEEPIN' IN THE GUTTER, WHEN SOME KID CAME UP AN' JUS' GAVE THAT TO ME.
THEN ALL OF A SUDDEN, HE STARTED SHOUTIN' AND SHOUTIN'. "HE'S GOT AN AMPULE!"
DIDN'T KNOW WHAT THE HELL HE WAS TALKIN' ABOUT, BUT IT GOT HALF THE CITY RUNNIN' AFTER ME!
SO HE SET THIS POOR SAP UP AS A PATSY AND RAN THE OTHER WAY, HUH?
HE IS QUITE CLEVER, THAT IS FOR SURE.
ENOUGH SO THAT IT IS A PITY HE IS ONLY A HUMAN.
THE GUY YOU'RE LOOKING FOR IS A HUMAN?
I THINK I SAW HIM!
WHAT ?!
HE WAS WANDERING AROUND THE FANGLESS APARTMENTS, LOOKING REALLY LOST. WE DECIDED TO HELP HIM OUT AND TAKE HIM TO THE POLICE STATION, SO HE COULD GET DIRECTIONS.
WE WERE ON OUR WAY THERE WHEN YOU CALLED, SO I CAME, WHILE ANNA AND CLARA TOOK HIM THE REST OF THE WAY.
GUH... I KNEW I SHOULD'VE MENTIONED IT EARLIER!
SORRRRY.
IT'S OKAY.

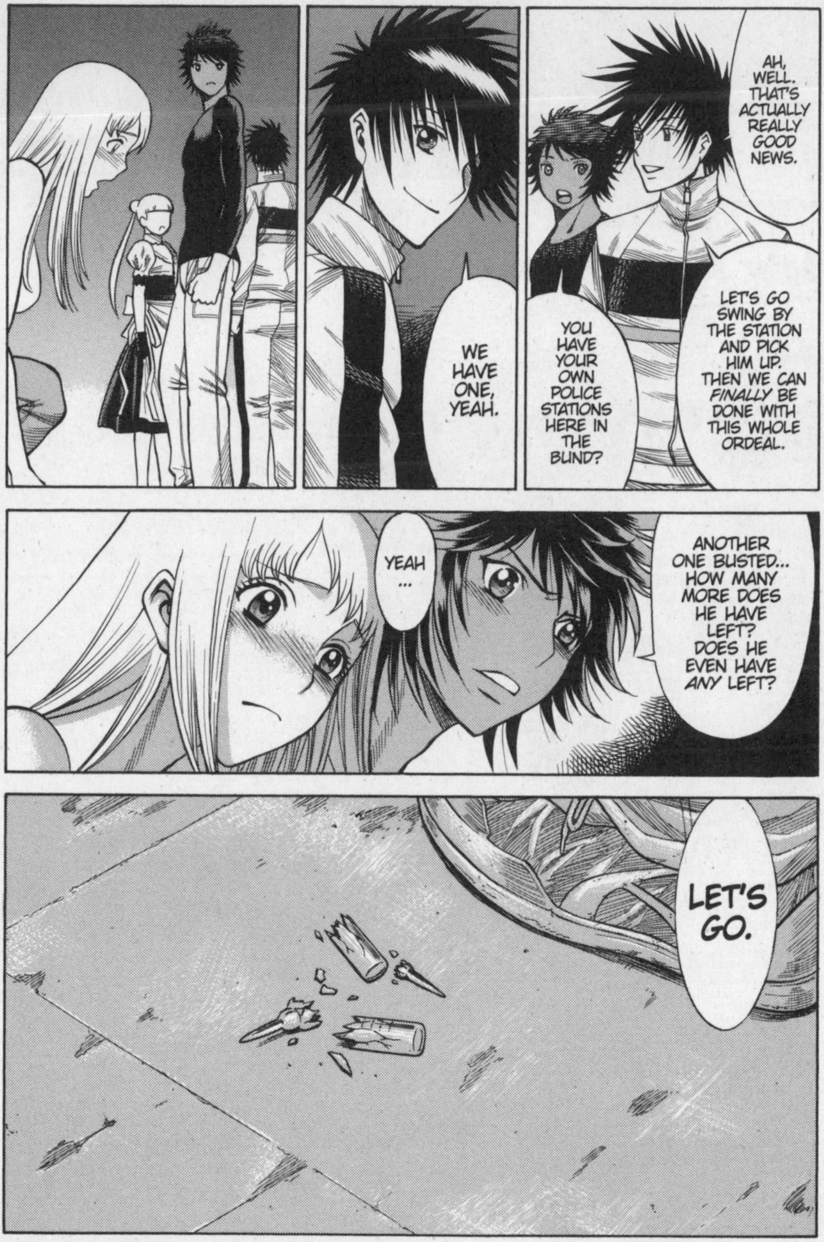
AH, WELL. THAT'S ACTUALLY REALLY GOOD NEWS.
LET'S GO SWING BY THE STATION AND PICK HIM UP. THEN WE CAN *FINALLY* BE DONE WITH THIS WHOLE ORDEAL.
YOU HAVE YOUR OWN POLICE STATIONS HERE IN THE BUND?
WE HAVE ONE, YEAH.
ANOTHER ONE BUSTED... HOW MANY MORE DOES HE HAVE LEFT? DOES HE EVEN HAVE *ANY* LEFT?
YEAH ...
LET'S GO.

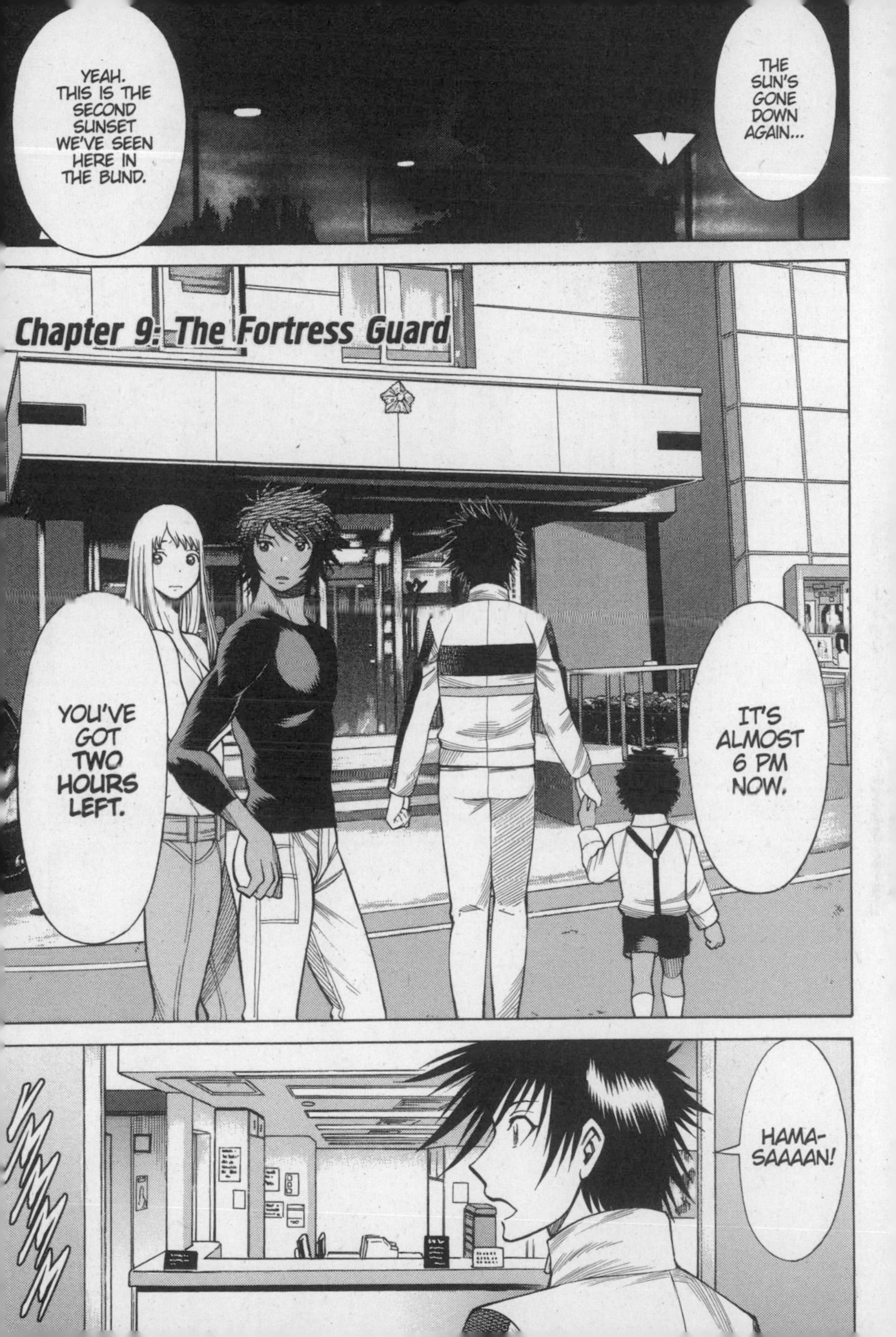
THE SUN'S GONE DOWN AGAIN...
YEAH. THIS IS THE SECOND SUNSET WE'VE SEEN HERE IN THE BUND.
Chapter 9: The Fortress Guard
IT'S ALMOST 6 PM NOW.
YOU'VE GOT TWO HOURS LEFT.
HAMA-SAAAAN!

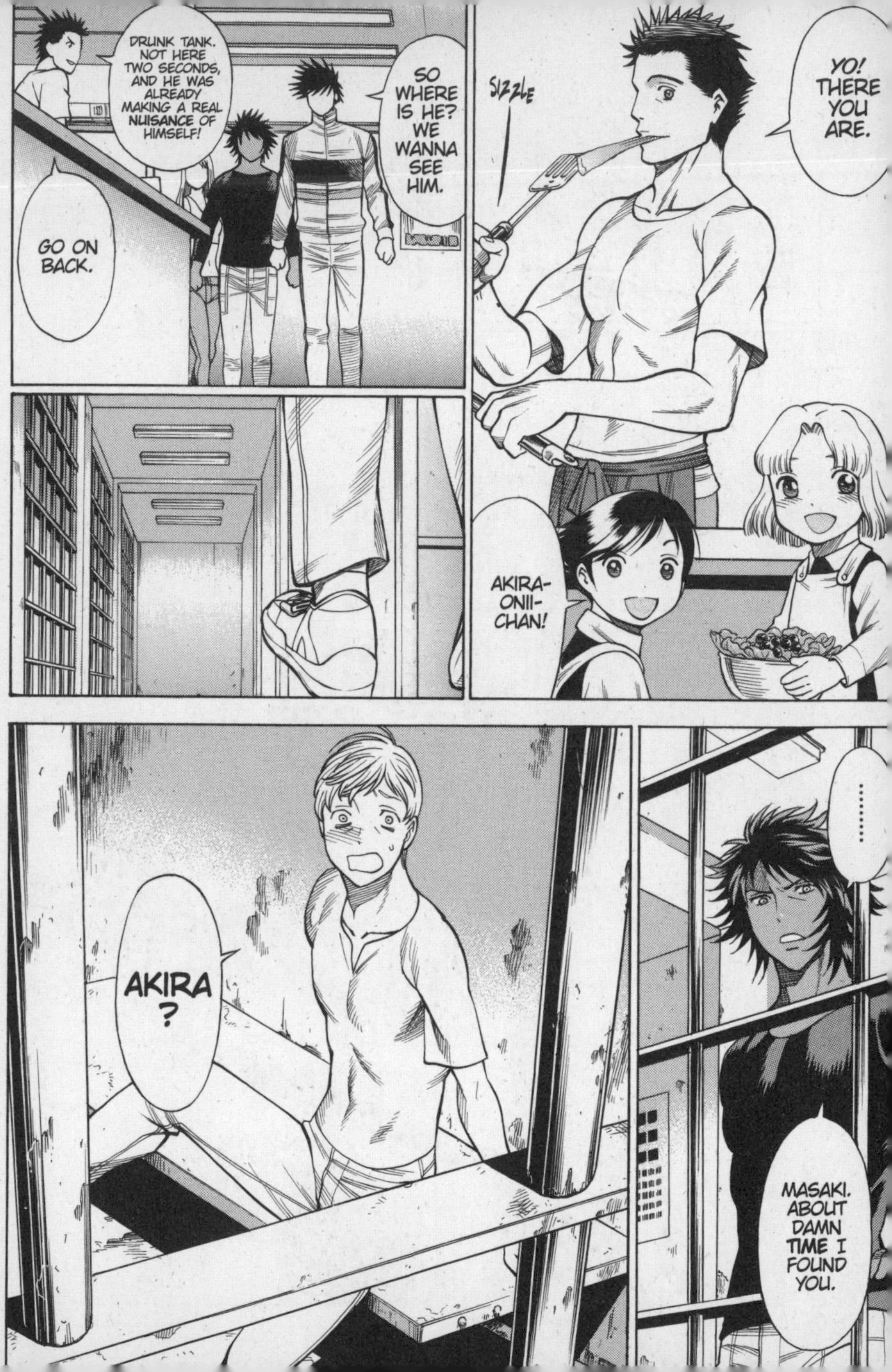
YO! THERE YOU ARE.
SIZZLE
AKIRA-ONII-CHAN!
SO WHERE IS HE? WE WANNA SEE HIM.
DRUNK TANK. NOT HERE TWO SECONDS, AND HE WAS ALREADY MAKING A REAL NUISANCE OF HIMSELF!
GO ON BACK.
....
MASAKI. ABOUT DAMN TIME I FOUND YOU.
AKIRA?

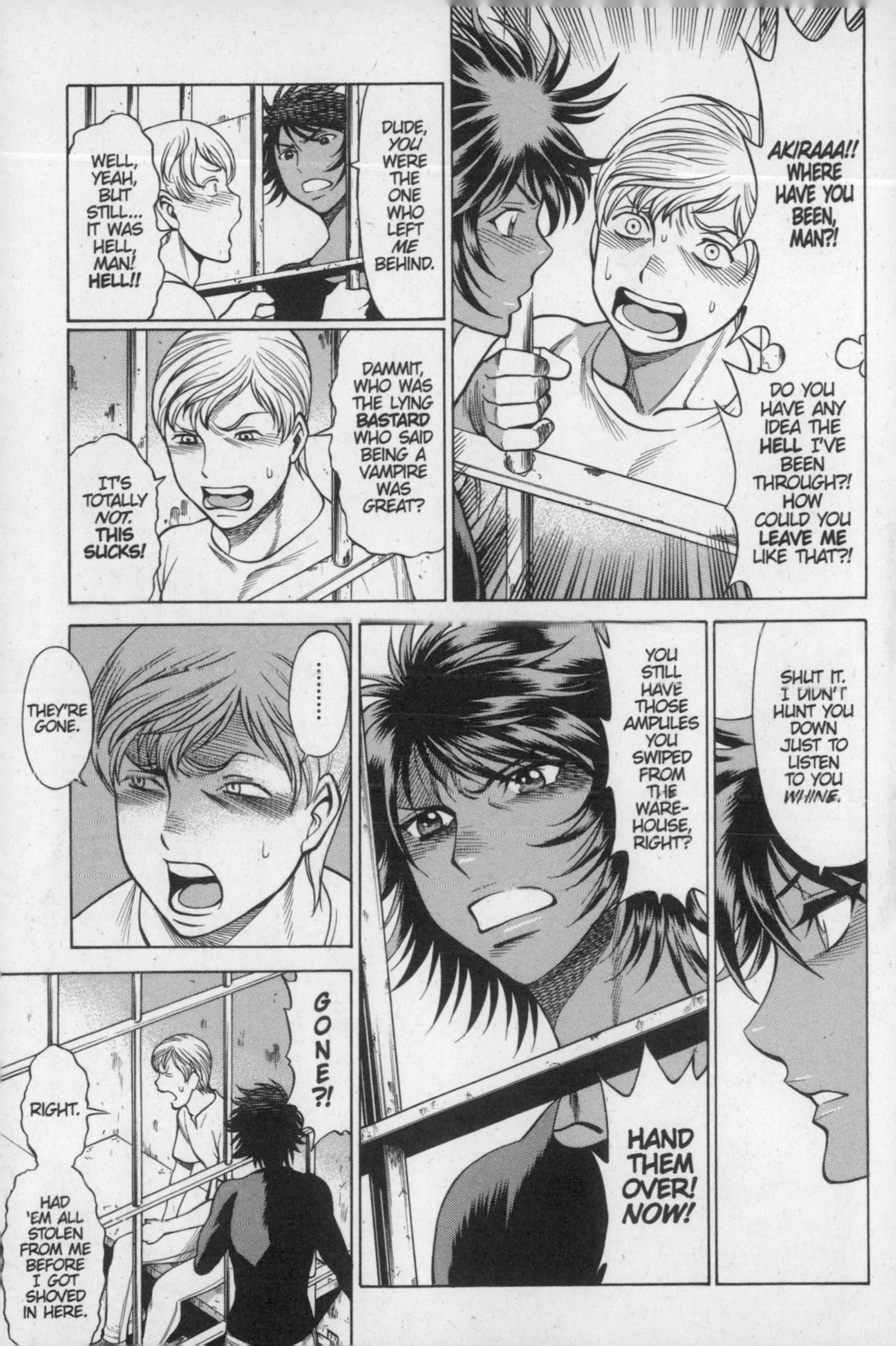
AKIRAAA!! WHERE HAVE YOU BEEN, MAN?!
DO YOU HAVE ANY IDEA THE HELL I'VE BEEN THROUGH?! HOW COULD YOU LEAVE ME LIKE THAT?!
DUDE, YOU WERE THE ONE WHO LEFT ME BEHIND.
WELL, YEAH, BUT STILL... IT WAS HELL, MAN! HELL!!
DAMMIT, WHO WAS THE LYING BASTARD WHO SAID BEING A VAMPIRE WAS GREAT?
IT'S TOTALLY NOT. THIS SUCKS!
SHUT IT. I DIDN'T HUNT YOU DOWN JUST TO LISTEN TO YOU WHINE.
YOU STILL HAVE THOSE AMPULES YOU SWIPED FROM THE WARE-HOUSE, RIGHT?
HAND THEM OVER! NOW!
....
THEY'RE GONE.
GONE?!
RIGHT.
HAD 'EM ALL STOLEN FROM ME BEFORE I GOT SHOVED IN HERE.

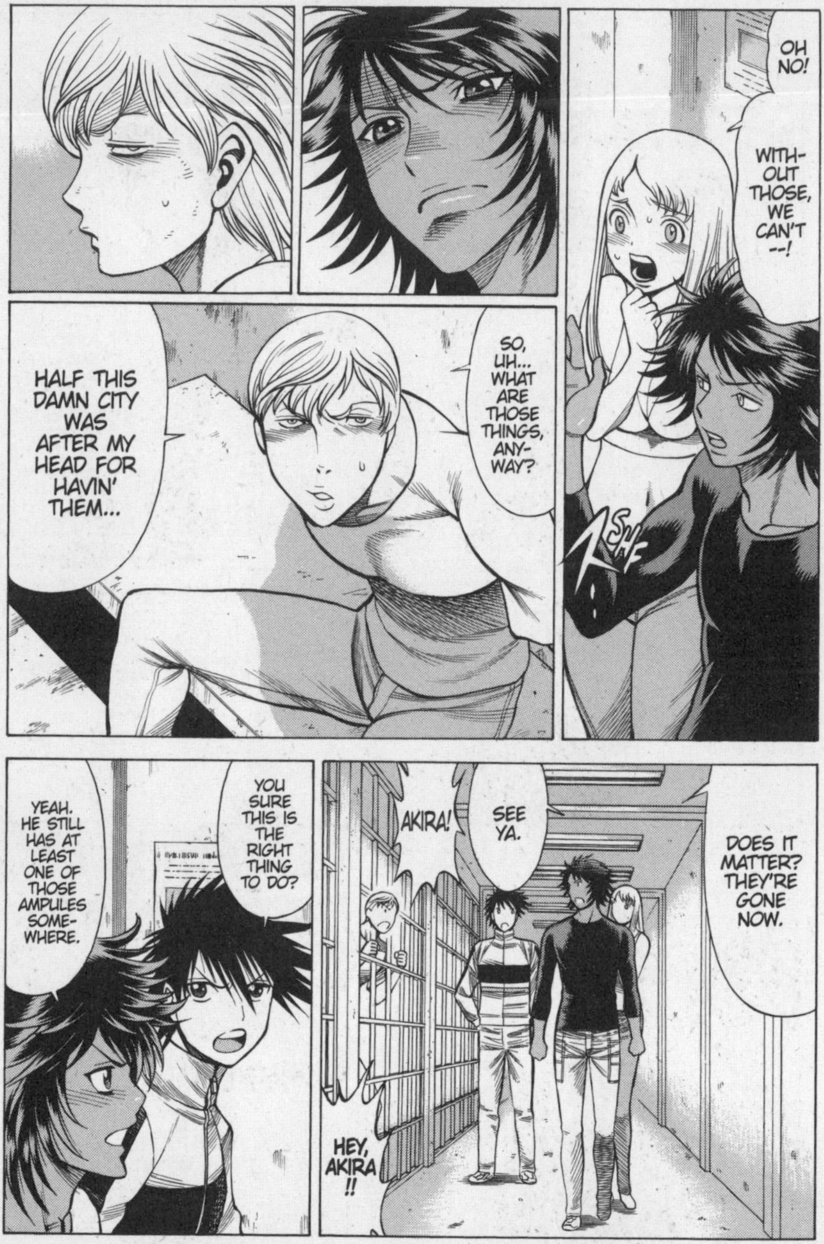
OH NO!
WITH-OUT THOSE, WE CAN'T --!
SHF
SO, UH... WHAT ARE THOSE THINGS, ANY-WAY?
HALF THIS DAMN CITY WAS AFTER MY HEAD FOR HAVIN' THEM...
DOES IT MATTER? THEY'RE GONE NOW.
SEE YA.
AKIRA!
HEY, AKIRA !!
YOU SURE THIS IS THE RIGHT THING TO DO?
YEAH. HE STILL HAS AT LEAST ONE OF THOSE AMPULES SOME-WHERE.

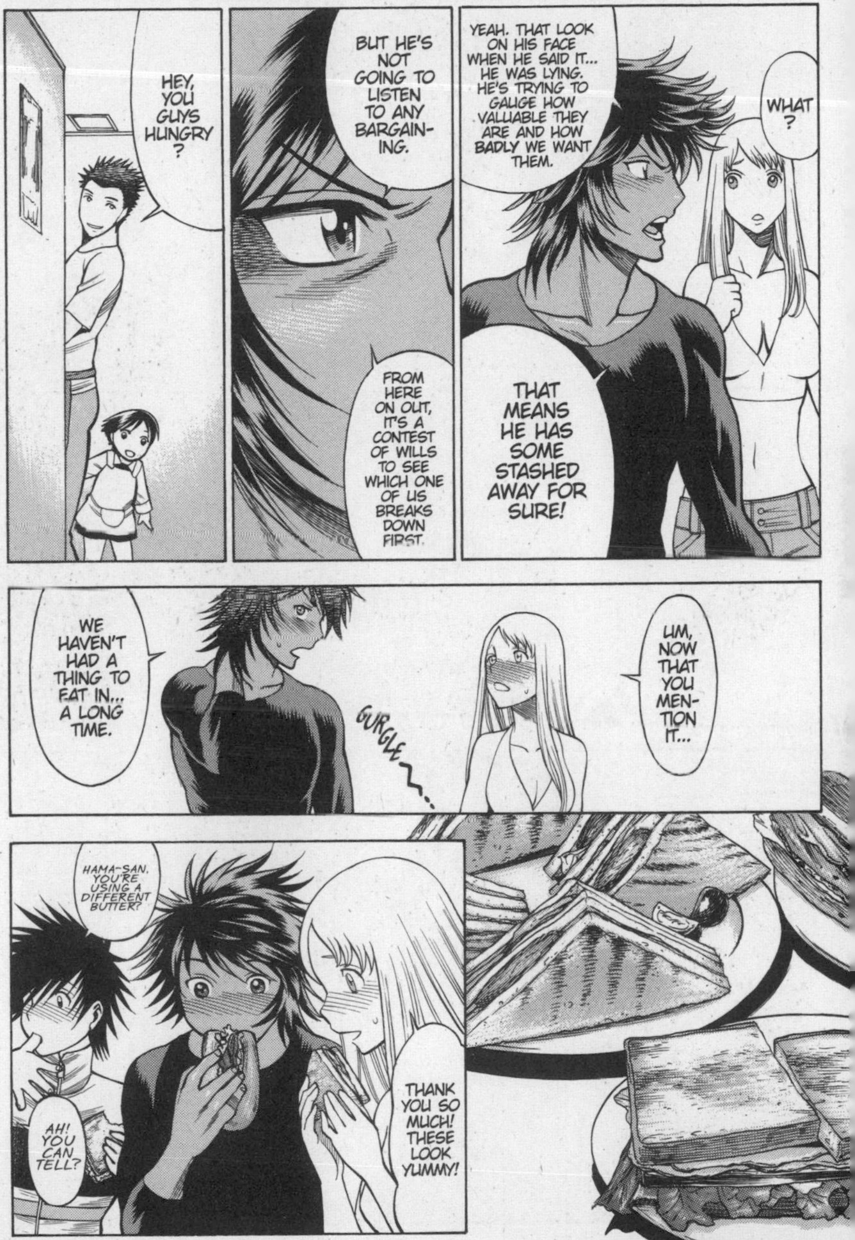
WHAT?
YEAH. THAT LOOK ON HIS FACE WHEN HE SAID IT... HE WAS LYING. HE'S TRYING TO GAUGE HOW VALUABLE THEY ARE AND HOW BADLY WE WANT THEM.
THAT MEANS HE HAS SOME STASHED AWAY FOR SURE!
BUT HE'S NOT GOING TO LISTEN TO ANY BARGAIN-ING.
FROM HERE ON OUT, IT'S A CONTEST OF WILLS TO SEE WHICH ONE OF US BREAKS DOWN FIRST.
HEY, YOU GUYS HUNGRY?
UM, NOW THAT YOU MEN-TION IT...
GURGLE...
WE HAVEN'T HAD A THING TO EAT IN... A LONG TIME.
THANK YOU SO MUCH! THESE LOOK YUMMY!
HAMA-SAN, YOU'RE USING A DIFFERENT BUTTER?
AH! YOU CAN TELL?

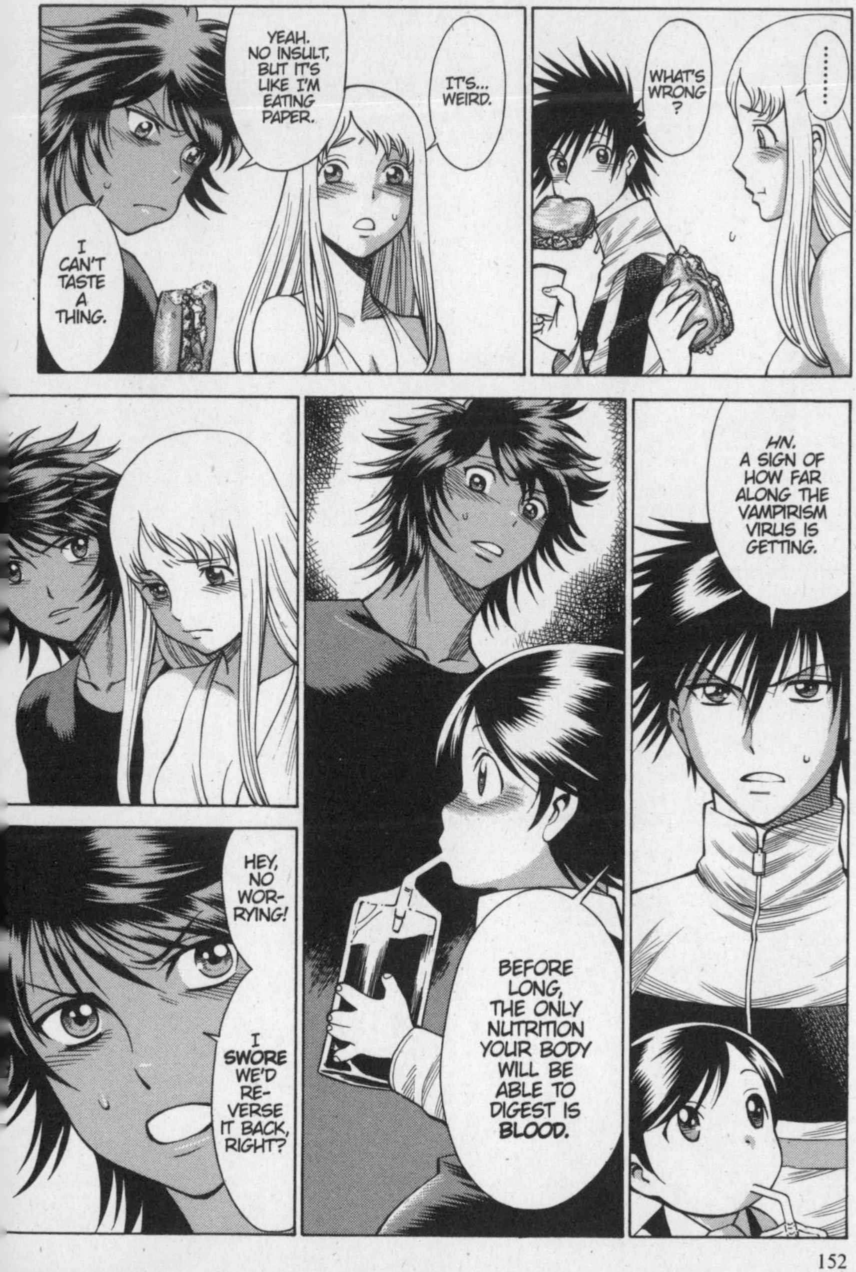
……
WHAT'S WRONG?
IT'S... WEIRD.
YEAH. NO INSULT, BUT IT'S LIKE I'M EATING PAPER.
I CAN'T TASTE A THING.
HN. A SIGN OF HOW FAR ALONG THE VAMPIRISM VIRUS IS GETTING.
BEFORE LONG, THE ONLY NUTRITION YOUR BODY WILL BE ABLE TO DIGEST IS BLOOD.
HEY, NO WOR-RYING!
I SWORE WE'D RE-VERSE IT BACK, RIGHT?

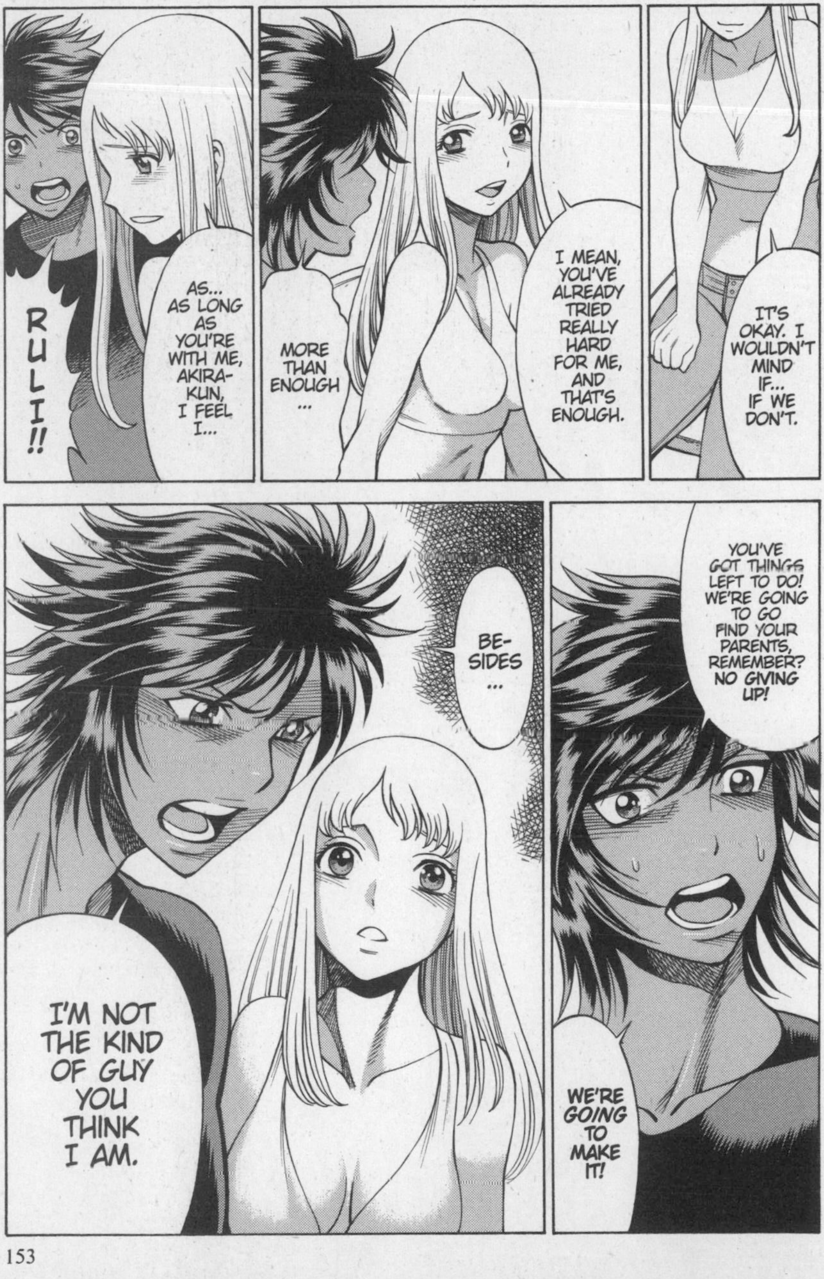
IT'S OKAY. I WOULDN'T MIND IF... IF WE DON'T.
I MEAN, YOU'VE ALREADY TRIED REALLY HARD FOR ME, AND THAT'S ENOUGH.
MORE THAN ENOUGH ...
AS... AS LONG AS YOU'RE WITH ME, AKIRA-KUN, I FEEL I...
RULI!!
YOU'VE GOT THINGS LEFT TO DO! WE'RE GOING TO GO FIND YOUR PARENTS, REMEMBER? NO GIVING UP!
WE'RE GOING TO MAKE IT!
BE-SIDES ...
I'M NOT THE KIND OF GUY YOU THINK I AM.

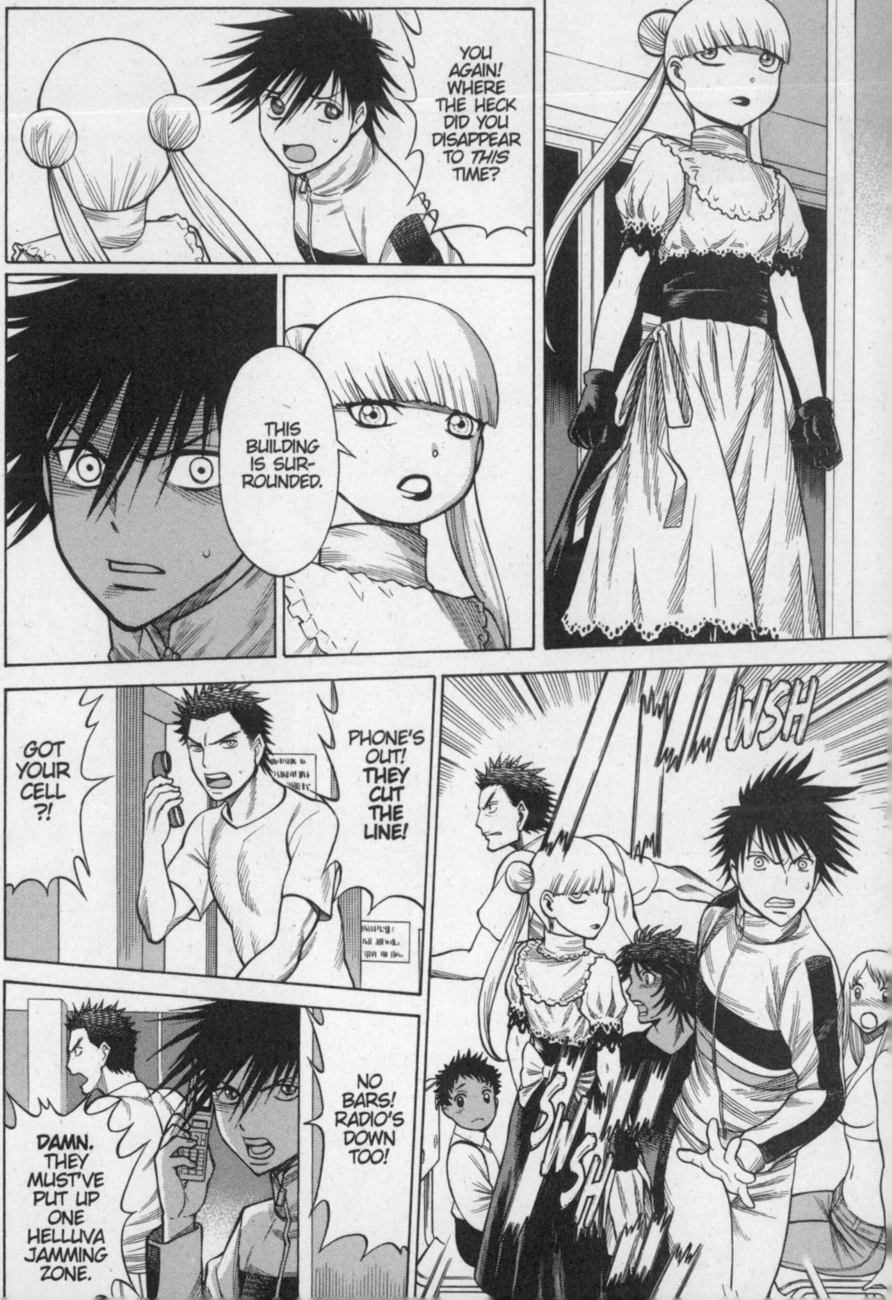
YOU AGAIN! WHERE THE HECK DID YOU DISAPPEAR TO *THIS* TIME?
THIS BUILDING IS SUR-ROUNDED.
WSH
PHONE'S OUT! THEY CUT THE LINE!
GOT YOUR CELL ?!
NO BARS! RADIO'S DOWN TOO!
DAMN. THEY MUST'VE PUT UP ONE HELLUVA JAMMING ZONE.

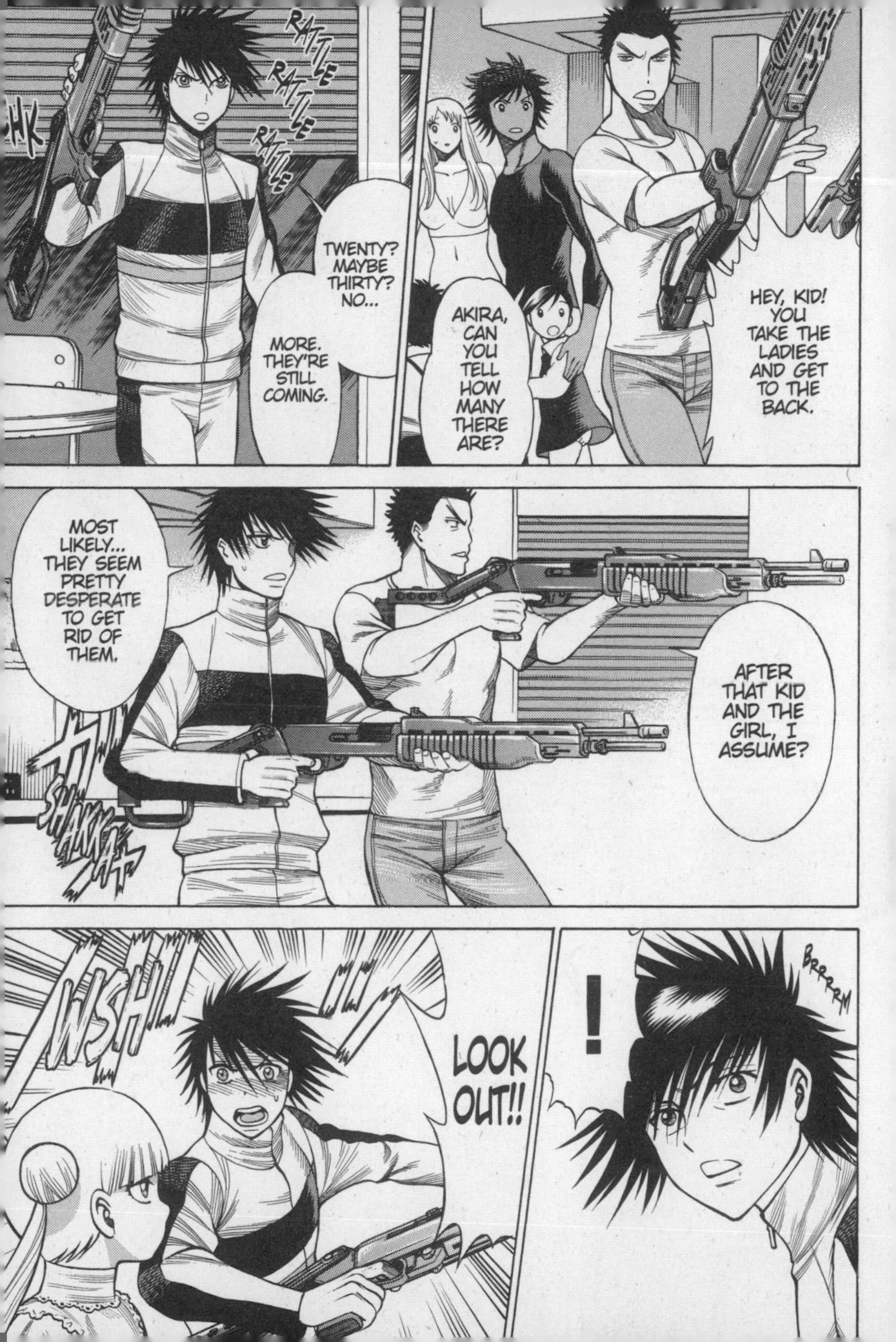
HEY, KID! YOU TAKE THE LADIES AND GET TO THE BACK.
AKIRA, CAN YOU TELL HOW MANY THERE ARE?
RATTLE RATTLE RATTLE
TWENTY? MAYBE THIRTY? NO...
MORE. THEY'RE STILL COMING.
AFTER THAT KID AND THE GIRL, I ASSUME?
MOST LIKELY... THEY SEEM PRETTY DESPERATE TO GET RID OF THEM.
!
LOOK OUT!!
WSH!!

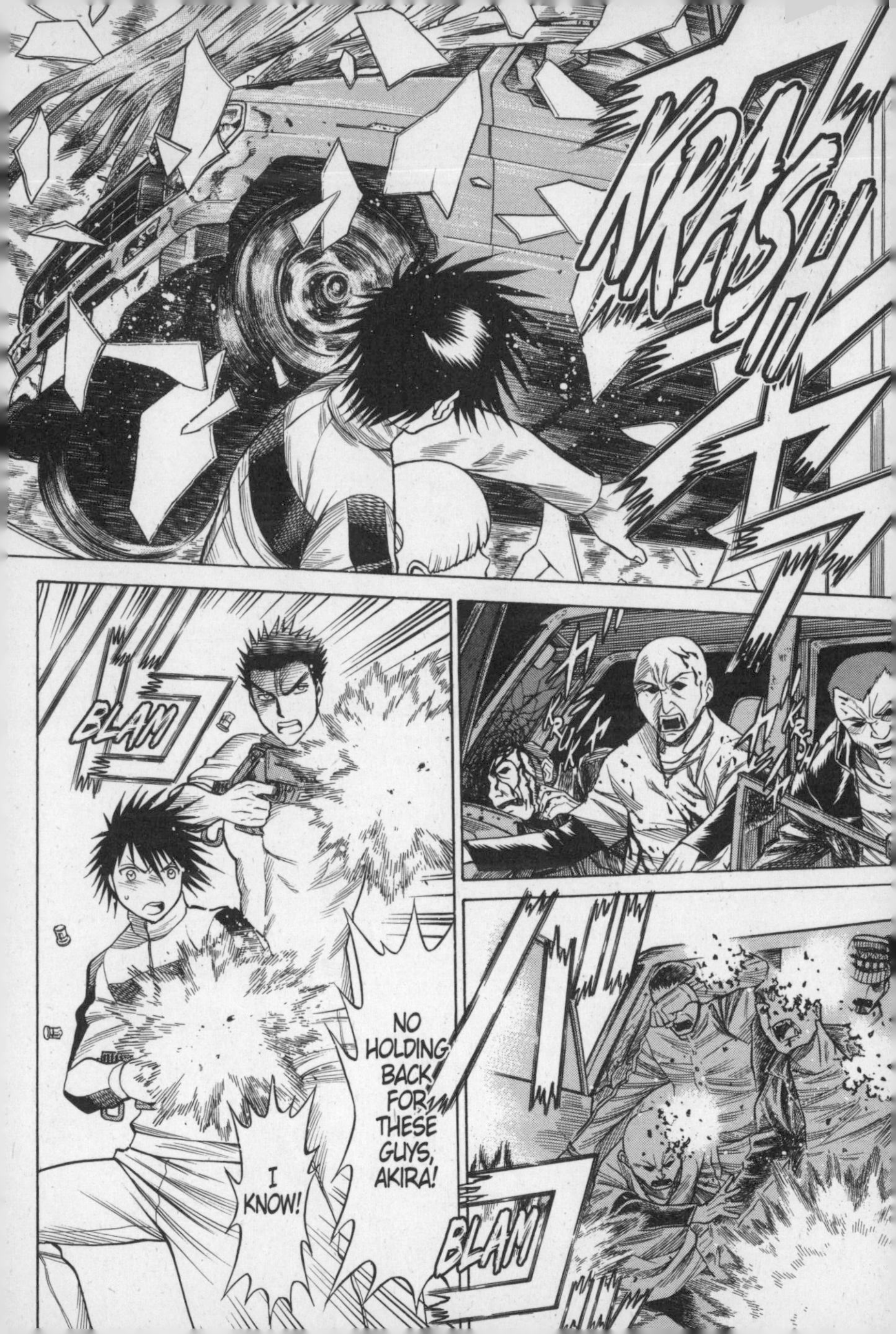
KRASH
KRSH
KRUK
BLAM
NO HOLDING BACK FOR THESE GUYS, AKIRA!
I KNOW!
BLAM

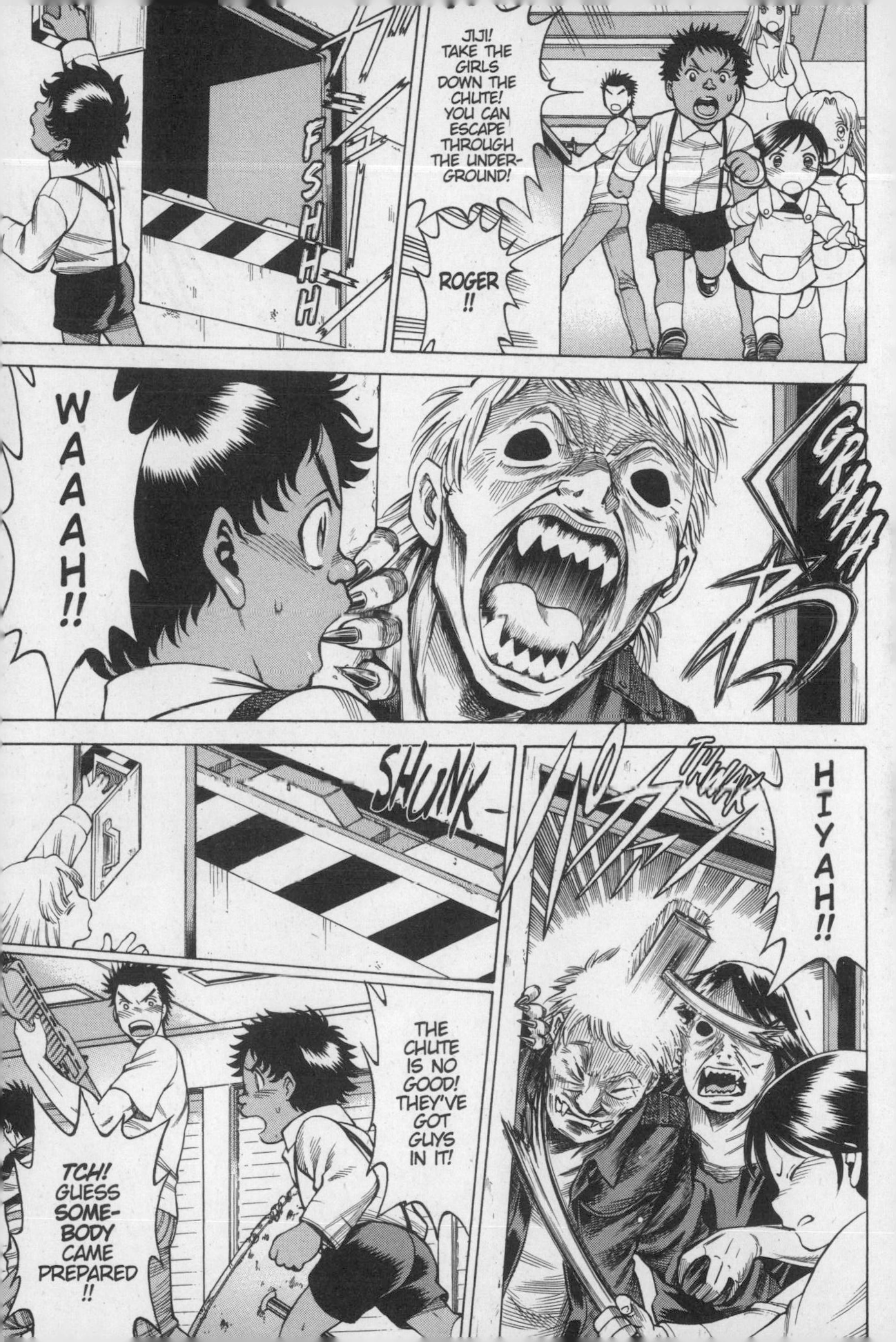
JIJI! TAKE THE GIRLS DOWN THE CHUTE! YOU CAN ESCAPE THROUGH THE UNDER-GROUND!
ROGER!!
FSHHHH
GRAAA
WAAAAH!!
HIYAH!!
SHUNK
THE CHUTE IS NO GOOD! THEY'VE GOT GUYS IN IT!
TCH! GUESS SOME-BODY CAME PREPARED!!

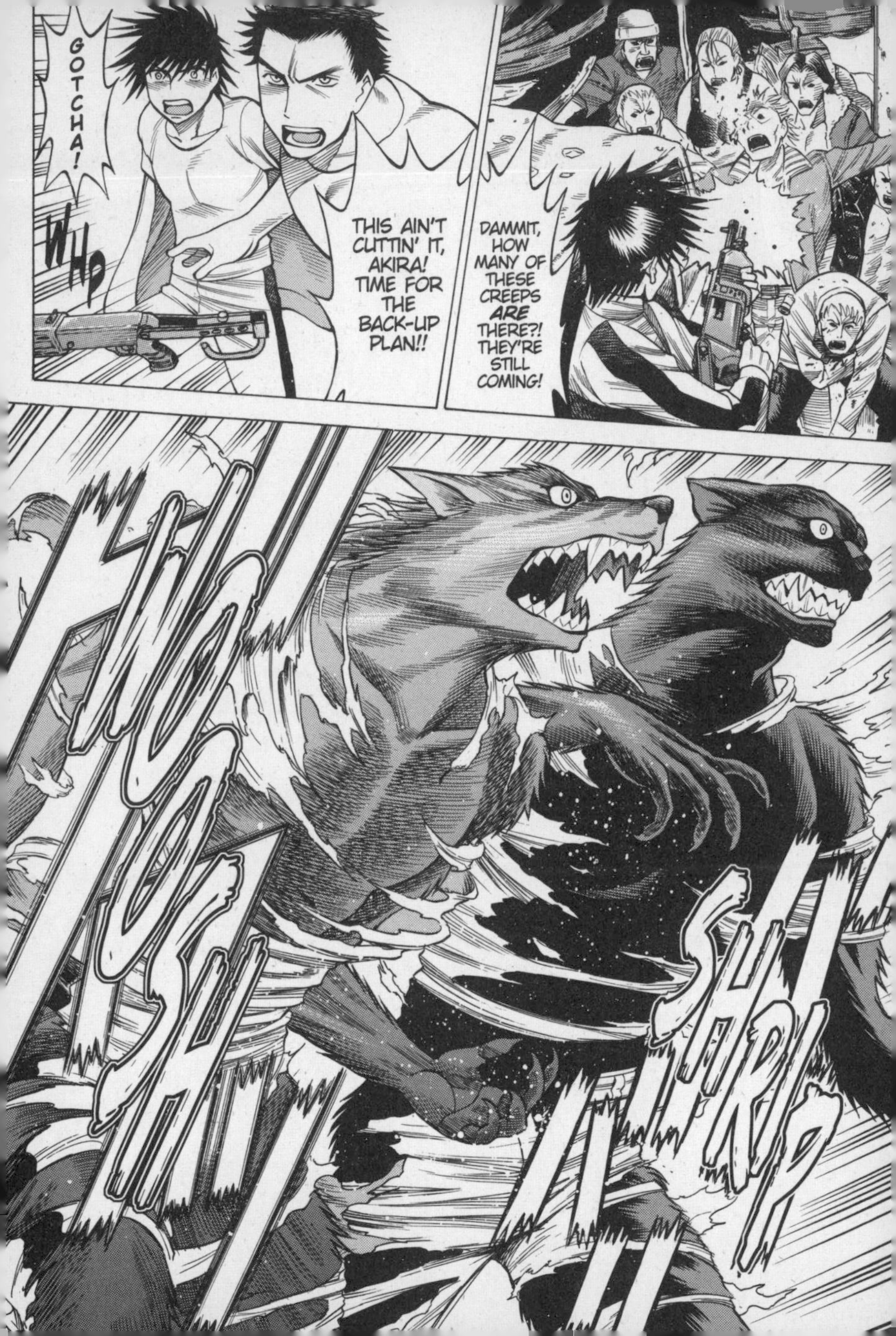
DAMMIT, HOW MANY OF THESE CREEPS ARE THERE?! THEY'RE STILL COMING!
THIS AIN'T CUTTIN' IT, AKIRA! TIME FOR THE BACK-UP PLAN!!
GOTCHA!
WHP

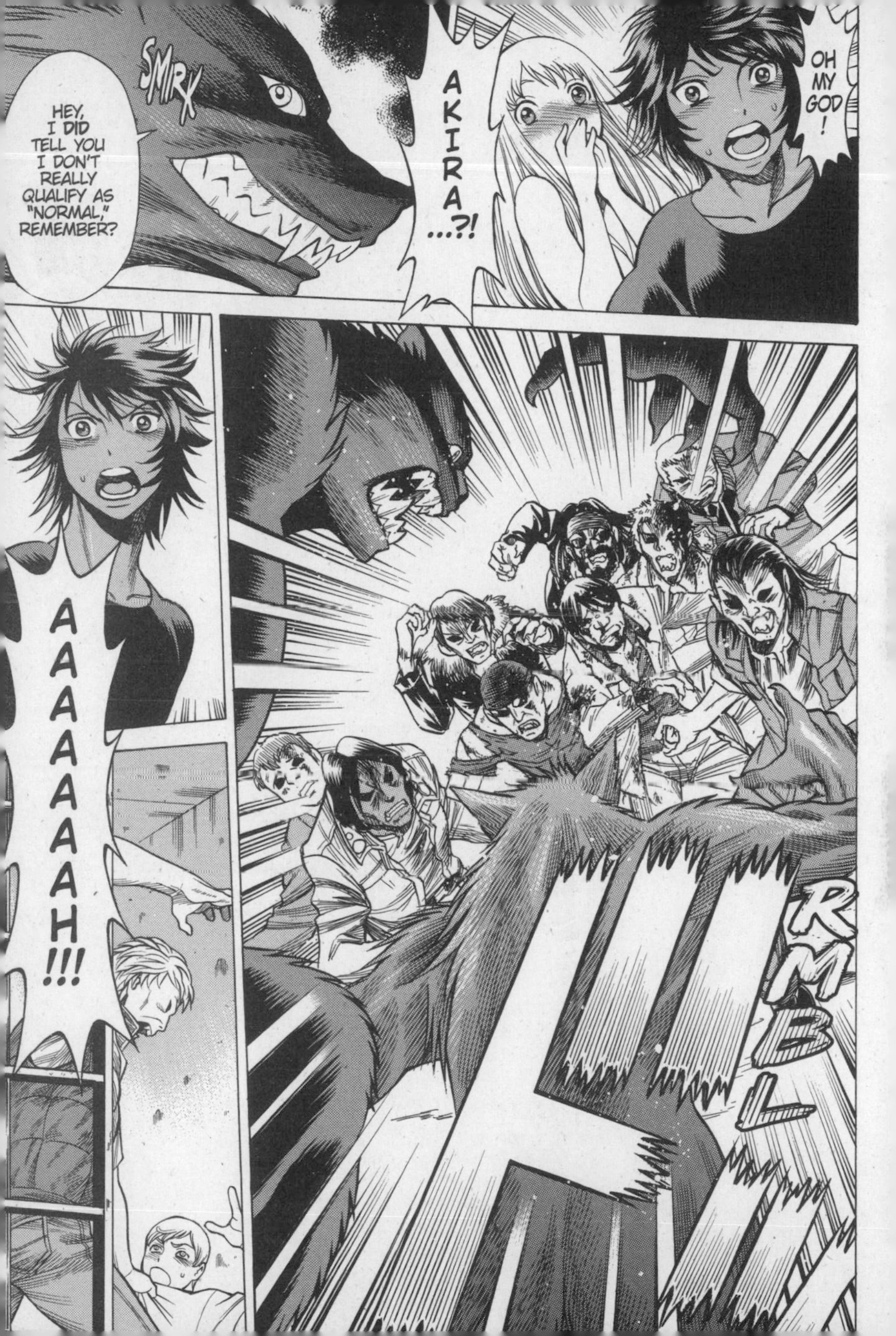
OH MY GOD!
AKIRA...?!
SMIRK
HEY, I DID TELL YOU I DON'T REALLY QUALIFY AS "NORMAL," REMEMBER?
RMBL
AAAAAAAAAAAH!!!

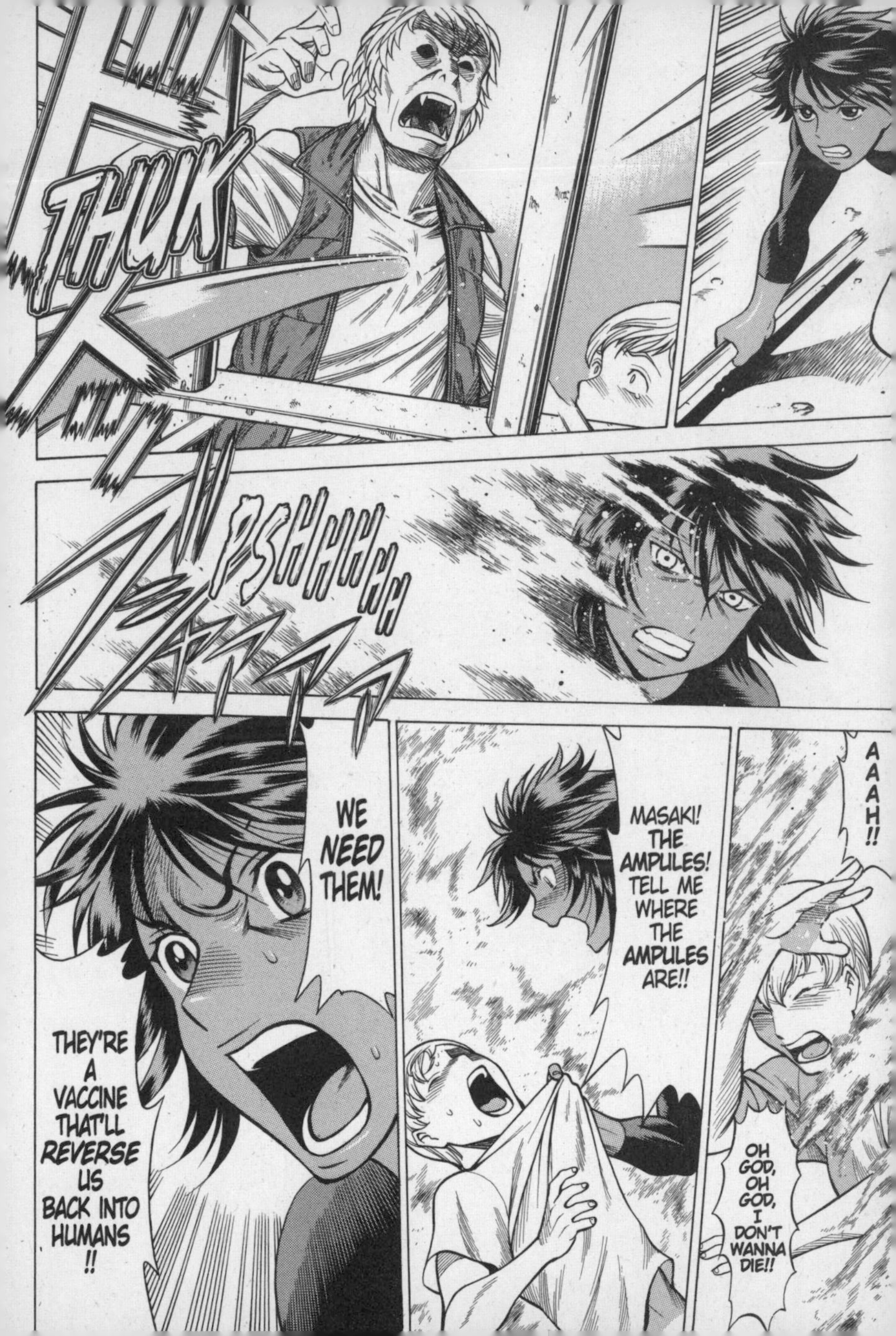

THUK
AAAAH!!
OH GOD, OH GOD, I DON'T WANNA DIE!!
MASAKI! THE AMPULES! TELL ME WHERE THE AMPULES ARE!!
WE NEED THEM!
THEY'RE A VACCINE THAT'LL REVERSE US BACK INTO HUMANS!!

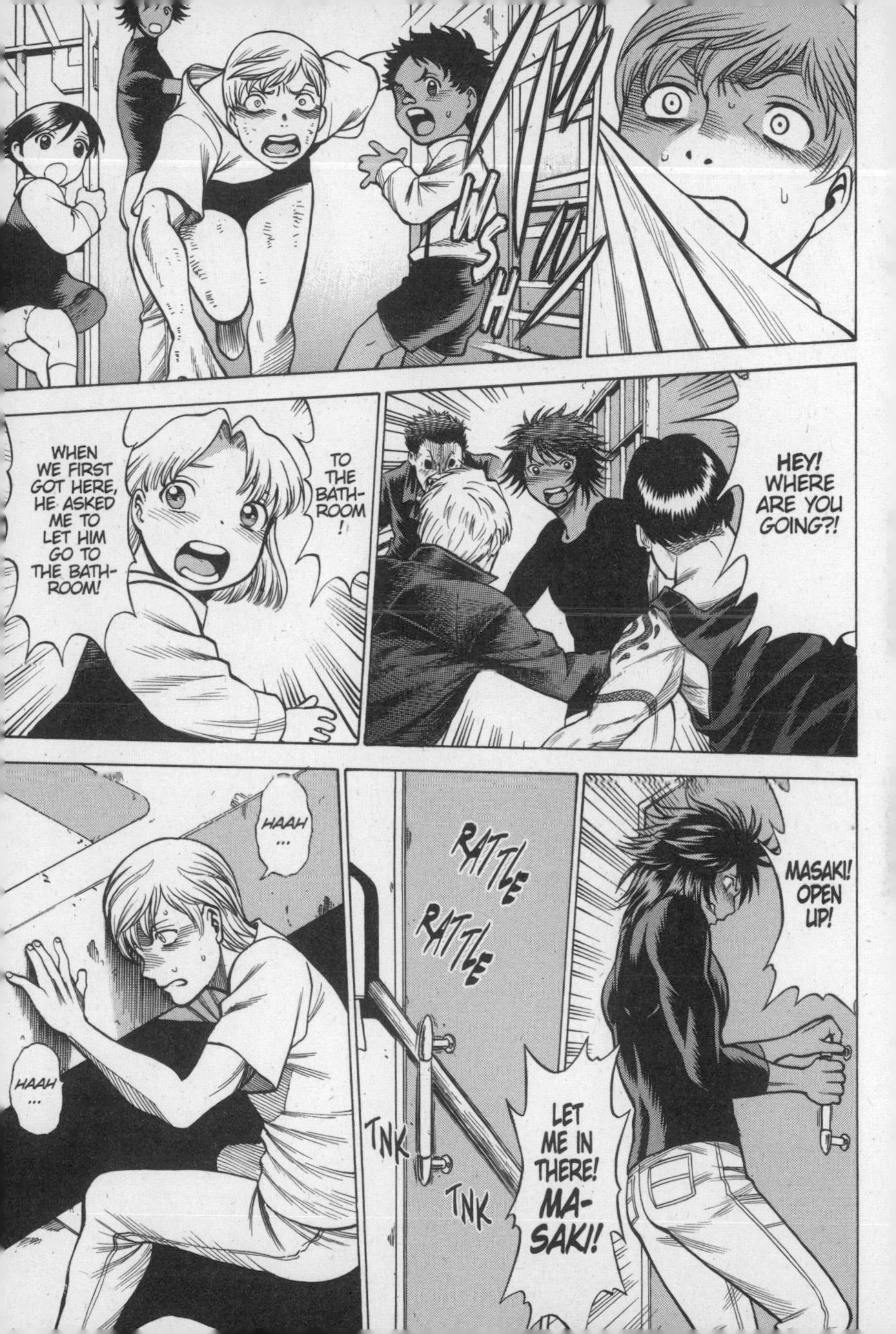
WHSH
HEY! WHERE ARE YOU GOING?!
TO THE BATH-ROOM!
WHEN WE FIRST GOT HERE, HE ASKED ME TO LET HIM GO TO THE BATH-ROOM!
MASAKI! OPEN UP!
RATTLE
RATTLE
LET ME IN THERE! MA-SAKI!
TNK
TNK
HAAH...
HAAH...

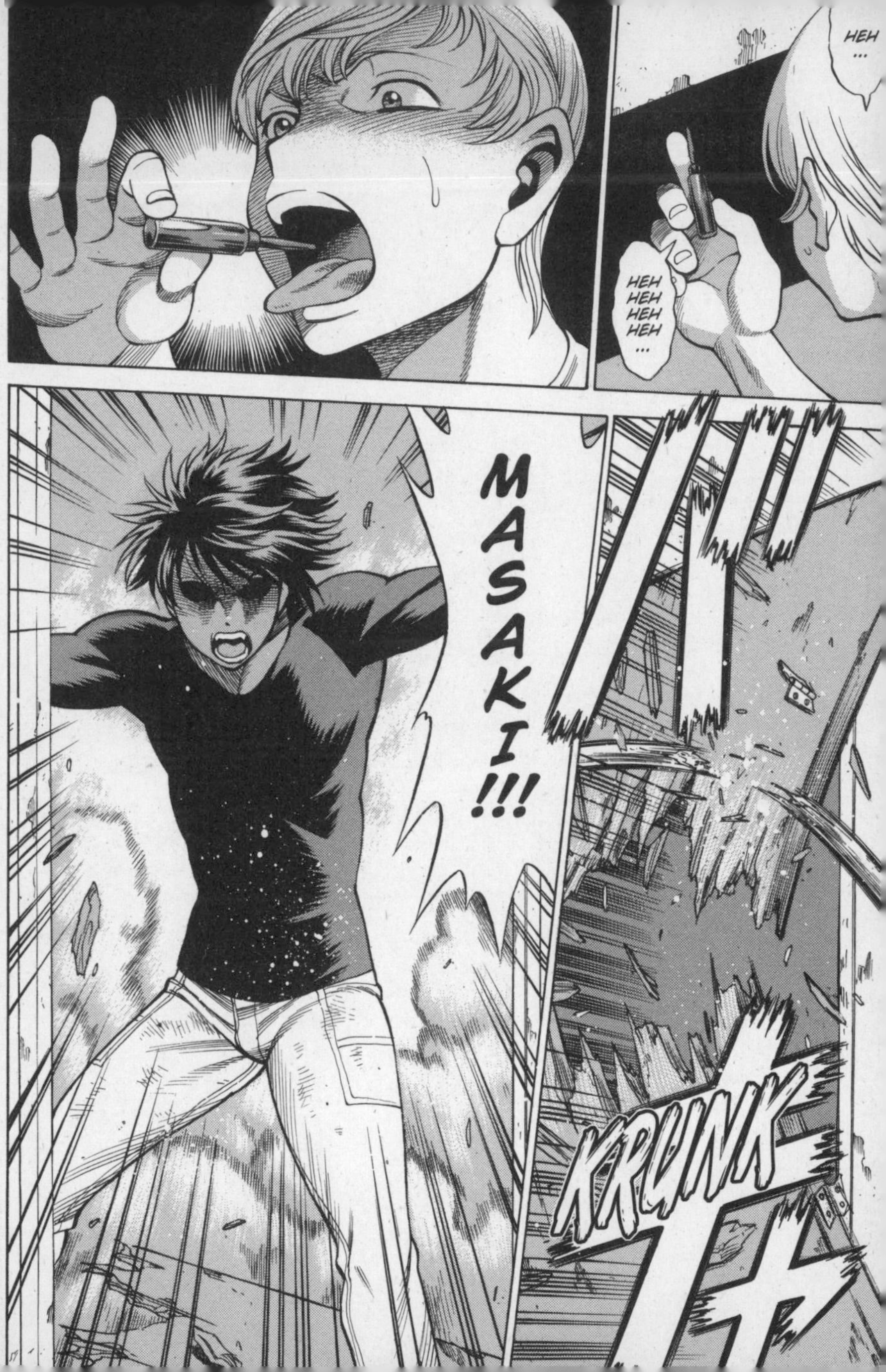
HEH ...
HEH HEH HEH HEH ...
MASAKI!!!
KRUNK

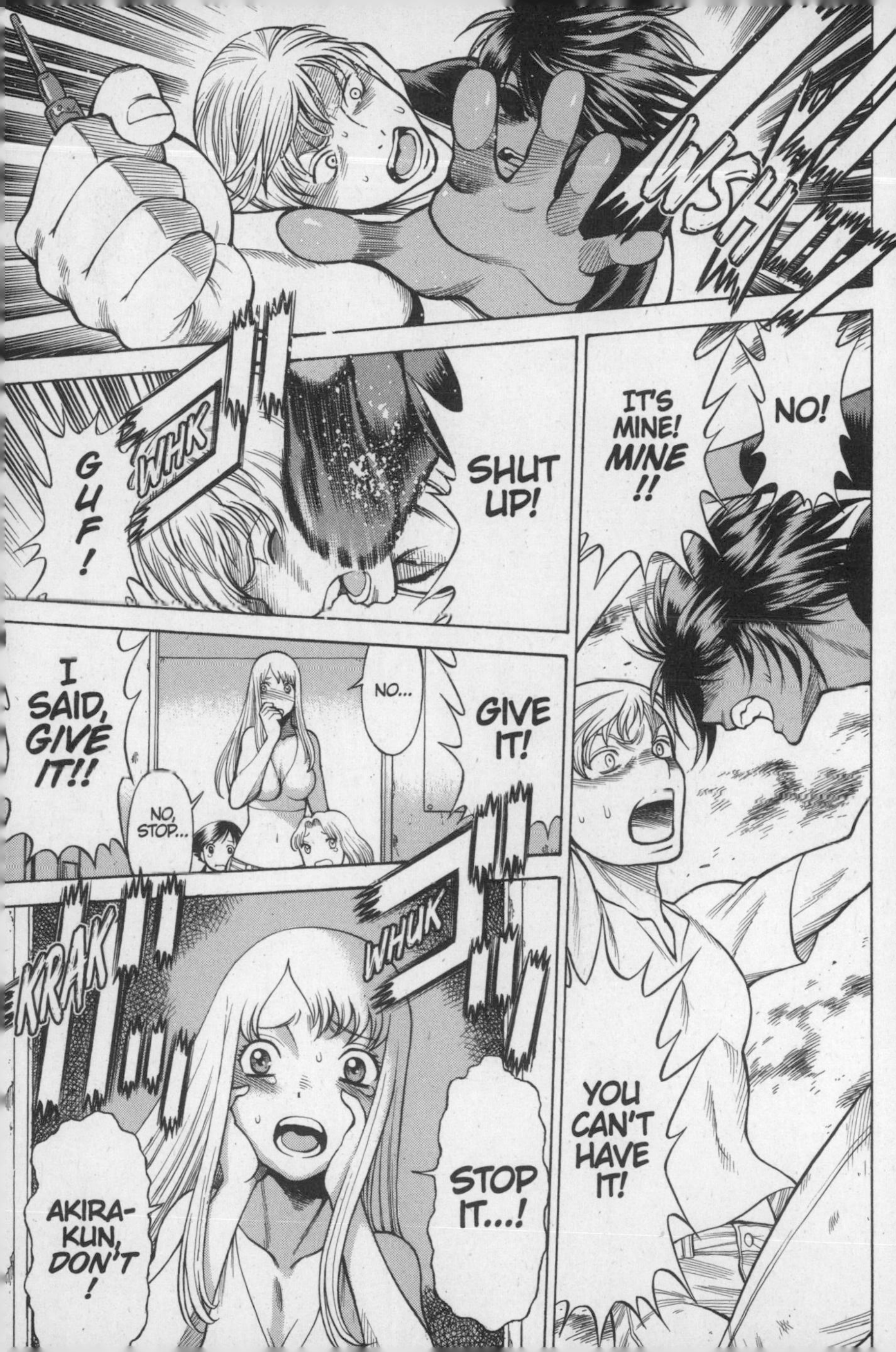
WSH
NO!
IT'S MINE! MINE!!
YOU CAN'T HAVE IT!
SHUT UP!
WHK
GUF!
GIVE IT!
NO...
I SAID, GIVE IT!!
NO, STOP...
STOP IT...!
WHUK
AKIRA-KUN, DON'T!
KRAK

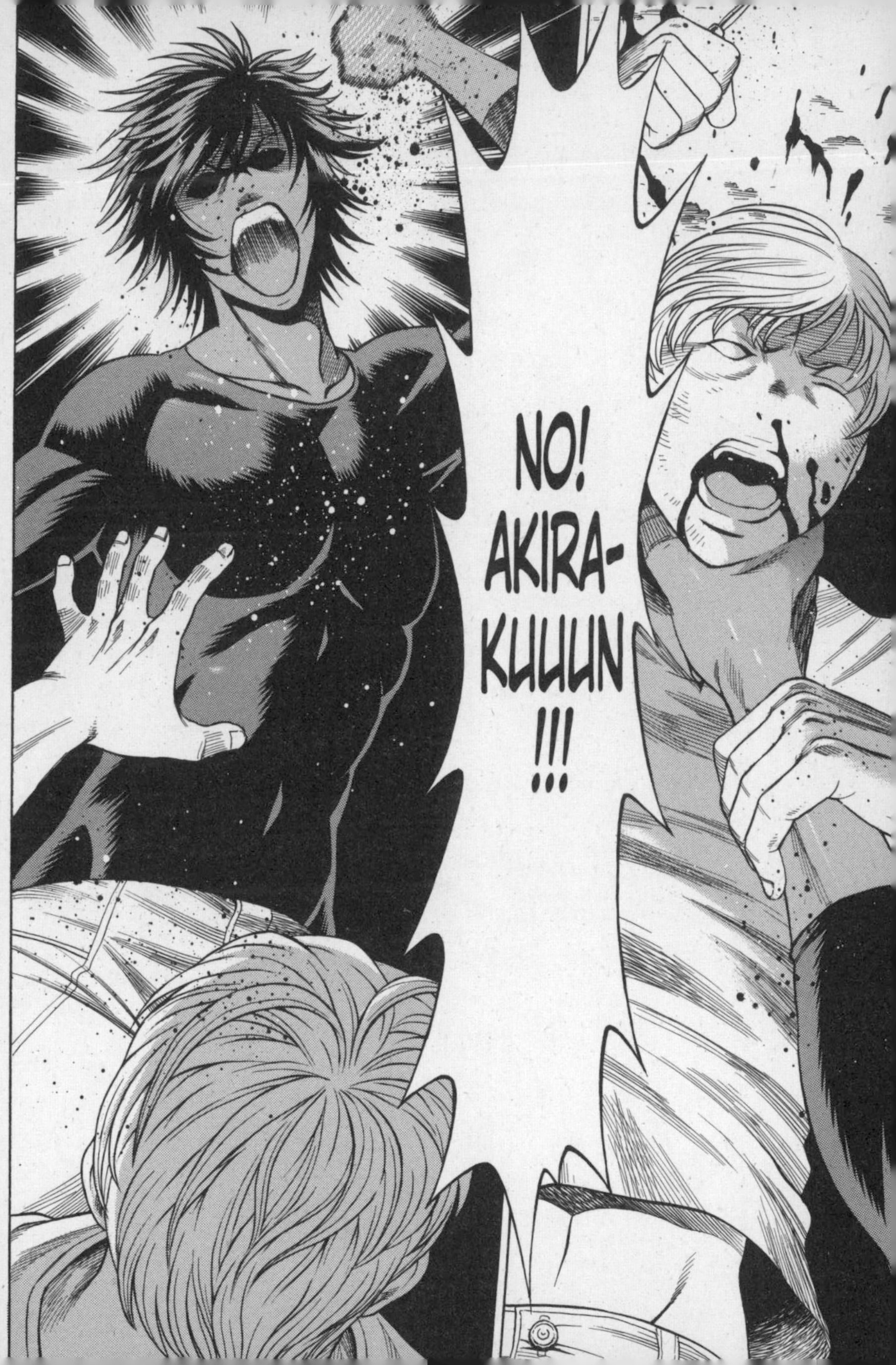
NO! AKIRA-KUUUN !!!

Chapter 10: The Rose in the Sky

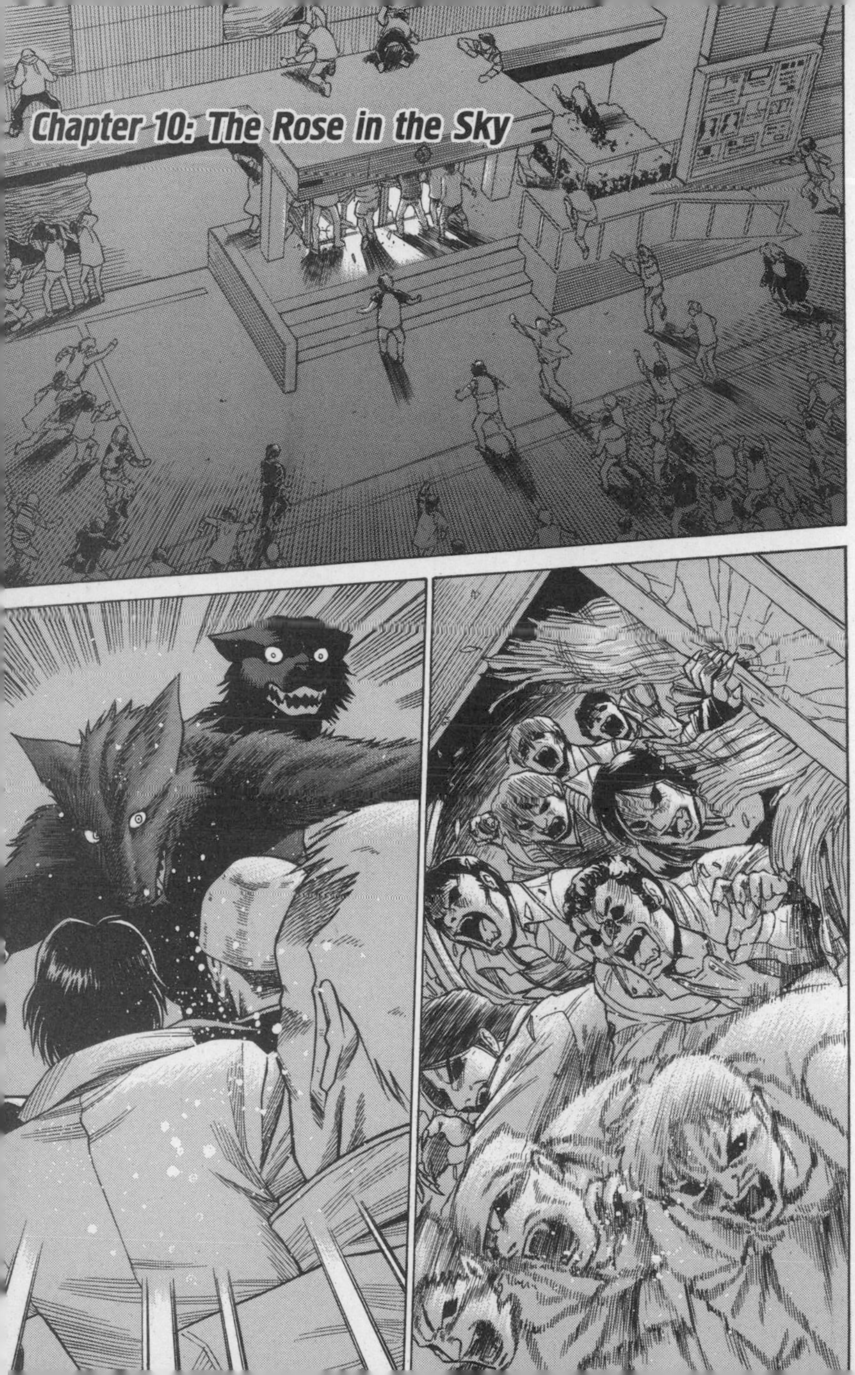

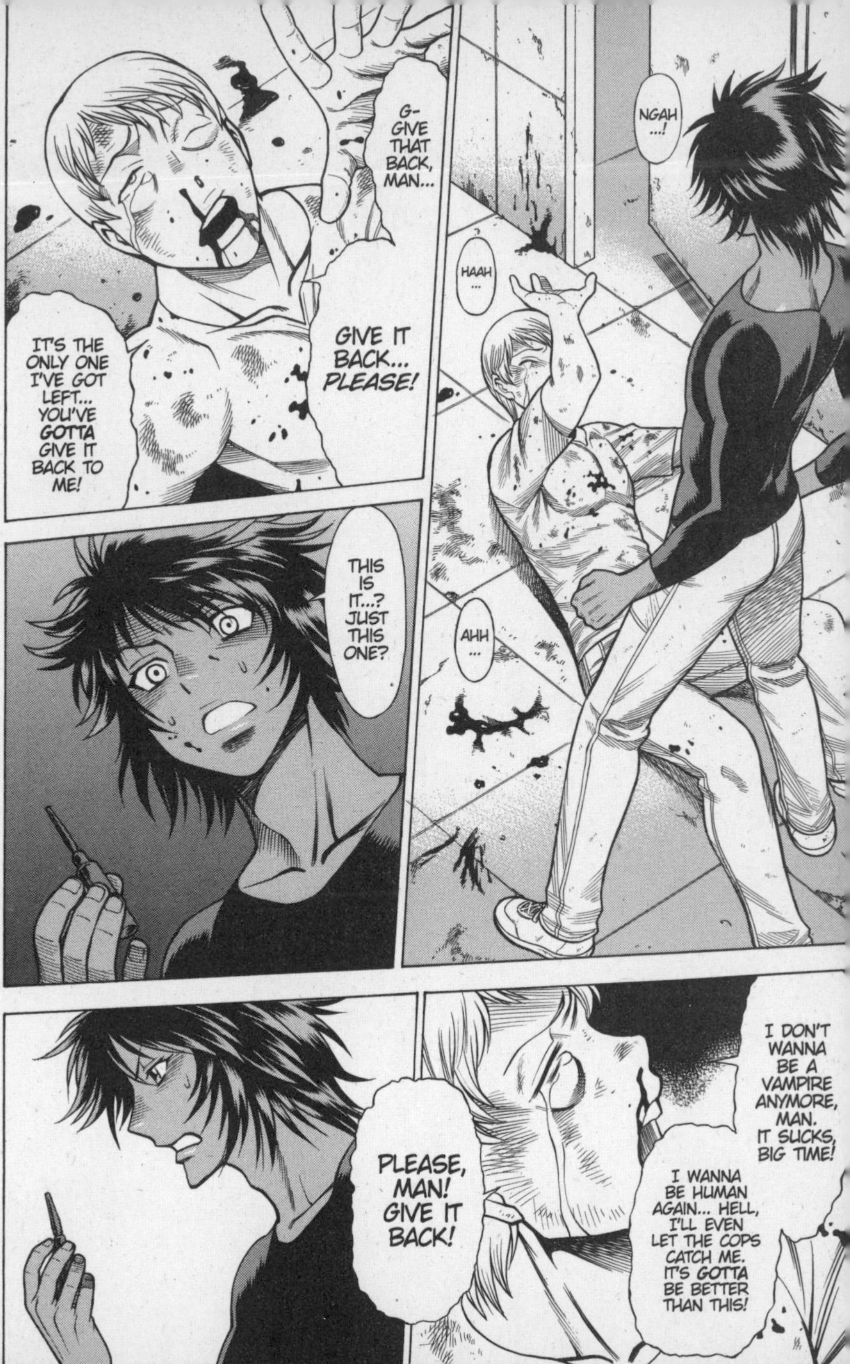
NGAH ...!
HAAH ...
AHH ...
G-GIVE THAT BACK, MAN...
GIVE IT BACK... *PLEASE!*
IT'S THE ONLY ONE I'VE GOT LEFT... YOU'VE **GOTTA** GIVE IT BACK TO ME!
THIS IS IT...? JUST THIS ONE?
I DON'T WANNA BE A VAMPIRE ANYMORE, MAN. IT SUCKS, BIG TIME!
I WANNA BE HUMAN AGAIN... HELL, I'LL EVEN LET THE COPS CATCH ME. IT'S **GOTTA** BE BETTER THAN THIS!
PLEASE, MAN! GIVE IT BACK!

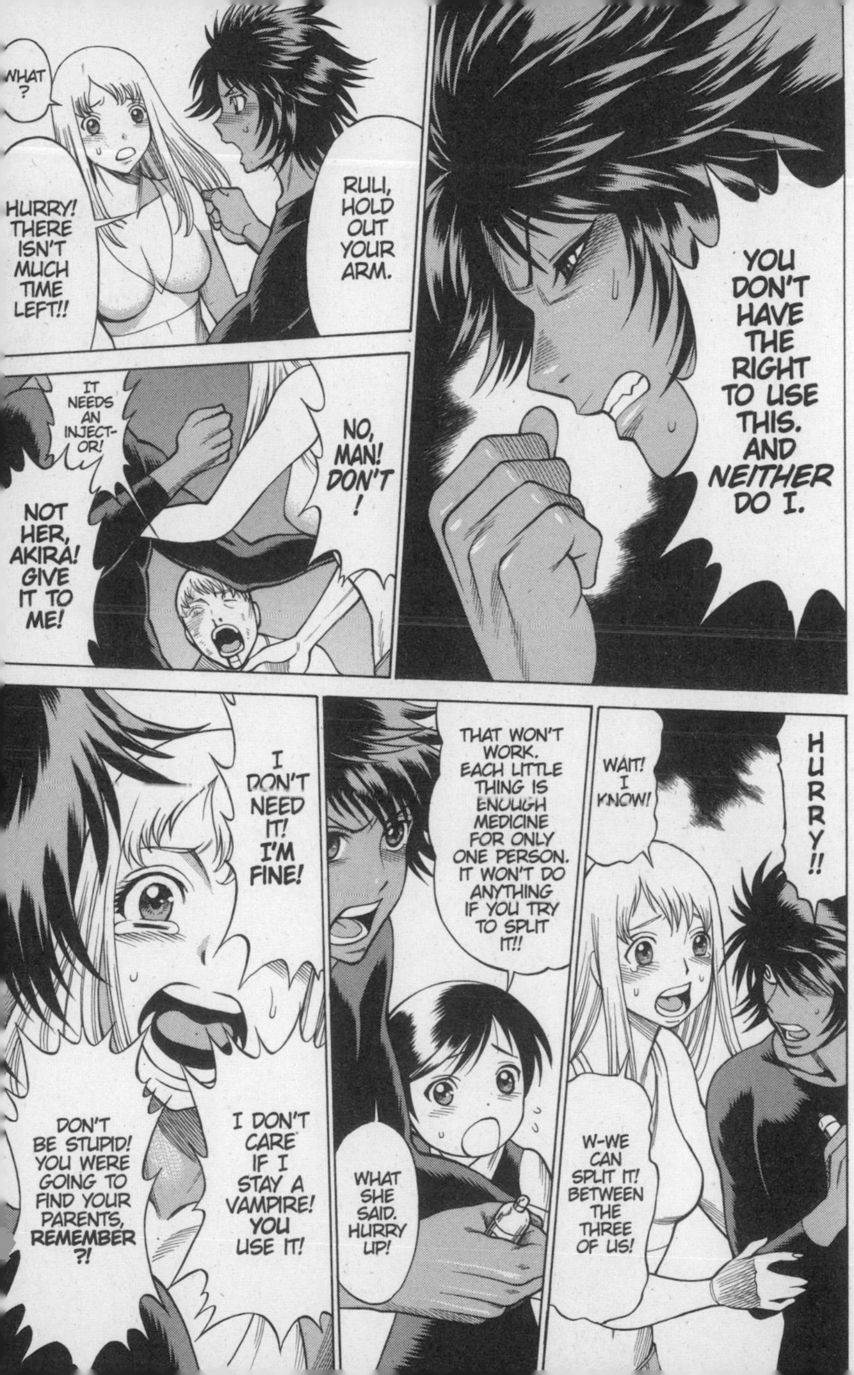
YOU DON'T HAVE THE RIGHT TO USE THIS. AND NEITHER DO I.
RULI, HOLD OUT YOUR ARM.
WHAT?
HURRY! THERE ISN'T MUCH TIME LEFT!!
NO, MAN! DON'T!
IT NEEDS AN INJECTOR!
NOT HER, AKIRA! GIVE IT TO ME!
HURRY!!
WAIT! I KNOW!
W-WE CAN SPLIT IT! BETWEEN THE THREE OF US!
THAT WON'T WORK. EACH LITTLE THING IS ENOUGH MEDICINE FOR ONLY ONE PERSON. IT WON'T DO ANYTHING IF YOU TRY TO SPLIT IT!!
WHAT SHE SAID. HURRY UP!
I DON'T NEED IT! I'M FINE!
I DON'T CARE IF I STAY A VAMPIRE! YOU USE IT!
DON'T BE STUPID! YOU WERE GOING TO FIND YOUR PARENTS, REMEMBER?!

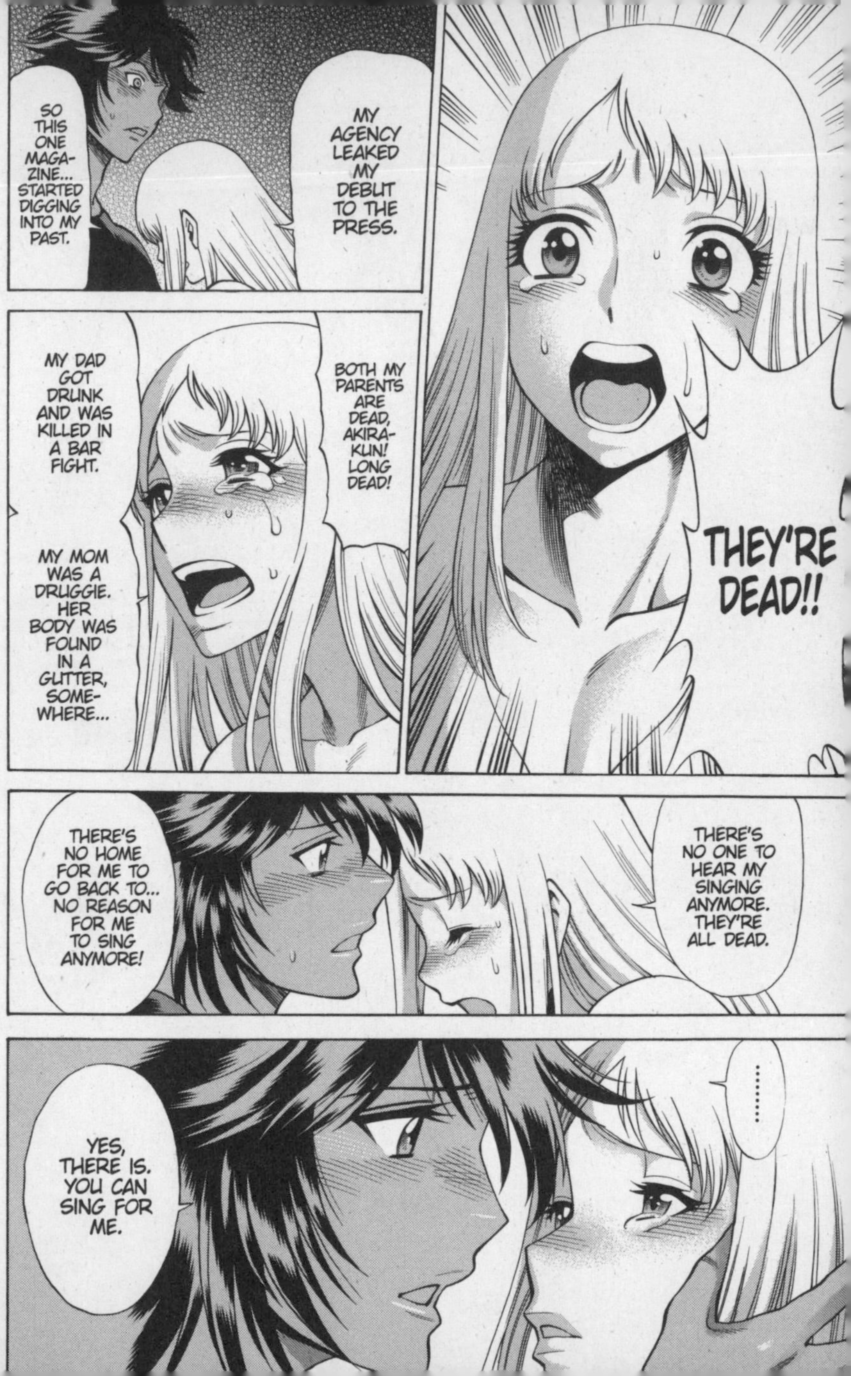
THEY'RE DEAD!!
MY AGENCY LEAKED MY DEBUT TO THE PRESS.
SO THIS ONE MAGAZINE... STARTED DIGGING INTO MY PAST.
BOTH MY PARENTS ARE DEAD, AKIRA-KUN! LONG DEAD!
MY DAD GOT DRUNK AND WAS KILLED IN A BAR FIGHT.
MY MOM WAS A DRUGGIE. HER BODY WAS FOUND IN A GUTTER, SOMEWHERE...
THERE'S NO ONE TO HEAR MY SINGING ANYMORE. THEY'RE ALL DEAD.
THERE'S NO HOME FOR ME TO GO BACK TO... NO REASON FOR ME TO SING ANYMORE!
......
YES, THERE IS. YOU CAN SING FOR ME.

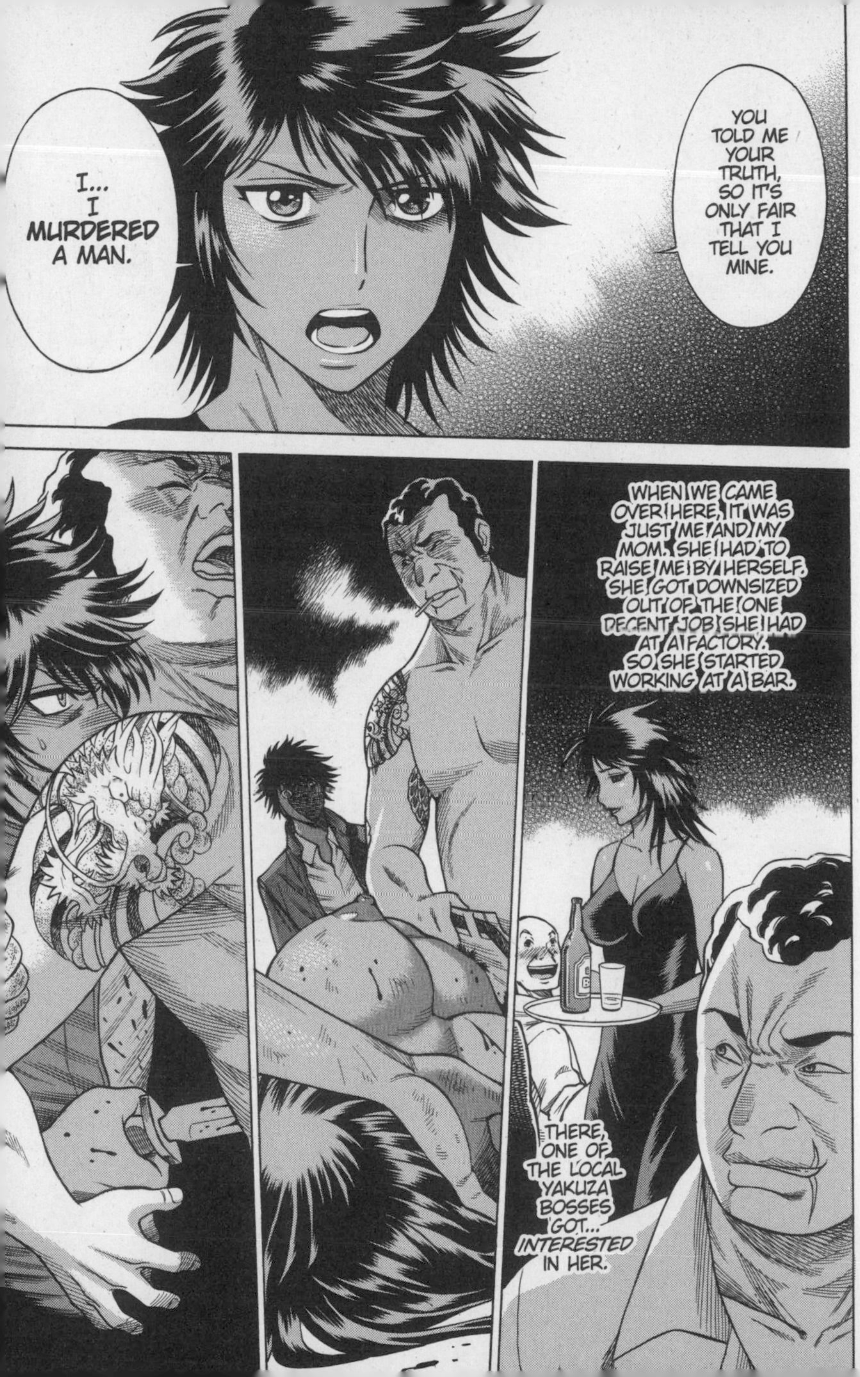
YOU TOLD ME YOUR TRUTH, SO IT'S ONLY FAIR THAT I TELL YOU MINE.
I... I MURDERED A MAN.
WHEN WE CAME OVER HERE, IT WAS JUST ME AND MY MOM. SHE HAD TO RAISE ME BY HERSELF. SHE GOT DOWNSIZED OUT OF THE ONE DECENT JOB SHE HAD AT A FACTORY. SO SHE STARTED WORKING AT A BAR.
THERE, ONE OF THE LOCAL YAKUZA BOSSES GOT... INTERESTED IN HER.

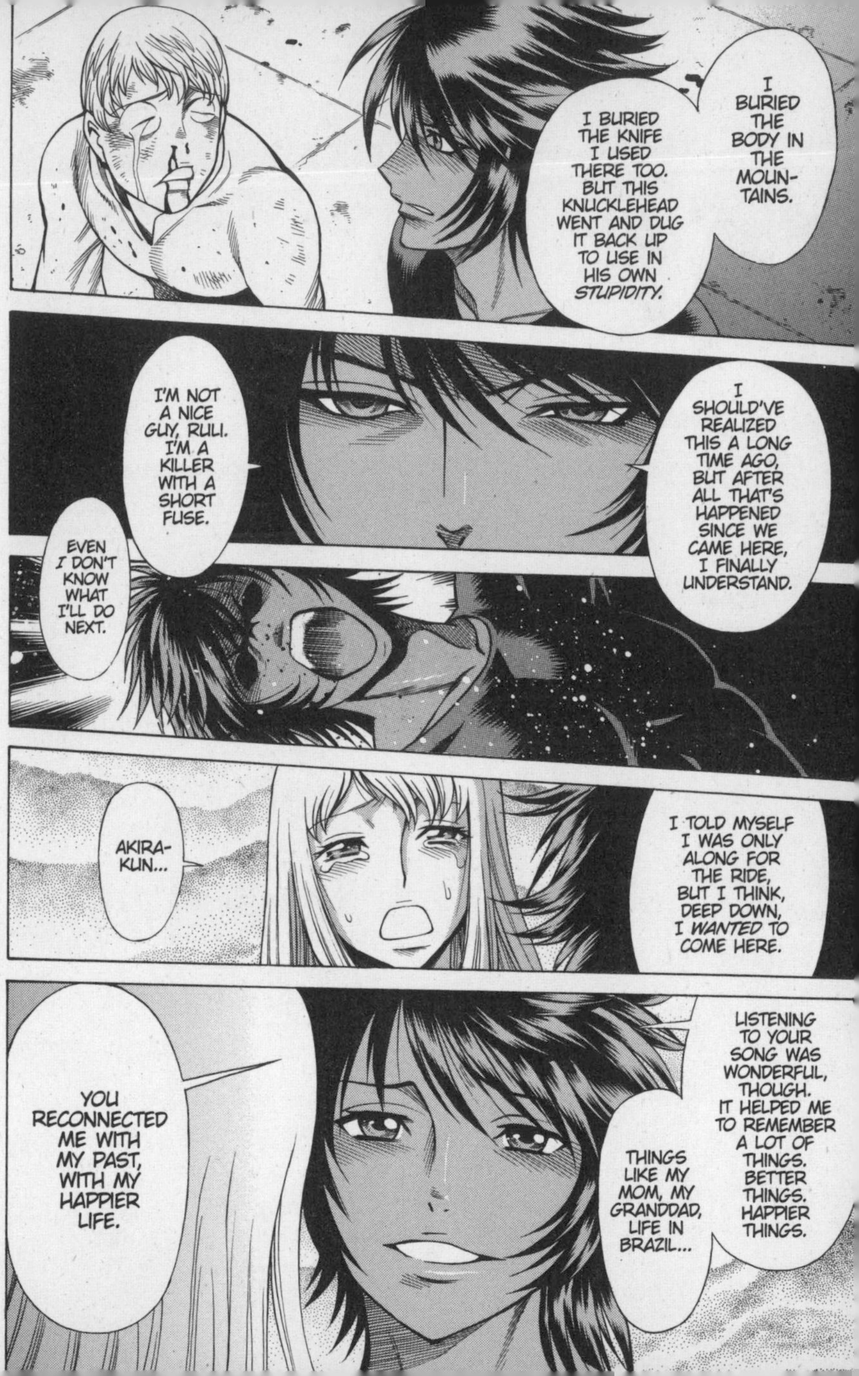
I BURIED THE BODY IN THE MOUN-TAINS.
I BURIED THE KNIFE I USED THERE TOO. BUT THIS KNUCKLEHEAD WENT AND DUG IT BACK UP TO USE IN HIS OWN *STUPIDITY.*
I SHOULD'VE REALIZED THIS A LONG TIME AGO, BUT AFTER ALL THAT'S HAPPENED SINCE WE CAME HERE, I FINALLY UNDERSTAND.
I'M NOT A NICE GUY, RULI. I'M A KILLER WITH A SHORT FUSE.
EVEN *I* DON'T KNOW WHAT I'LL DO NEXT.
I TOLD MYSELF I WAS ONLY ALONG FOR THE RIDE, BUT I THINK, DEEP DOWN, I *WANTED* TO COME HERE.
AKIRA-KUN...
LISTENING TO YOUR SONG WAS WONDERFUL, THOUGH. IT HELPED ME TO REMEMBER A LOT OF THINGS. BETTER THINGS. HAPPIER THINGS.
THINGS LIKE MY MOM, MY GRANDDAD, LIFE IN BRAZIL...
YOU RECONNECTED ME WITH MY PAST, WITH MY HAPPIER LIFE.

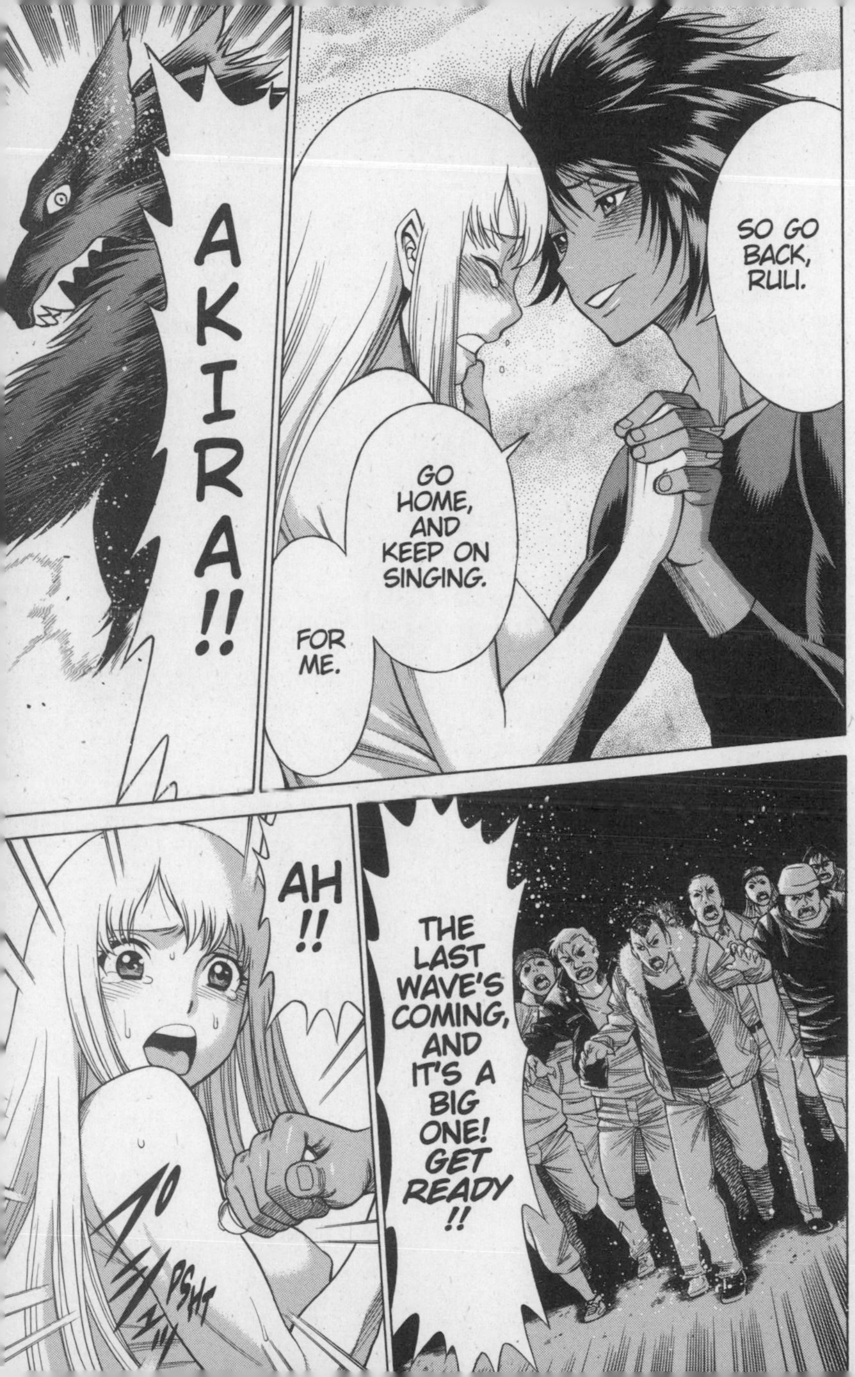
SO GO BACK, RULI.
GO HOME, AND KEEP ON SINGING.
FOR ME.
AKIRA!!
THE LAST WAVE'S COMING, AND IT'S A BIG ONE! GET READY!!
AH!!
PSHT

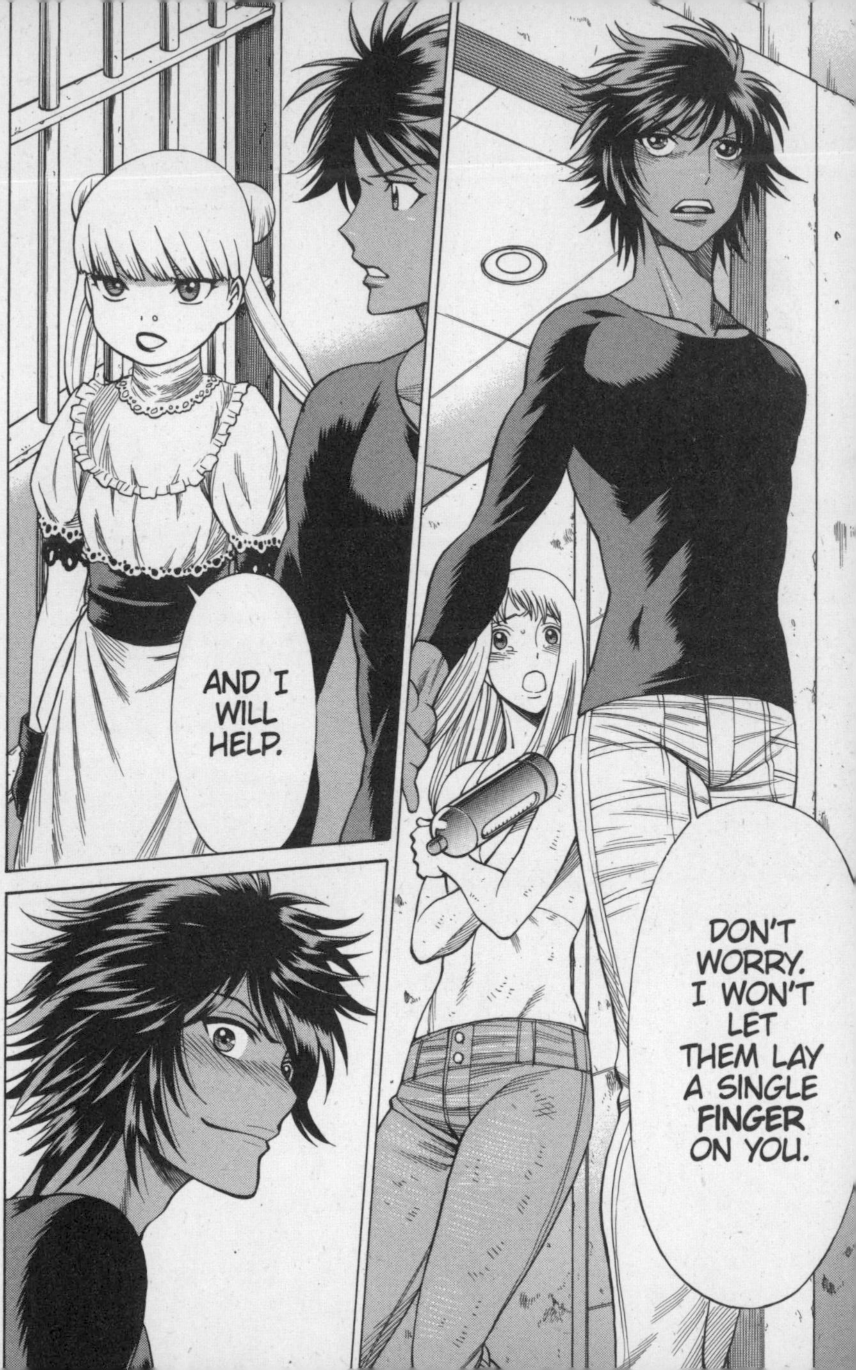
DON'T WORRY. I WON'T LET THEM LAY A SINGLE FINGER ON YOU.
AND I WILL HELP.

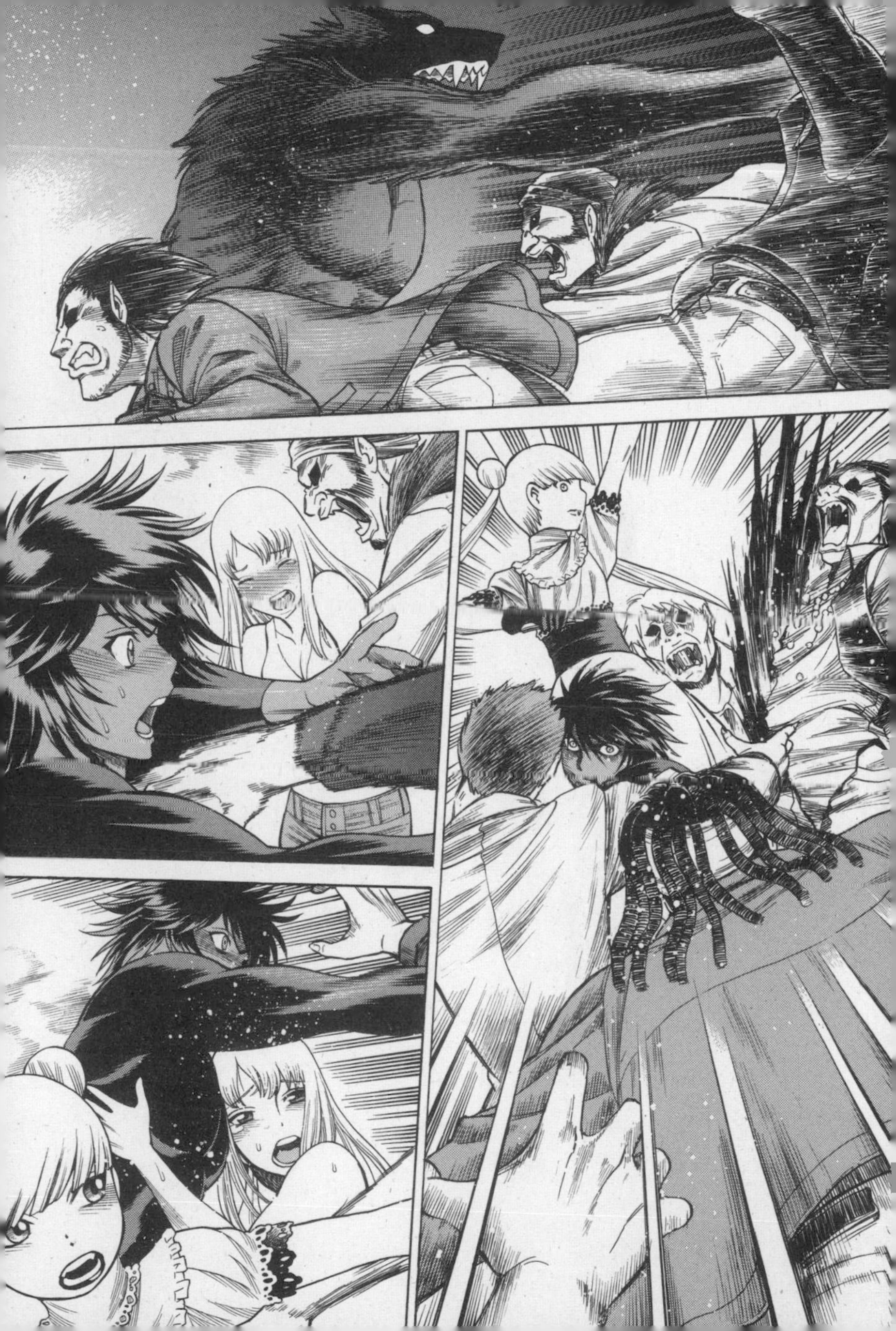

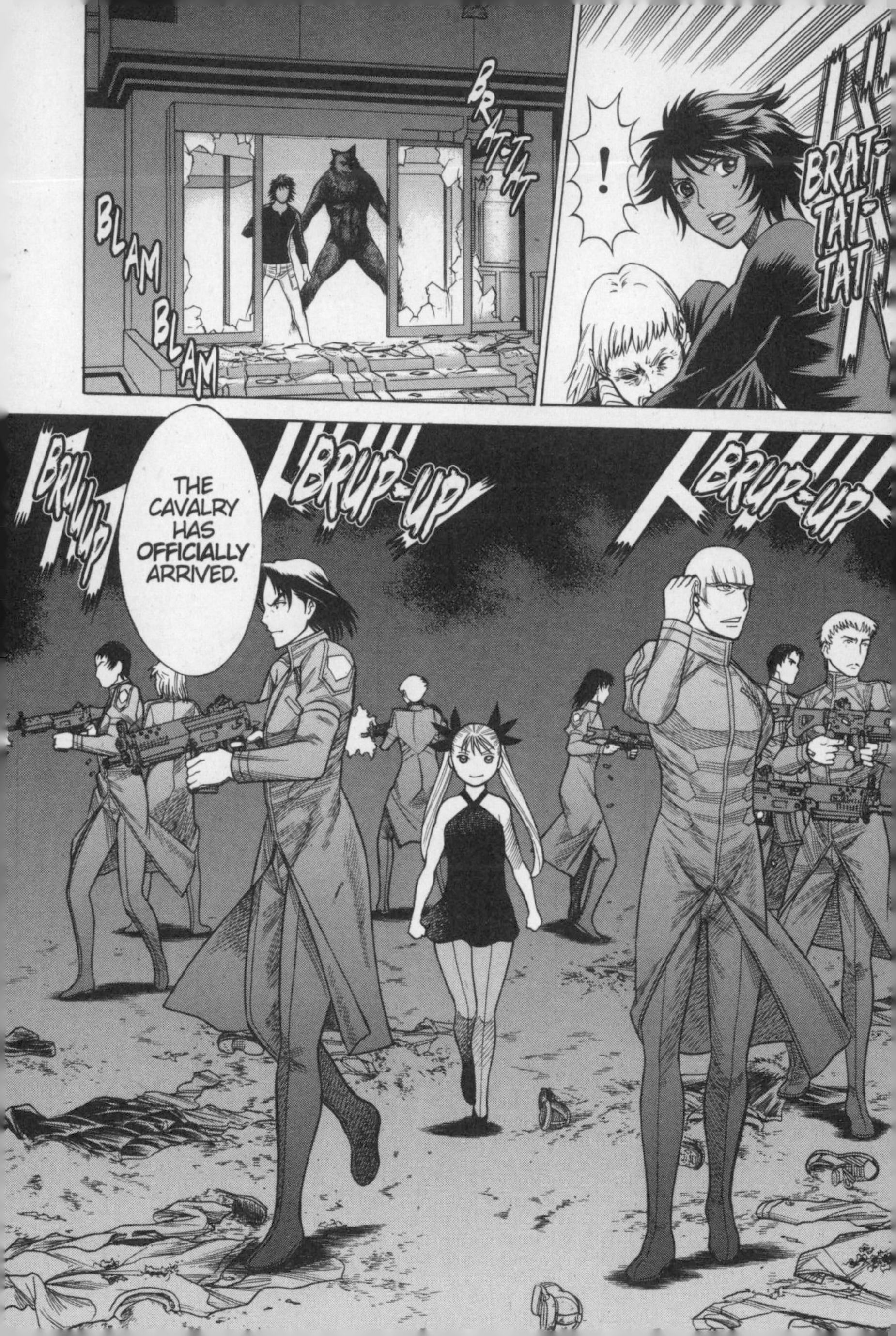
!
BRAT-TAT-TAT
BRATATAT
BLAM
BLAM
BLAM
BRUP-UP
BRUP-UP
THE CAVALRY HAS OFFICIALLY ARRIVED.
BRUUUP

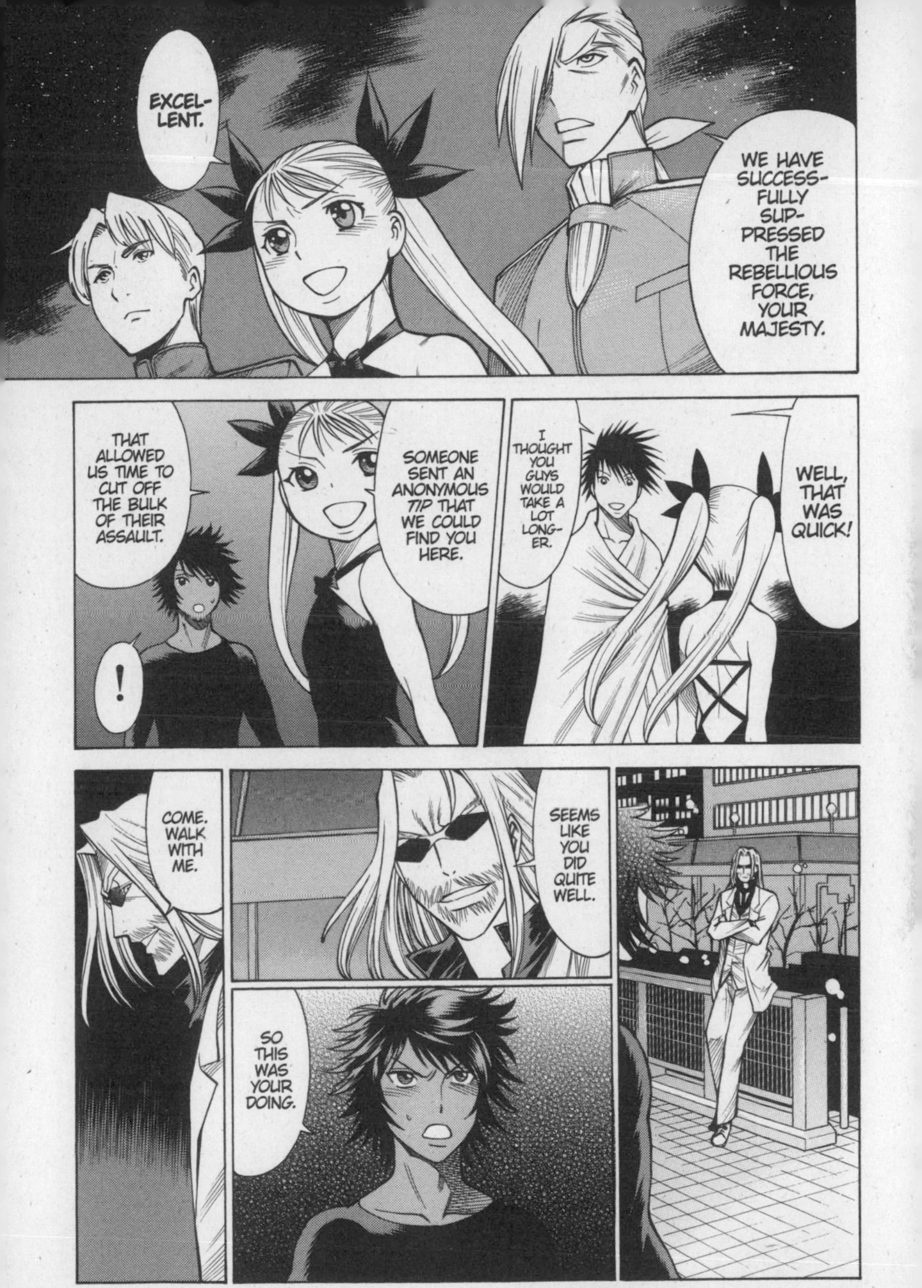
WE HAVE SUCCESS-FULLY SUP-PRESSED THE REBELLIOUS FORCE, YOUR MAJESTY.
EXCEL-LENT.
WELL, THAT WAS QUICK!
I THOUGHT YOU GUYS WOULD TAKE A LOT LONG-ER.
SOMEONE SENT AN ANONYMOUS *TIP* THAT WE COULD FIND YOU HERE.
THAT ALLOWED US TIME TO CUT OFF THE BULK OF THEIR ASSAULT.
!
SEEMS LIKE YOU DID QUITE WELL.
SO THIS WAS YOUR DOING.
COME. WALK WITH ME.

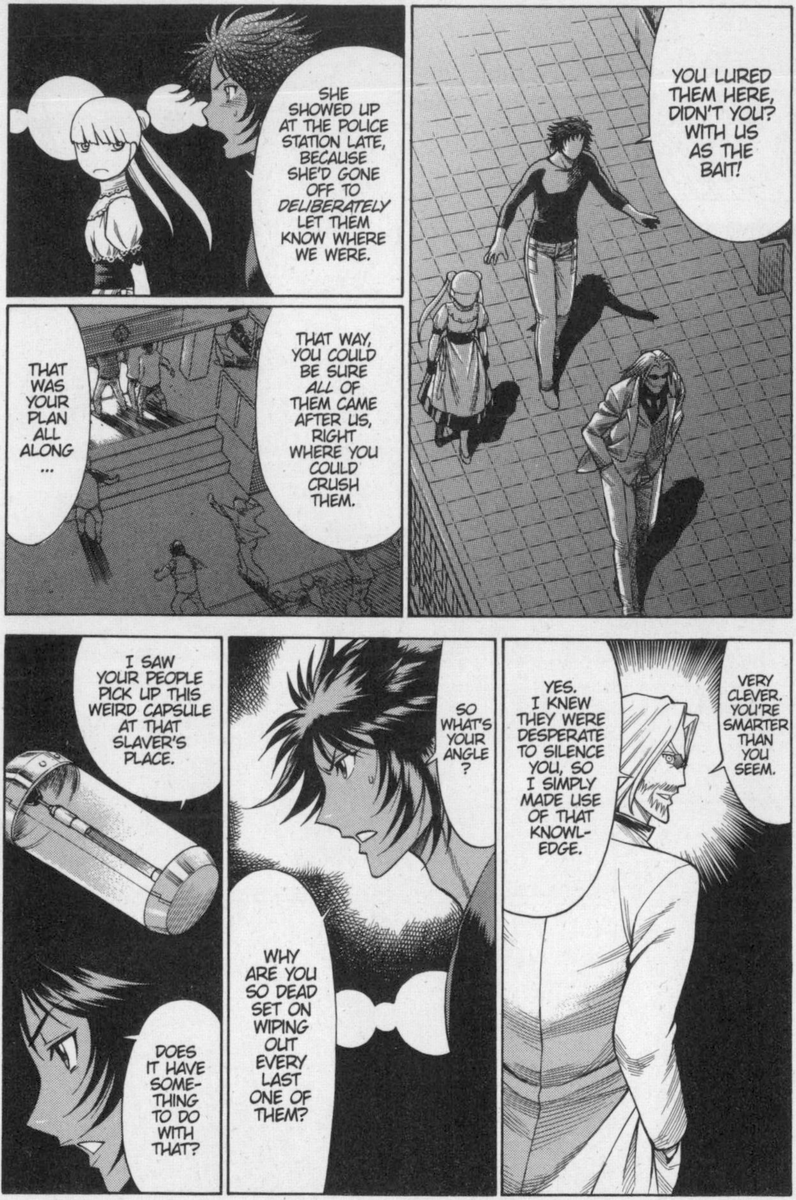
YOU LURED THEM HERE, DIDN'T YOU? WITH US AS THE BAIT!
SHE SHOWED UP AT THE POLICE STATION LATE, BECAUSE SHE'D GONE OFF TO *DELIBERATELY* LET THEM KNOW WHERE WE WERE.
THAT WAY, YOU COULD BE SURE *ALL* OF THEM CAME AFTER US, RIGHT WHERE YOU COULD CRUSH THEM.
THAT WAS YOUR PLAN ALL ALONG ...
VERY CLEVER. YOU'RE SMARTER THAN YOU SEEM.
YES. I KNEW THEY WERE DESPERATE TO SILENCE YOU, SO I SIMPLY MADE USE OF THAT KNOWL-EDGE.
SO WHAT'S YOUR ANGLE?
WHY ARE YOU SO DEAD SET ON WIPING OUT EVERY LAST ONE OF THEM?
I SAW YOUR PEOPLE PICK UP THIS WEIRD CAPSULE AT THAT SLAVER'S PLACE.
DOES IT HAVE SOME-THING TO DO WITH THAT?

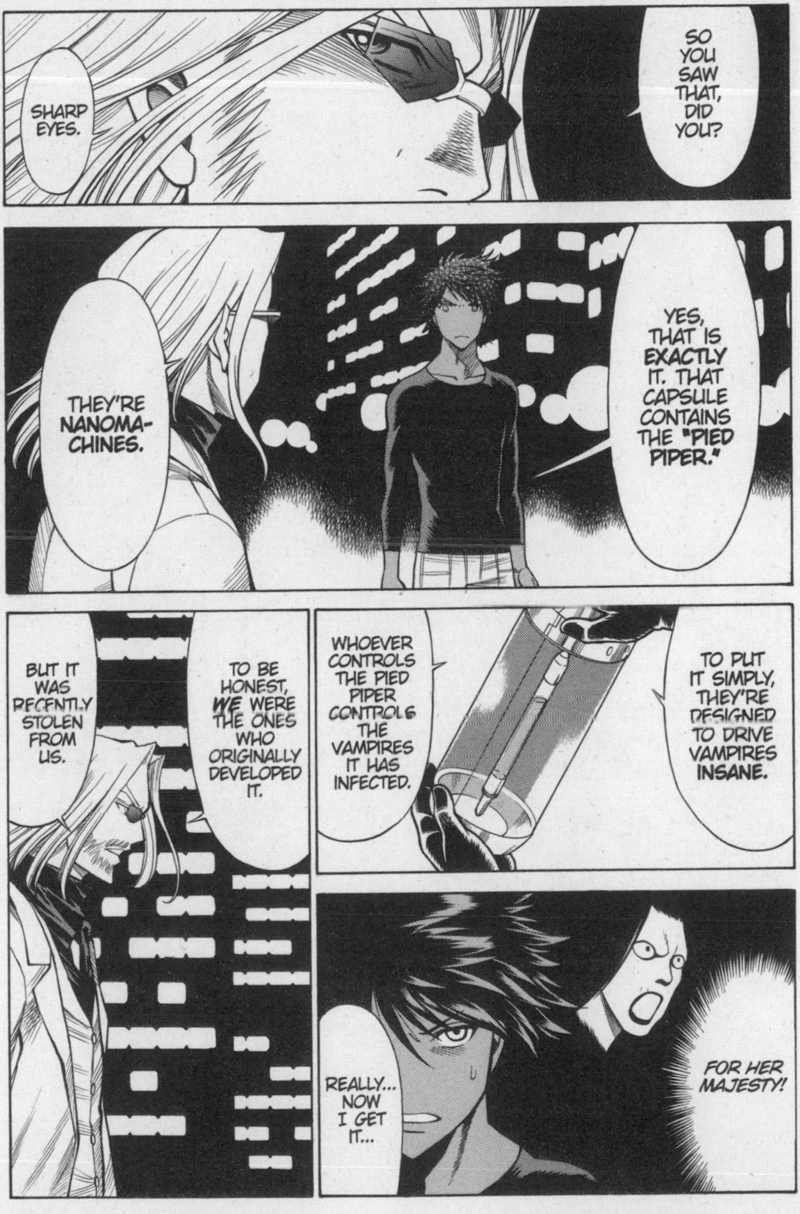
SO YOU SAW THAT, DID YOU?
SHARP EYES.
YES, THAT IS EXACTLY IT. THAT CAPSULE CONTAINS THE "PIED PIPER."
THEY'RE NANOMA-CHINES.
TO PUT IT SIMPLY, THEY'RE DESIGNED TO DRIVE VAMPIRES INSANE.
WHOEVER CONTROLS THE PIED PIPER CONTROLS THE VAMPIRES IT HAS INFECTED.
FOR HER MAJESTY!
REALLY... NOW I GET IT...
TO BE HONEST, WE WERE THE ONES WHO ORIGINALLY DEVELOPED IT.
BUT IT WAS RECENTLY STOLEN FROM US.

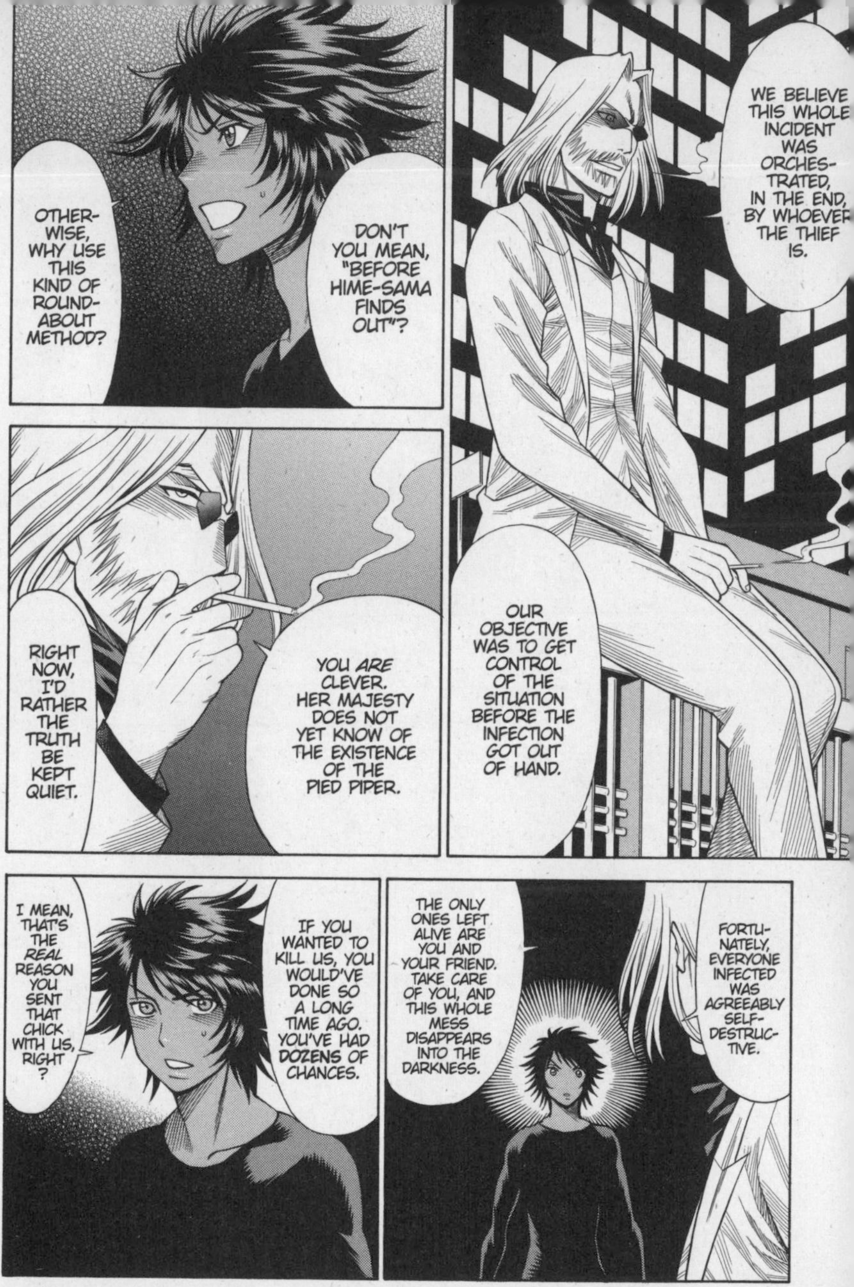
WE BELIEVE THIS WHOLE INCIDENT WAS ORCHES-TRATED, IN THE END, BY WHOEVER THE THIEF IS.
OUR OBJECTIVE WAS TO GET CONTROL OF THE SITUATION BEFORE THE INFECTION GOT OUT OF HAND.
DON'T YOU MEAN, "BEFORE HIME-SAMA FINDS OUT"?
OTHER-WISE, WHY USE THIS KIND OF ROUND-ABOUT METHOD?
YOU *ARE* CLEVER. HER MAJESTY DOES NOT YET KNOW OF THE EXISTENCE OF THE PIED PIPER.
RIGHT NOW, I'D RATHER THE TRUTH BE KEPT QUIET.
FORTU-NATELY, EVERYONE INFECTED WAS AGREEABLY SELF-DESTRUC-TIVE.
THE ONLY ONES LEFT ALIVE ARE YOU AND YOUR FRIEND. TAKE CARE OF YOU, AND THIS WHOLE MESS DISAPPEARS INTO THE DARKNESS.
IF YOU WANTED TO KILL US, YOU WOULD'VE DONE SO A LONG TIME AGO. YOU'VE HAD DOZENS OF CHANCES.
I MEAN, THAT'S THE *REAL* REASON YOU SENT THAT CHICK WITH US, RIGHT?

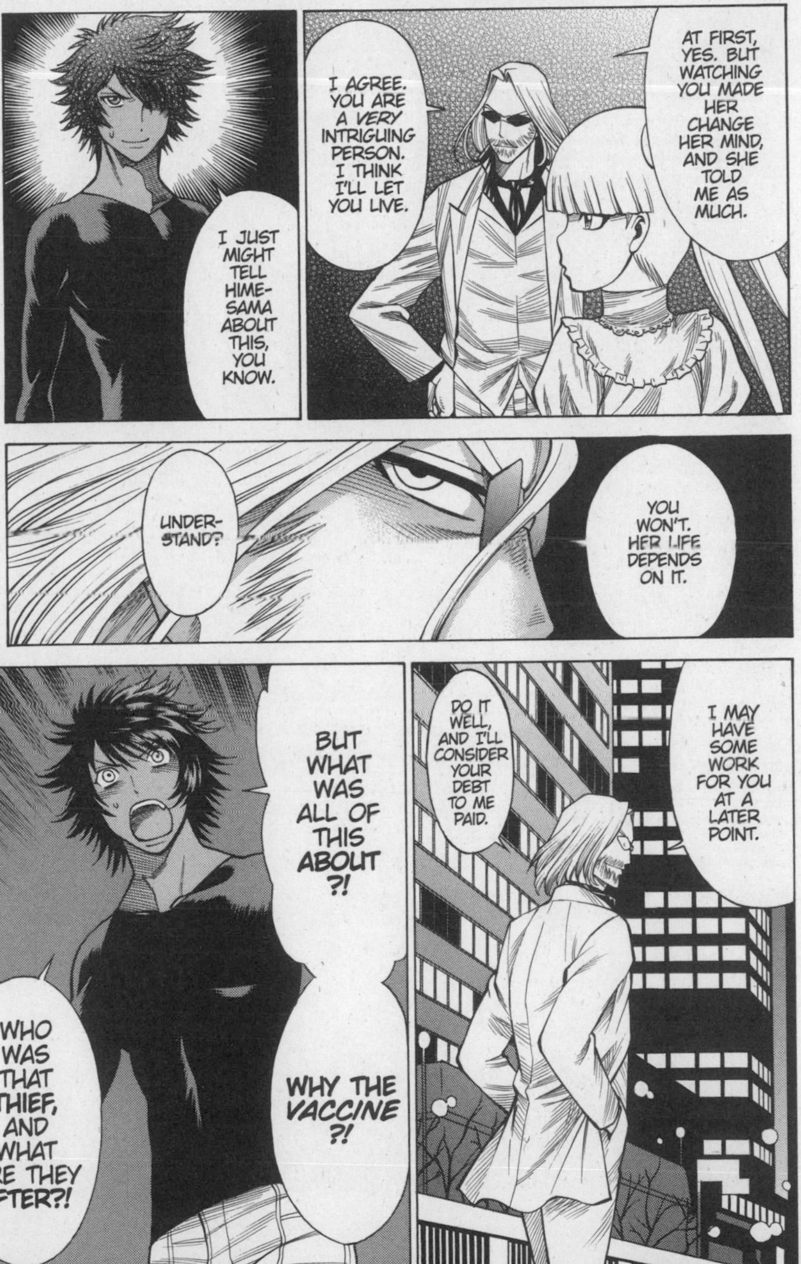
AT FIRST, YES. BUT WATCHING YOU MADE HER CHANGE HER MIND, AND SHE TOLD ME AS MUCH.
I AGREE. YOU ARE A *VERY* INTRIGUING PERSON. I THINK I'LL LET YOU LIVE.
I JUST MIGHT TELL HIME-SAMA ABOUT THIS, YOU KNOW.
YOU WON'T. HER LIFE DEPENDS ON IT.
UNDER-STAND?
I MAY HAVE SOME WORK FOR YOU AT A LATER POINT.
DO IT WELL, AND I'LL CONSIDER YOUR DEBT TO ME PAID.
BUT WHAT WAS ALL OF THIS ABOUT?!
WHY THE *VACCINE*?!
WHO WAS THAT THIEF, AND WHAT ARE THEY AFTER?!

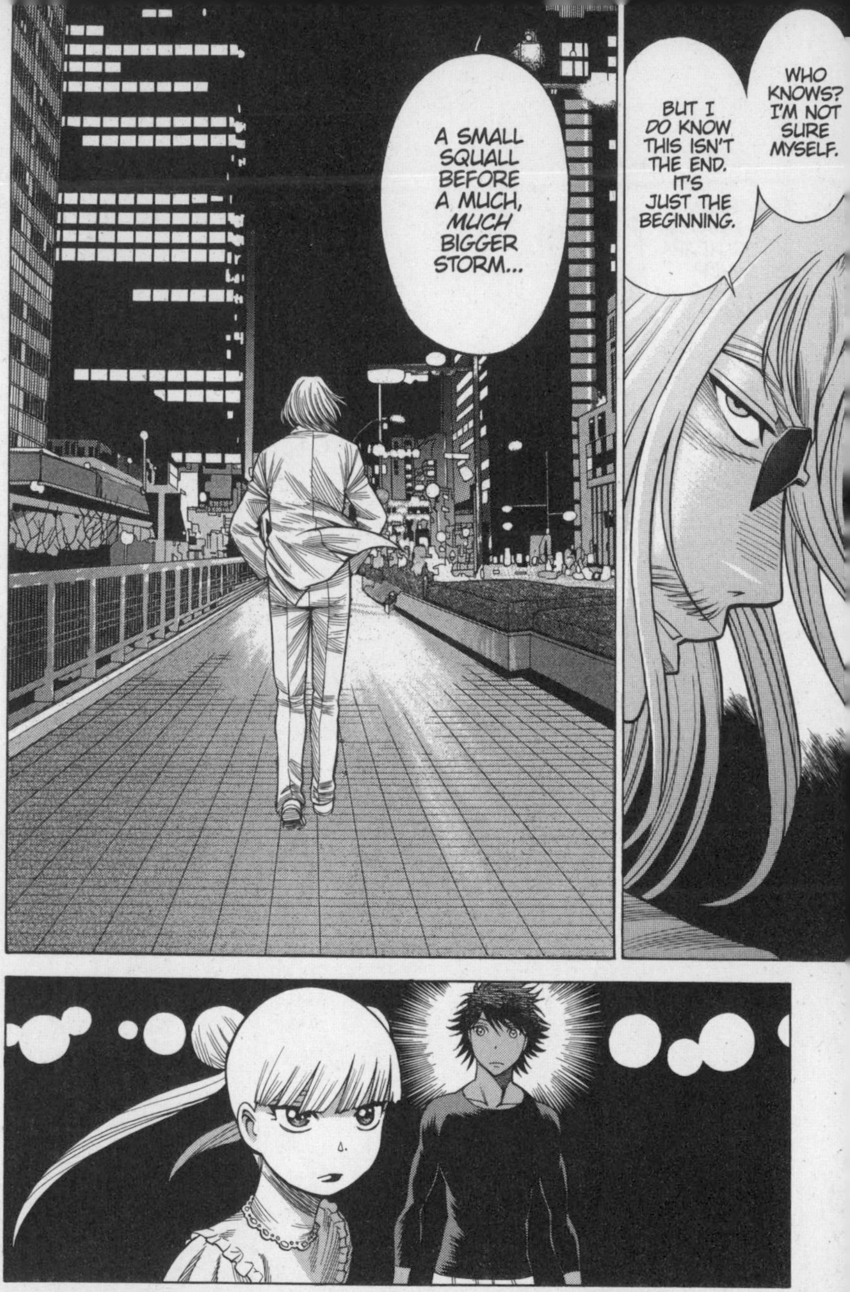
WHO KNOWS? I'M NOT SURE MYSELF.
BUT I DO KNOW THIS ISN'T THE END. IT'S JUST THE BEGINNING.
A SMALL SQUALL BEFORE A MUCH, *MUCH* BIGGER STORM...

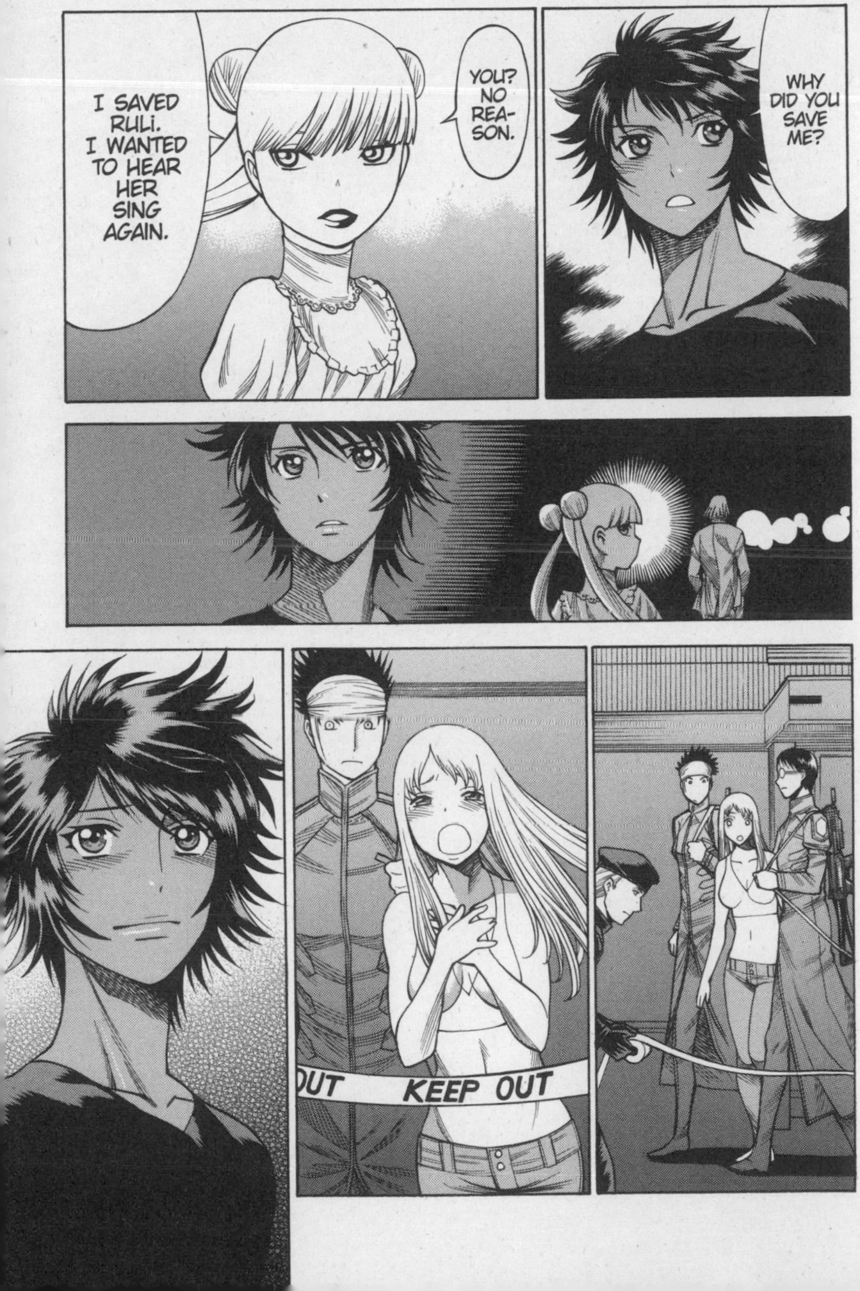
WHY DID YOU SAVE ME?
YOU? NO REA-SON.
I SAVED RULi. I WANTED TO HEAR HER SING AGAIN.
OUT KEEP OUT

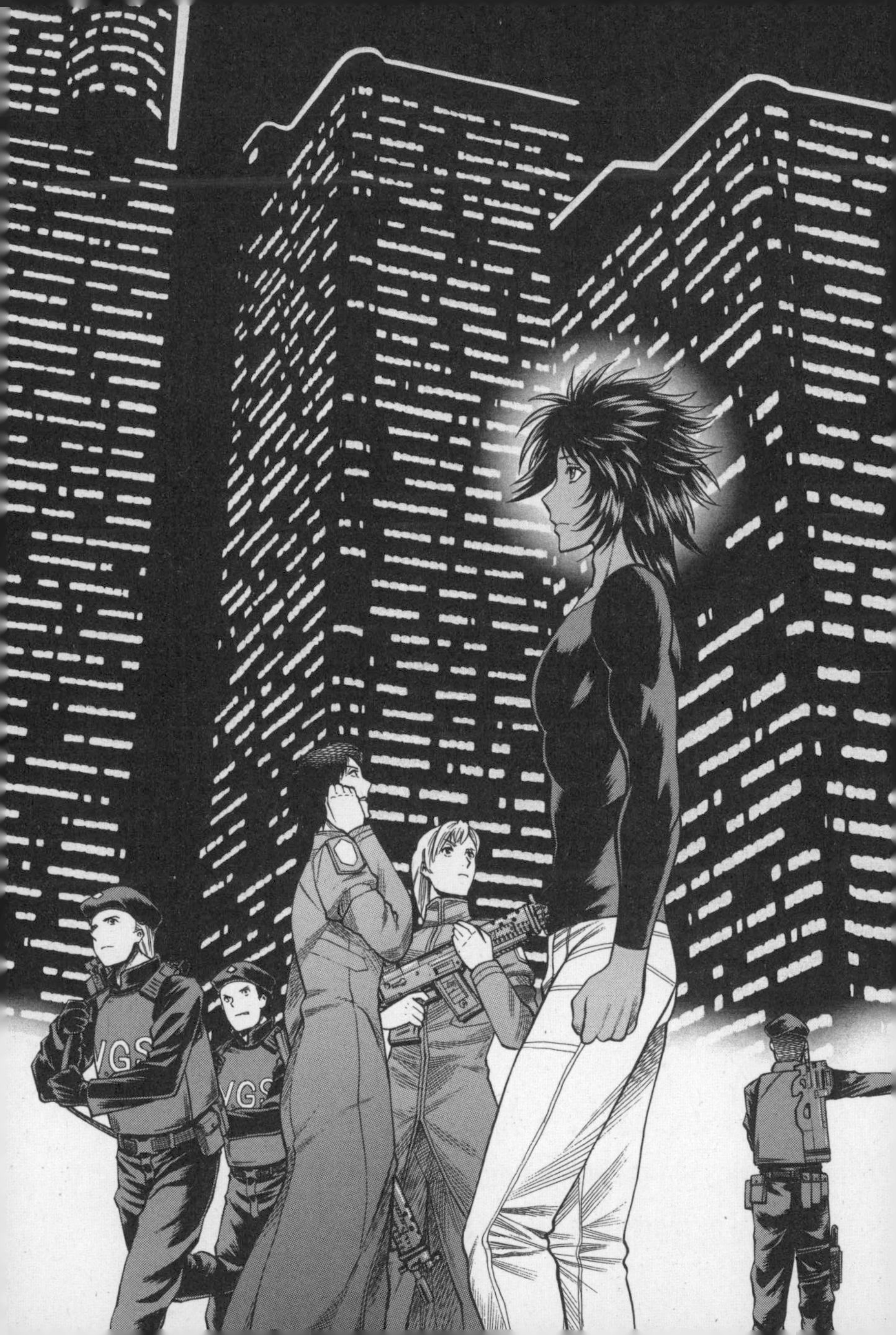
VGS
VGS

La sesta compagnia in due si scema:
per altra via mi mena il solvo duca,
fuor de la queta, ne l'aura che trema.

In two, the six associates part. Another way
My sage guide leads me, from that air serene
Into a climate ever vex'd with storms.
                    —Dante's Inferno, Canto IV

Epilogue: What a Wonderful World

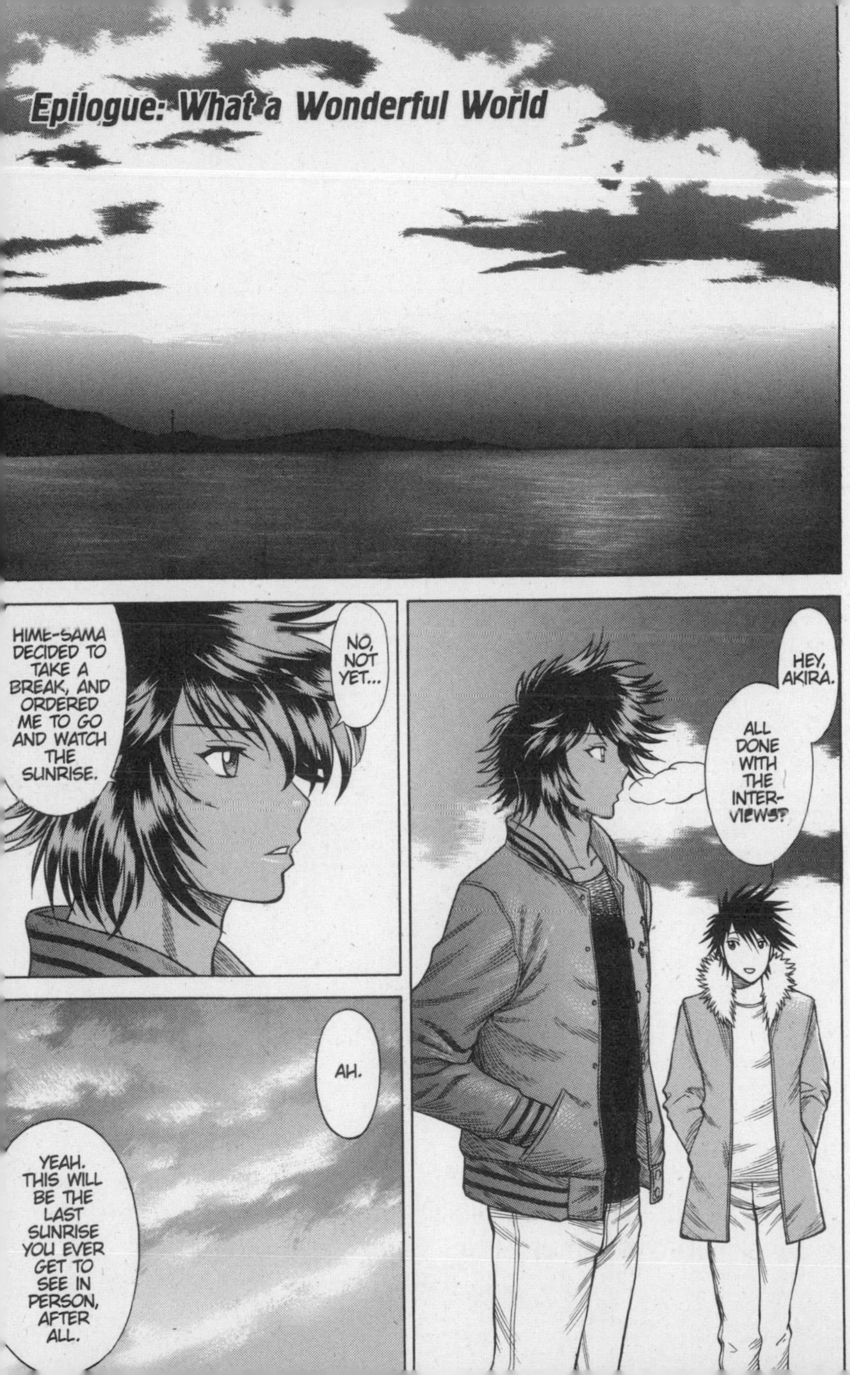
HEY, AKIRA.
ALL DONE WITH THE INTER-VIEWS?
NO, NOT YET...
HIME-SAMA DECIDED TO TAKE A BREAK, AND ORDERED ME TO GO AND WATCH THE SUNRISE.
AH.
YEAH. THIS WILL BE THE LAST SUNRISE YOU EVER GET TO SEE IN PERSON, AFTER ALL.

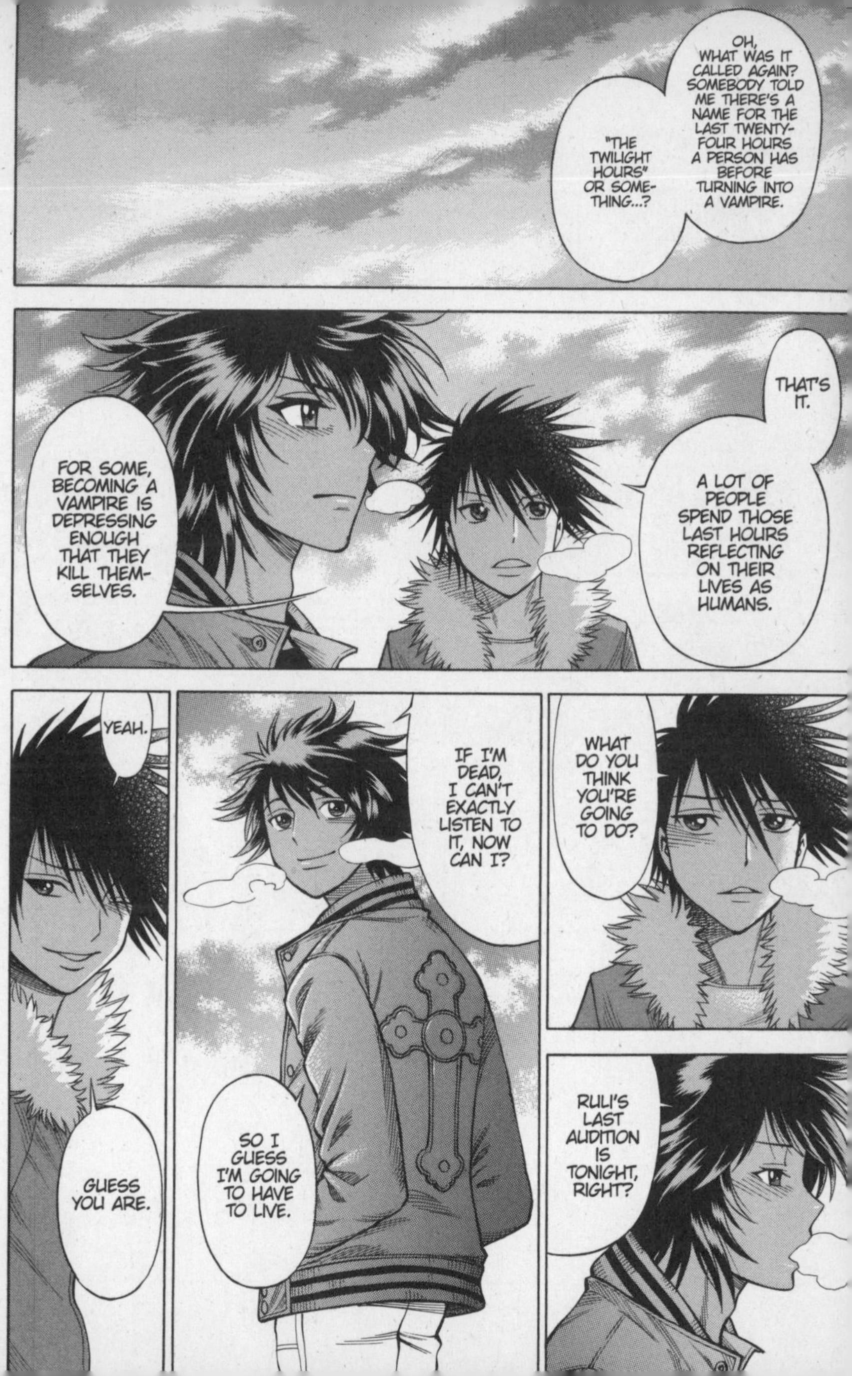
OH, WHAT WAS IT CALLED AGAIN? SOMEBODY TOLD ME THERE'S A NAME FOR THE LAST TWENTY-FOUR HOURS A PERSON HAS BEFORE TURNING INTO A VAMPIRE.
"THE TWILIGHT HOURS" OR SOME-THING...?
THAT'S IT.
A LOT OF PEOPLE SPEND THOSE LAST HOURS REFLECTING ON THEIR LIVES AS HUMANS.
FOR SOME, BECOMING A VAMPIRE IS DEPRESSING ENOUGH THAT THEY KILL THEM-SELVES.
WHAT DO YOU THINK YOU'RE GOING TO DO?
RULI'S LAST AUDITION IS TONIGHT, RIGHT?
IF I'M DEAD, I CAN'T EXACTLY LISTEN TO IT, NOW CAN I?
SO I GUESS I'M GOING TO HAVE TO LIVE.
YEAH.
GUESS YOU ARE.

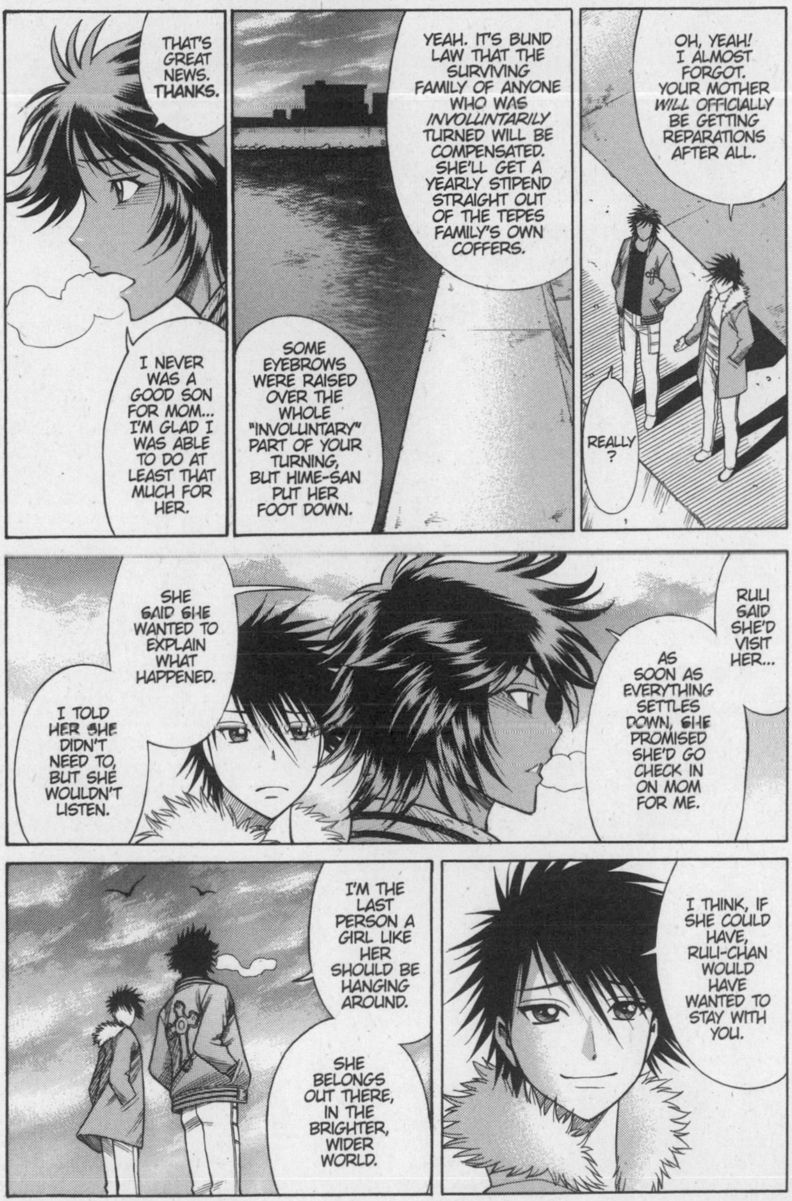
OH, YEAH! I ALMOST FORGOT. YOUR MOTHER *WILL* OFFICIALLY BE GETTING REPARATIONS AFTER ALL.
REALLY?
YEAH. IT'S BUND LAW THAT THE SURVIVING FAMILY OF ANYONE WHO WAS *INVOLUNTARILY* TURNED WILL BE COMPENSATED. SHE'LL GET A YEARLY STIPEND STRAIGHT OUT OF THE TEPES FAMILY'S OWN COFFERS.
SOME EYEBROWS WERE RAISED OVER THE WHOLE "INVOLUNTARY" PART OF YOUR TURNING, BUT HIME-SAN PUT HER FOOT DOWN.
THAT'S GREAT NEWS. THANKS.
I NEVER WAS A GOOD SON FOR MOM... I'M GLAD I WAS ABLE TO DO AT LEAST THAT MUCH FOR HER.
RULI SAID SHE'D VISIT HER...
AS SOON AS EVERYTHING SETTLES DOWN, SHE PROMISED SHE'D GO CHECK IN ON MOM FOR ME.
SHE SAID SHE WANTED TO EXPLAIN WHAT HAPPENED.
I TOLD HER SHE DIDN'T NEED TO, BUT SHE WOULDN'T LISTEN.
I THINK, IF SHE COULD HAVE, RULI-CHAN WOULD HAVE WANTED TO STAY WITH YOU.
I'M THE LAST PERSON A GIRL LIKE HER SHOULD BE HANGING AROUND.
SHE BELONGS OUT THERE, IN THE BRIGHTER, WIDER WORLD.

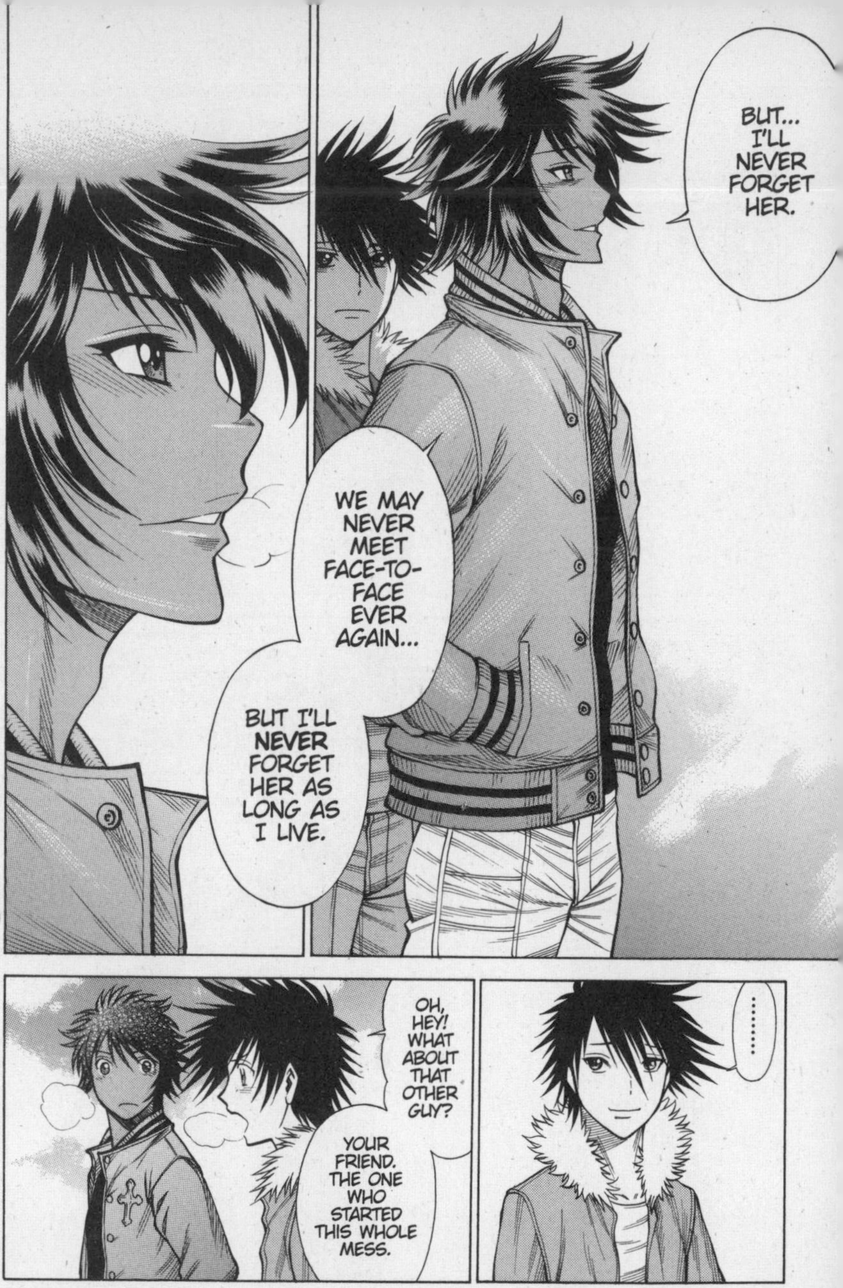
BUT... I'LL NEVER FORGET HER.
WE MAY NEVER MEET FACE-TO-FACE EVER AGAIN...
BUT I'LL NEVER FORGET HER AS LONG AS I LIVE.
....
OH, HEY! WHAT ABOUT THAT OTHER GUY?
YOUR FRIEND. THE ONE WHO STARTED THIS WHOLE MESS.

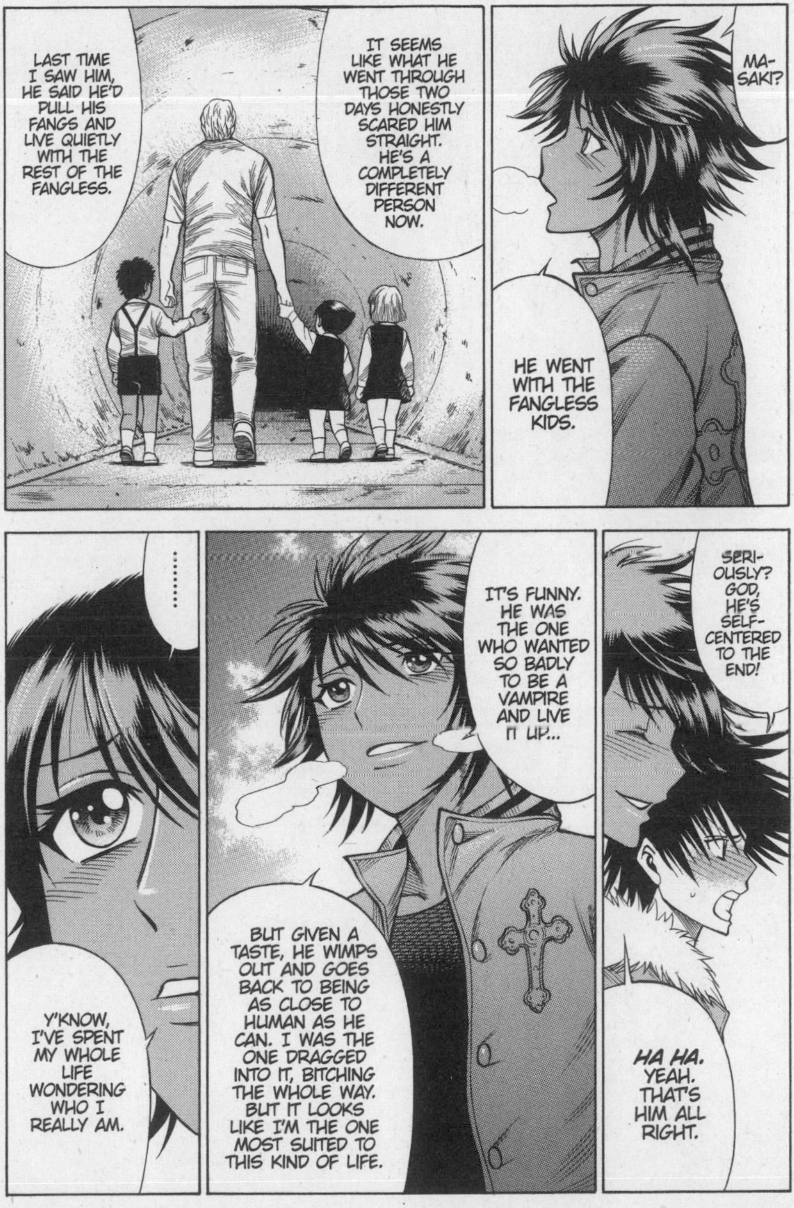
MA-SAKI?
HE WENT WITH THE FANGLESS KIDS.
IT SEEMS LIKE WHAT HE WENT THROUGH THOSE TWO DAYS HONESTLY SCARED HIM STRAIGHT. HE'S A COMPLETELY DIFFERENT PERSON NOW.
LAST TIME I SAW HIM, HE SAID HE'D PULL HIS FANGS AND LIVE QUIETLY WITH THE REST OF THE FANGLESS.
SERI-OUSLY? GOD, HE'S SELF-CENTERED TO THE END!
HA HA. YEAH. THAT'S HIM ALL RIGHT.
IT'S FUNNY. HE WAS THE ONE WHO WANTED SO BADLY TO BE A VAMPIRE AND LIVE IT UP...
BUT GIVEN A TASTE, HE WIMPS OUT AND GOES BACK TO BEING AS CLOSE TO HUMAN AS HE CAN. I WAS THE ONE DRAGGED INTO IT, BITCHING THE WHOLE WAY. BUT IT LOOKS LIKE I'M THE ONE MOST SUITED TO THIS KIND OF LIFE.
....
Y'KNOW, I'VE SPENT MY WHOLE LIFE WONDERING WHO I REALLY AM.

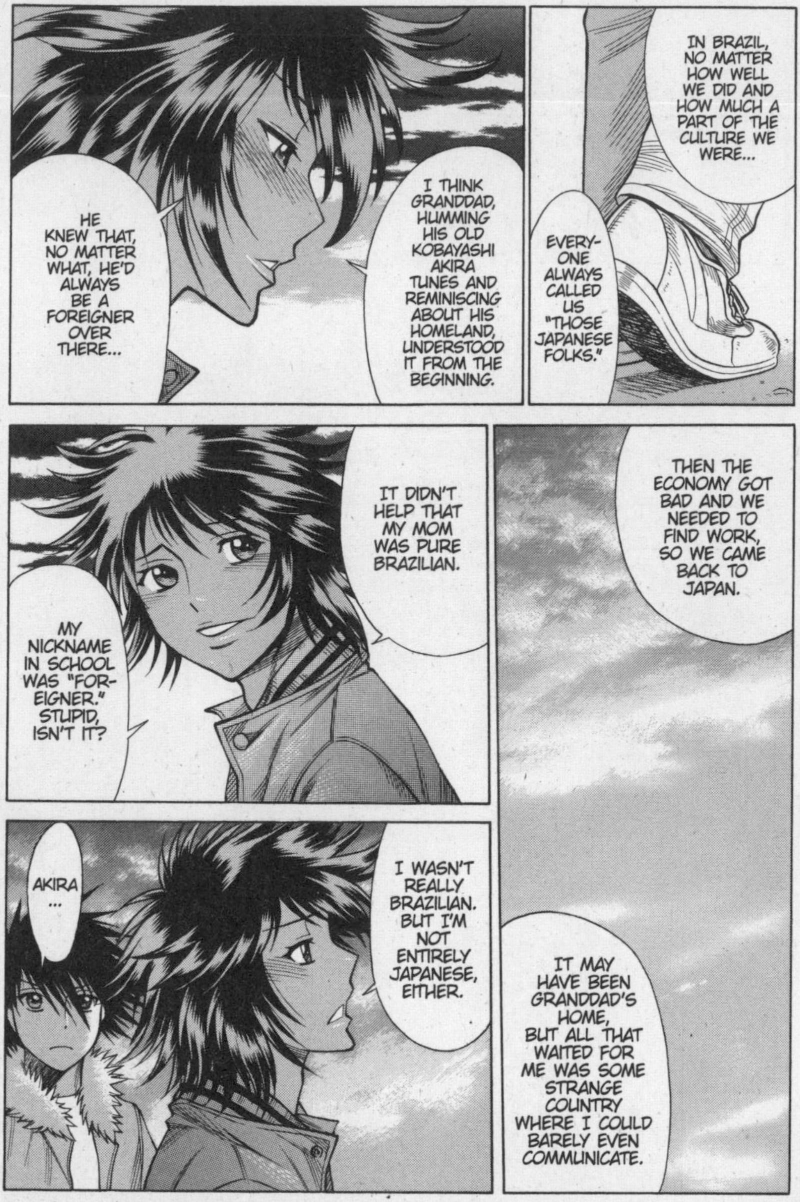
IN BRAZIL, NO MATTER HOW WELL WE DID AND HOW MUCH A PART OF THE CULTURE WE WERE...
EVERY-ONE ALWAYS CALLED US "THOSE JAPANESE FOLKS."
I THINK GRANDDAD, HUMMING HIS OLD KOBAYASHI AKIRA TUNES AND REMINISCING ABOUT HIS HOMELAND, UNDERSTOOD IT FROM THE BEGINNING.
HE KNEW THAT, NO MATTER WHAT, HE'D ALWAYS BE A FOREIGNER OVER THERE...
THEN THE ECONOMY GOT BAD AND WE NEEDED TO FIND WORK, SO WE CAME BACK TO JAPAN.
IT MAY HAVE BEEN GRANDDAD'S HOME, BUT ALL THAT WAITED FOR ME WAS SOME STRANGE COUNTRY WHERE I COULD BARELY EVEN COMMUNICATE.
IT DIDN'T HELP THAT MY MOM WAS PURE BRAZILIAN.
MY NICKNAME IN SCHOOL WAS "FOR-EIGNER." STUPID, ISN'T IT?
I WASN'T REALLY BRAZILIAN. BUT I'M NOT ENTIRELY JAPANESE, EITHER.
AKIRA ...

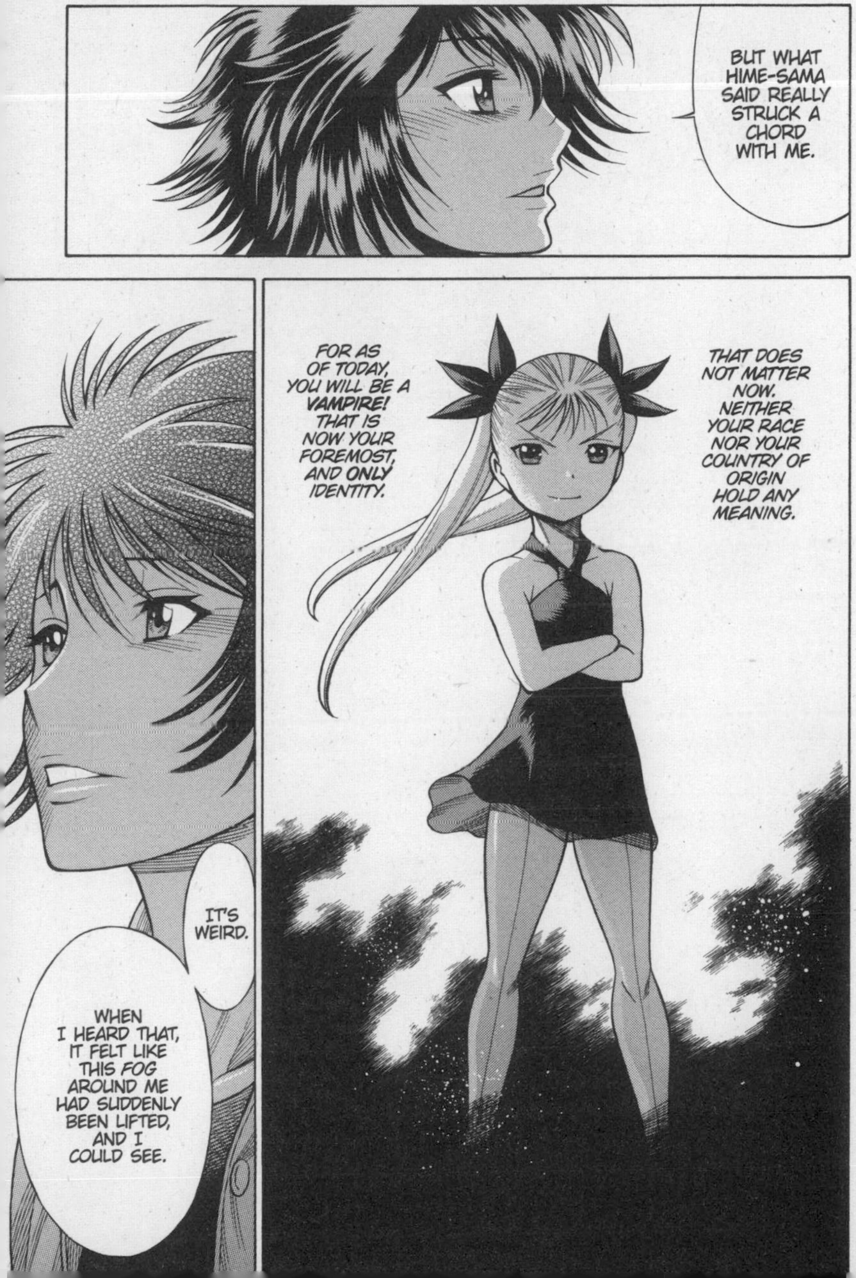
BUT WHAT HIME-SAMA SAID REALLY STRUCK A CHORD WITH ME.
THAT DOES NOT MATTER NOW. NEITHER YOUR RACE NOR YOUR COUNTRY OF ORIGIN HOLD ANY MEANING.
FOR AS OF TODAY, YOU WILL BE A VAMPIRE! THAT IS NOW YOUR FOREMOST, AND ONLY IDENTITY.
IT'S WEIRD.
WHEN I HEARD THAT, IT FELT LIKE THIS FOG AROUND ME HAD SUDDENLY BEEN LIFTED, AND I COULD SEE.

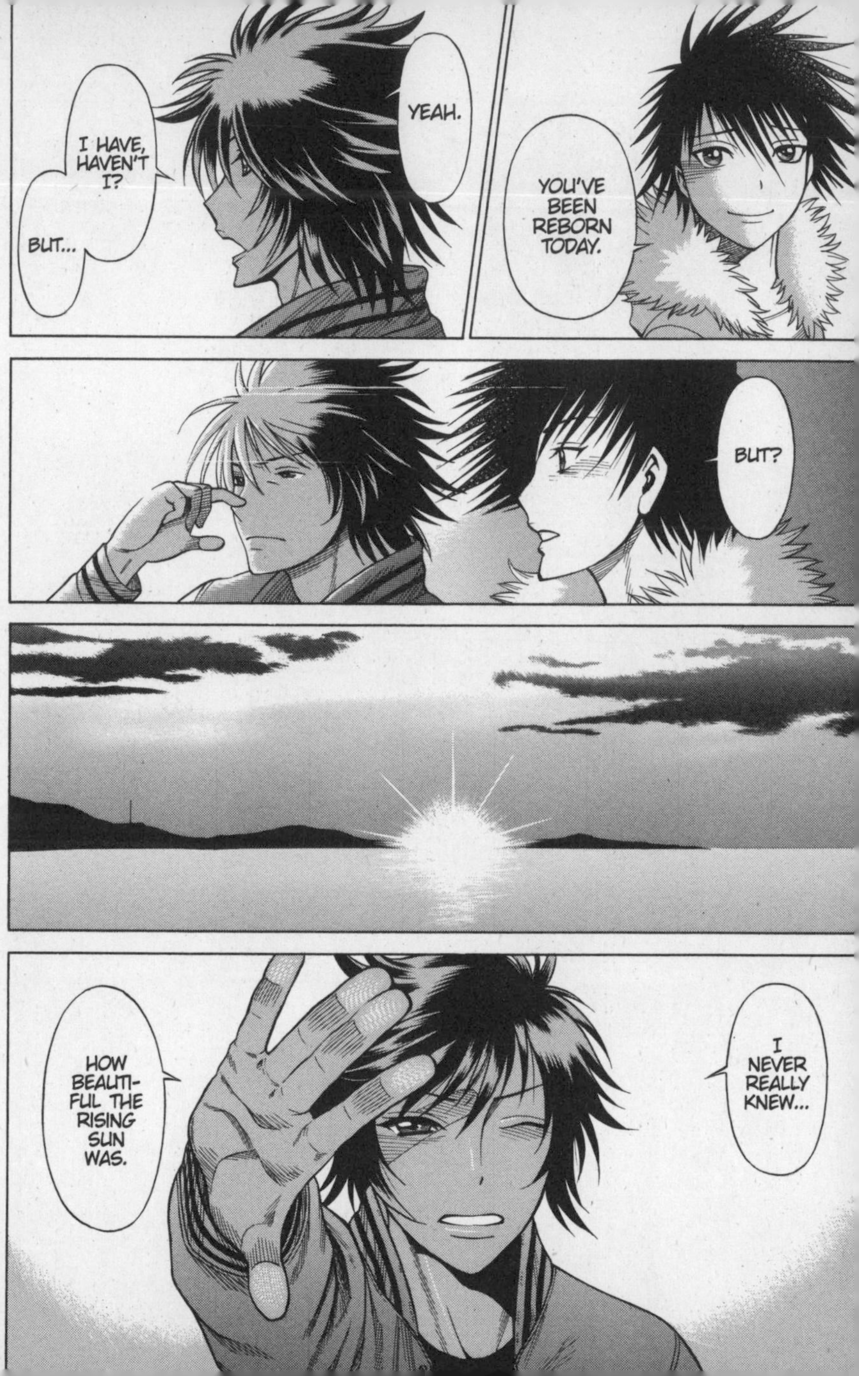
YOU'VE BEEN REBORN TODAY.
YEAH.
I HAVE, HAVEN'T I?
BUT...
BUT?
I NEVER REALLY KNEW...
HOW BEAUTI- FUL THE RISING SUN WAS.

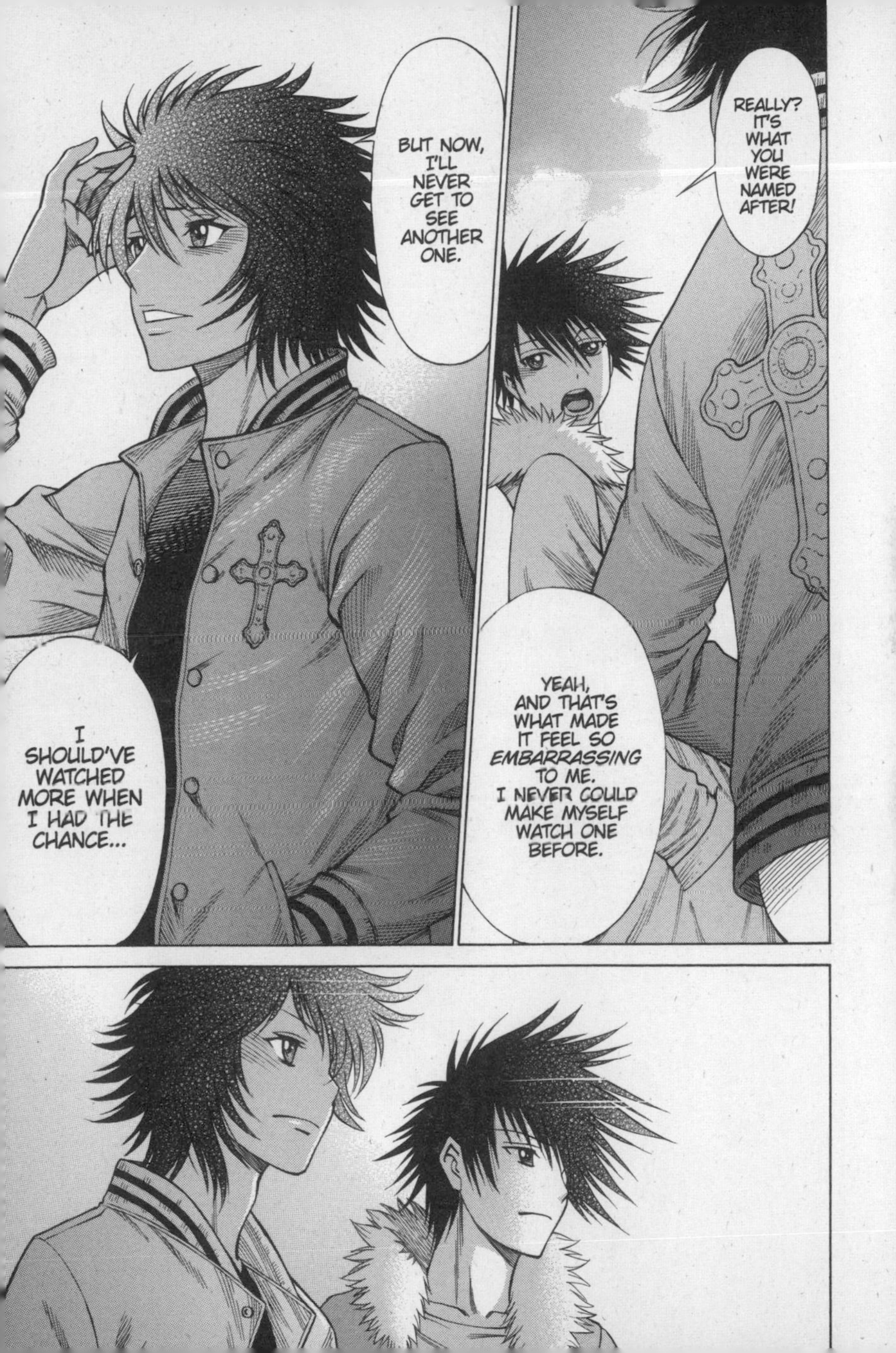
REALLY? IT'S WHAT YOU WERE NAMED AFTER!
YEAH, AND THAT'S WHAT MADE IT FEEL SO *EMBARRASSING* TO ME. I NEVER COULD MAKE MYSELF WATCH ONE BEFORE.
BUT NOW, I'LL NEVER GET TO SEE ANOTHER ONE.
I SHOULD'VE WATCHED MORE WHEN I HAD THE CHANCE...

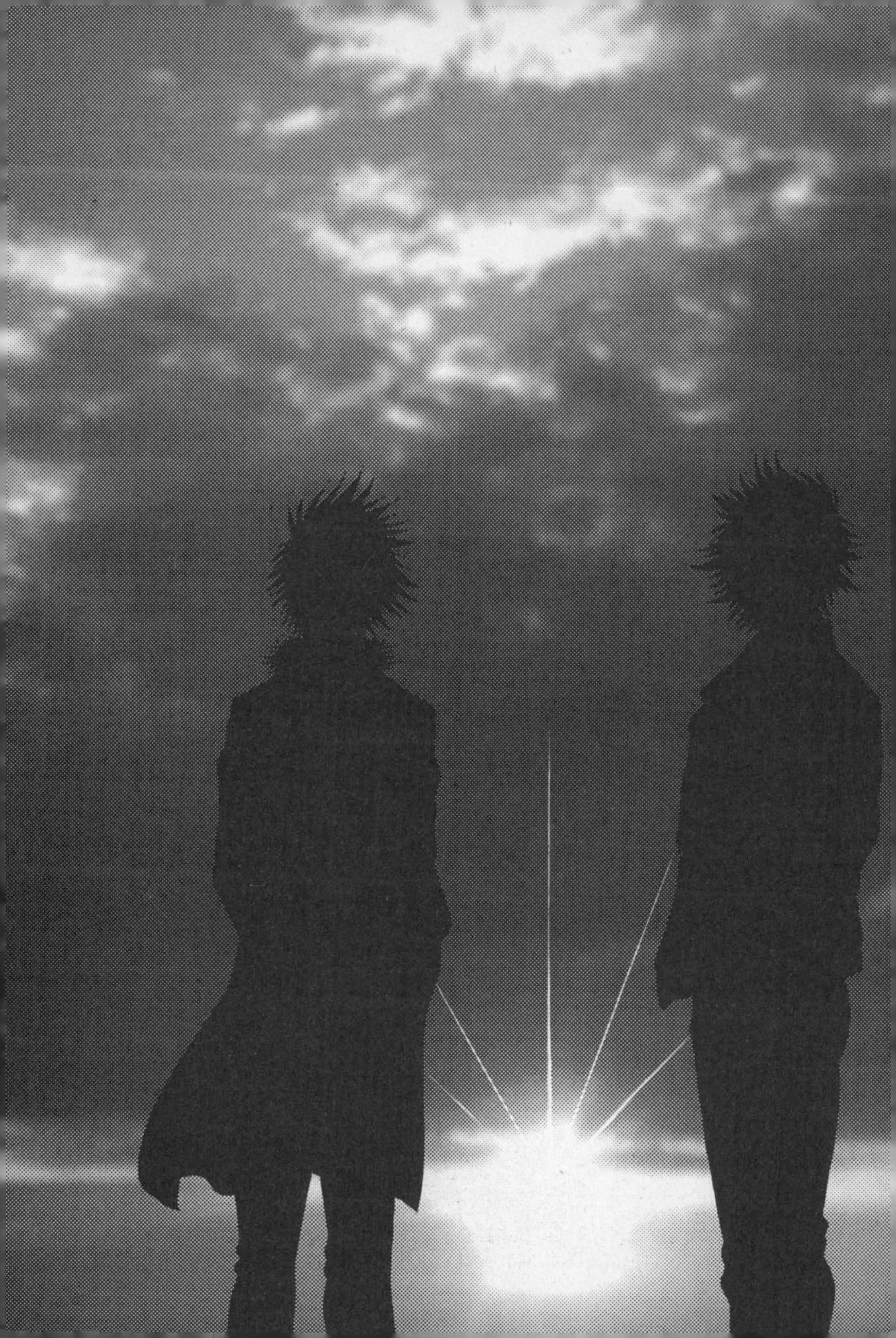

DIVE IN THE VAMPIRE BUND

THE SHOW MUST GO ON

TRANSLATION NOTES

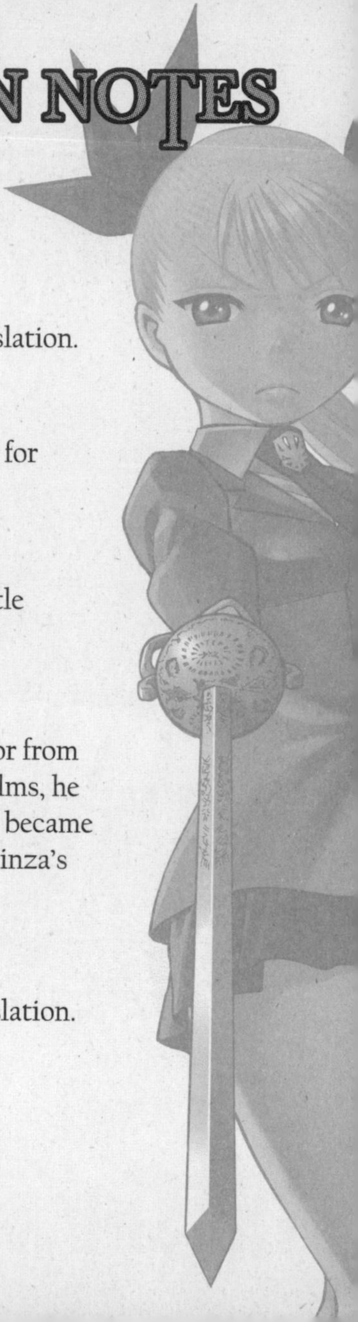

1.3
Dante's Inferno, Canto III. H.F. Cary translation.

101.4.4
"Favela" is the Brazilian-Portuguese word for "slum."

115.5.9
On a related, interesting note-- Akira's little brother's name, Yuuhi, means "sunset."

115.6.11
Kobayashi Akira is a famous Japanese actor from the 1960s. Aside from starring in several films, he also sang their theme songs, two of which became hits: "The Guitar-Toting Rambler" and "Ginza's Whirlwind Child."

184.1
Dante's Inferno, Canto IV. H.F. Cary translation.

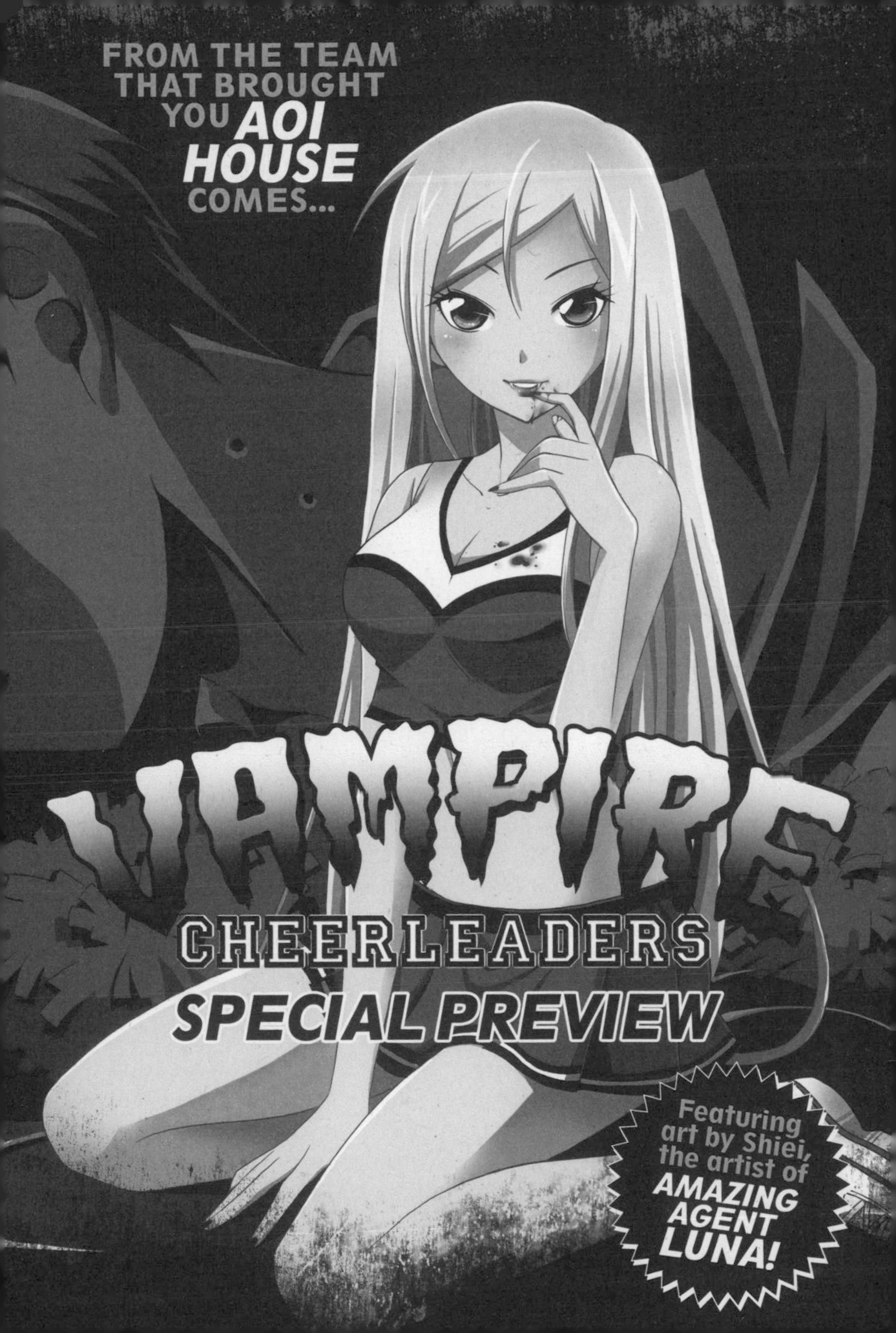
FROM THE TEAM THAT BROUGHT YOU AOI HOUSE COMES...
VAMPIRE
CHEERLEADERS
SPECIAL PREVIEW
Featuring art by Shiei, the artist of AMAZING AGENT LUNA!

VAMPIRE CHEERLEADERS
VOLUME 1
COMING MARCH 2011

Story by
ADAM ARNOLD

Art by
SHIEI

The Bakertown High School cheerleading squad has a secret: behind all their pretty makeup and short skirts are five hungry vampires who sure know how to show their school spirit!

When one of their own turns up missing, the vampire cheerleaders have no other choice but to induct one of the eleventh grade girls from B Squad into their vixenous ranks. Siring new recruit Heather Hartley may be the easy part, but keeping her from turning into a vamp-gone-wild and draining the entire football team on the eve of the big homecoming game is another matter!

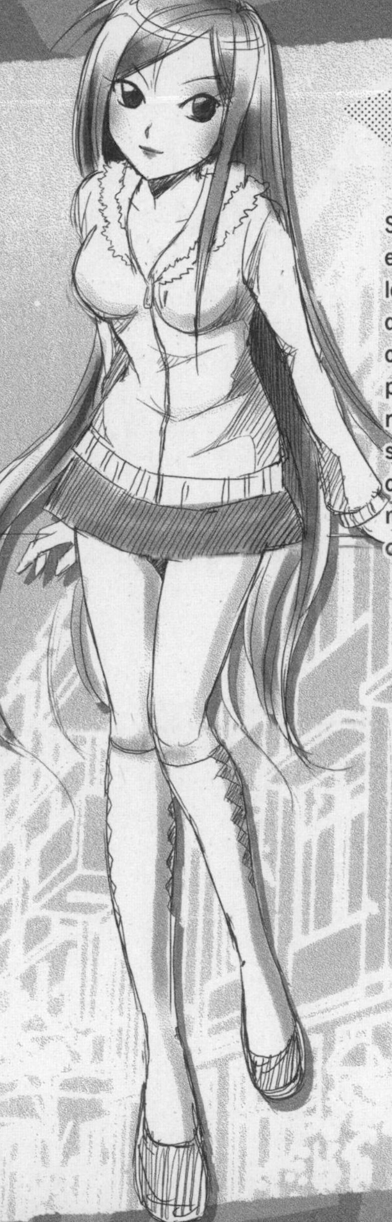

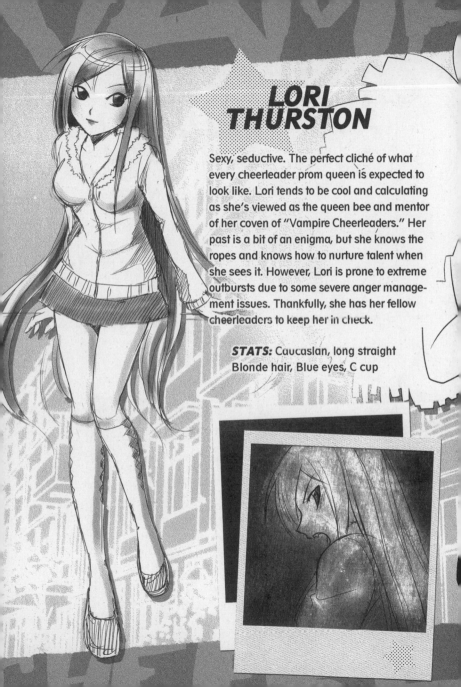

LORI THURSTON

Sexy, seductive. The perfect cliché of what every cheerleader prom queen is expected to look like. Lori tends to be cool and calculating as she's viewed as the queen bee and mentor of her coven of "Vampire Cheerleaders." Her past is a bit of an enigma, but she knows the ropes and knows how to nurture talent when she sees it. However, Lori is prone to extreme outbursts due to some severe anger management issues. Thankfully, she has her fellow cheerleaders to keep her in check.

STATS: Caucasian, long straight Blonde hair, Blue eyes, C cup

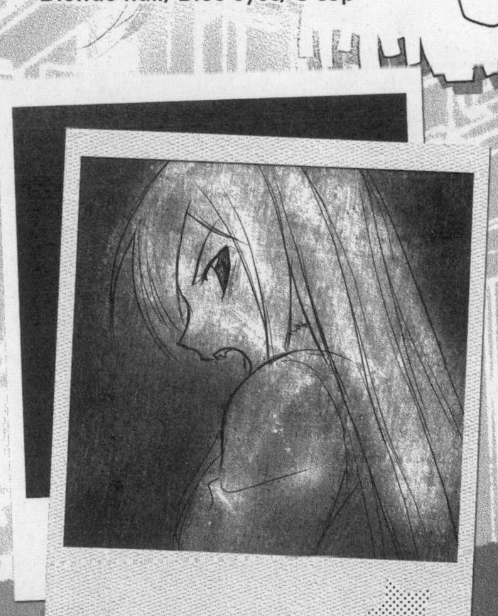

HEATHER HARTLEY

An eleventh grader on the B Squad who is seen as a goodie-two-shoes. Indeed, Heather's parents are overbearing and avid churchgoers, so Heather has lived a sheltered life. Once Heather gets turned into a vampire, however, a whole new world opens up for her.

STATS: Caucasian, Short (Petite), Brown hair done in a single pony tail in the back, Green eyes, B cup

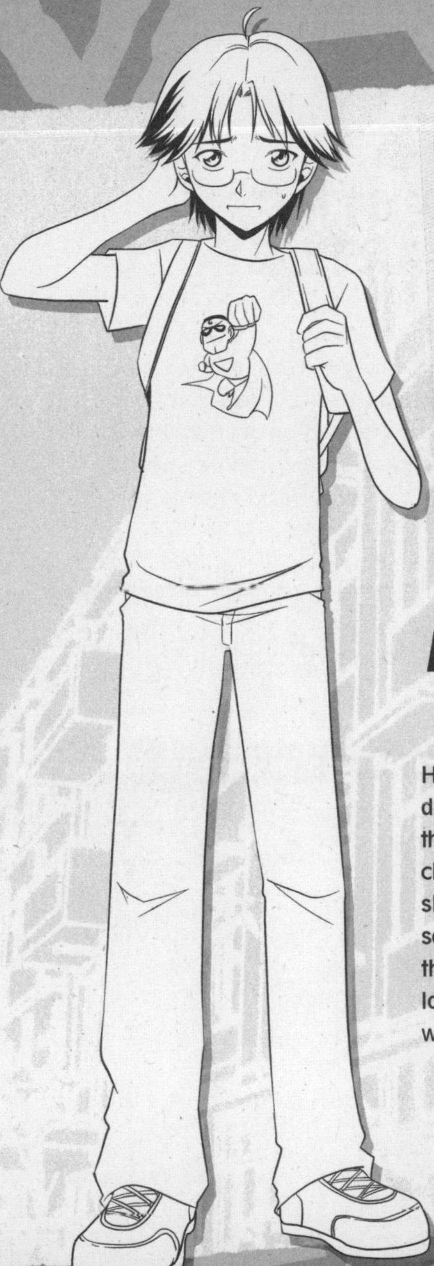

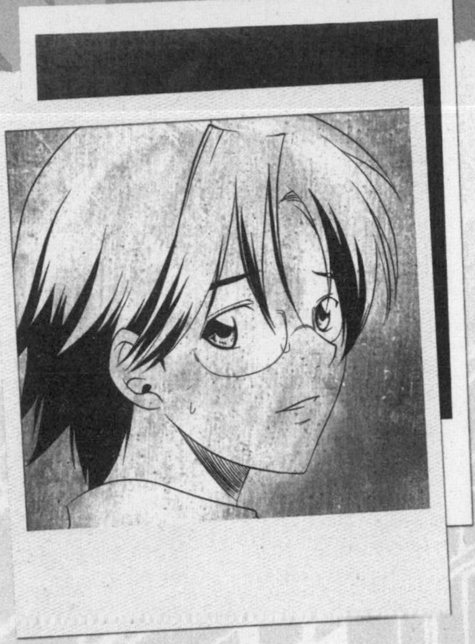

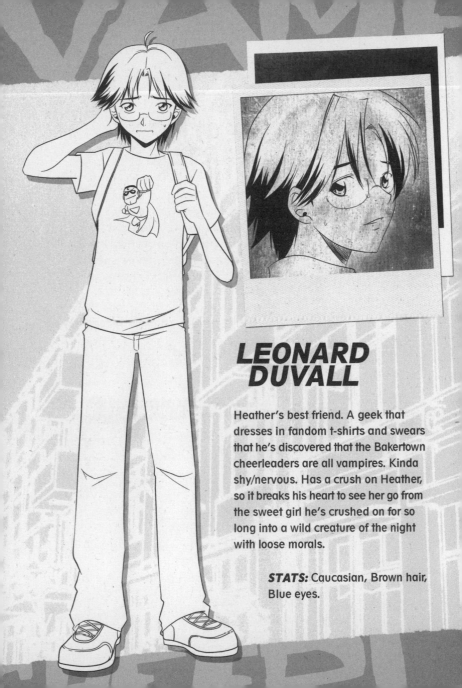

LEONARD DUVALL

Heather's best friend. A geek that dresses in fandom t-shirts and swears that he's discovered that the Bakertown cheerleaders are all vampires. Kinda shy/nervous. Has a crush on Heather, so it breaks his heart to see her go from the sweet girl he's crushed on for so long into a wild creature of the night with loose morals.

STATS: Caucasian, Brown hair, Blue eyes.

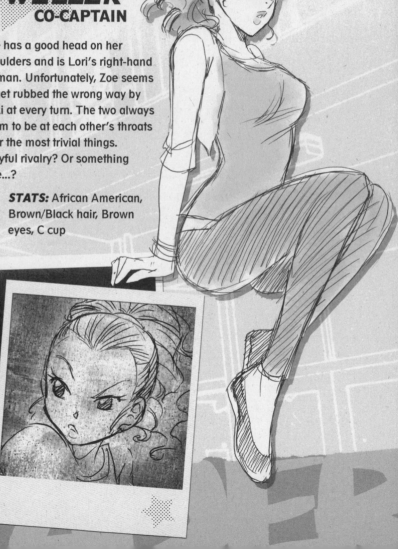

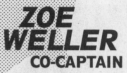

ZOE WELLER
CO-CAPTAIN

Zoe has a good head on her shoulders and is Lori's right-hand woman. Unfortunately, Zoe seems to get rubbed the wrong way by Suki at every turn. The two always seem to be at each other's throats over the most trivial things. Playful rivalry? Or something else...?

STATS: African American, Brown/Black hair, Brown eyes, C cup

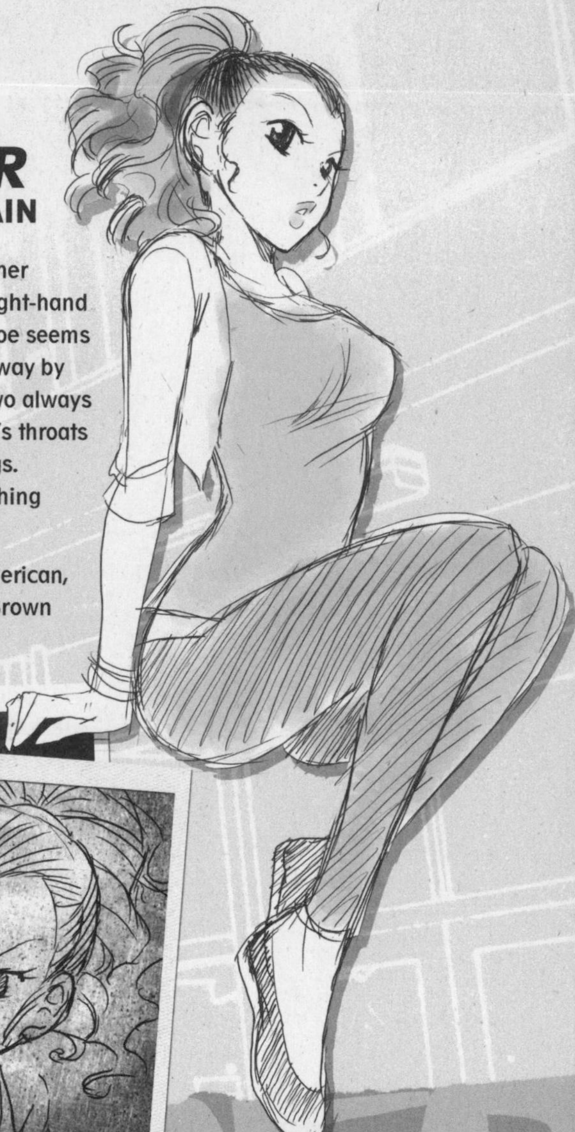

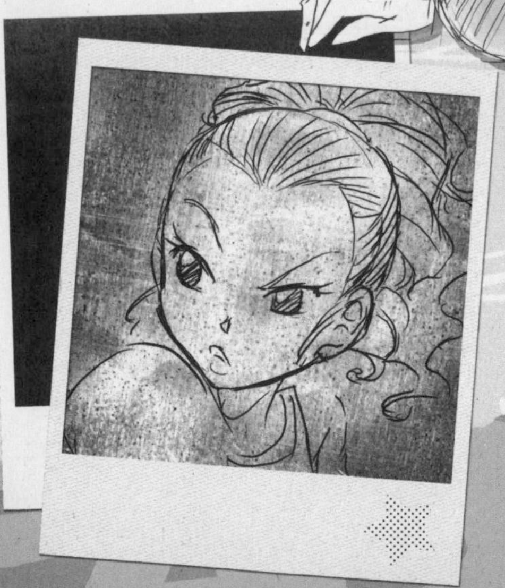

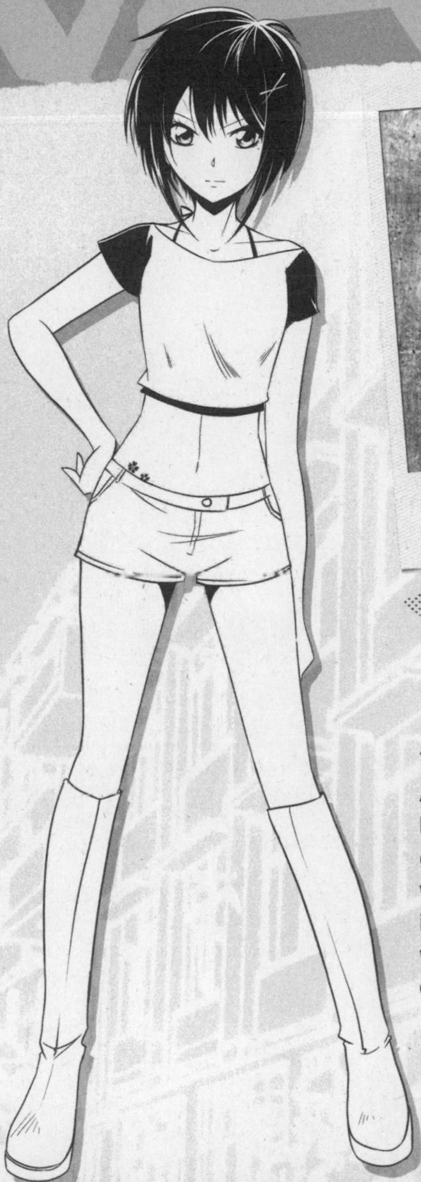

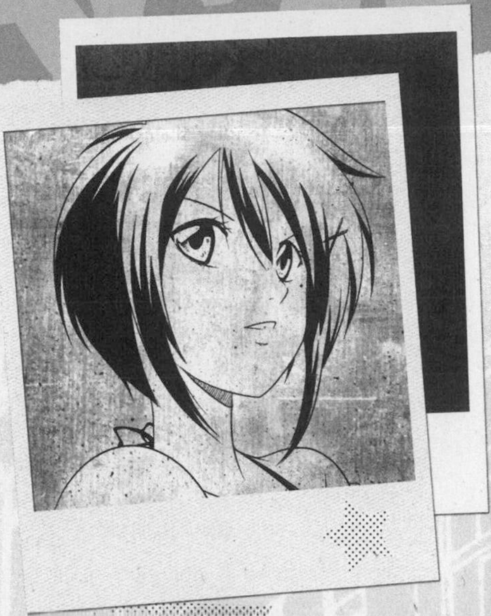

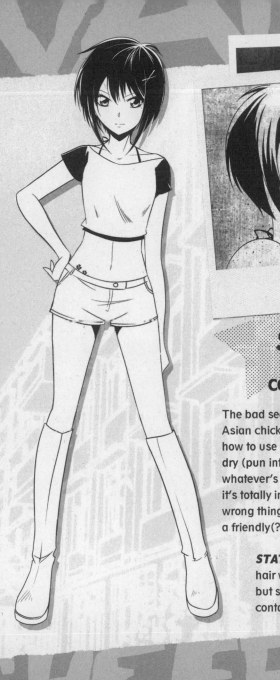

SUKI TAFT
CO-CAPTAIN

The bad seed. She knows guys dig Asian chicks and she knows just how to use her talents to bleed 'em dry (pun intended). Always saying whatever's on her mind...even when it's totally inappropriate and the wrong thing at the wrong time. Has a friendly(?) rivalry with Zoe.

STATS: Asian American, Black hair with highlights, Brown eyes but sometimes wears colored contacts, A cup

LESLEY CHANDRA

TEAM TREASURER

Pleasant personality, friendly. The voice of reason in the group. Probably the smartest of all the girls. But she's also got a wild side. In fact, you'd be surprised to know that she's "Ms. Kama Sutra" in a cheerleading costume.

STATS: East Indian American, Black/Brown hair, Brown eyes, D cup

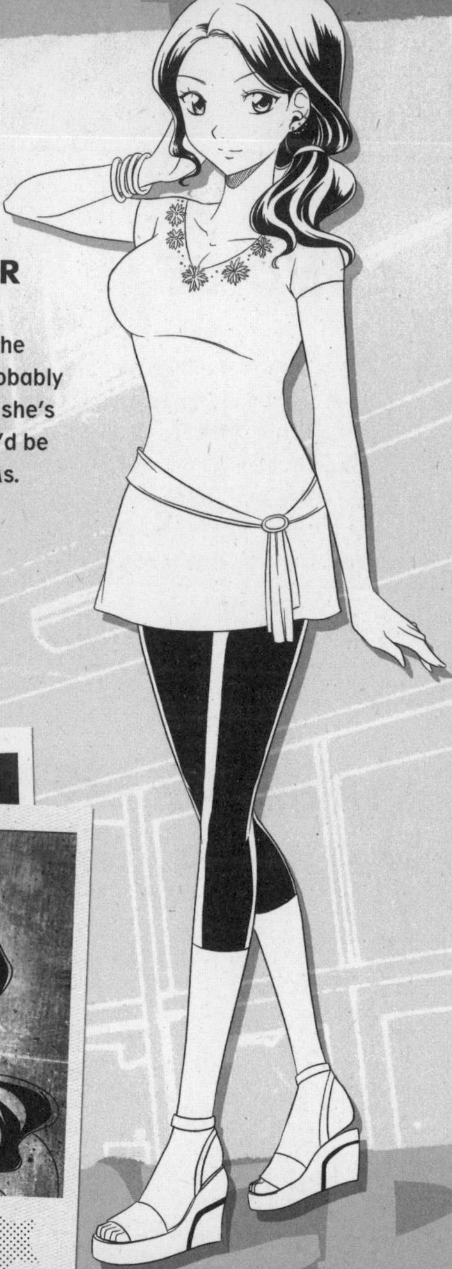

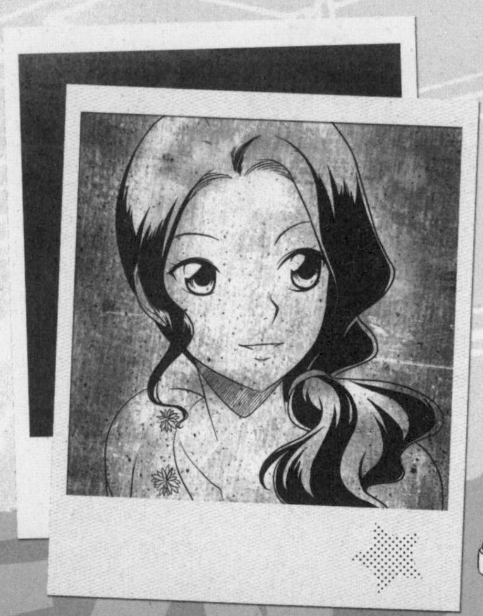

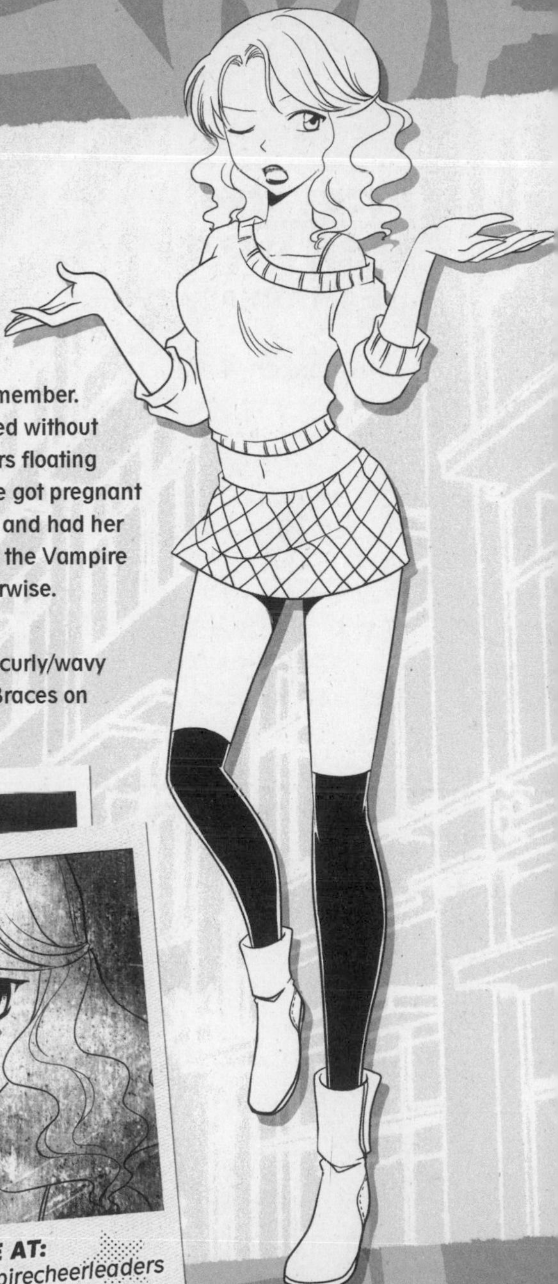

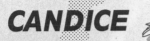

CANDICE

The team's former fifth member. She's up and disappeared without a trace. One of the rumors floating around school is that she got pregnant and her parents freaked and had her sent to a monastery. But the Vampire Cheerleaders know otherwise.

STATS: Caucasian, semi-curly/wavy hair, Brown eyes, C cup, Braces on her teeth.

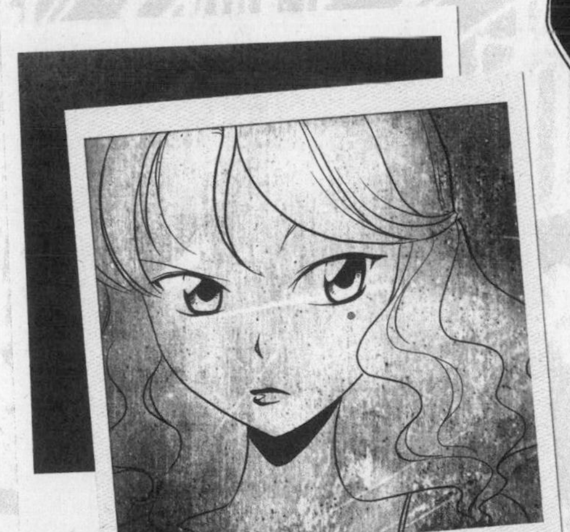

FIND OUT MORE AT:
facebook.com/vampirecheerleaders

Dance in the Vampire Bund GAIDEN

story & art by Nozomu Tamaki

STAFF CREDITS

translation	Adrienne Beck
adaptation	Janet Houck
retouch & lettering	Roland Amago
cover design	Nicky Lim
layout	Bambi Eloriaga-Amago
copy editor	Shanti Whitesides
editor	Adam Arnold

publisher	Jason DeAngelis
	Seven Seas Entertainment

DIVE IN THE VAMPIRE BUND VOL. 1
© 2010 Nozomu Tamaki
First published in Japan in 2010 by MEDIA FACTORY, Inc.
English translation rights reserved by Seven Seas Entertainment, LLC.
Under the license from MEDIA FACTORY, Inc., Tokyo.

Seven Seas and the Seven Seas logo are trademarks of
Seven Seas Entertainment, LLC. All rights reserved.

Visit us online at www.gomanga.com

ISBN: 978-1-934876-38-1

Printed in Canada

First printing: April 2011

10 9 8 7 6 5 4 3 2 1

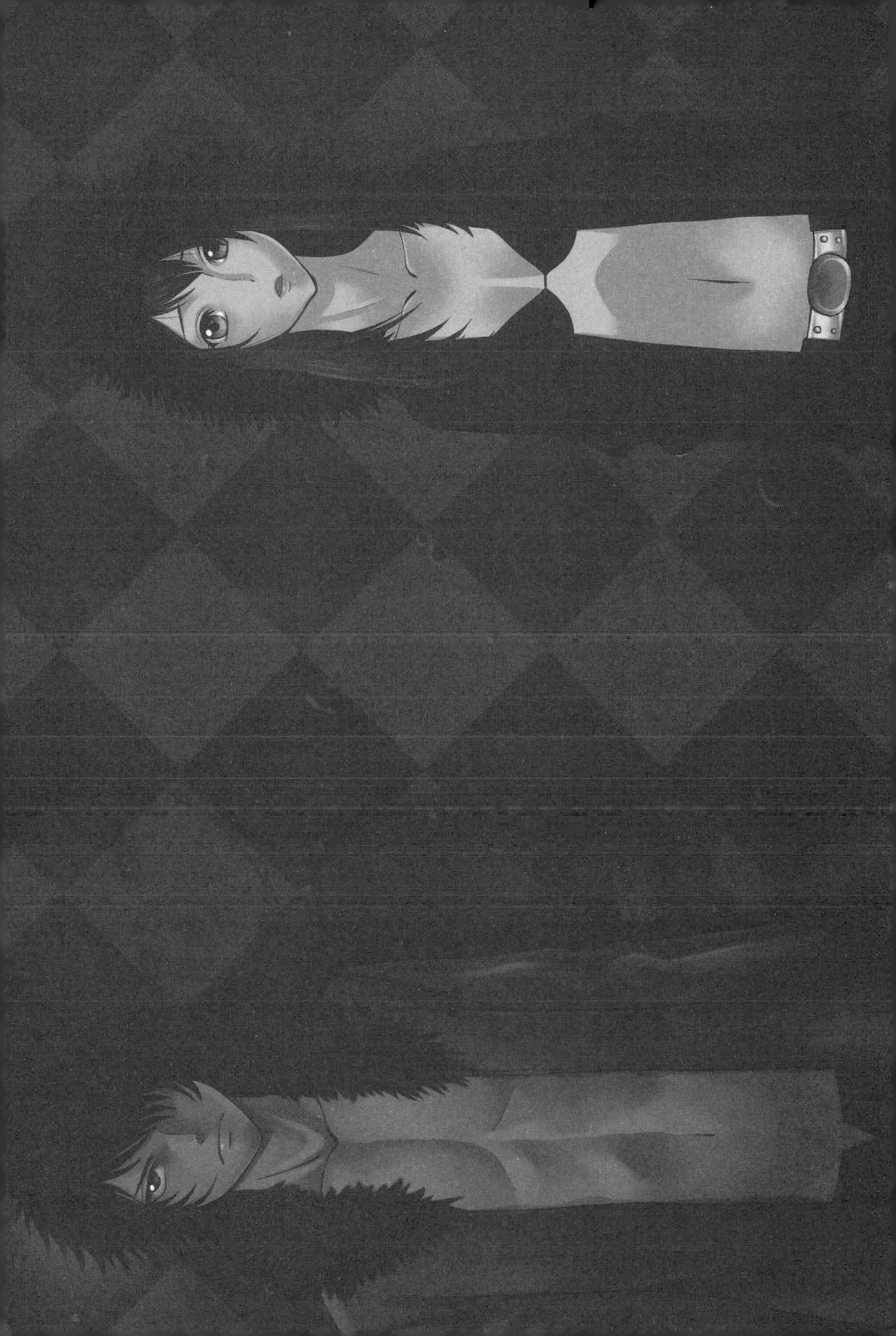

YOU'RE READING THE WRONG WAY

This is the last page of
Dance in the Vampire Bund Gaiden:
Dive in the Vampire Bund

This book reads from right to left, Japanese style. To read from the beginning, flip the book over to the other side, start with the top right panel, and take it from there.

If this is your first time reading manga, just follow the diagram. It may seem backwards at first, but you'll get used to it! Have fun!